BLACK PANTHER
ENEMY OF THE STATE

WRITER
Christopher Priest

ARTISTS
Joe Jusko, Mike Manley, Mark Bright,
Jimmy Palmiotti, Nelson DeCastro,
Amanda Connor and Vince Evans

COLORISTS
Avalon Studios, Chris Sotomayor,
Drew and Matt Yackey

LETTERERS
Richard Starkings and Comicraft

EDITOR
Joe Quesada, Jimmy Palmiotti
and Nanci Dakesian

BLACK PANTHER ® ENEMY OF THE STATE. Contains material originally published in magazine form as BLACK PANTHER Vol. 2 #s 6-12. First Printing, FEBRUARY 2001. ISBN # 0-7851-0829-7 GST. #R127032852. Published by MARVEL COMICS, a division of MARVEL ENTERTAINMENT GROUP, INC. OFFICE OF PUBLICATION: 10 EAST 40th STREET, NEW YORK, NY 10016. Copyright © 1998 and 2001 Marvel Characters, Inc. No similarity between any of the names, characters, persons, and/or institutions in this publication with those of any living or dead person or institutions is intended, and any such similarity which may exist is purely coincidental. This publication may not be sold except by authorized dealers and is sold subject to the conditions that it shall not be sold or distributed with any part of its cover or markings removed, nor in a mutilated condition. BLACK PANTHER (including all prominent characters featured in this publication and the distinctive likenesses thereof) is a trademark of MARVEL CHARACTERS, INC. Printed in Canada. PETER CUNEO, Chief Executive Officer; AVI ARAD, Chief Creative Officer; GUI KARYO, Chief Information Officer; BOB GREEN-BERGER, Director – Publishing Operations; STAN LEE, Chairman Emeritus.

10 9 8 7 6 5 4 3 2 1

BLACK PANTHER
ISSUE 6

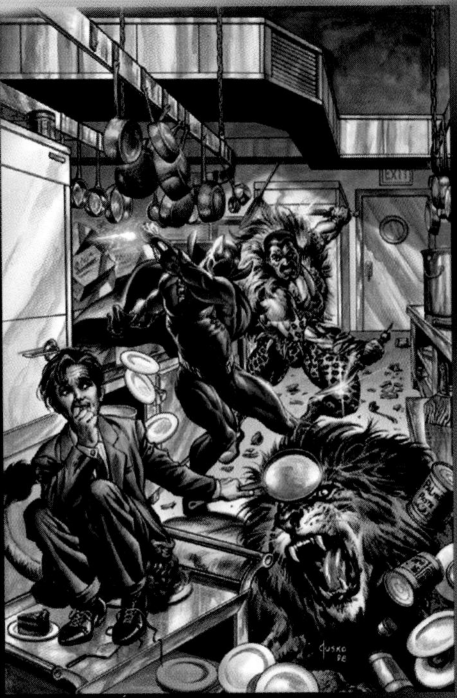
EXIT

BLACK PANTHER
ISSUE 7

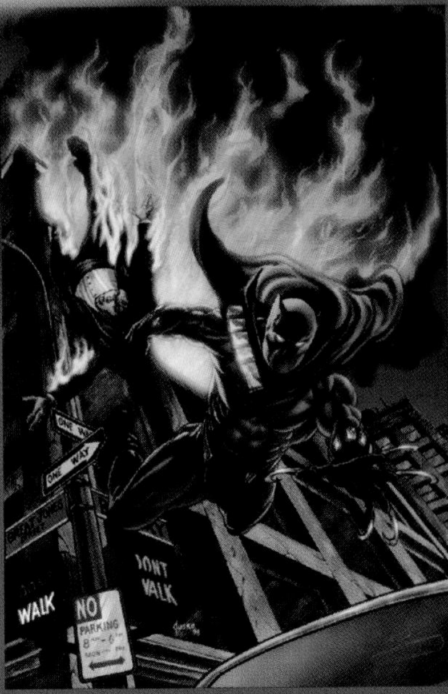
DONT
WALK
WALK
NO
PARKING

BLACK PANTHER
ISSUE 8

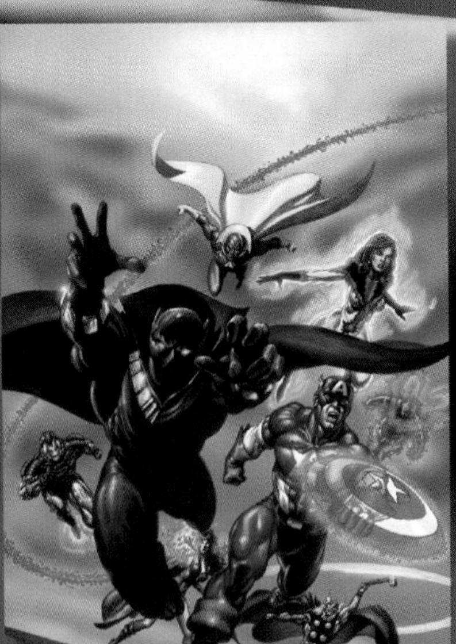

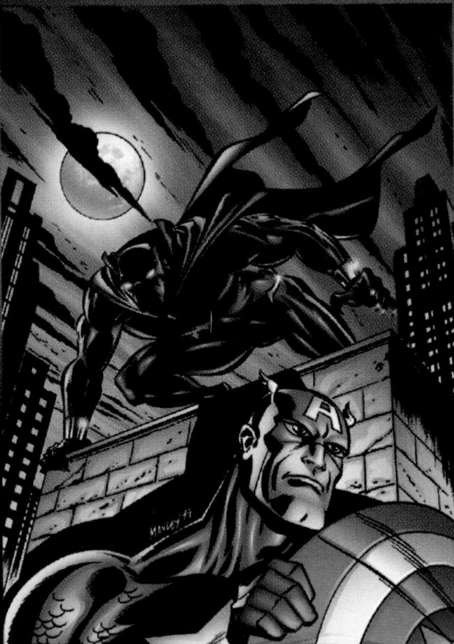

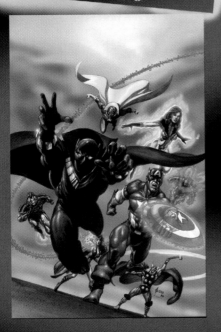

BLACK PANTHER
ISSUE 9

BLACK PANTHER
ISSUE 10

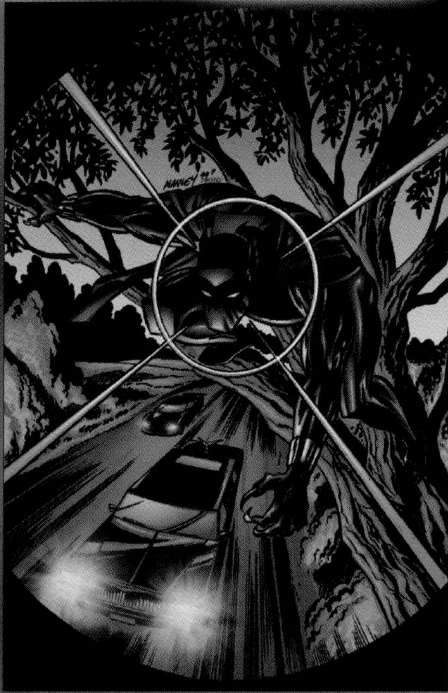

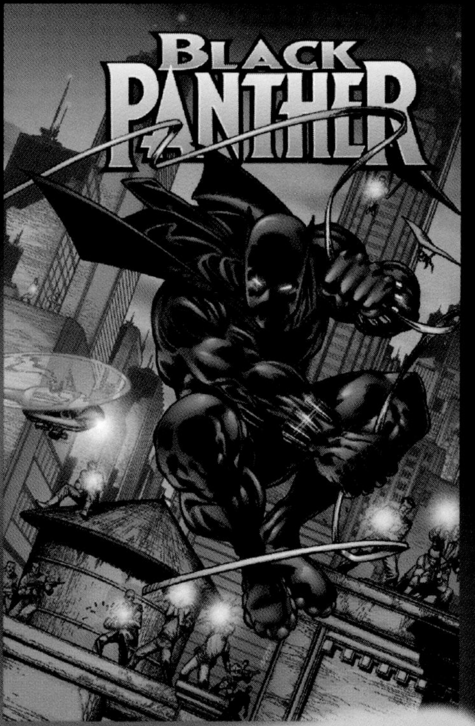
BLACK PANTHER

BLACK PANTHER
ISSUE 11

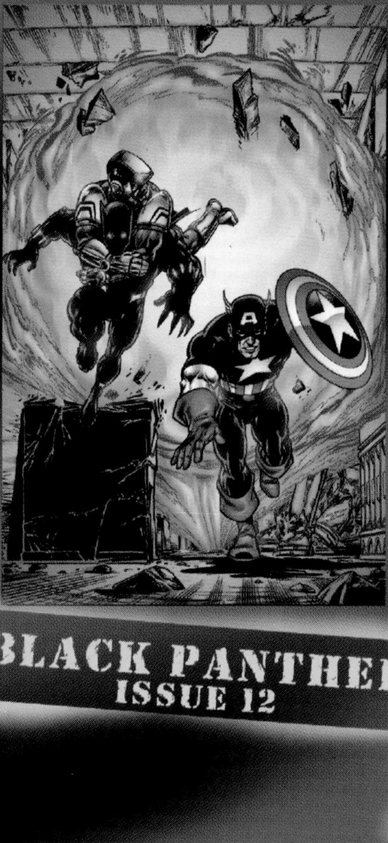

BLACK PANTHER
ISSUE 12

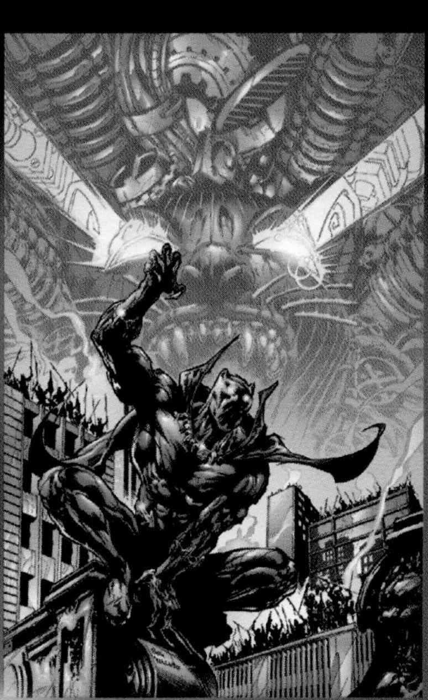

BLACK PANTHER
ISSUE 13

GREAT BALLS OF SPIT

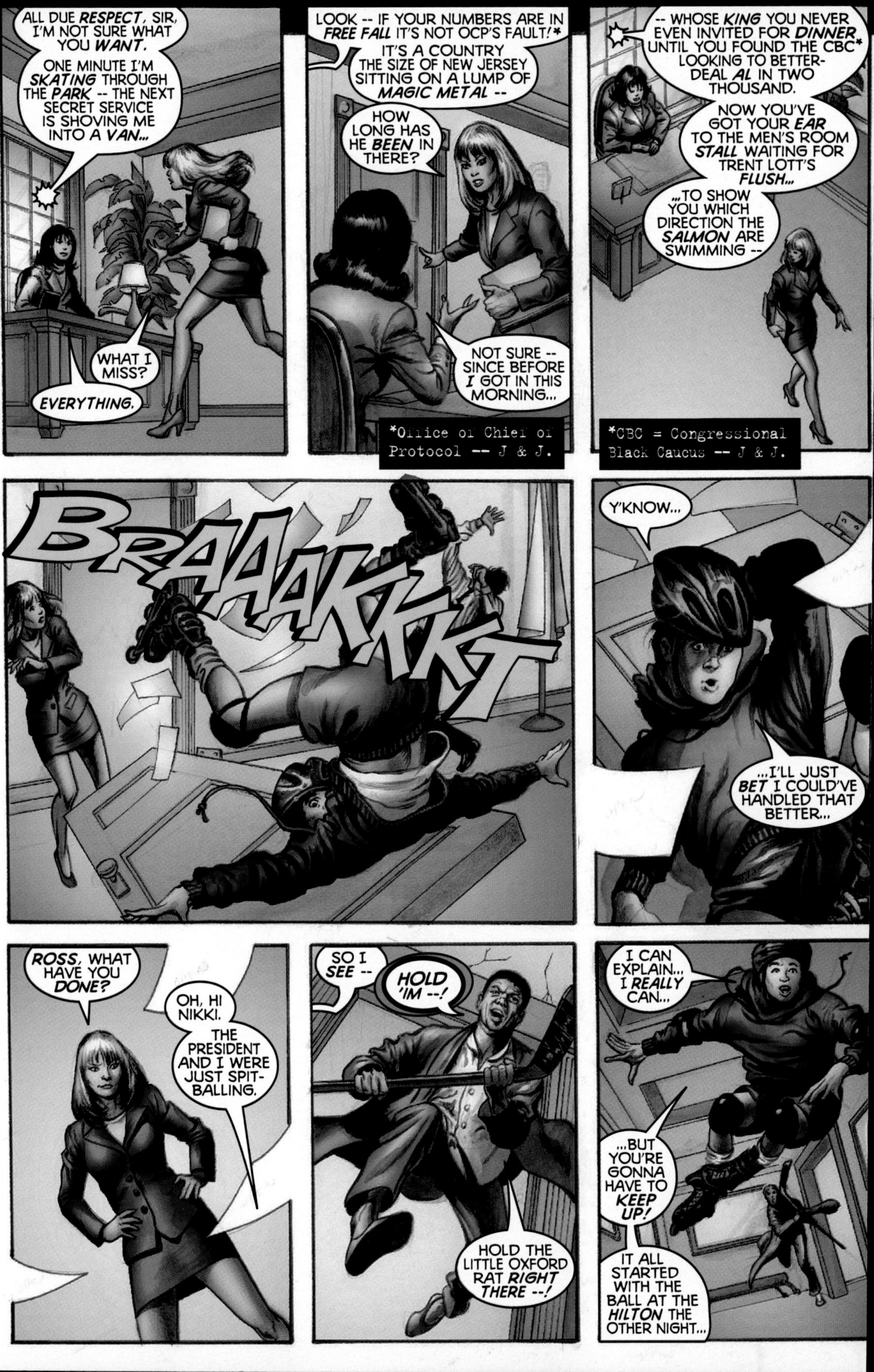
ALL DUE RESPECT, SIR, I'M NOT SURE WHAT YOU WANT.
ONE MINUTE I'M SKATING THROUGH THE PARK -- THE NEXT SECRET SERVICE IS SHOVING ME INTO A VAN...
WHAT I MISS?
EVERYTHING.
LOOK -- IF YOUR NUMBERS ARE IN FREE FALL IT'S NOT OCP'S FAULT!*
IT'S A COUNTRY THE SIZE OF NEW JERSEY SITTING ON A LUMP OF MAGIC METAL --
HOW LONG HAS HE BEEN IN THERE?
NOT SURE -- SINCE BEFORE I GOT IN THIS MORNING...
*Office of Chief of Protocol -- J & J.
-- WHOSE KING YOU NEVER EVEN INVITED FOR DINNER UNTIL YOU FOUND THE CBC* LOOKING TO BETTER-DEAL AL IN TWO THOUSAND.
NOW YOU'VE GOT YOUR EAR TO THE MEN'S ROOM STALL WAITING FOR TRENT LOTT'S FLUSH...
...TO SHOW YOU WHICH DIRECTION THE SALMON ARE SWIMMING --
*CBC = Congressional Black Caucus -- J & J.
BRAAAKKKT
Y'KNOW...
...I'LL JUST BET I COULD'VE HANDLED THAT BETTER...
ROSS, WHAT HAVE YOU DONE?
OH, HI NIKKI.
THE PRESIDENT AND I WERE JUST SPIT-BALLING.
SO I SEE --
HOLD 'IM --!
HOLD THE LITTLE OXFORD RAT RIGHT THERE --!
I CAN EXPLAIN... I REALLY CAN...
...BUT YOU'RE GONNA HAVE TO KEEP UP!
IT ALL STARTED WITH THE BALL AT THE HILTON THE OTHER NIGHT...

DUCK TIME

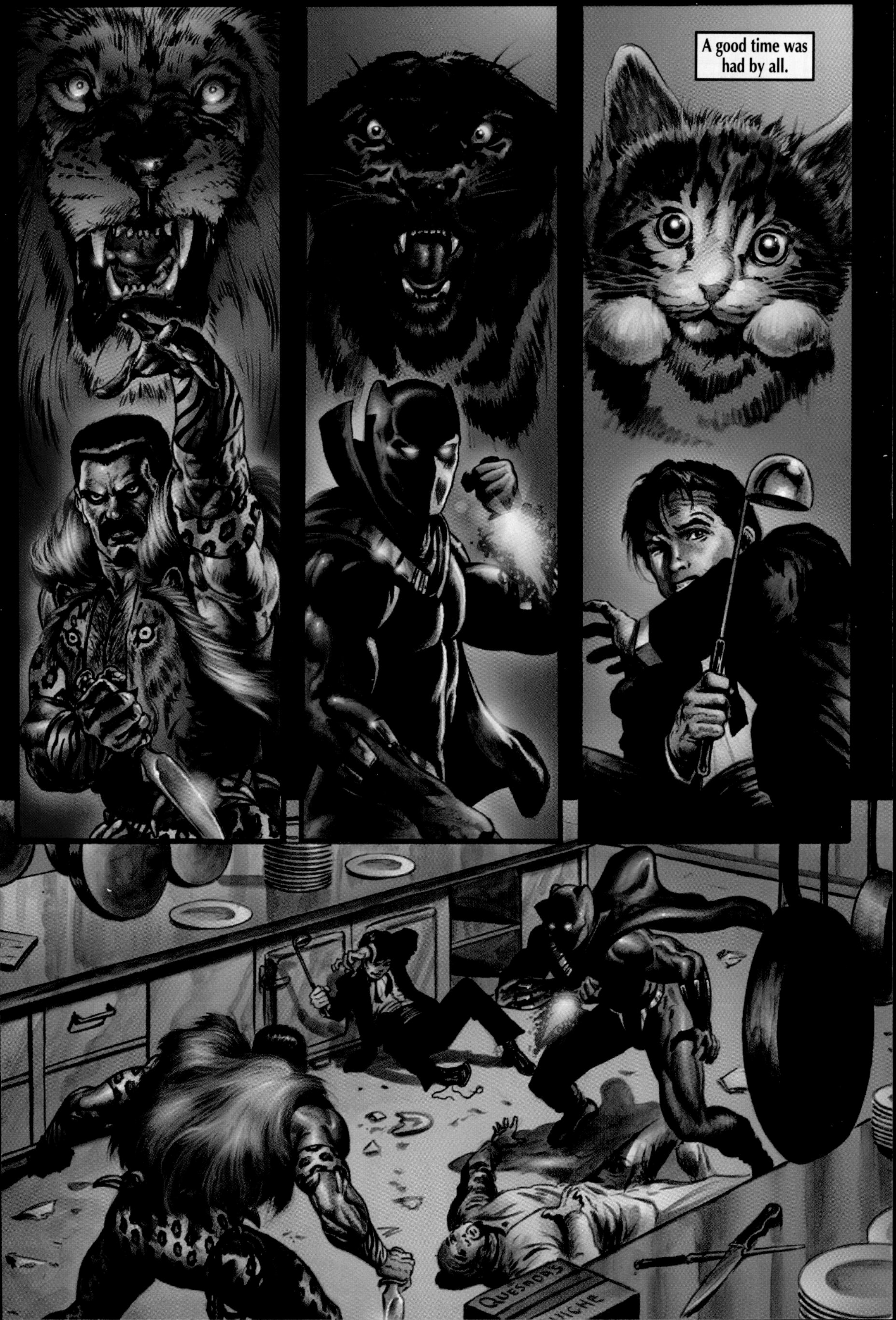
A good time was had by all.

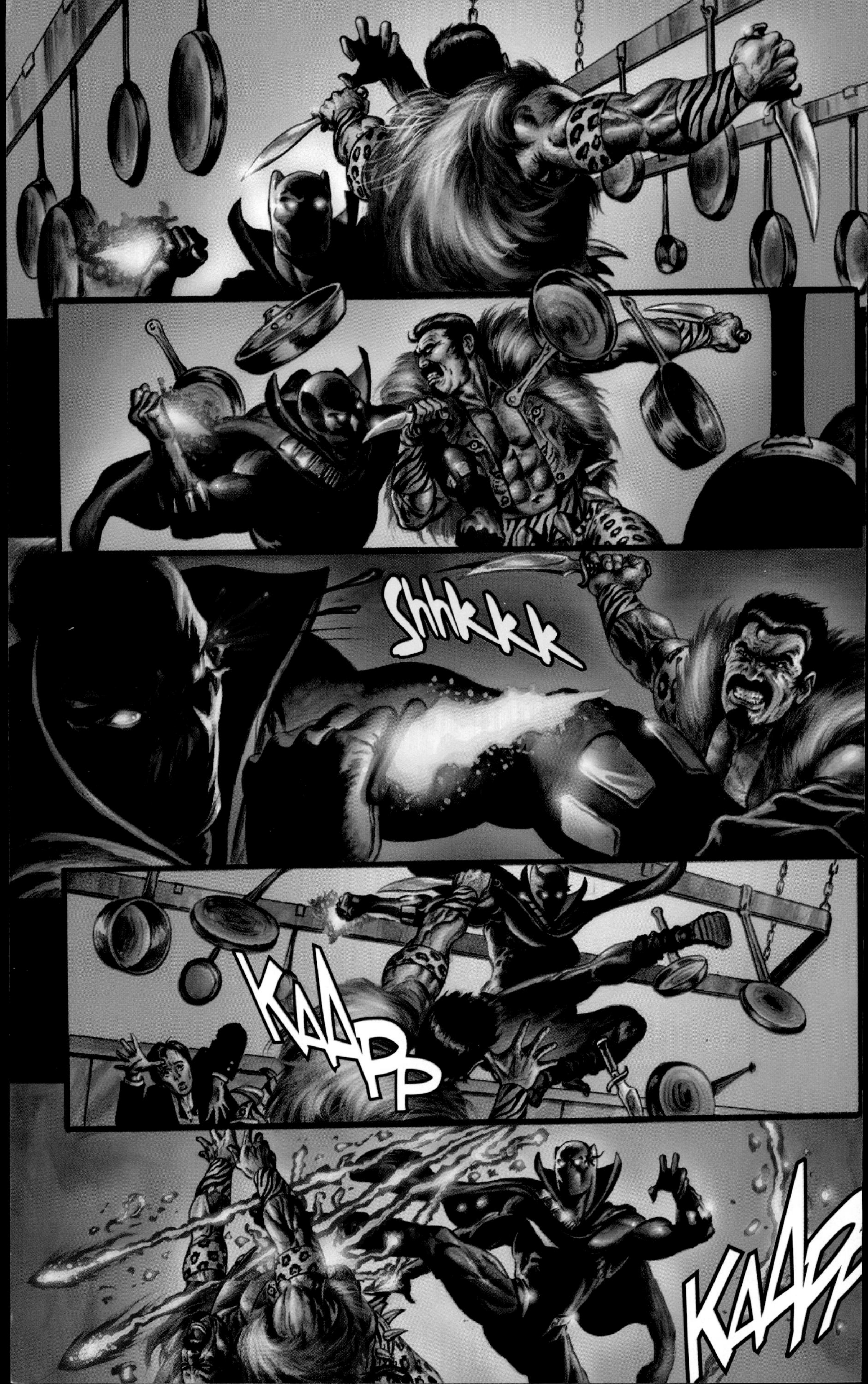

Shhkkk
KAAPP
KAAP

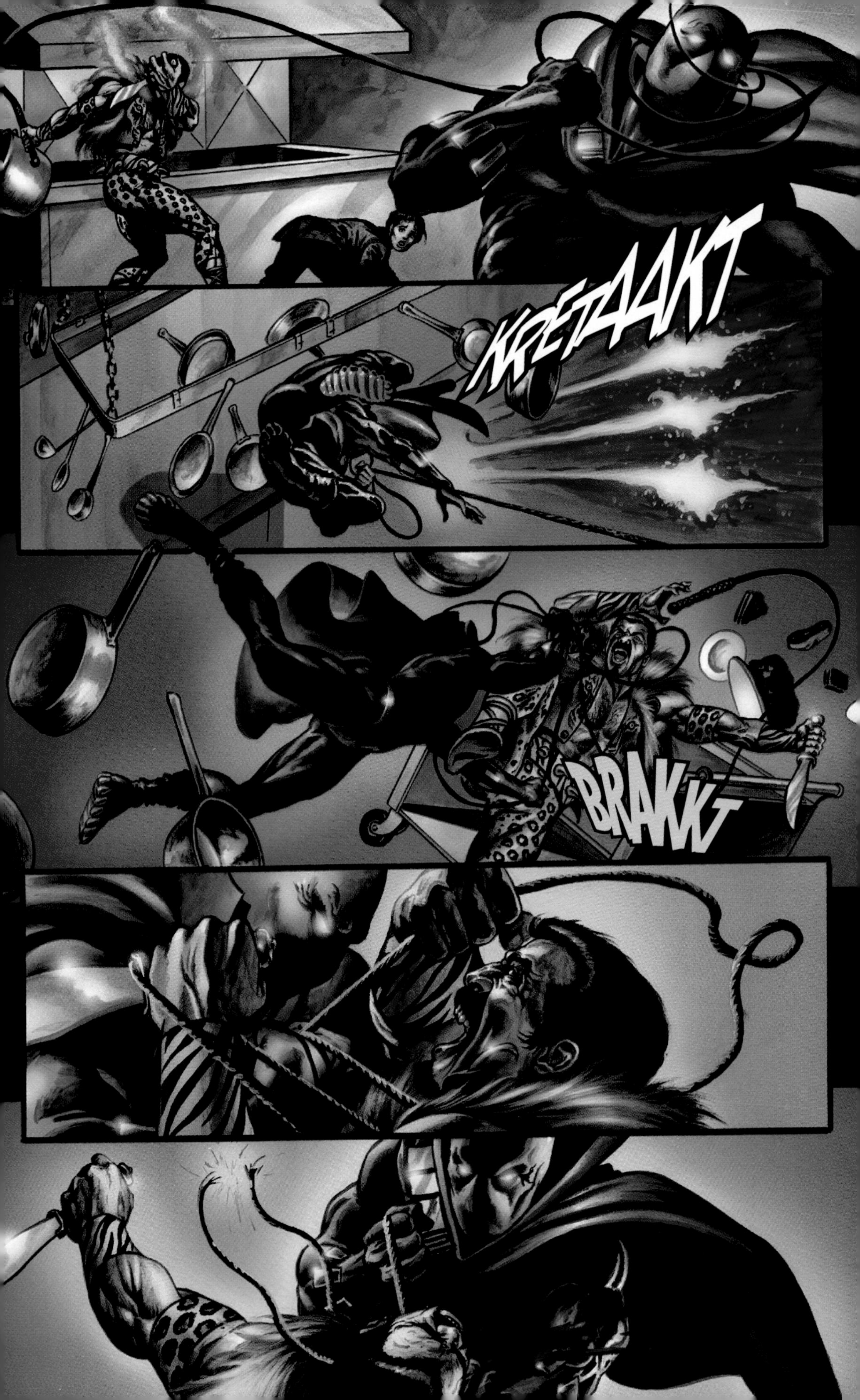
KREEAAKT
BRAKKT

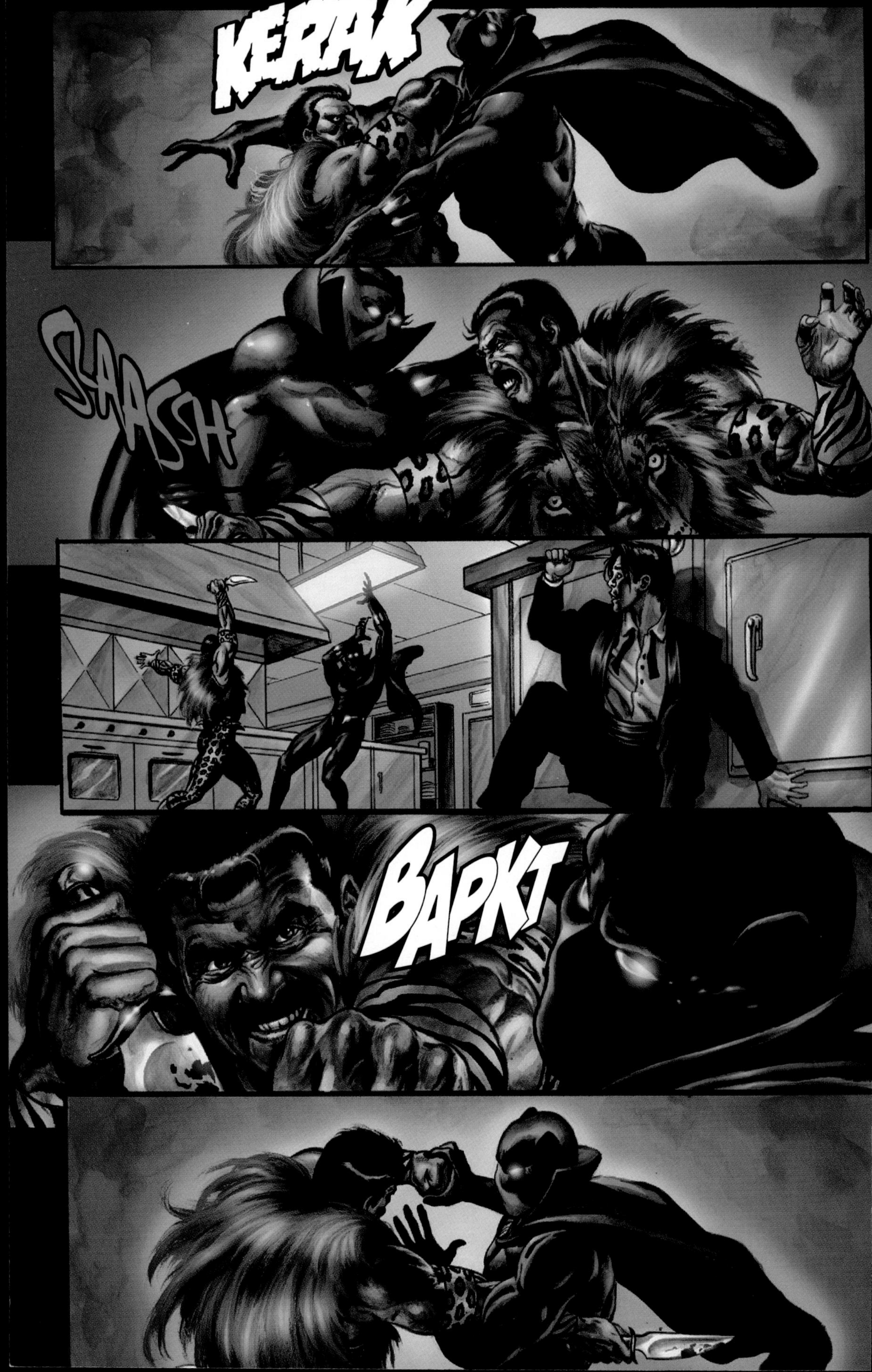
KERAK
SLASH
BAPKT

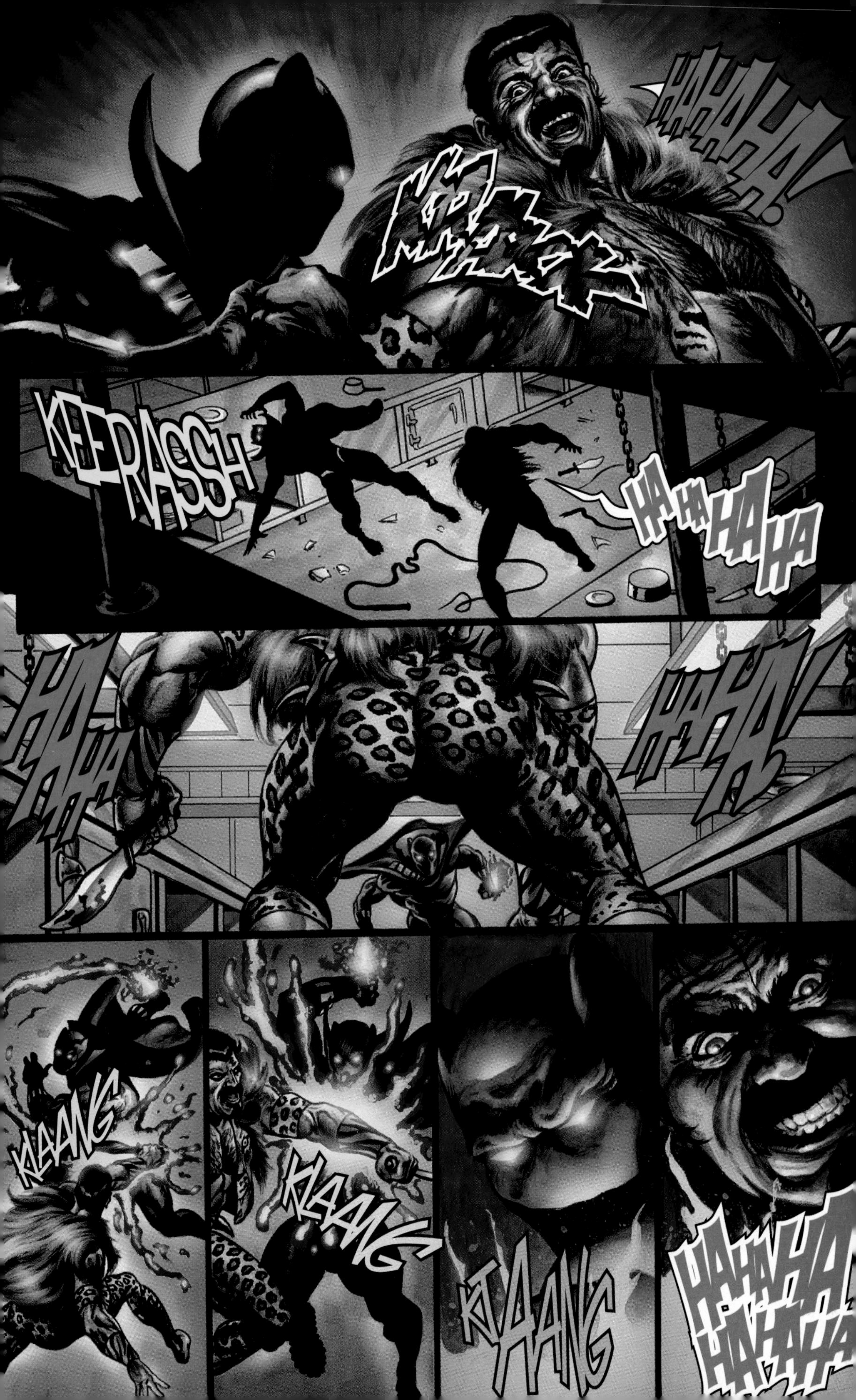
HAHAHA!
KEERASSH
HA HA HAHAHA
HAHA
HAHA!
KLAANG
KLAANG
KLAANG
HAHAHA
HAHAHA

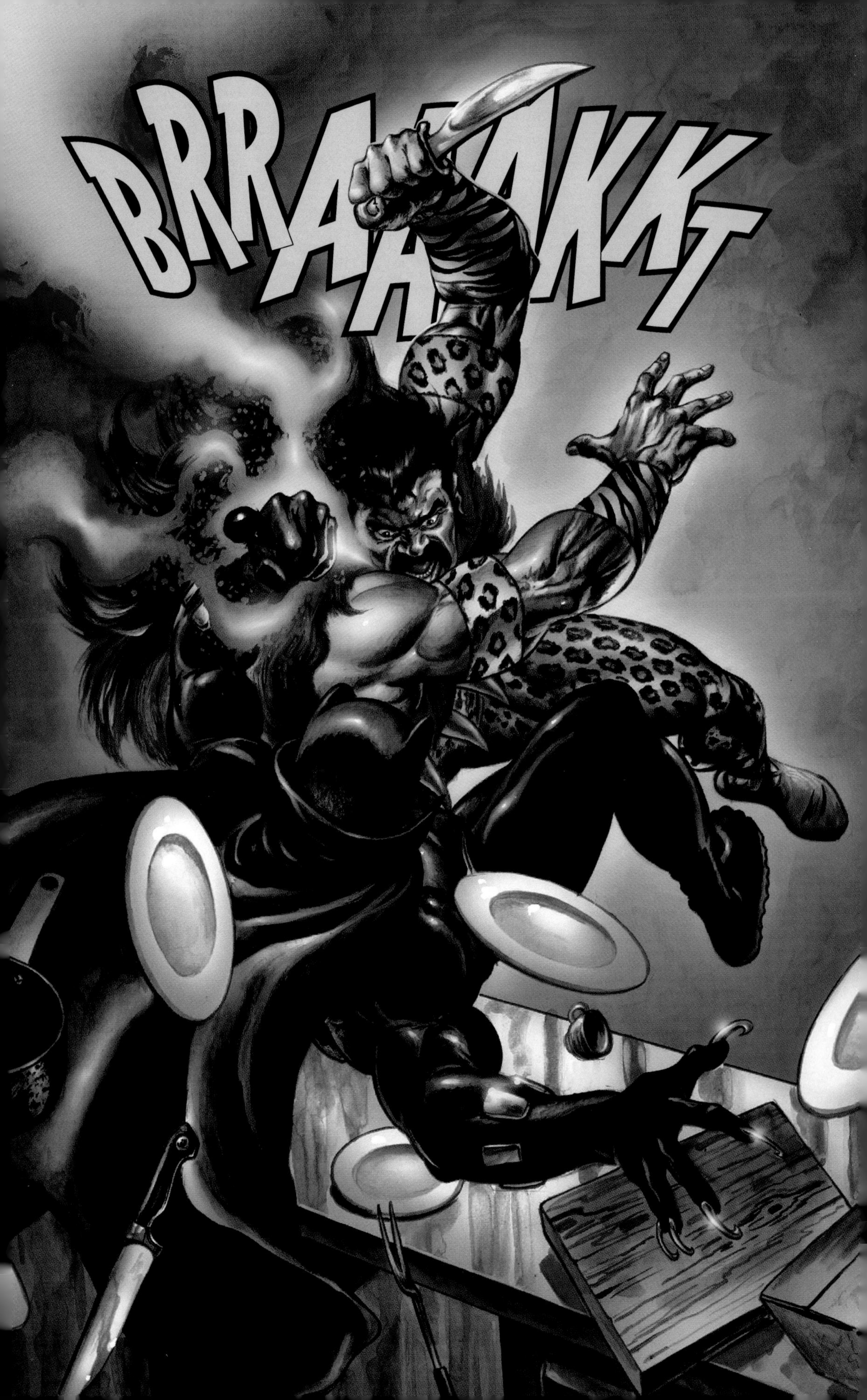
BRRAAAKKT

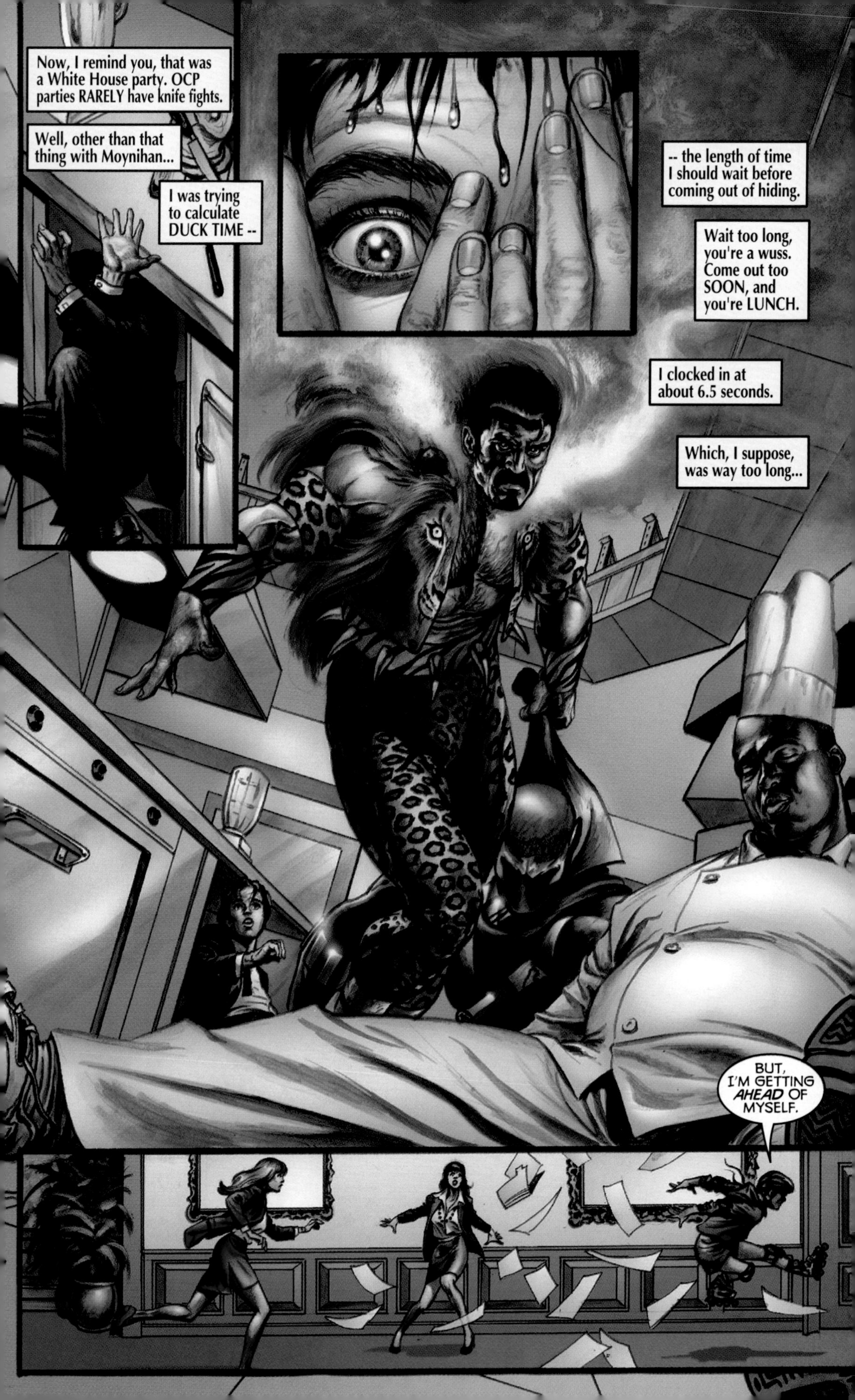
Now, I remind you, that was a White House party. OCP parties RARELY have knife fights.
Well, other than that thing with Moynihan...
I was trying to calculate DUCK TIME --
-- the length of time I should wait before coming out of hiding.
Wait too long, you're a wuss. Come out too SOON, and you're LUNCH.
I clocked in at about 6.5 seconds.
Which, I suppose, was way too long...
BUT, I'M GETTING AHEAD OF MYSELF.

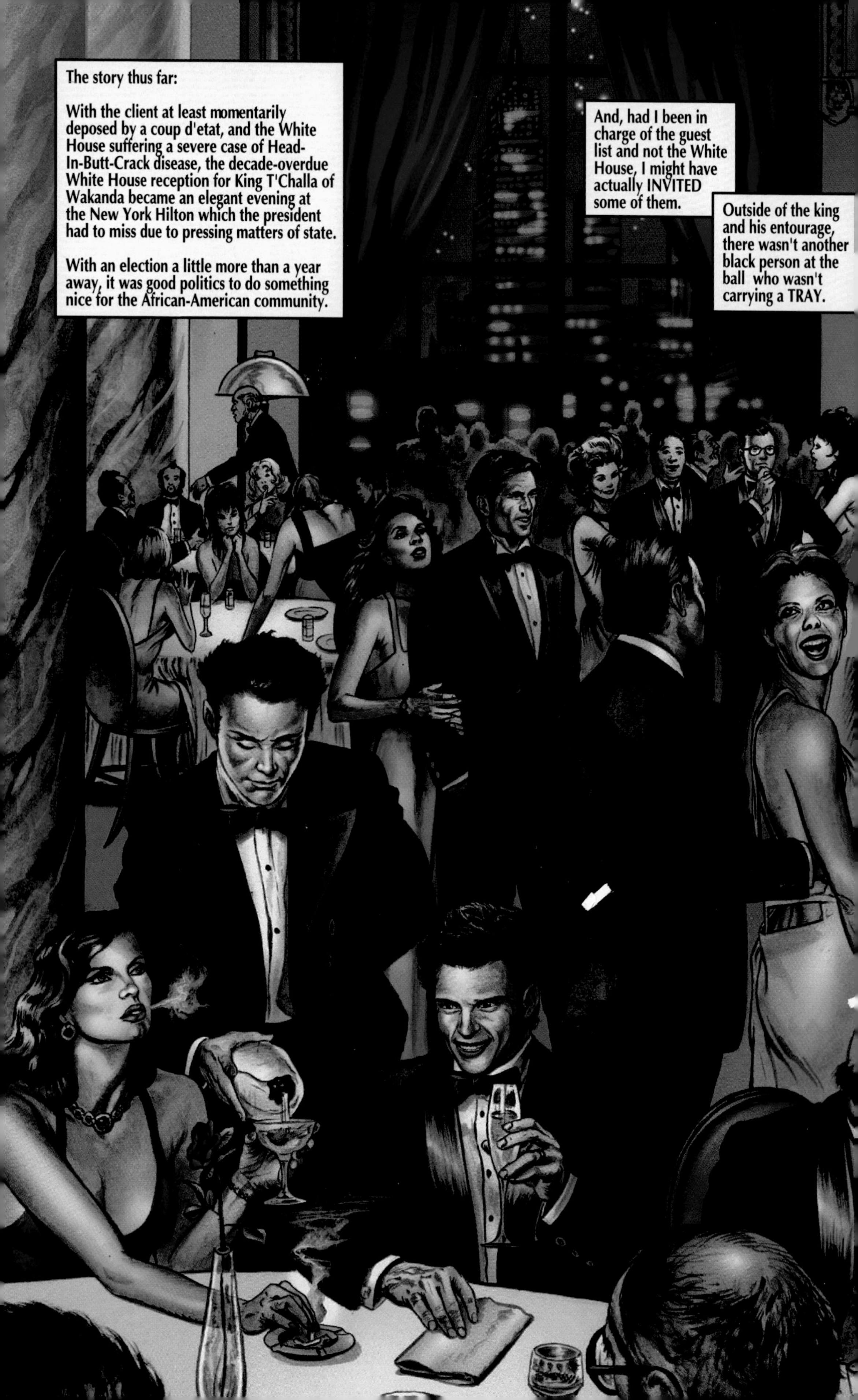
The story thus far:
With the client at least momentarily deposed by a coup d'etat, and the White House suffering a severe case of Head-In-Butt-Crack disease, the decade-overdue White House reception for King T'Challa of Wakanda became an elegant evening at the New York Hilton which the president had to miss due to pressing matters of state.
With an election a little more than a year away, it was good politics to do something nice for the African-American community.
And, had I been in charge of the guest list and not the White House, I might have actually INVITED some of them.
Outside of the king and his entourage, there wasn't another black person at the ball who wasn't carrying a TRAY.

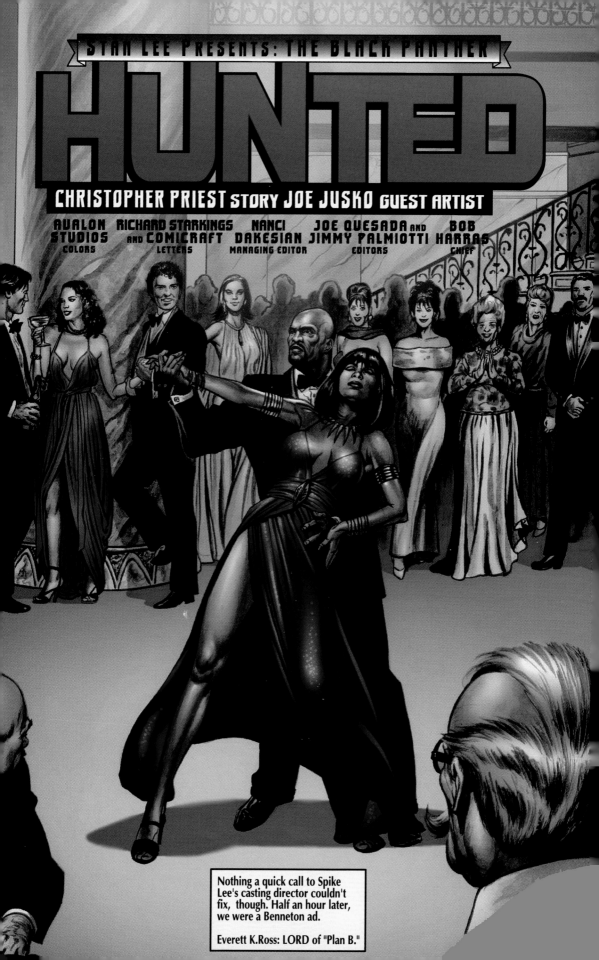

STAN LEE PRESENTS: THE BLACK PANTHER

HUNTED

CHRISTOPHER PRIEST STORY JOE JUSKO GUEST ARTIST

AVALON STUDIOS COLORS — RICHARD STARKINGS AND COMICRAFT LETTERS — NANCI DAKESIAN MANAGING EDITOR — JOE QUESADA AND JIMMY PALMIOTTI EDITORS — BOB HARRAS CHIEF

Nothing a quick call to Spike Lee's casting director couldn't fix, though. Half an hour later, we were a Benneton ad.

Everett K. Ross: LORD of "Plan B."

LAST TANGO IN WAKANDA

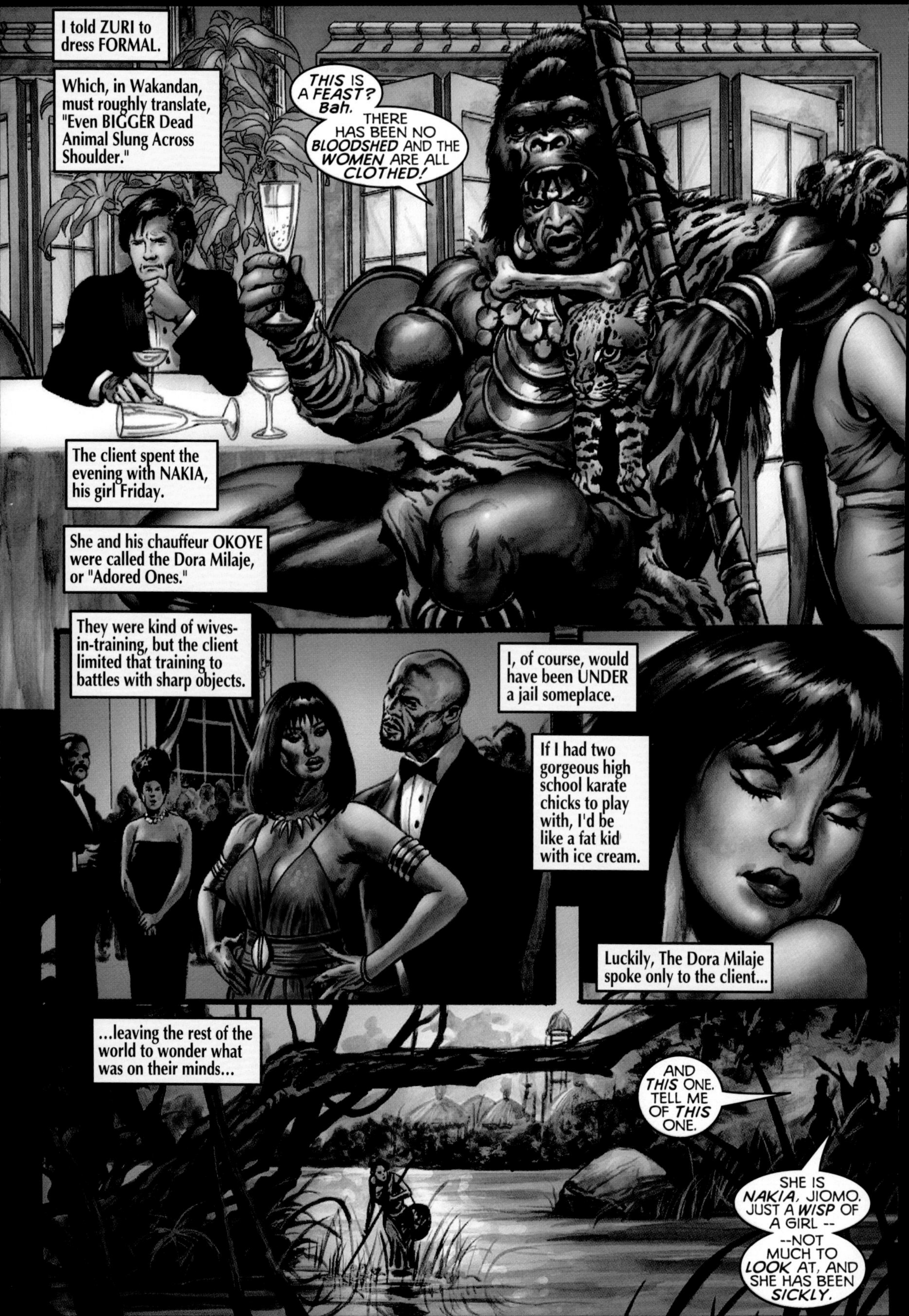
I told ZURI to dress FORMAL.
Which, in Wakandan, must roughly translate, "Even BIGGER Dead Animal Slung Across Shoulder."
THIS IS A FEAST? Bah. THERE HAS BEEN NO BLOODSHED AND THE WOMEN ARE ALL CLOTHED!
The client spent the evening with NAKIA, his girl Friday.
She and his chauffeur OKOYE were called the Dora Milaje, or "Adored Ones."
They were kind of wives-in-training, but the client limited that training to battles with sharp objects.
I, of course, would have been UNDER a jail someplace.
If I had two gorgeous high school karate chicks to play with, I'd be like a fat kid with ice cream.
Luckily, The Dora Milaje spoke only to the client...
...leaving the rest of the world to wonder what was on their minds...
AND THIS ONE. TELL ME OF THIS ONE.
SHE IS NAKIA, JIOMO. JUST A WISP OF A GIRL --
--NOT MUCH TO LOOK AT, AND SHE HAS BEEN SICKLY.

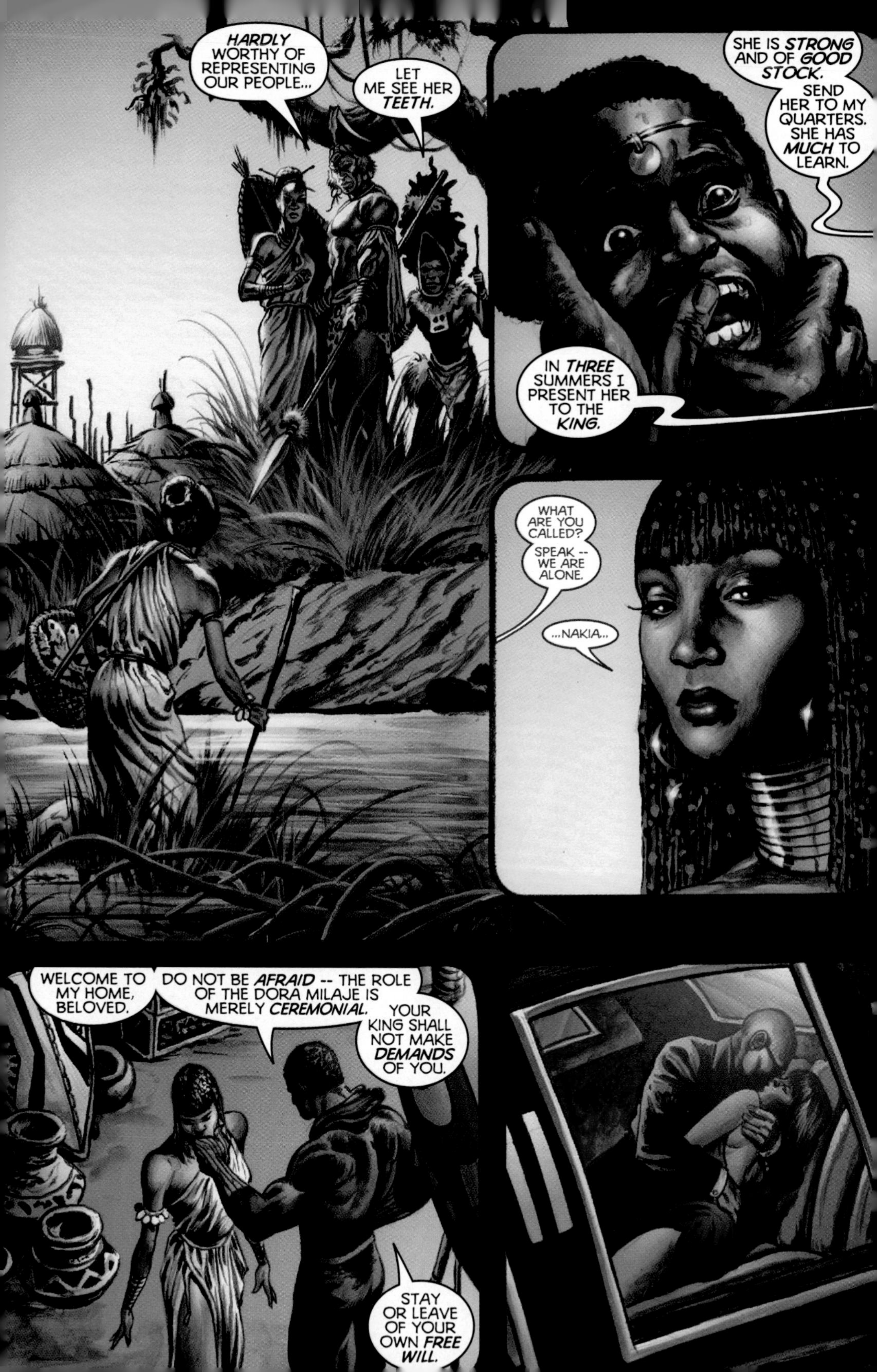
HARDLY WORTHY OF REPRESENTING OUR PEOPLE...
LET ME SEE HER TEETH.
SHE IS STRONG AND OF GOOD STOCK.
SEND HER TO MY QUARTERS. SHE HAS MUCH TO LEARN.
IN THREE SUMMERS I PRESENT HER TO THE KING.
WHAT ARE YOU CALLED?
SPEAK -- WE ARE ALONE.
...NAKIA...
WELCOME TO MY HOME, BELOVED.
DO NOT BE AFRAID -- THE ROLE OF THE DORA MILAJE IS MERELY CEREMONIAL.
YOUR KING SHALL NOT MAKE DEMANDS OF YOU.
STAY OR LEAVE OF YOUR OWN FREE WILL.

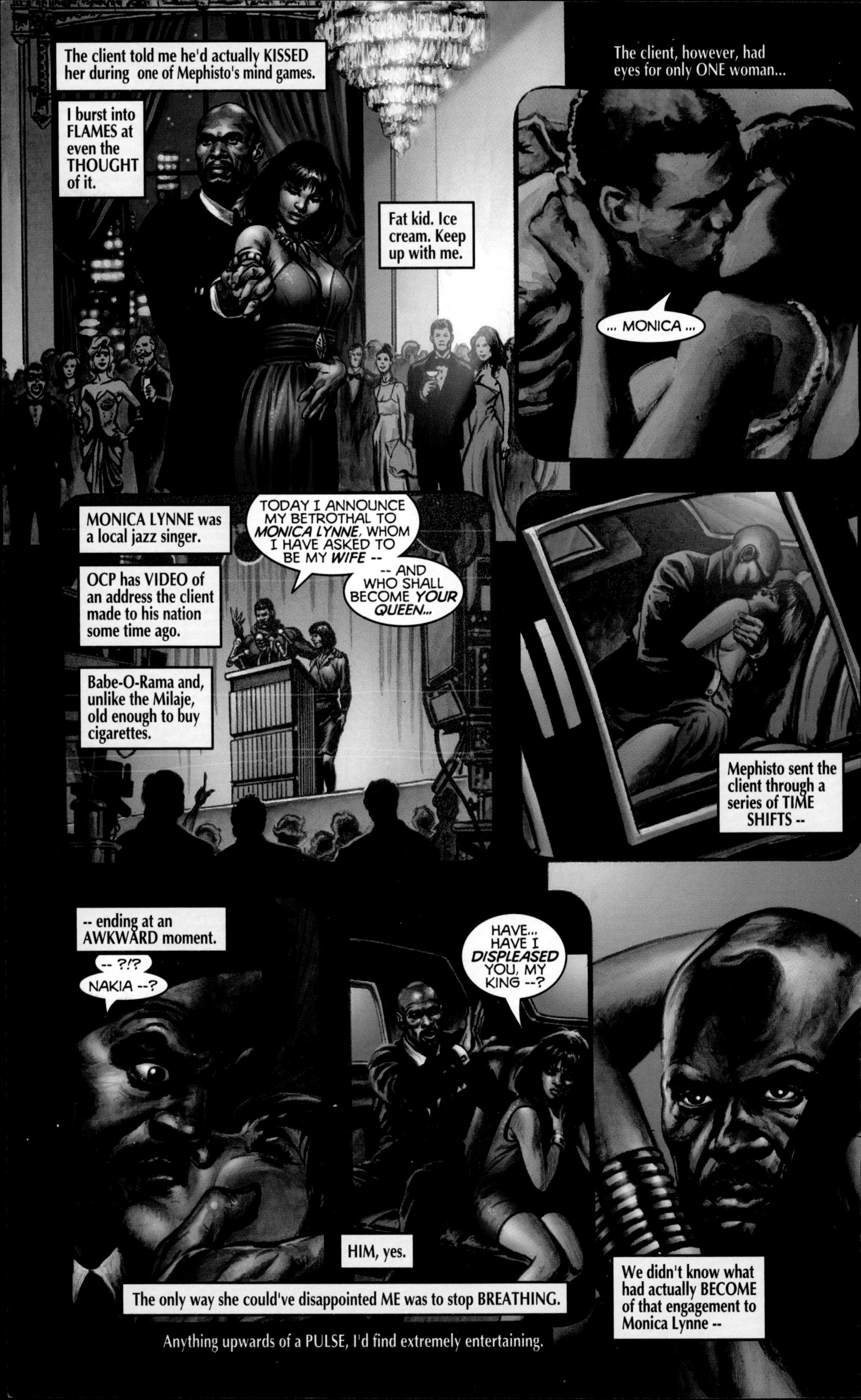
The client told me he'd actually KISSED her during one of Mephisto's mind games.
I burst into FLAMES at even the THOUGHT of it.
Fat kid. Ice cream. Keep up with me.
The client, however, had eyes for only ONE woman...
... MONICA ...
MONICA LYNNE was a local jazz singer.
OCP has VIDEO of an address the client made to his nation some time ago.
Babe-O-Rama and, unlike the Milaje, old enough to buy cigarettes.
TODAY I ANNOUNCE MY BETROTHAL TO MONICA LYNNE, WHOM I HAVE ASKED TO BE MY WIFE --
-- AND WHO SHALL BECOME YOUR QUEEN...
Mephisto sent the client through a series of TIME SHIFTS --
-- ending at an AWKWARD moment.
-- ?!? NAKIA --?
HAVE.. HAVE I DISPLEASED YOU, MY KING --?
HIM, yes.
The only way she could've disappointed ME was to stop BREATHING.
Anything upwards of a PULSE, I'd find extremely entertaining.
We didn't know what had actually BECOME of that engagement to Monica Lynne --

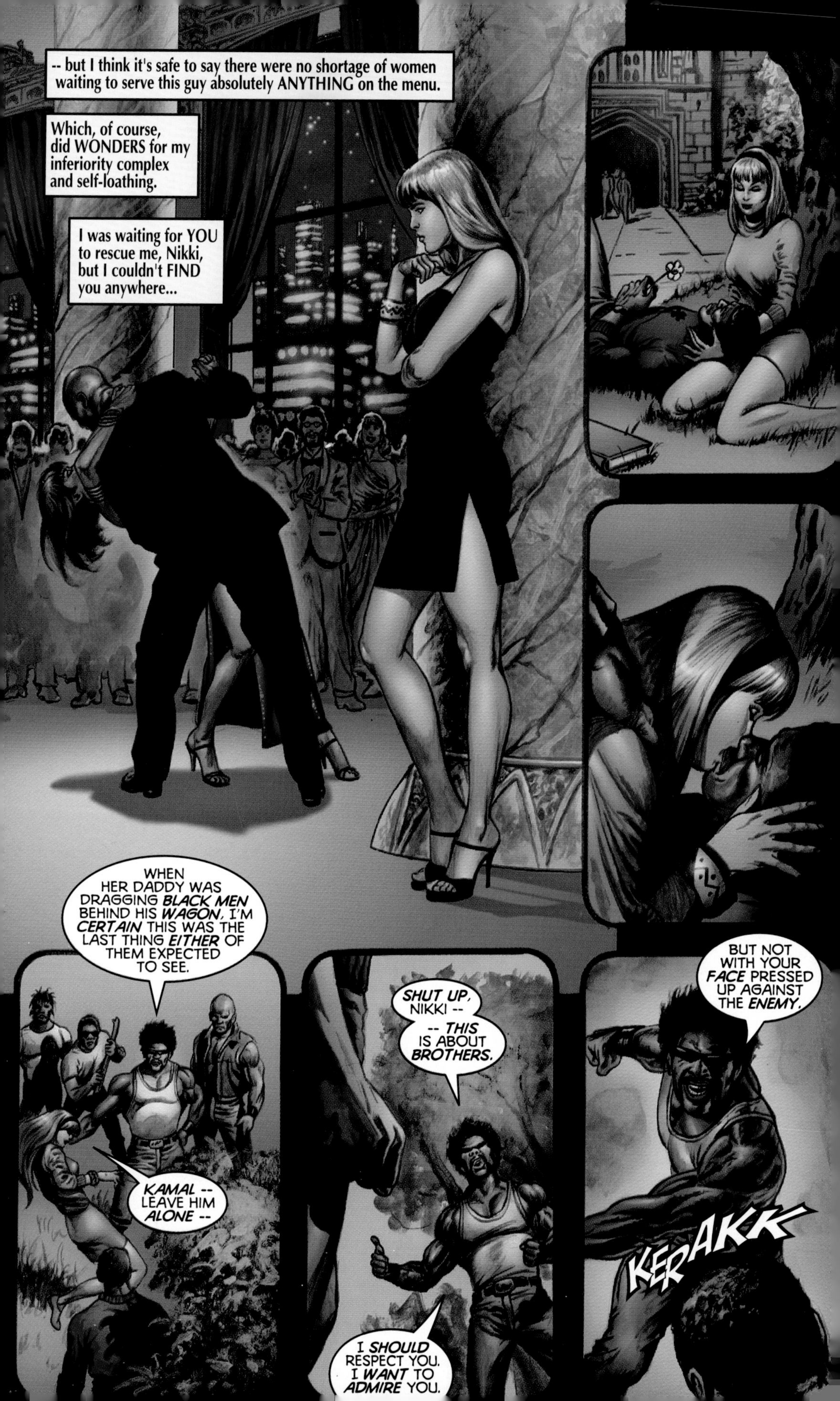

-- but I think it's safe to say there were no shortage of women waiting to serve this guy absolutely ANYTHING on the menu.
Which, of course, did WONDERS for my inferiority complex and self-loathing.
I was waiting for YOU to rescue me, Nikki, but I couldn't FIND you anywhere...
WHEN HER DADDY WAS DRAGGING BLACK MEN BEHIND HIS WAGON, I'M CERTAIN THIS WAS THE LAST THING EITHER OF THEM EXPECTED TO SEE.
KAMAL -- LEAVE HIM ALONE --
SHUT UP, NIKKI --
-- THIS IS ABOUT BROTHERS.
I SHOULD RESPECT YOU. I WANT TO ADMIRE YOU.
BUT NOT WITH YOUR FACE PRESSED UP AGAINST THE ENEMY.
KERAKK

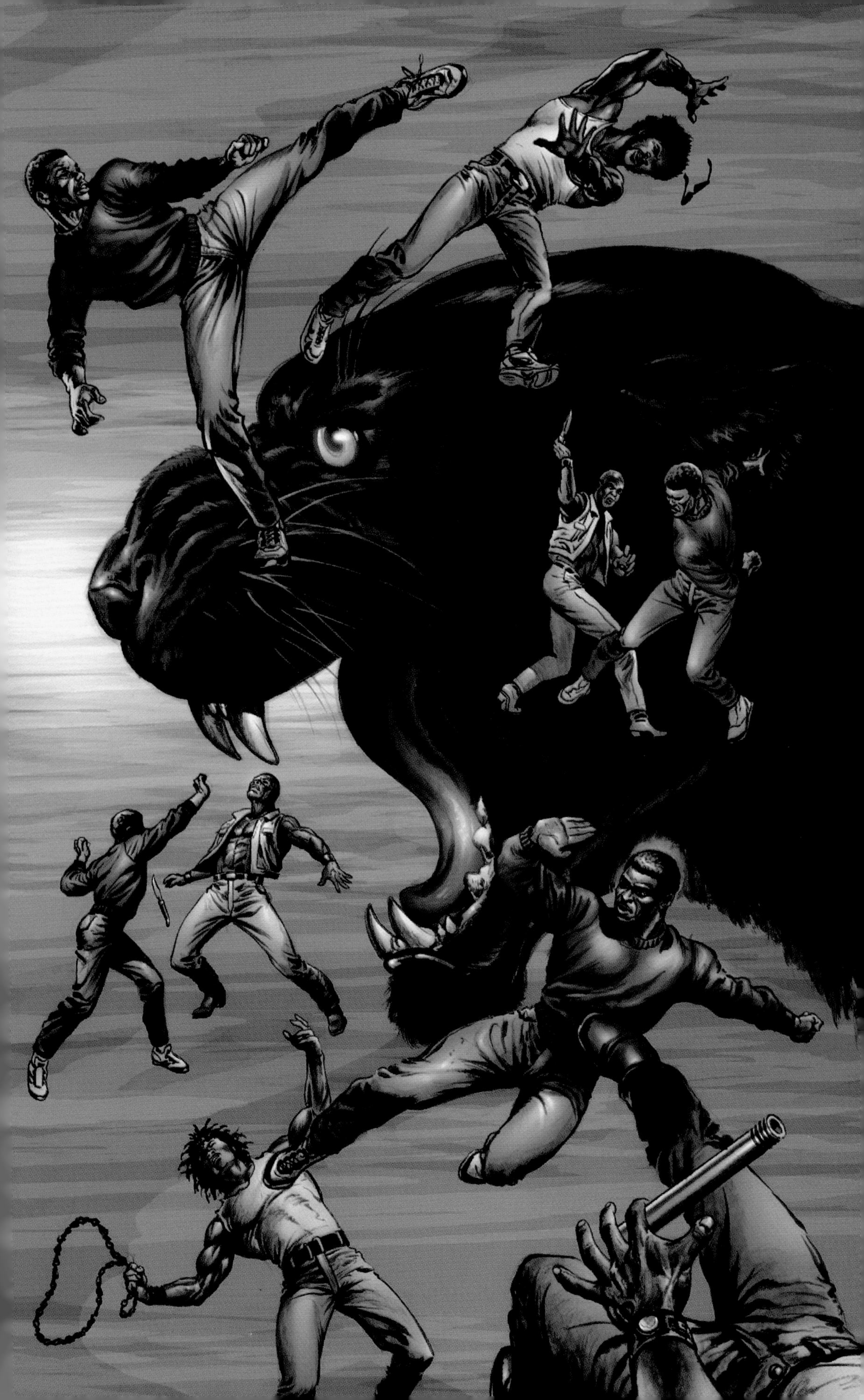

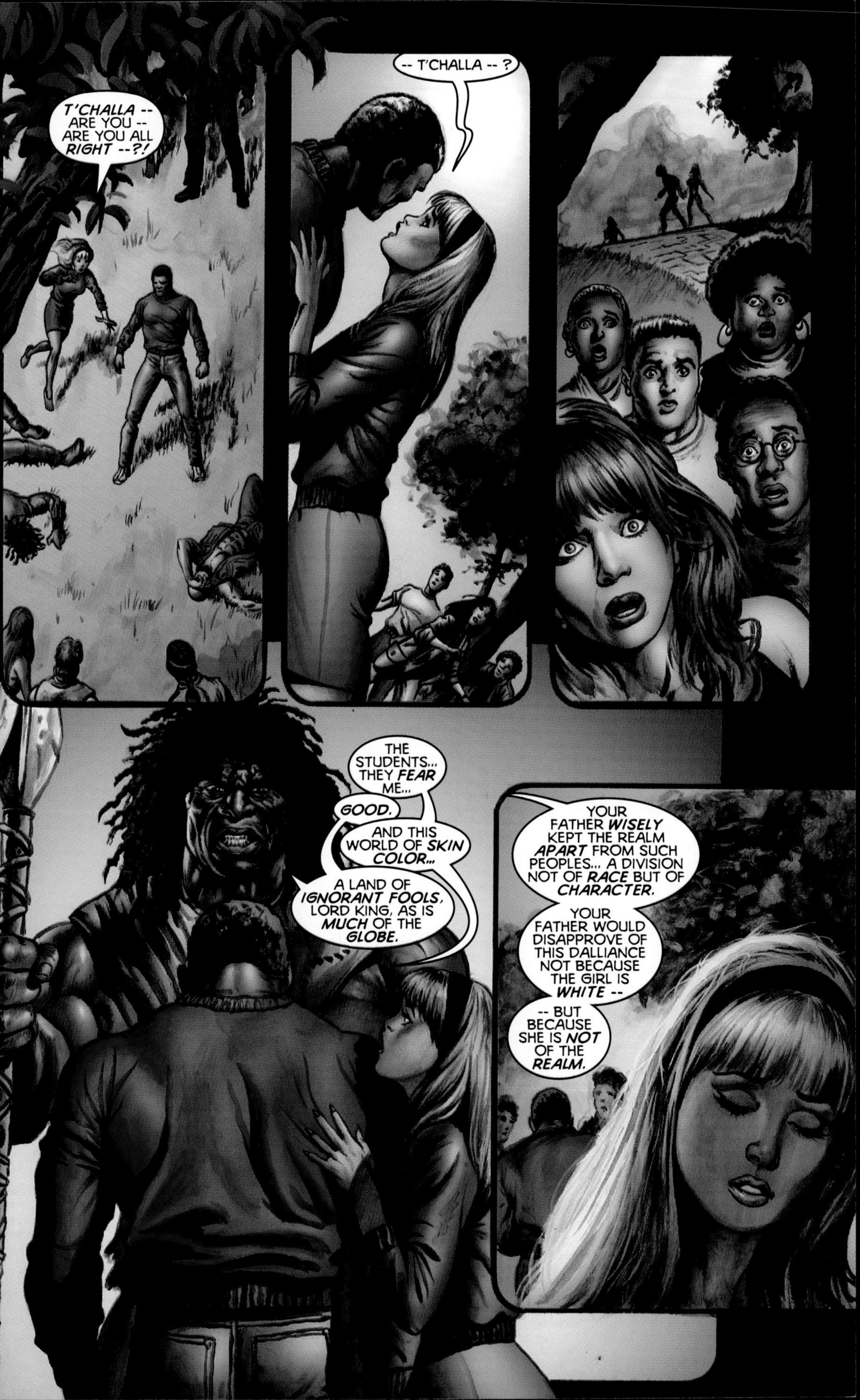

T'CHALLA -- ARE YOU -- ARE YOU ALL RIGHT --?!
-- T'CHALLA -- ?
THE STUDENTS... THEY FEAR ME...
GOOD.
AND THIS WORLD OF SKIN COLOR...
A LAND OF IGNORANT FOOLS, LORD KING, AS IS MUCH OF THE GLOBE.
YOUR FATHER WISELY KEPT THE REALM APART FROM SUCH PEOPLES... A DIVISION NOT OF RACE BUT OF CHARACTER.
YOUR FATHER WOULD DISAPPROVE OF THIS DALLIANCE NOT BECAUSE THE GIRL IS WHITE --
-- BUT BECAUSE SHE IS NOT OF THE REALM.

CLAP CLAP CLAP CLAP
CLAP CLAP CLAP
CLAP

CLAP CLAP CLAP CLAP
CLAP CLAP
CLAP

CLAP
CLAP
CLAP
CLAP

And who KNEW he could TANGO -- ?

< BELOVED... WE MUST SPEAK... >

KING T'CHALLA -- EXCUSE ME FOR INTERRUPTING --

-- BUT IT'S BEEN A *VERY* LONG TIME. AND I OWE YOU A LONG-OVERDUE *APOLOGY.*

DON'T BE RIDICULOUS, SENATOR RAKIM.

-- ?! I'M *IMPRESSED,* YOUR HIGHNESS. AFTER ALL --

-- IT'S BEEN A *LONG TIME* SINCE COLLEGE.

I KNOW THE NAMES OF *ALL* U.S. SENATORS AND CONGRESSMEN, SENATOR.

IT'S STILL *KAMAL,* YOUR HIGHNESS.

AND I AM *STILL* T'CHALLA, KAMAL.

YOU KNOW *NIKK* IS WITH OCP NOW SAW HER HER A *MINUTE* AGO --

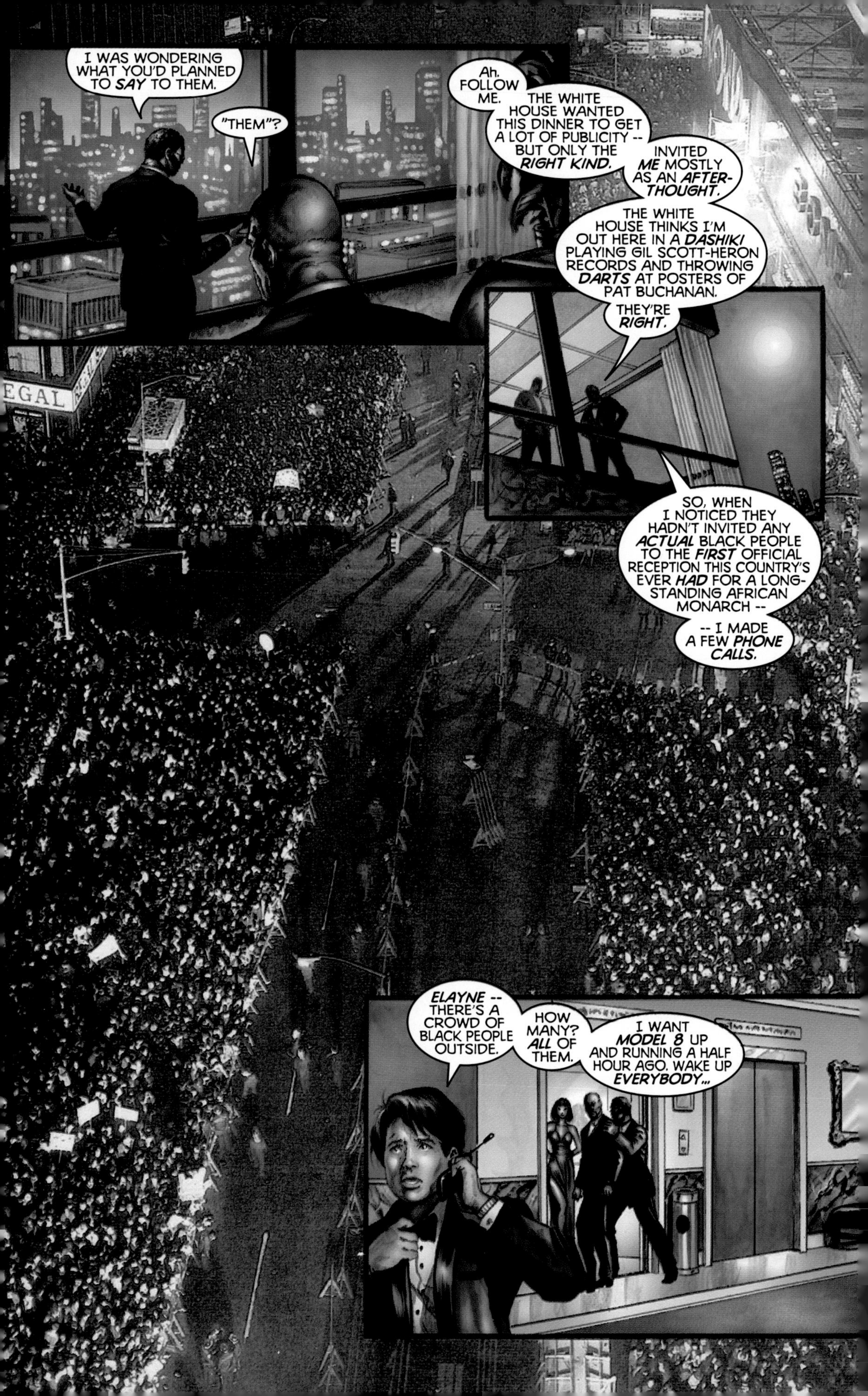
I WAS WONDERING WHAT YOU'D PLANNED TO *SAY* TO THEM.
"THEM"?
Ah. FOLLOW ME.
THE WHITE HOUSE WANTED THIS DINNER TO GET A LOT OF PUBLICITY -- BUT ONLY THE *RIGHT KIND.*
INVITED *ME* MOSTLY AS AN *AFTER-THOUGHT.*
THE WHITE HOUSE THINKS I'M OUT HERE IN A *DASHIKI* PLAYING GIL SCOTT-HERON RECORDS AND THROWING *DARTS* AT POSTERS OF PAT BUCHANAN.
THEY'RE *RIGHT.*
SO, WHEN I NOTICED THEY HADN'T INVITED ANY *ACTUAL* BLACK PEOPLE TO THE *FIRST* OFFICIAL RECEPTION THIS COUNTRY'S EVER *HAD* FOR A LONG-STANDING AFRICAN MONARCH --
-- I MADE A FEW *PHONE CALLS.*
EGAL
ELAYNE -- THERE'S A CROWD OF BLACK PEOPLE OUTSIDE.
HOW MANY? *ALL* OF THEM.
I WANT *MODEL 8* UP AND RUNNING A HALF HOUR AGO. WAKE UP *EVERYBODY*...

EVERYBODY

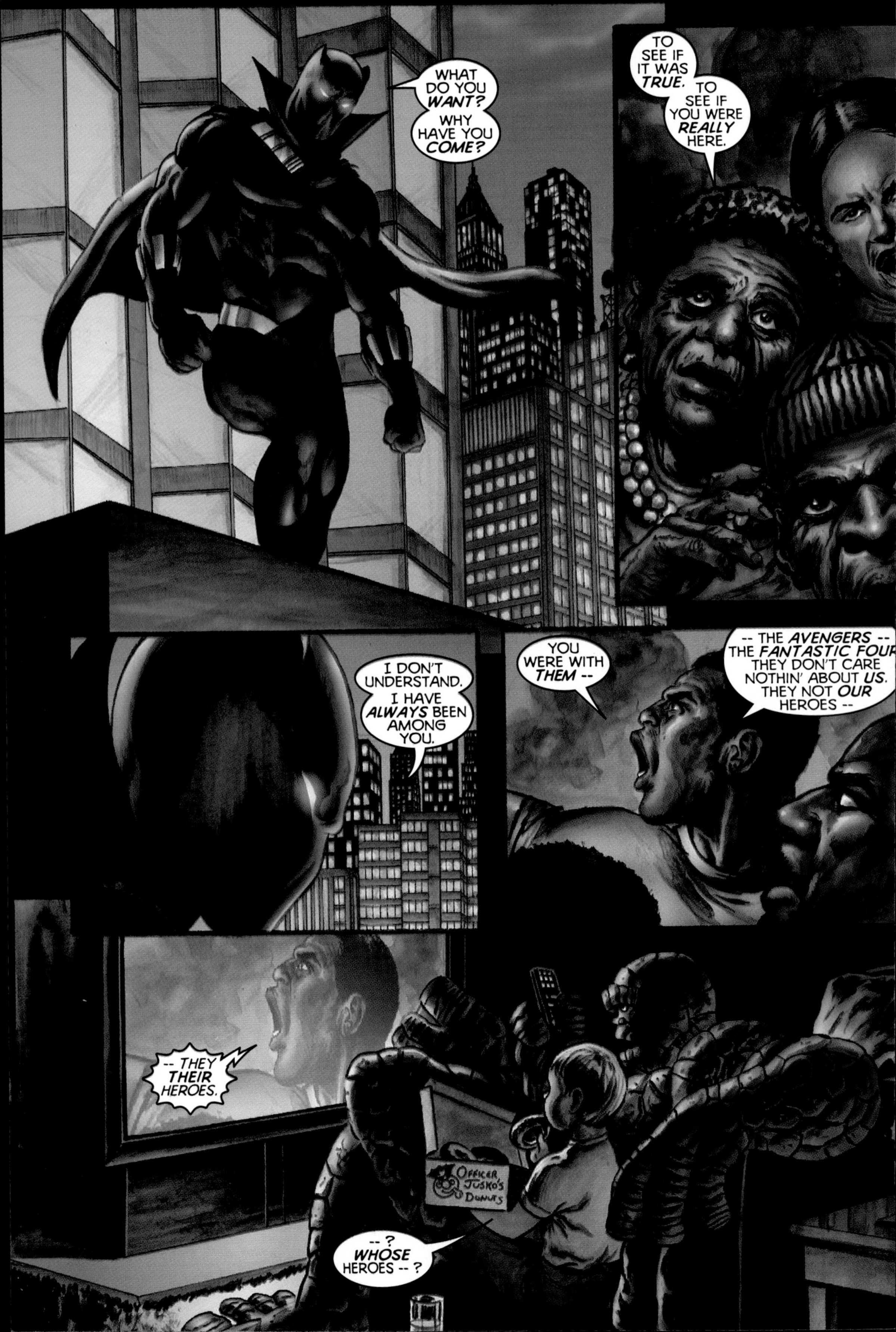
WHAT DO YOU WANT? WHY HAVE YOU COME?
TO SEE IF IT WAS TRUE.
TO SEE IF YOU WERE REALLY HERE.
I DON'T UNDERSTAND. I HAVE ALWAYS BEEN AMONG YOU.
YOU WERE WITH THEM --
-- THE AVENGERS -- THE FANTASTIC FOUR THEY DON'T CARE NOTHIN' ABOUT US. THEY NOT OUR HEROES --
-- THEY THEIR HEROES.
OFFICER JUSKO'S DONUTS
-- ? WHOSE HEROES -- ?

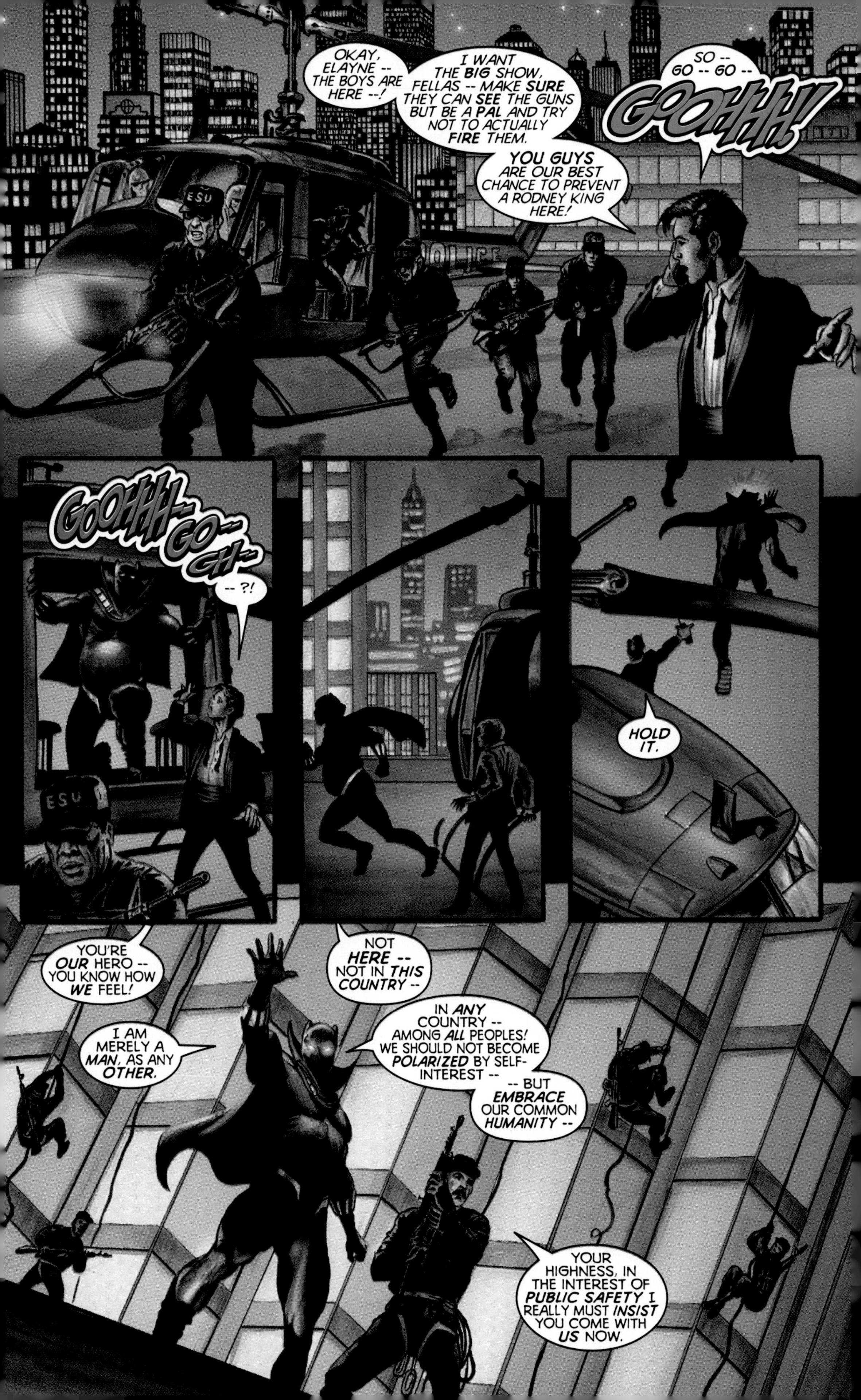
OKAY, ELAYNE -- THE BOYS ARE HERE --!
I WANT THE BIG SHOW, FELLAS -- MAKE SURE THEY CAN SEE THE GUNS BUT BE A PAL AND TRY NOT TO ACTUALLY FIRE THEM.
YOU GUYS ARE OUR BEST CHANCE TO PREVENT A RODNEY KING HERE!
SO -- GO -- GO -- GOOHHH!
GOOHHH-- GO-- GH--
-- ?!
HOLD IT.
YOU'RE OUR HERO -- YOU KNOW HOW WE FEEL!
I AM MERELY A MAN, AS ANY OTHER.
NOT HERE -- NOT IN THIS COUNTRY --
IN ANY COUNTRY -- AMONG ALL PEOPLES! WE SHOULD NOT BECOME POLARIZED BY SELF-INTEREST --
-- BUT EMBRACE OUR COMMON HUMANITY --
YOUR HIGHNESS, IN THE INTEREST OF PUBLIC SAFETY I REALLY MUST INSIST YOU COME WITH US NOW.

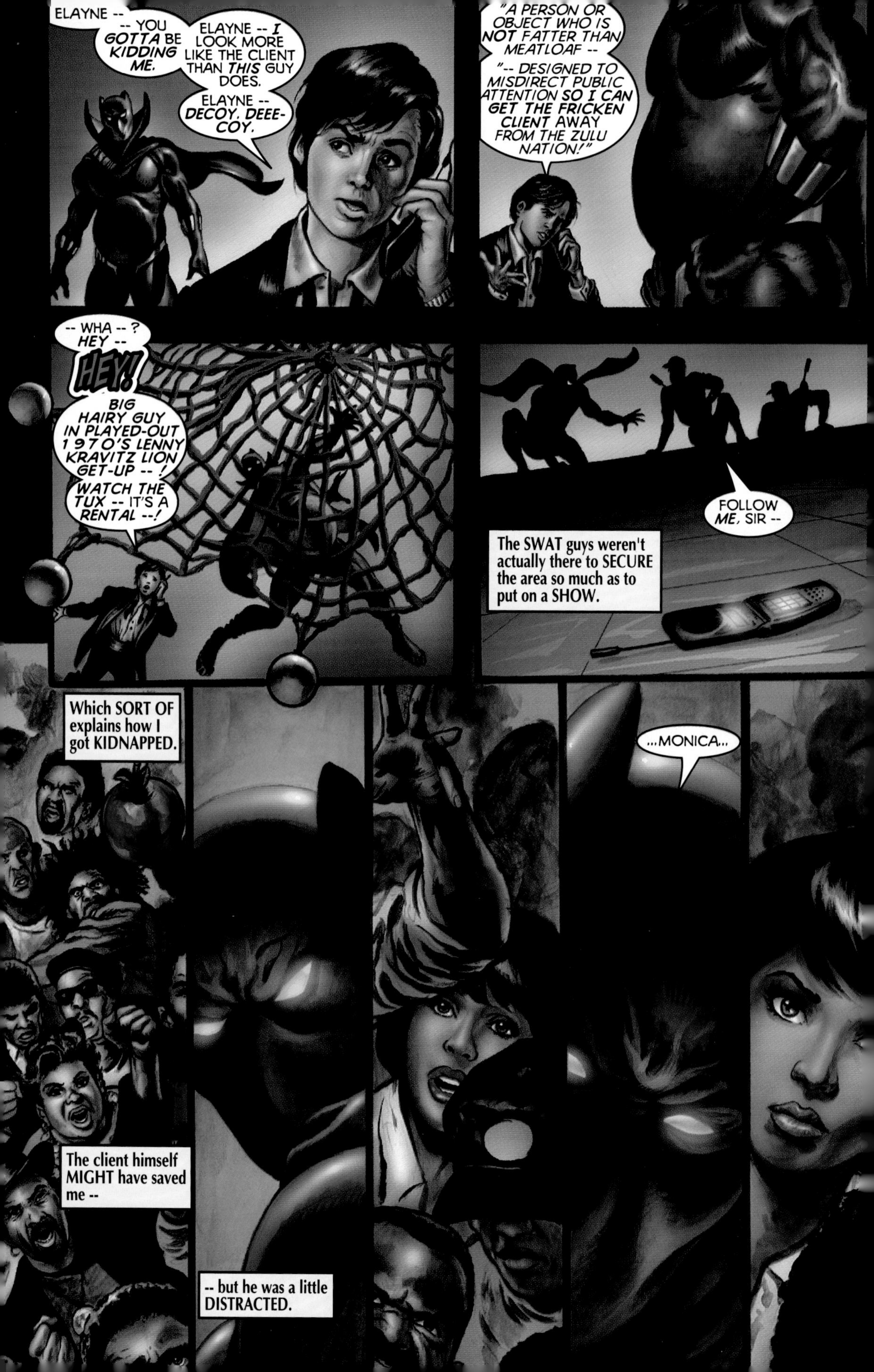
ELAYNE --
-- YOU *GOTTA* BE *KIDDING ME.*
ELAYNE -- *I* LOOK MORE LIKE THE CLIENT THAN *THIS* GUY DOES.
ELAYNE -- *DECOY. DEEE-COY.*
"A PERSON OR OBJECT WHO IS *NOT* FATTER THAN MEATLOAF --
"-- DESIGNED TO MISDIRECT PUBLIC ATTENTION *SO I CAN GET THE FRICKEN CLIENT* AWAY FROM THE ZULU NATION!"
-- WHA -- ? *HEY* --
HEY!
BIG HAIRY GUY IN PLAYED-OUT 1970'S LENNY KRAVITZ LION GET-UP -- !
WATCH THE TUX -- IT'S A *RENTAL* --!
FOLLOW *ME,* SIR --
The SWAT guys weren't actually there to SECURE the area so much as to put on a SHOW.
Which SORT OF explains how I got KIDNAPPED.
...MONICA...
The client himself MIGHT have saved me --
-- but he was a little DISTRACTED.

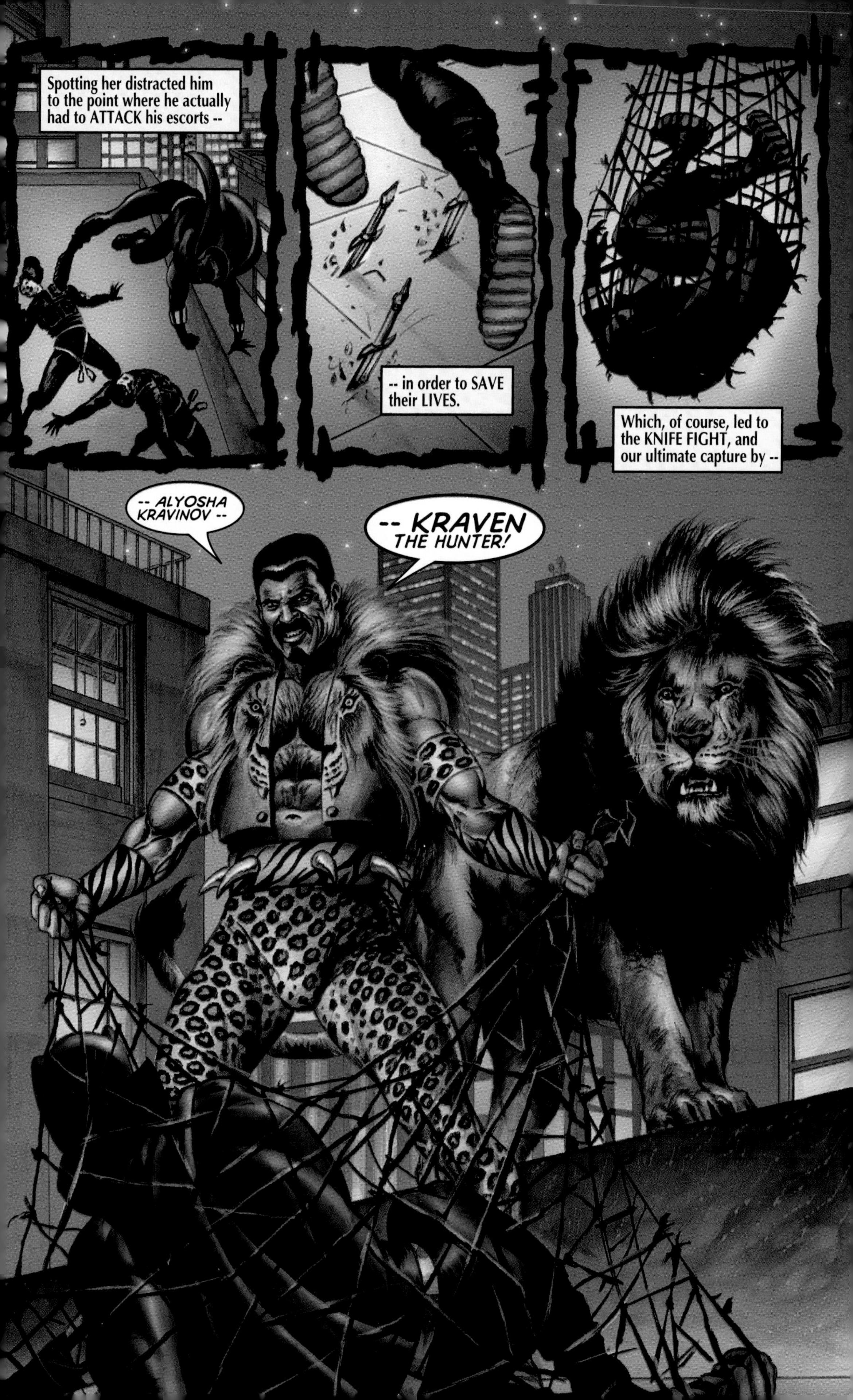

Spotting her distracted him to the point where he actually had to ATTACK his escorts --
-- in order to SAVE their LIVES.
Which, of course, led to the KNIFE FIGHT, and our ultimate capture by --
-- ALYOSHA KRAVINOV --
-- KRAVEN THE HUNTER!

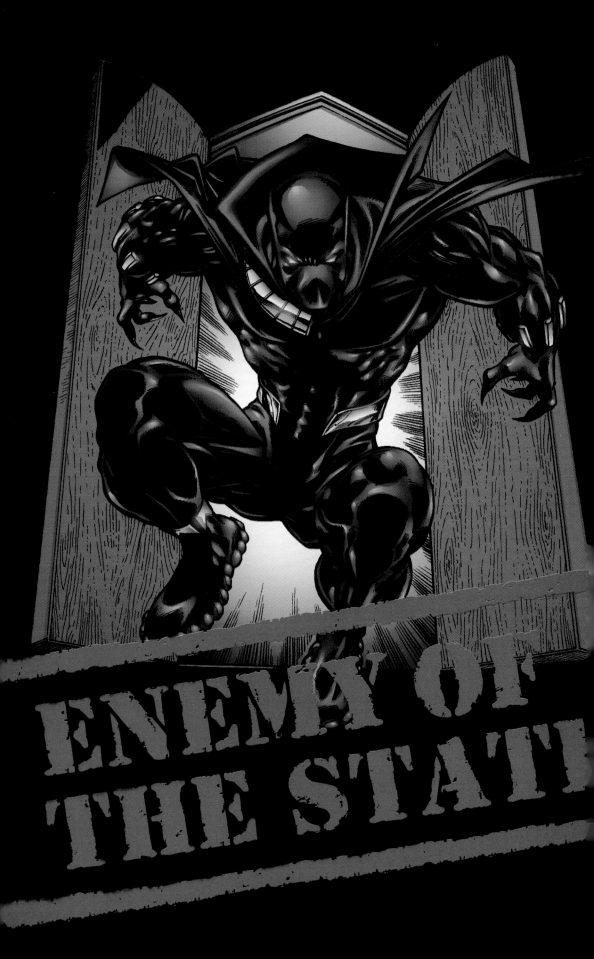

ENEMY OF THE STATE

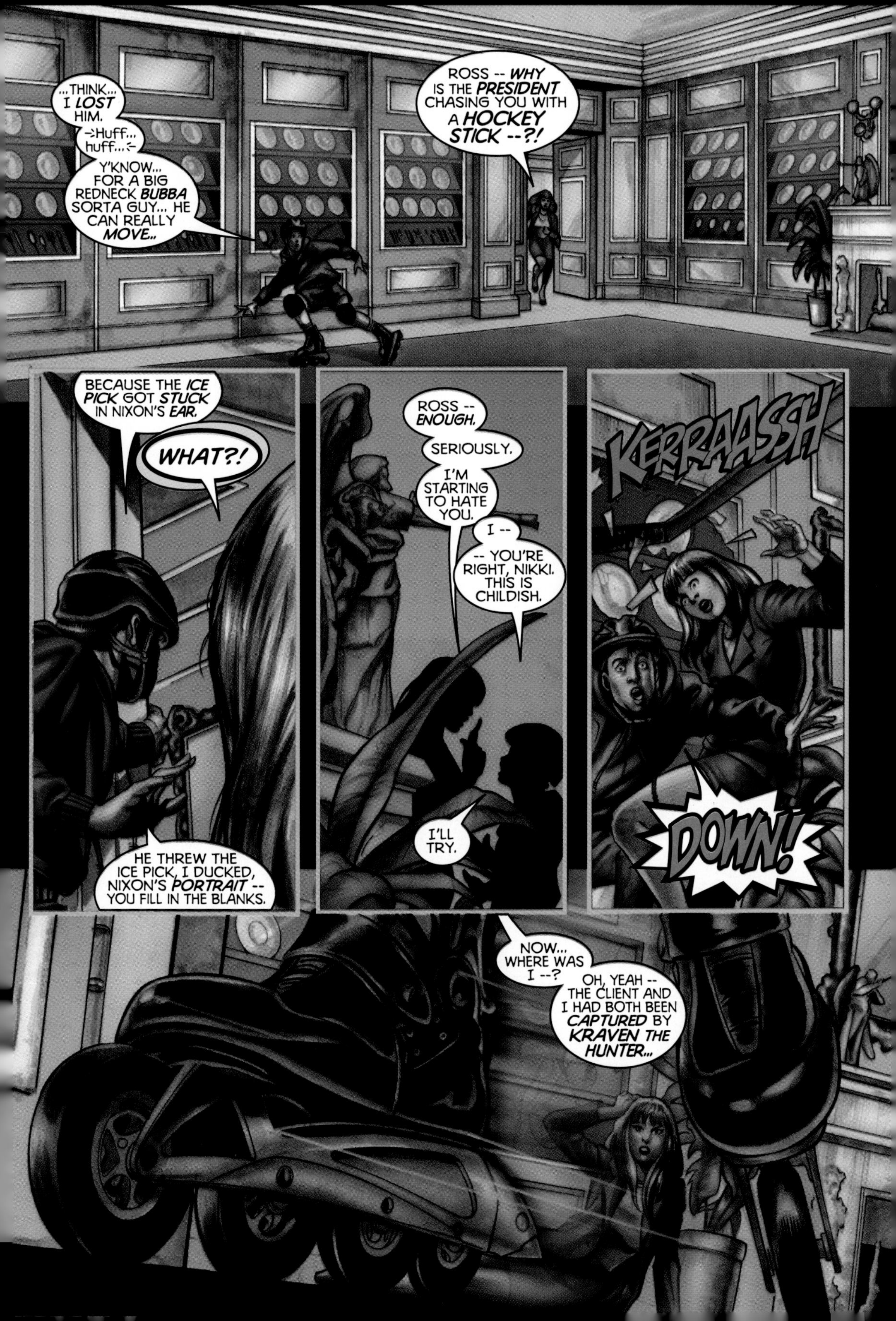
...THINK... I LOST HIM.
->Huff... huff...<-
Y'KNOW... FOR A BIG REDNECK BUBBA SORTA GUY... HE CAN REALLY MOVE...
ROSS -- WHY IS THE PRESIDENT CHASING YOU WITH A HOCKEY STICK --?!
BECAUSE THE ICE PICK GOT STUCK IN NIXON'S EAR.
WHAT?!
HE THREW THE ICE PICK, I DUCKED, NIXON'S PORTRAIT -- YOU FILL IN THE BLANKS.
ROSS -- ENOUGH.
SERIOUSLY.
I'M STARTING TO HATE YOU.
I --
-- YOU'RE RIGHT, NIKKI. THIS IS CHILDISH.
I'LL TRY.
KERRAASSH
DOWN!
NOW... WHERE WAS I --?
OH, YEAH -- THE CLIENT AND I HAD BOTH BEEN CAPTURED BY KRAVEN THE HUNTER...

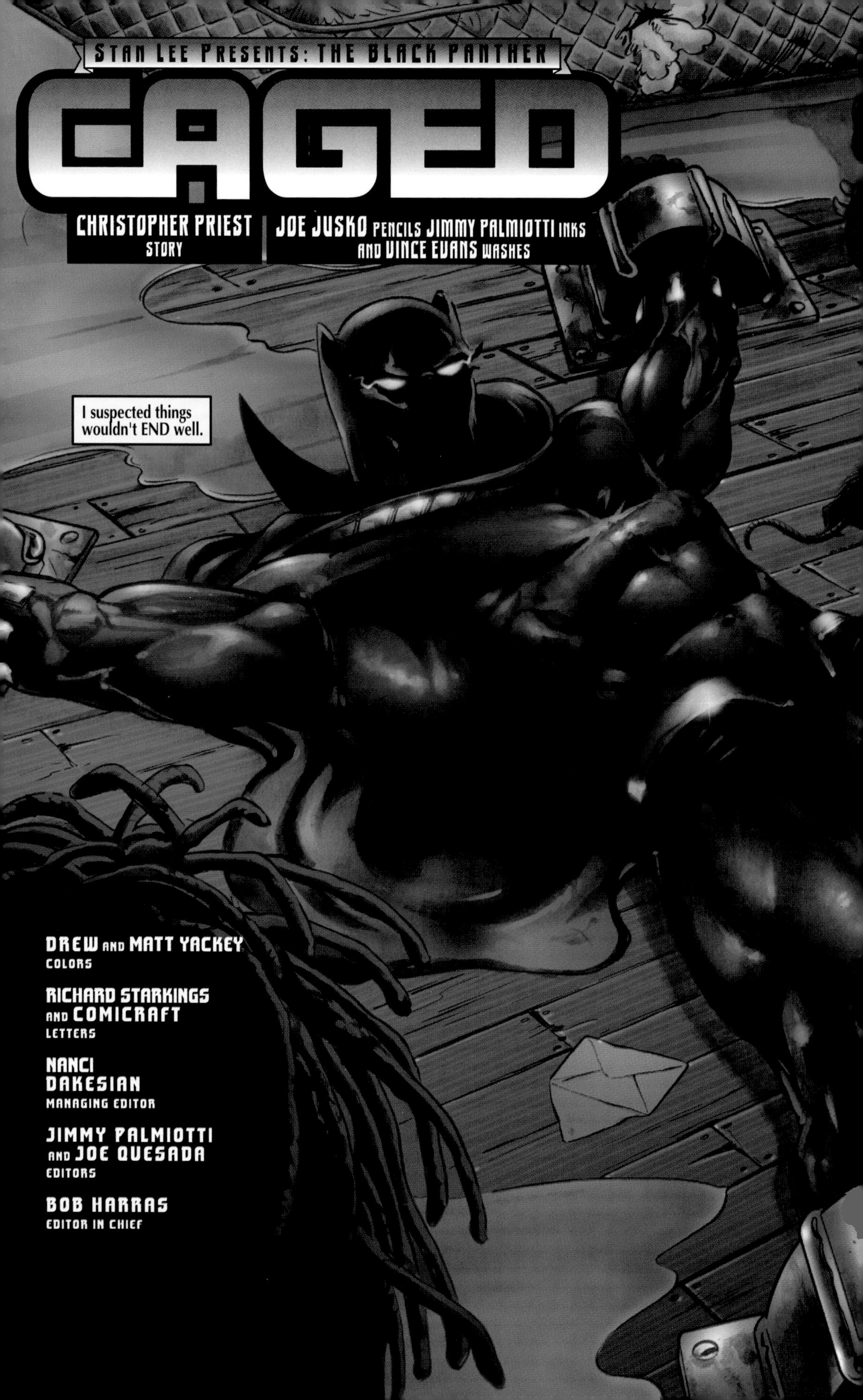
STAN LEE PRESENTS: THE BLACK PANTHER
CAGED
CHRISTOPHER PRIEST STORY
JOE JUSKO PENCILS JIMMY PALMIOTTI INKS AND VINCE EVANS WASHES
I suspected things wouldn't END well.
DREW AND MATT YACKEY COLORS
RICHARD STARKINGS AND COMICRAFT LETTERS
NANCI DAKESIAN MANAGING EDITOR
JIMMY PALMIOTTI AND JOE QUESADA EDITORS
BOB HARRAS EDITOR IN CHIEF

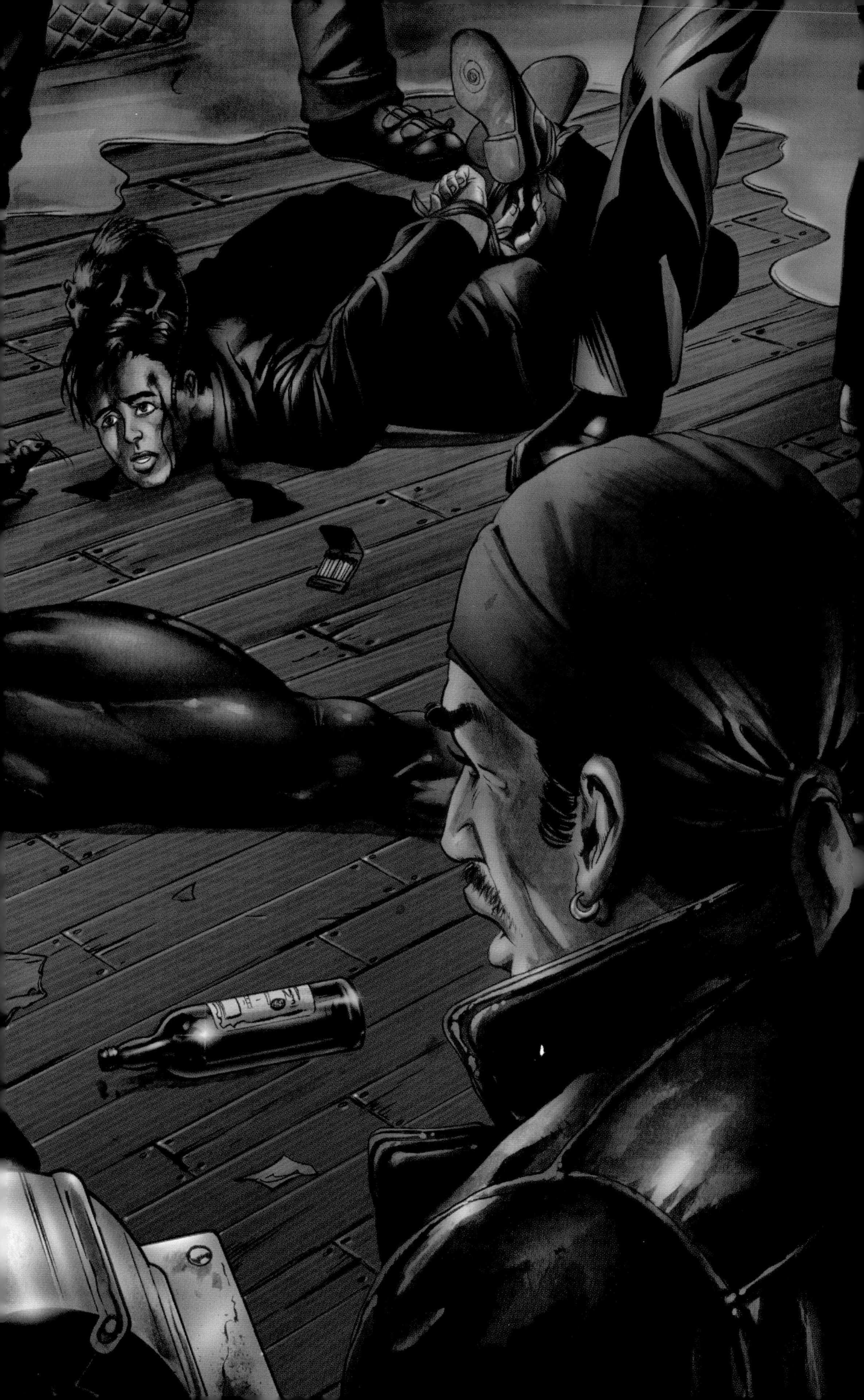

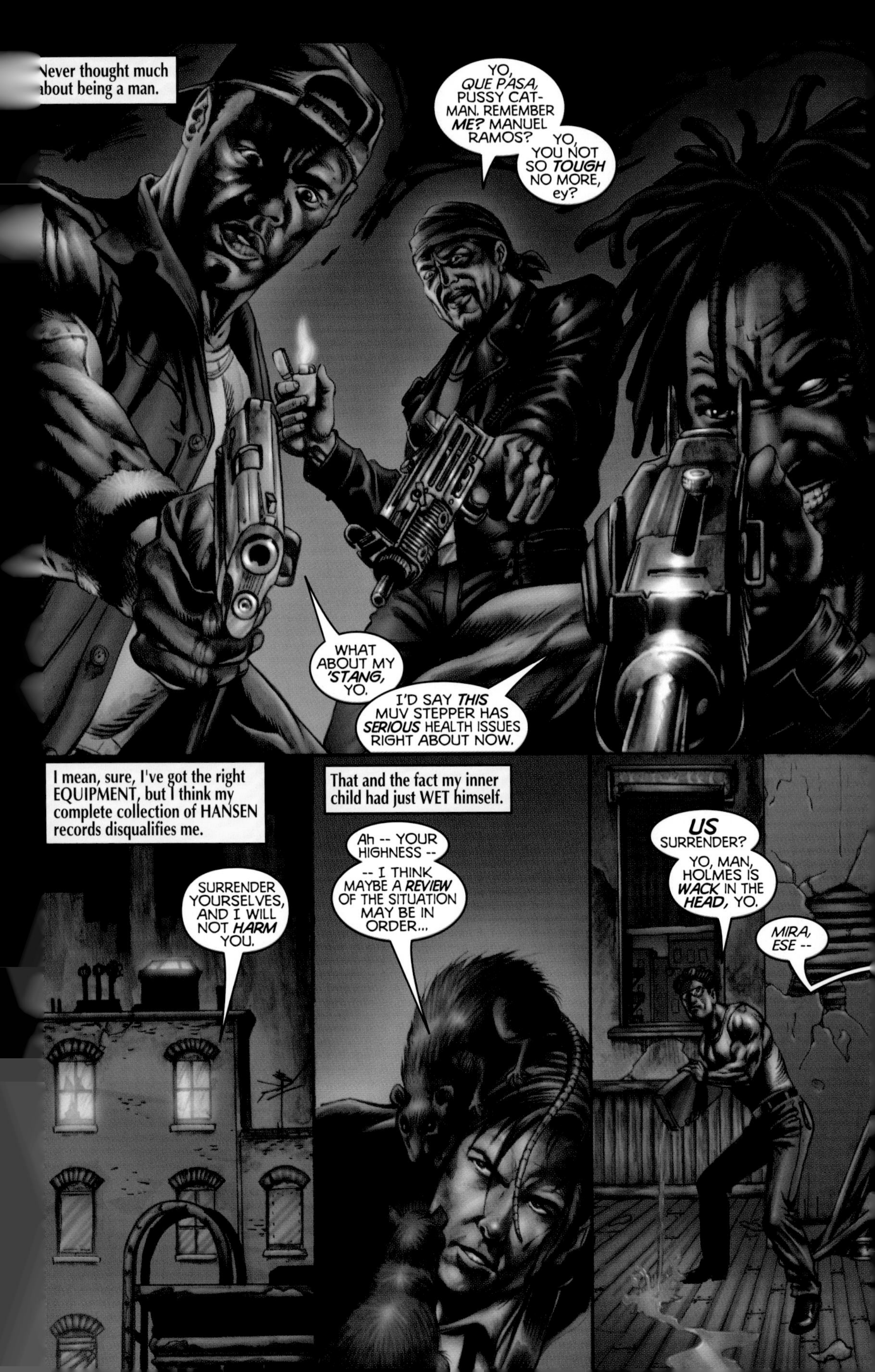
Never thought much about being a man.
YO, QUE PASA, PUSSY CAT-MAN. REMEMBER ME? MANUEL RAMOS?
YO, YOU NOT SO TOUGH NO MORE, ey?
WHAT ABOUT MY 'STANG, YO.
I'D SAY THIS MUV STEPPER HAS SERIOUS HEALTH ISSUES RIGHT ABOUT NOW.
I mean, sure, I've got the right EQUIPMENT, but I think my complete collection of HANSEN records disqualifies me.
SURRENDER YOURSELVES, AND I WILL NOT HARM YOU.
That and the fact my inner child had just WET himself.
Ah -- YOUR HIGHNESS --
-- I THINK MAYBE A REVIEW OF THE SITUATION MAY BE IN ORDER...
US SURRENDER?
YO, MAN, HOLMES IS WACK IN THE HEAD, YO.
MIRA, ESE --

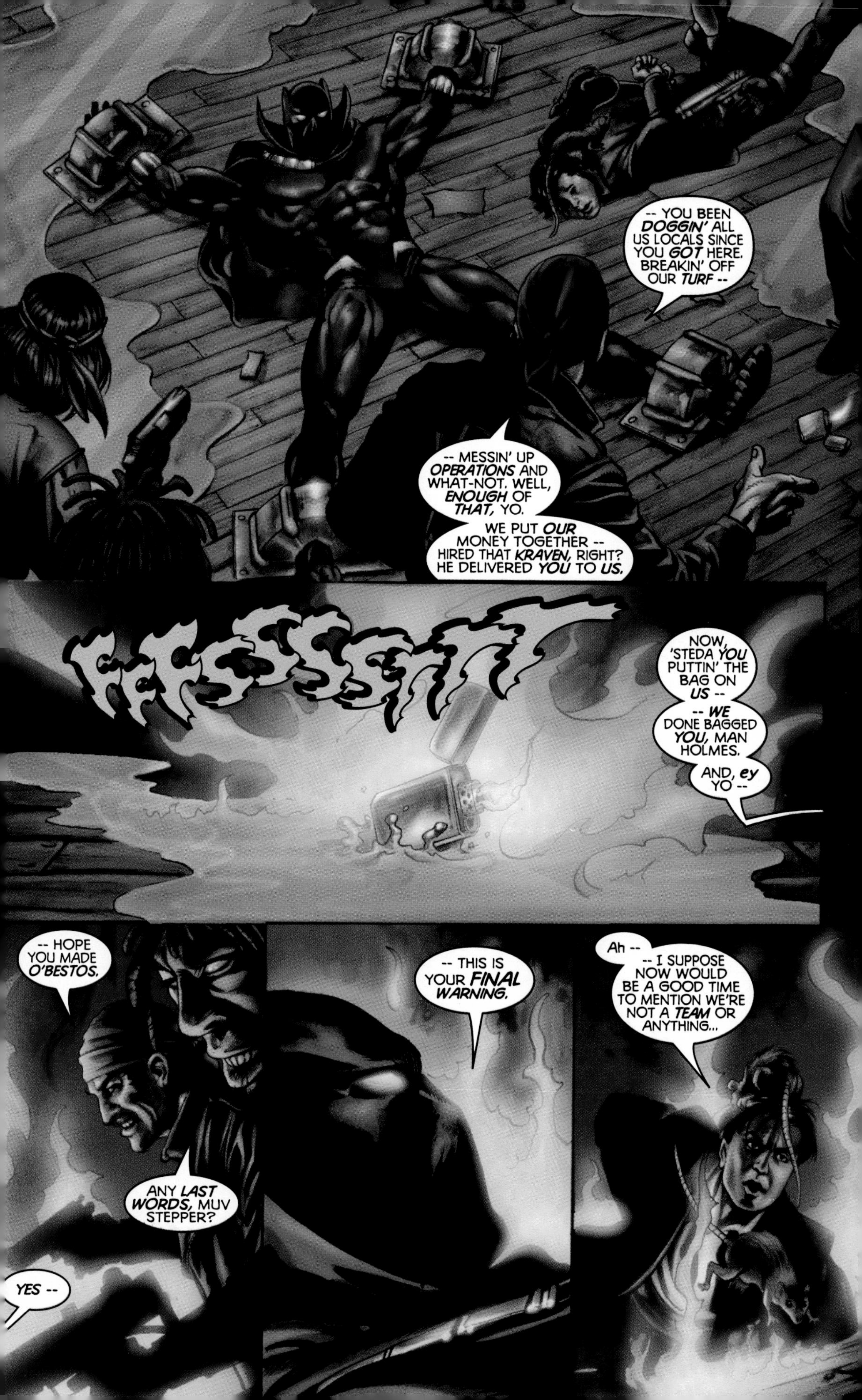
-- YOU BEEN DOGGIN' ALL US LOCALS SINCE YOU GOT HERE. BREAKIN' OFF OUR TURF --
-- MESSIN' UP OPERATIONS AND WHAT-NOT. WELL, ENOUGH OF THAT, YO.
WE PUT OUR MONEY TOGETHER -- HIRED THAT KRAVEN, RIGHT? HE DELIVERED YOU TO US.
NOW, 'STEDA YOU PUTTIN' THE BAG ON US --
-- WE DONE BAGGED YOU, MAN HOLMES.
AND, ey YO --
-- HOPE YOU MADE O'BESTOS.
ANY LAST WORDS, MUV STEPPER?
YES --
-- THIS IS YOUR FINAL WARNING.
Ah --
-- I SUPPOSE NOW WOULD BE A GOOD TIME TO MENTION WE'RE NOT A TEAM OR ANYTHING...

BLAM
BLAAAM
BBRRAATATATATAT
BLAMM
BLAM
BLAAAM
KAPP KAPP KAPP
DIRT NAP TIME, PUSSY CAT-MAN.
BLAM
BLAMM
BLAAAM
BBRRAATATATATAT
KAPP KAPP
BLAM
I screamed like a little girl.
AAAAAHHHHHH
BBRRAATATATATAT
BLAM
KAPP KAPP
BLAM
It had both RANGE and SUSTENANCE --
BBRRAATATATATAT
BLAM
KAPP KAPP
BLAAAM
BLAMM
-- just like the BLUE CHICK in Fifth Element.
I held the note until they ran out of bullets.
AAAAAHHHHHH!
About TWO YEARS by my count.
KLIK
KLIK
KLIK
KK-KLAAAKKK
They looked almost ANNOYED. Like 316 rounds wasn't quite ENOUGH to take out two guys.

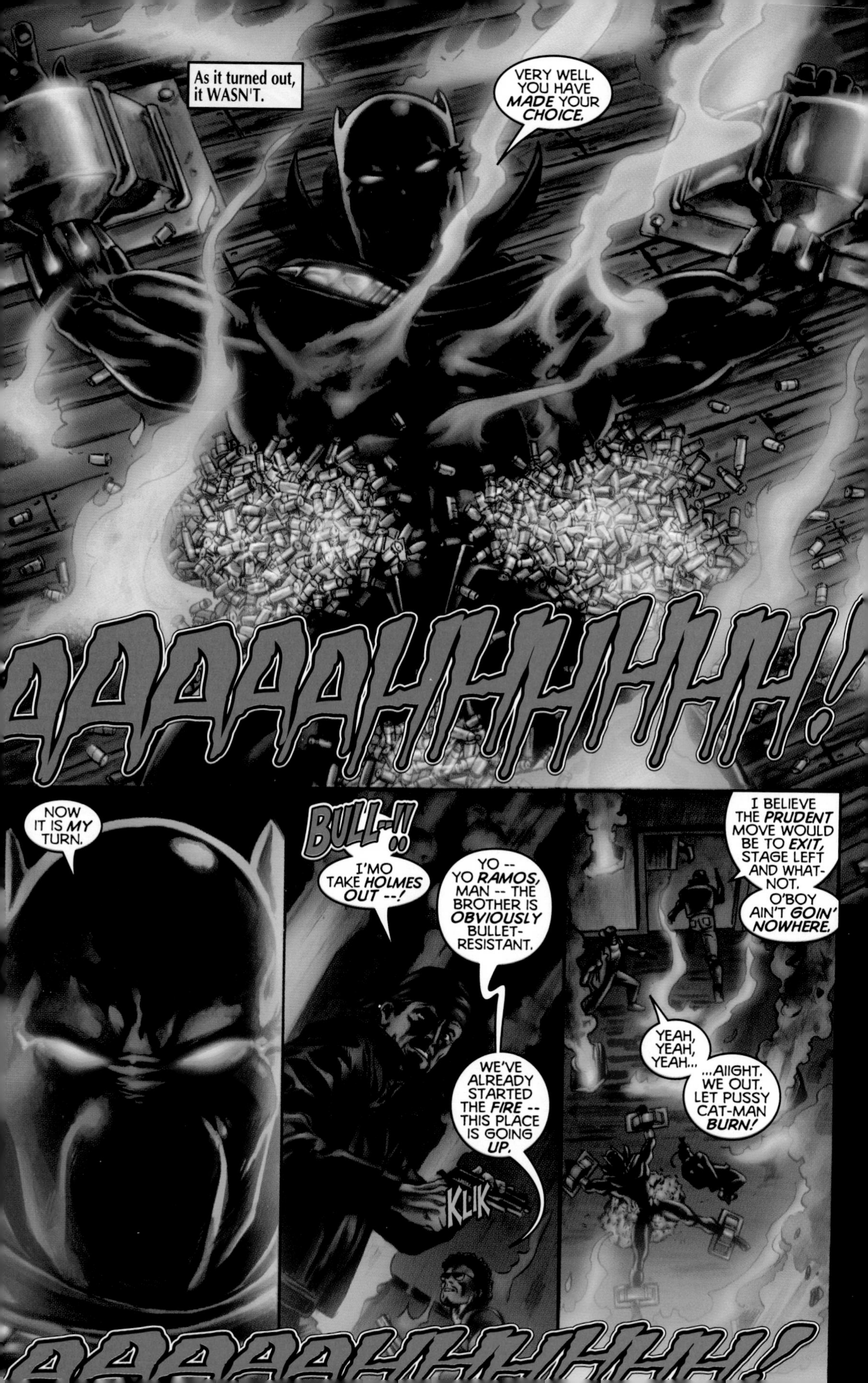
As it turned out, it WASN'T.
VERY WELL. YOU HAVE MADE YOUR CHOICE.
AAAAAHHHHHHH!
NOW IT IS MY TURN.
BULL--!!
I'MO TAKE HOLMES OUT --!
YO -- YO RAMOS, MAN -- THE BROTHER IS OBVIOUSLY BULLET-RESISTANT.
WE'VE ALREADY STARTED THE FIRE -- THIS PLACE IS GOING UP.
KLIK
I BELIEVE THE PRUDENT MOVE WOULD BE TO EXIT, STAGE LEFT AND WHAT-NOT.
O'BOY AIN'T GOIN' NOWHERE.
YEAH, YEAH, YEAH...
...AIIGHT. WE OUT. LET PUSSY CAT-MAN BURN!
AAAAAHHHHHHH!

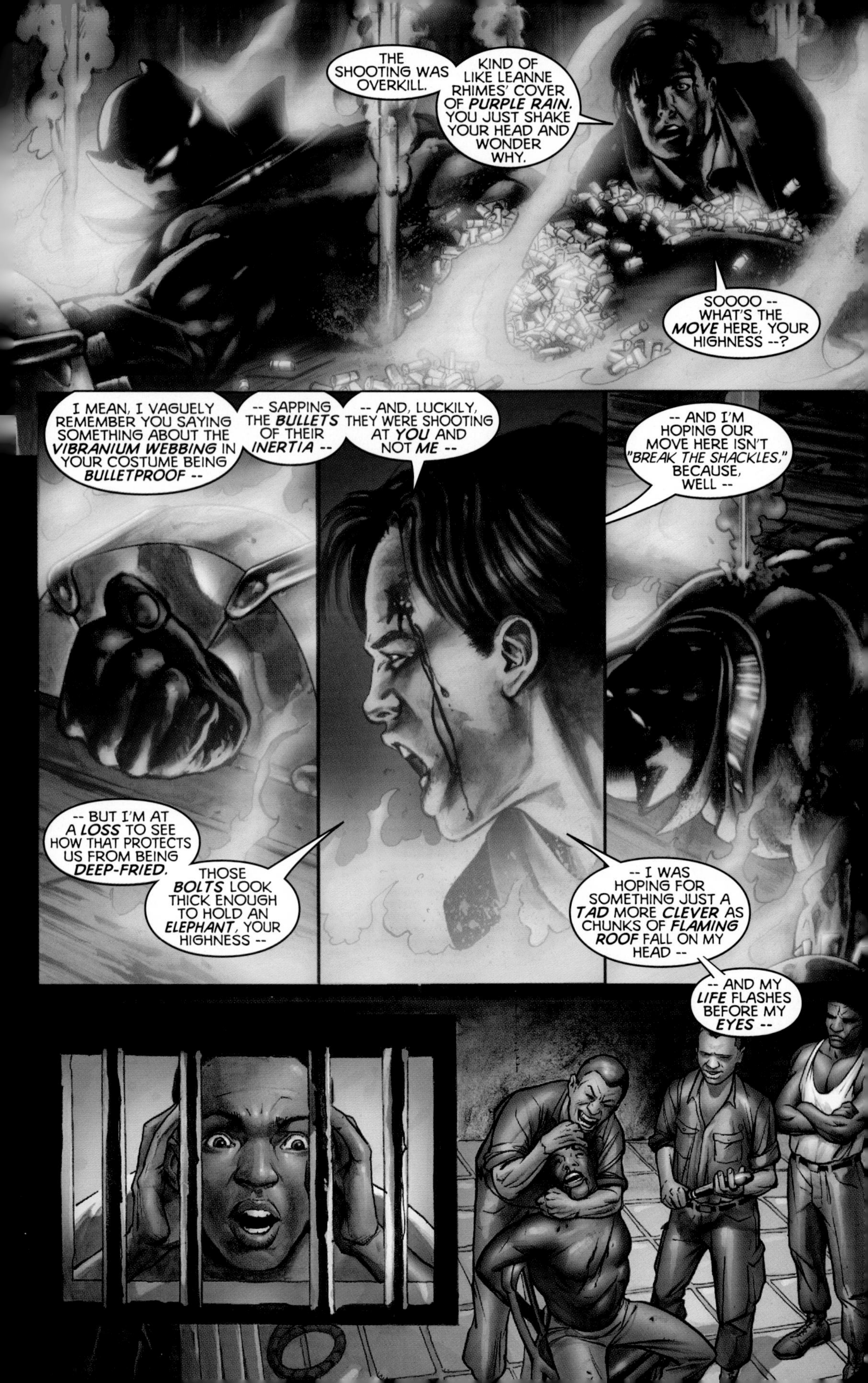
THE SHOOTING WAS OVERKILL.
KIND OF LIKE LEANNE RHIMES' COVER OF PURPLE RAIN. YOU JUST SHAKE YOUR HEAD AND WONDER WHY.
SOOOO -- WHAT'S THE MOVE HERE, YOUR HIGHNESS --?
I MEAN, I VAGUELY REMEMBER YOU SAYING SOMETHING ABOUT THE VIBRANIUM WEBBING IN YOUR COSTUME BEING BULLETPROOF --
-- SAPPING THE BULLETS OF THEIR INERTIA --
-- AND, LUCKILY, THEY WERE SHOOTING AT YOU AND NOT ME --
-- BUT I'M AT A LOSS TO SEE HOW THAT PROTECTS US FROM BEING DEEP-FRIED.
THOSE BOLTS LOOK THICK ENOUGH TO HOLD AN ELEPHANT, YOUR HIGHNESS --
-- AND I'M HOPING OUR MOVE HERE ISN'T "BREAK THE SHACKLES," BECAUSE, WELL --
-- I WAS HOPING FOR SOMETHING JUST A TAD MORE CLEVER AS CHUNKS OF FLAMING ROOF FALL ON MY HEAD --
-- AND MY LIFE FLASHES BEFORE MY EYES --

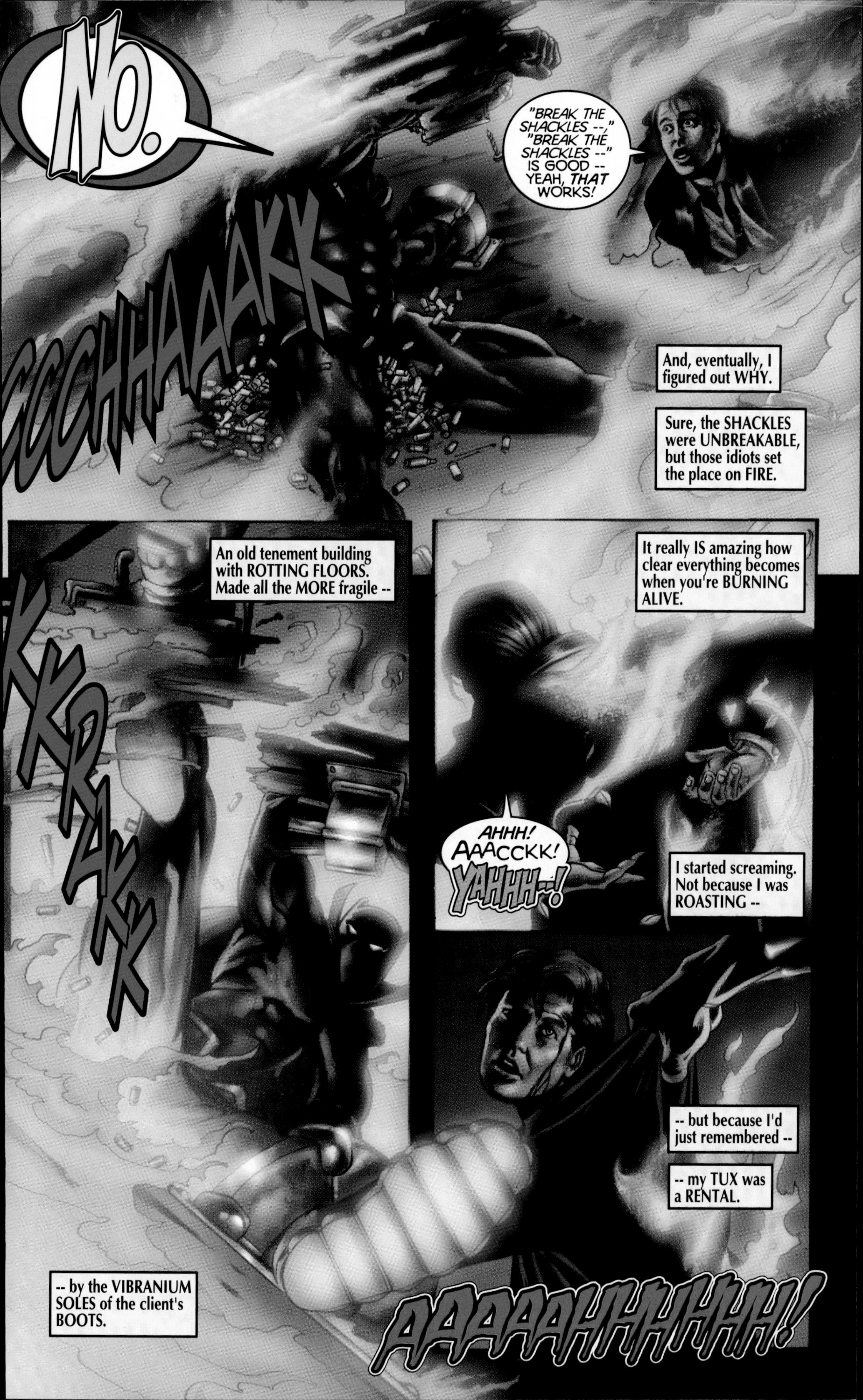
NO.
"BREAK THE SHACKLES --," "BREAK THE SHACKLES --" IS GOOD -- YEAH, THAT WORKS!
CCCHHAAAKK
And, eventually, I figured out WHY.
Sure, the SHACKLES were UNBREAKABLE, but those idiots set the place on FIRE.
An old tenement building with ROTTING FLOORS. Made all the MORE fragile --
KKRAKK
-- by the VIBRANIUM SOLES of the client's BOOTS.
It really IS amazing how clear everything becomes when you're BURNING ALIVE.
AHHH! AAACCKK! YAHHH--!
I started screaming. Not because I was ROASTING --
-- but because I'd just remembered --
-- my TUX was a RENTAL.
AAAAAHHHHHHH!

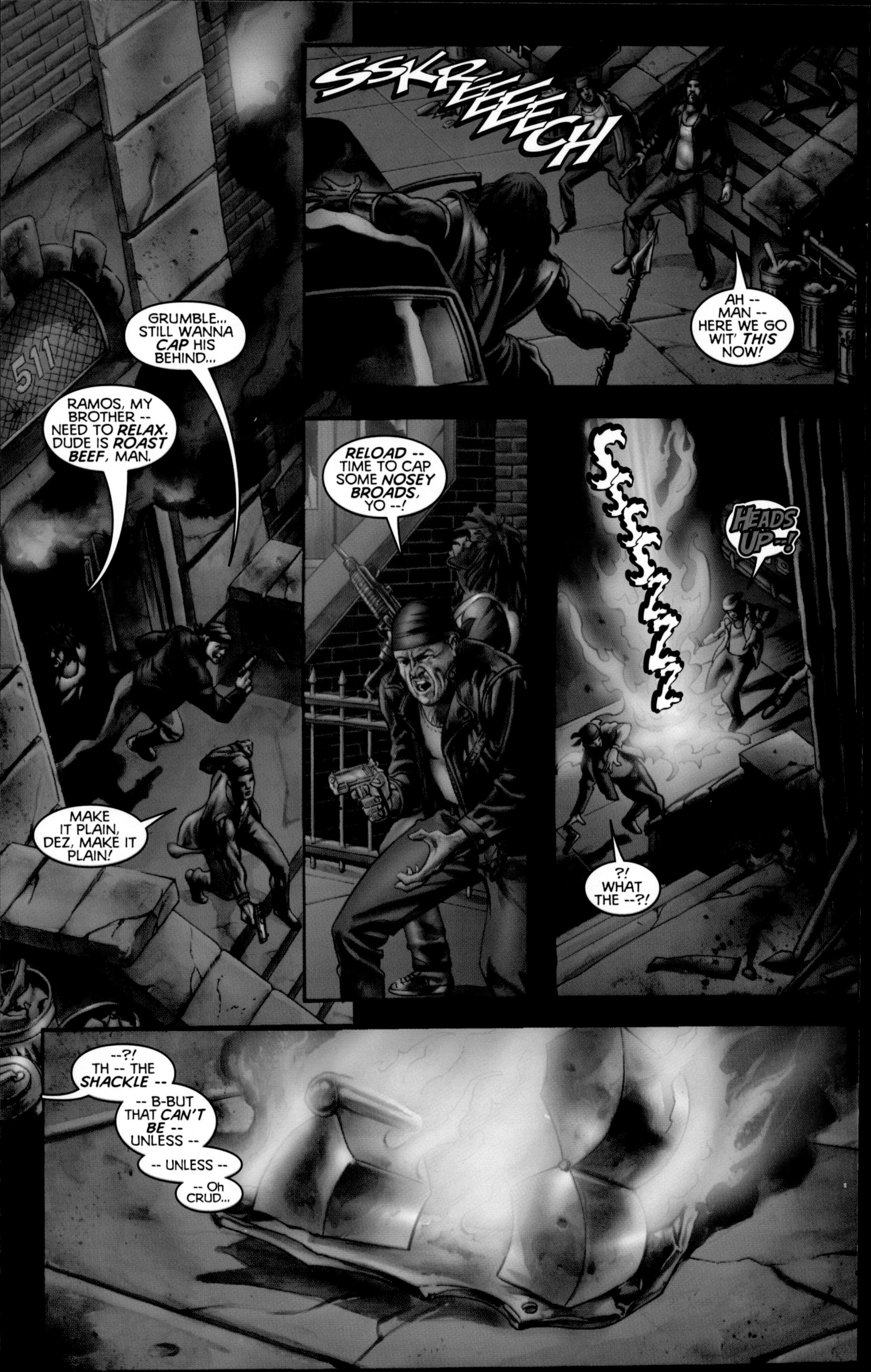
SSKREEEECH
AH -- MAN -- HERE WE GO WIT' THIS NOW!
GRUMBLE... STILL WANNA CAP HIS BEHIND...
RAMOS, MY BROTHER -- NEED TO RELAX. DUDE IS ROAST BEEF, MAN.
MAKE IT PLAIN, DEZ, MAKE IT PLAIN!
RELOAD -- TIME TO CAP SOME NOSEY BROADS, YO --!
SSSSZZZZ
HEADS UP--!
?! WHAT THE --?!
--?! TH -- THE SHACKLE --
-- B-BUT THAT CAN'T BE -- UNLESS --
-- UNLESS --
-- Oh CRUD...

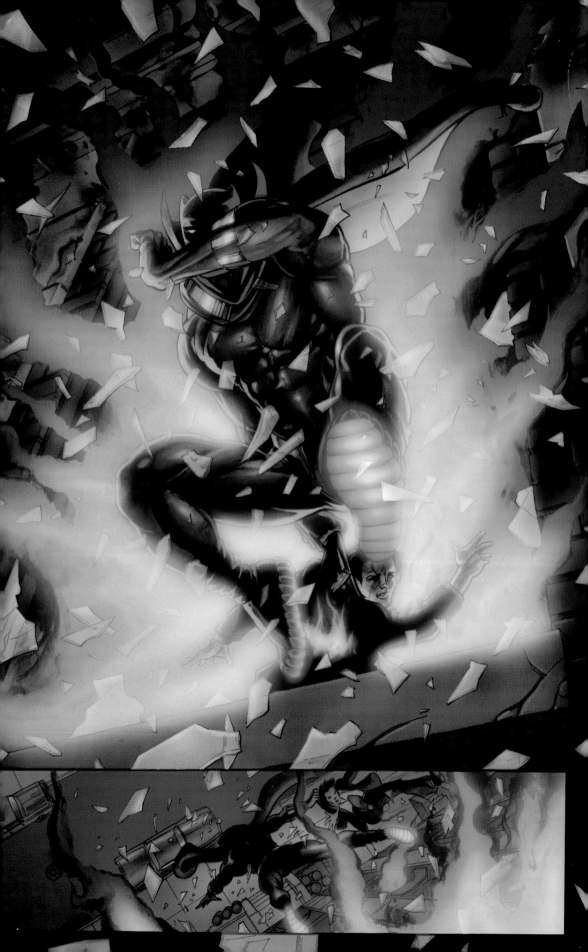

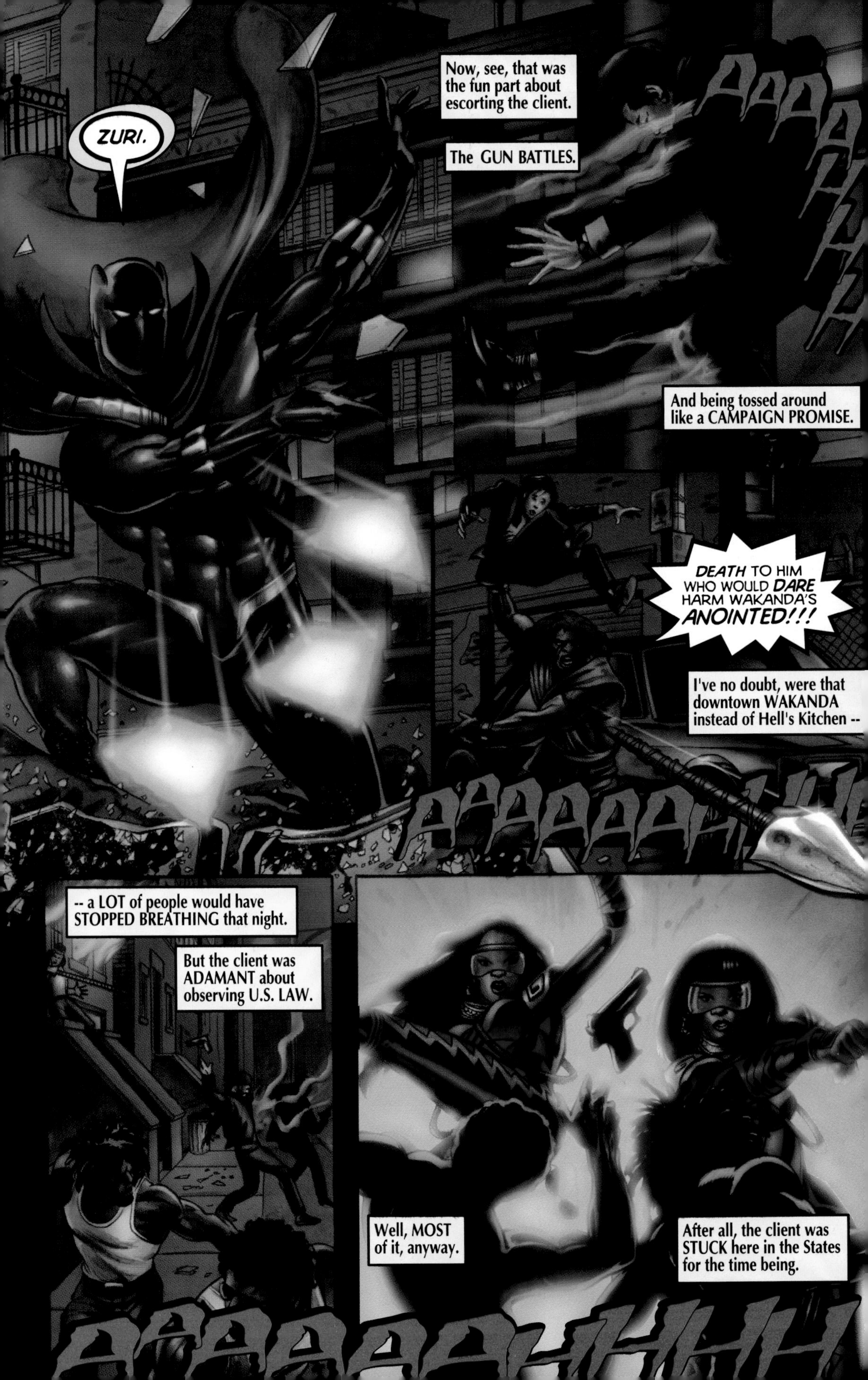
ZURI.
Now, see, that was the fun part about escorting the client.
The GUN BATTLES.
AAAAAAHHHHH
And being tossed around like a CAMPAIGN PROMISE.
DEATH TO HIM WHO WOULD DARE HARM WAKANDA'S ANOINTED!!!
I've no doubt, were that downtown WAKANDA instead of Hell's Kitchen --
AAAAAAHHH
-- a LOT of people would have STOPPED BREATHING that night.
But the client was ADAMANT about observing U.S. LAW.
Well, MOST of it, anyway.
After all, the client was STUCK here in the States for the time being.
AAAAAAHHHHH

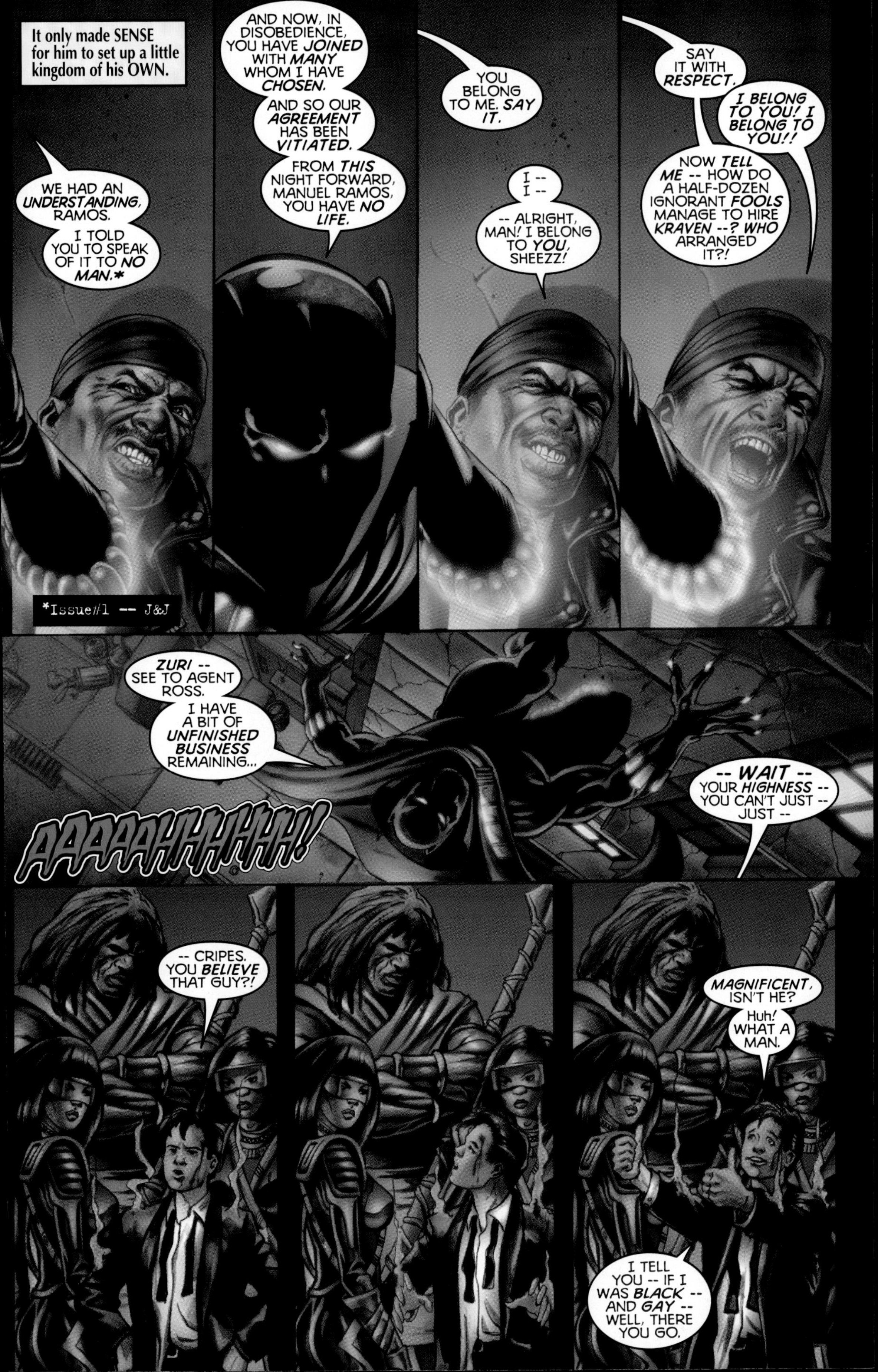
It only made SENSE for him to set up a little kingdom of his OWN.
WE HAD AN UNDERSTANDING, RAMOS.
I TOLD YOU TO SPEAK OF IT TO NO MAN.*
*Issue#1 -- J&J
AND NOW, IN DISOBEDIENCE, YOU HAVE JOINED WITH MANY WHOM I HAVE CHOSEN.
AND SO OUR AGREEMENT HAS BEEN VITIATED.
FROM THIS NIGHT FORWARD, MANUEL RAMOS, YOU HAVE NO LIFE.
YOU BELONG TO ME. SAY IT.
I -- I --
-- ALRIGHT, MAN! I BELONG TO YOU, SHEEZZ!
SAY IT WITH RESPECT.
I BELONG TO YOU! I BELONG TO YOU!!
NOW TELL ME -- HOW DO A HALF-DOZEN IGNORANT FOOLS MANAGE TO HIRE KRAVEN --? WHO ARRANGED IT?!
ZURI -- SEE TO AGENT ROSS.
I HAVE A BIT OF UNFINISHED BUSINESS REMAINING...
AAAAAHHHHHH!
-- WAIT -- YOUR HIGHNESS -- YOU CAN'T JUST -- JUST --
-- CRIPES. YOU BELIEVE THAT GUY?!
MAGNIFICENT, ISN'T HE?
Huh! WHAT A MAN.
I TELL YOU -- IF I WAS BLACK -- AND GAY -- WELL, THERE YOU GO.

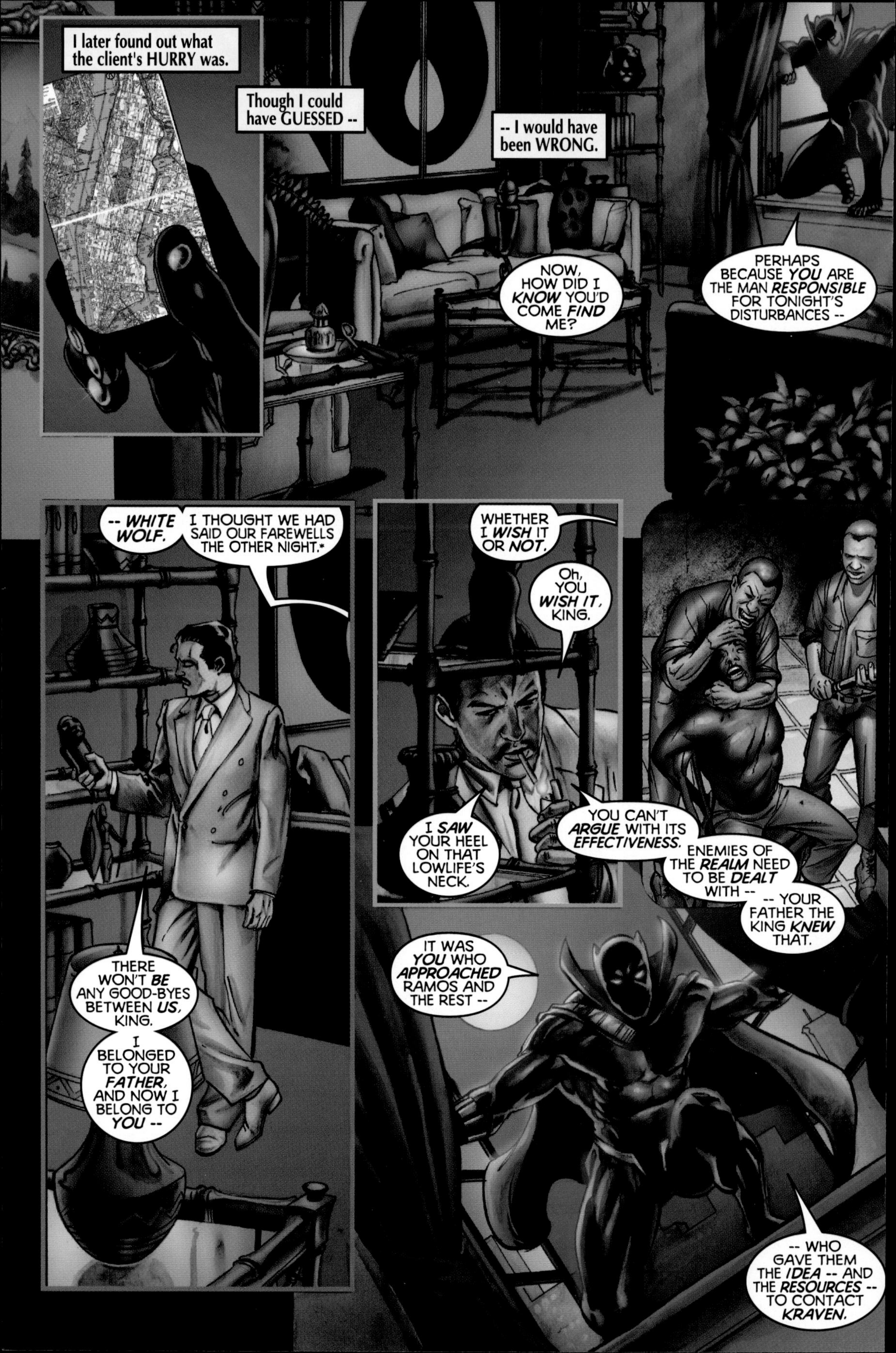

I later found out what the client's HURRY was.
Though I could have GUESSED --
-- I would have been WRONG.
NOW, HOW DID I KNOW YOU'D COME FIND ME?
PERHAPS BECAUSE YOU ARE THE MAN RESPONSIBLE FOR TONIGHT'S DISTURBANCES --
-- WHITE WOLF.
I THOUGHT WE HAD SAID OUR FAREWELLS THE OTHER NIGHT.*
THERE WON'T BE ANY GOOD-BYES BETWEEN US, KING.
I BELONGED TO YOUR FATHER, AND NOW I BELONG TO YOU --
WHETHER I WISH IT OR NOT.
Oh, YOU WISH IT, KING.
I SAW YOUR HEEL ON THAT LOWLIFE'S NECK.
YOU CAN'T ARGUE WITH ITS EFFECTIVENESS.
ENEMIES OF THE REALM NEED TO BE DEALT WITH --
-- YOUR FATHER THE KING KNEW THAT.
IT WAS YOU WHO APPROACHED RAMOS AND THE REST --
-- WHO GAVE THEM THE IDEA -- AND THE RESOURCES -- TO CONTACT KRAVEN.

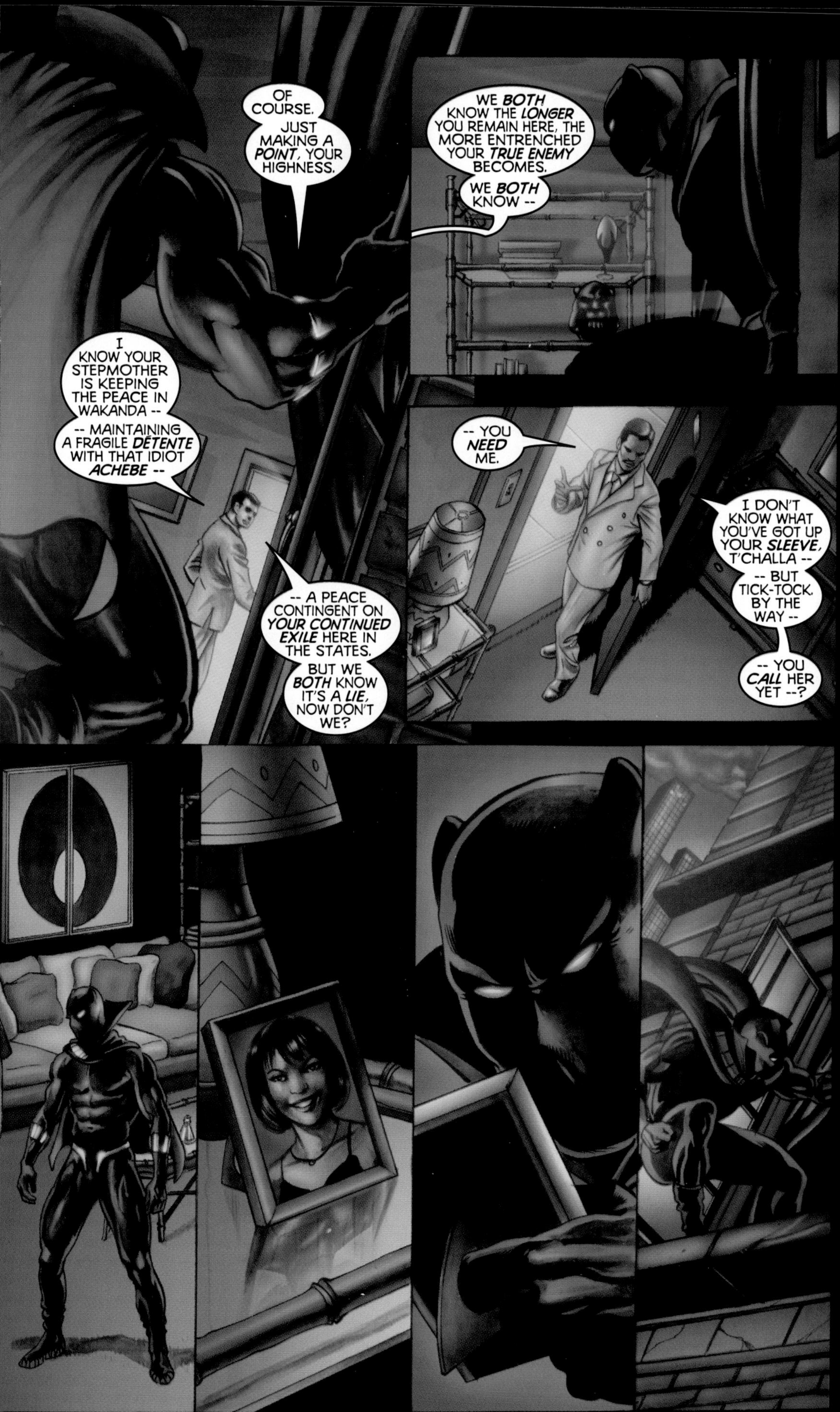

OF COURSE. JUST MAKING A POINT, YOUR HIGHNESS.
WE BOTH KNOW THE LONGER YOU REMAIN HERE, THE MORE ENTRENCHED YOUR TRUE ENEMY BECOMES.
WE BOTH KNOW --
I KNOW YOUR STEPMOTHER IS KEEPING THE PEACE IN WAKANDA --
-- MAINTAINING A FRAGILE DÉTENTE WITH THAT IDIOT ACHEBE --
-- A PEACE CONTINGENT ON YOUR CONTINUED EXILE HERE IN THE STATES.
BUT WE BOTH KNOW IT'S A LIE, NOW DON'T WE?
-- YOU NEED ME.
I DON'T KNOW WHAT YOU'VE GOT UP YOUR SLEEVE, T'CHALLA --
-- BUT TICK-TOCK. BY THE WAY --
-- YOU CALL HER YET --?

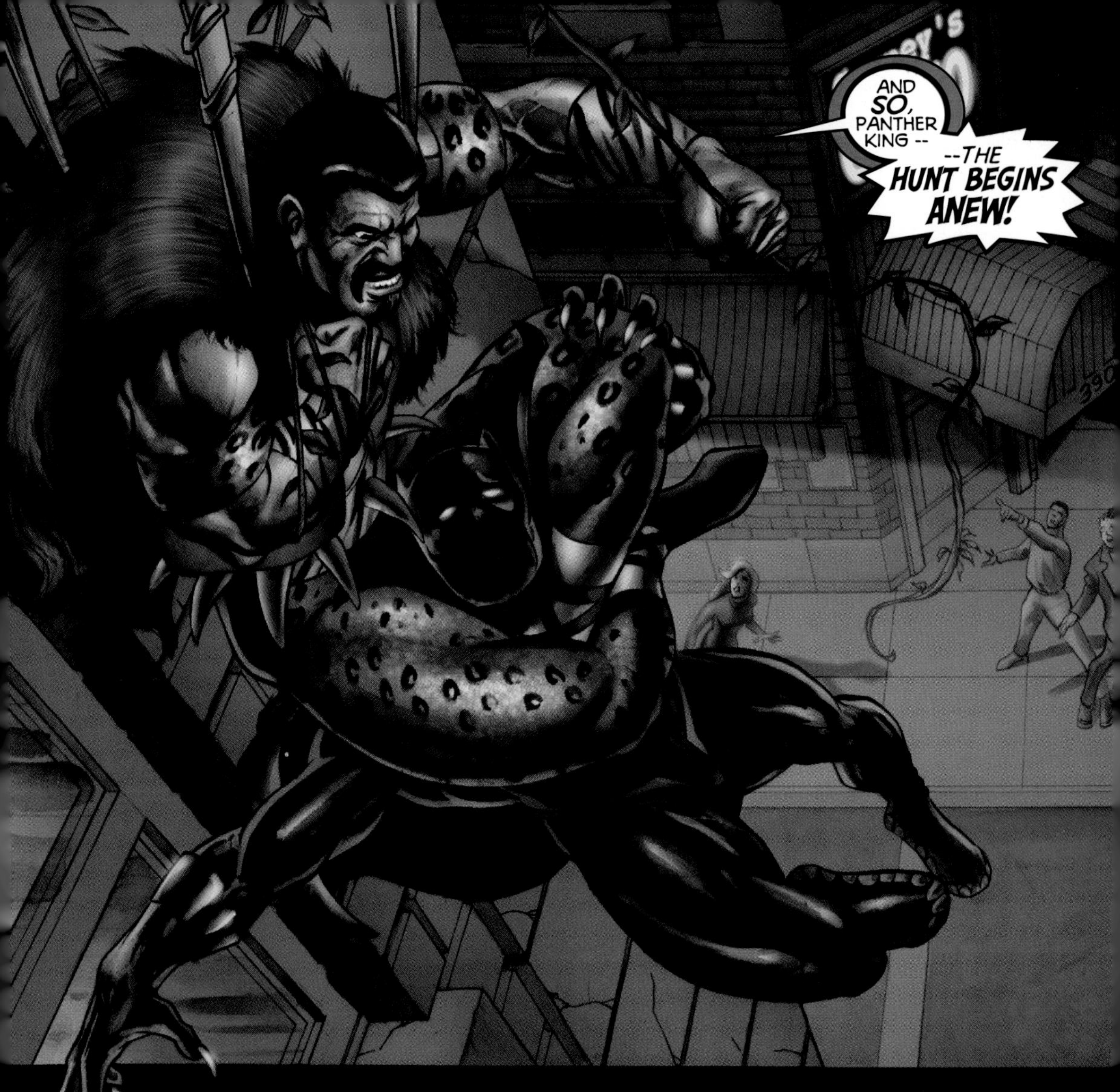
AND SO, PANTHER KING --
--THE HUNT BEGINS ANEW!

DON'T DROP THE SOAP

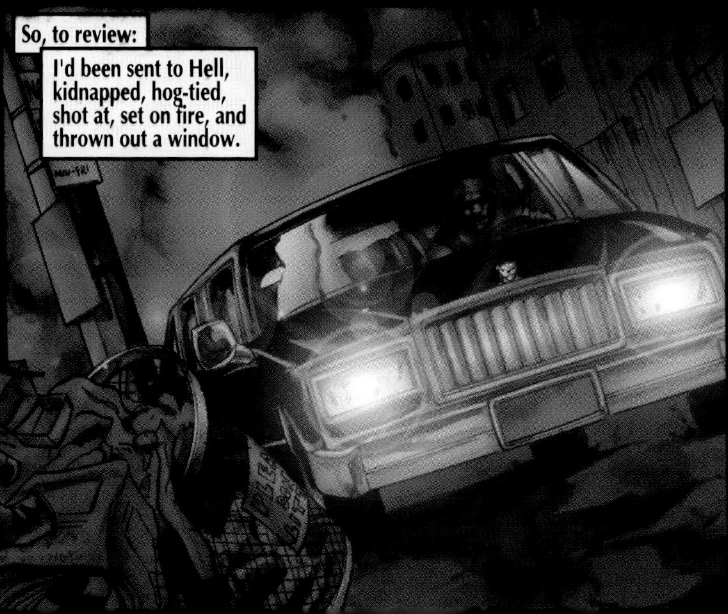
So, to review:
I'd been sent to Hell, kidnapped, hog-tied, shot at, set on fire, and thrown out a window.

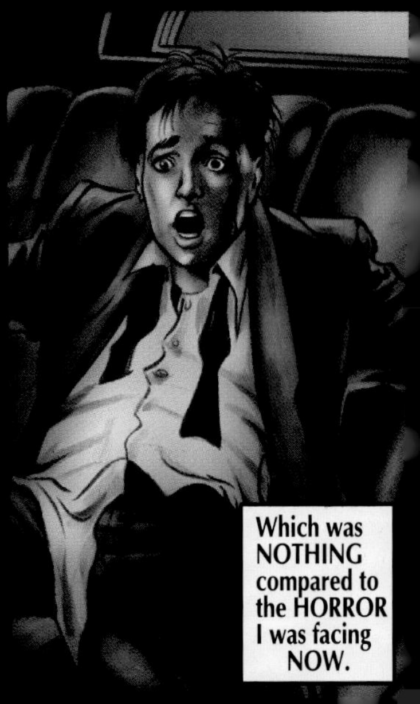
Which was NOTHING compared to the HORROR I was facing NOW.

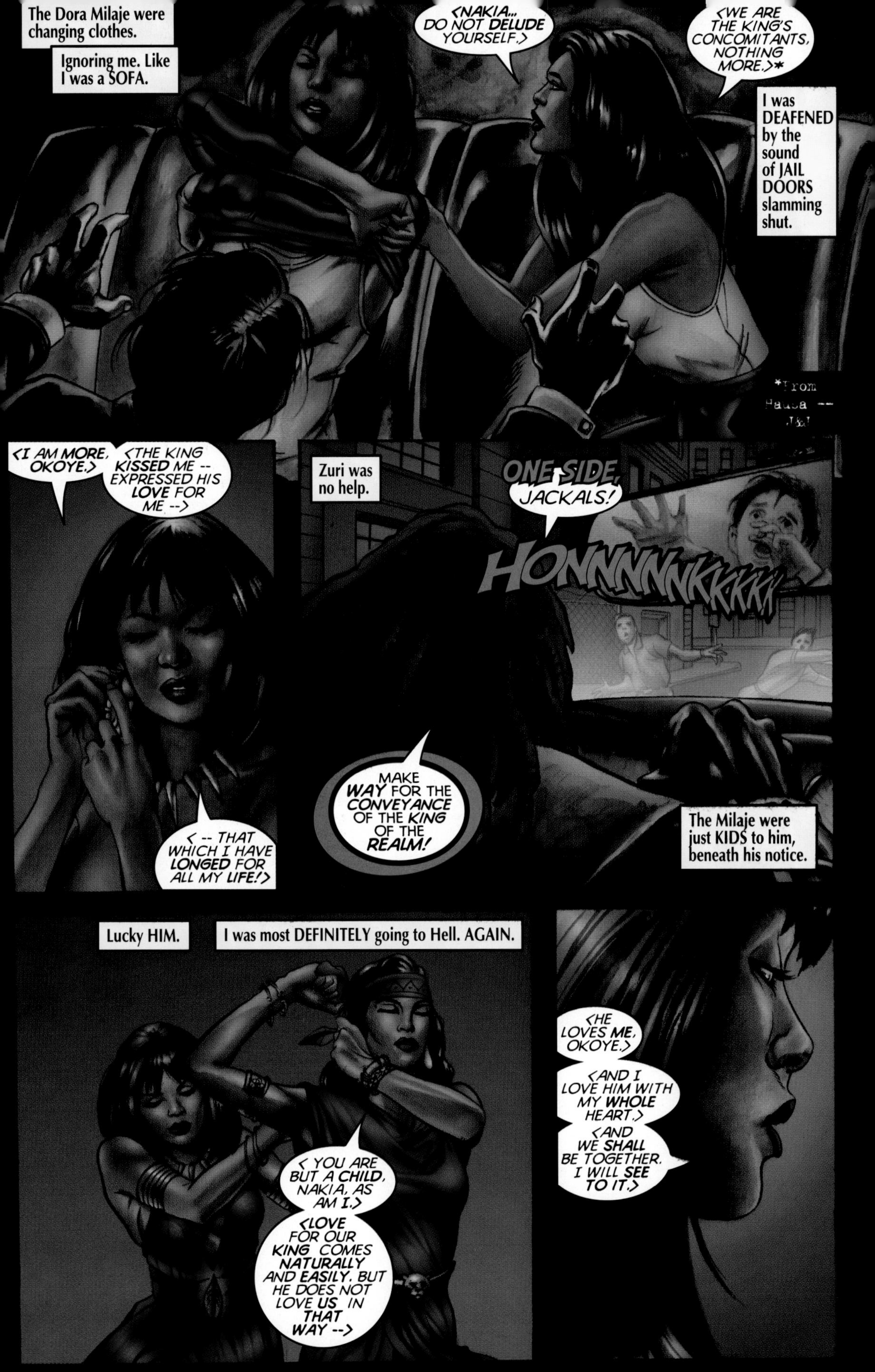

The Dora Milaje were changing clothes.
Ignoring me. Like I was a SOFA.
<NAKIA... DO NOT DELUDE YOURSELF.>
<WE ARE THE KING'S CONCOMITANTS, NOTHING MORE.>*
I was DEAFENED by the sound of JAIL DOORS slamming shut.
*From Hausa -- J&J
<I AM MORE, OKOYE.>
<THE KING KISSED ME -- EXPRESSED HIS LOVE FOR ME -->
< -- THAT WHICH I HAVE LONGED FOR ALL MY LIFE!>
Zuri was no help.
ONE SIDE, JACKALS!
HONNNNNKKKK
MAKE WAY FOR THE CONVEYANCE OF THE KING OF THE REALM!
The Milaje were just KIDS to him, beneath his notice.
Lucky HIM.
I was most DEFINITELY going to Hell. AGAIN.
< YOU ARE BUT A CHILD, NAKIA, AS AM I.>
<LOVE FOR OUR KING COMES NATURALLY AND EASILY. BUT HE DOES NOT LOVE US IN THAT WAY -->
<HE LOVES ME, OKOYE.>
<AND I LOVE HIM WITH MY WHOLE HEART.>
<AND WE SHALL BE TOGETHER. I WILL SEE TO IT.>

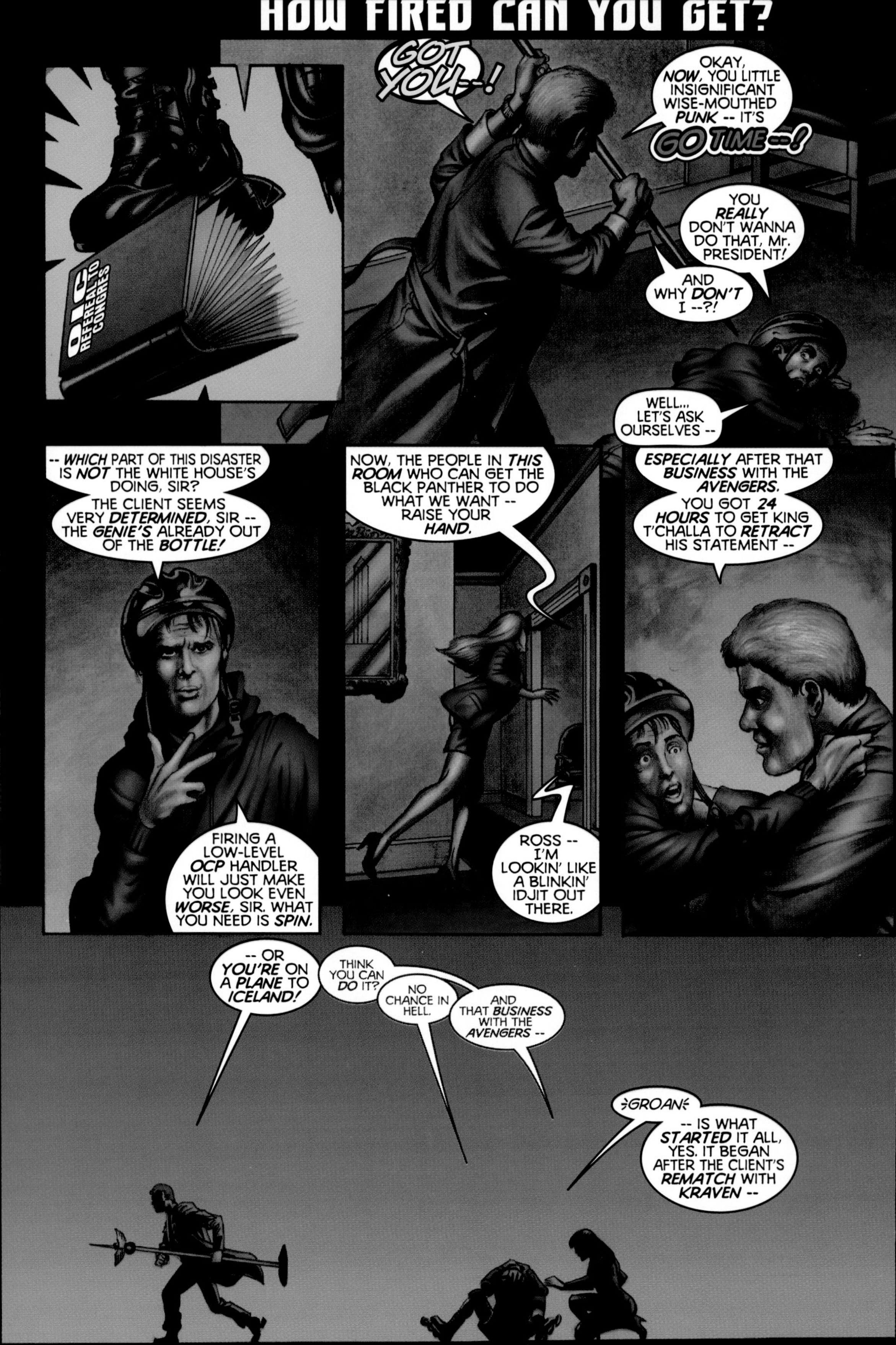
HOW FIRED CAN YOU GET?
OIC REFFEREAL TO CONGRES
GOT YOU--!
OKAY, NOW, YOU LITTLE INSIGNIFICANT WISE-MOUTHED PUNK -- IT'S GO TIME--!
YOU REALLY DON'T WANNA DO THAT, Mr. PRESIDENT!
AND WHY DON'T I --?!
WELL... LET'S ASK OURSELVES --
-- WHICH PART OF THIS DISASTER IS NOT THE WHITE HOUSE'S DOING, SIR?
THE CLIENT SEEMS VERY DETERMINED, SIR -- THE GENIE'S ALREADY OUT OF THE BOTTLE!
FIRING A LOW-LEVEL OCP HANDLER WILL JUST MAKE YOU LOOK EVEN WORSE, SIR. WHAT YOU NEED IS SPIN.
NOW, THE PEOPLE IN THIS ROOM WHO CAN GET THE BLACK PANTHER TO DO WHAT WE WANT -- RAISE YOUR HAND.
ROSS -- I'M LOOKIN' LIKE A BLINKIN' IDJIT OUT THERE.
ESPECIALLY AFTER THAT BUSINESS WITH THE AVENGERS.
YOU GOT 24 HOURS TO GET KING T'CHALLA TO RETRACT HIS STATEMENT --
-- OR YOU'RE ON A PLANE TO ICELAND!
THINK YOU CAN DO IT?
NO CHANCE IN HELL.
AND THAT BUSINESS WITH THE AVENGERS --
GROAN
-- IS WHAT STARTED IT ALL, YES. IT BEGAN AFTER THE CLIENT'S REMATCH WITH KRAVEN --

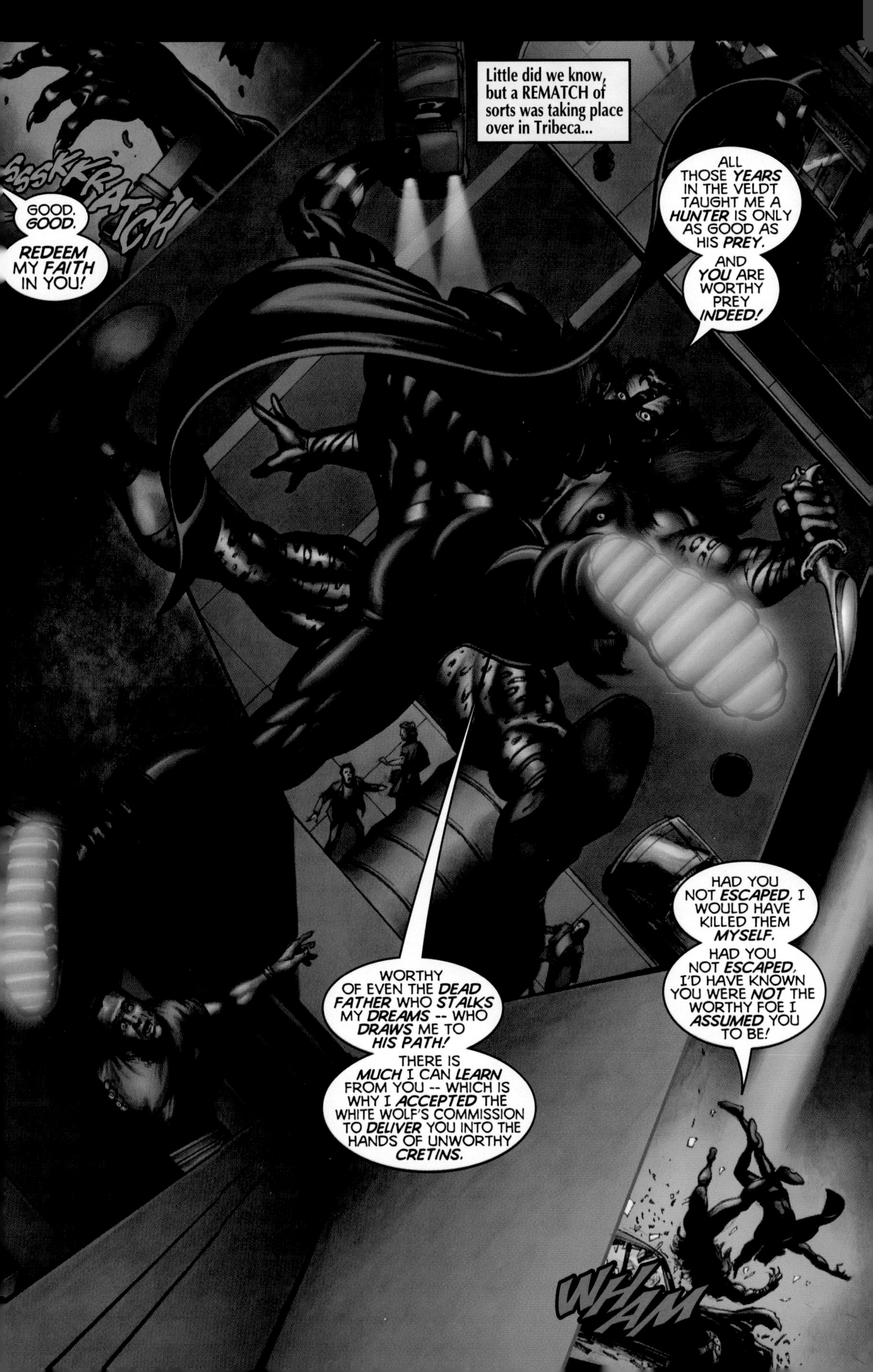
Little did we know, but a REMATCH of sorts was taking place over in Tribeca...
SSSKKRATCH
GOOD. GOOD.
REDEEM MY FAITH IN YOU!
ALL THOSE YEARS IN THE VELDT TAUGHT ME A HUNTER IS ONLY AS GOOD AS HIS PREY.
AND YOU ARE WORTHY PREY INDEED!
WORTHY OF EVEN THE DEAD FATHER WHO STALKS MY DREAMS -- WHO DRAWS ME TO HIS PATH!
THERE IS MUCH I CAN LEARN FROM YOU -- WHICH IS WHY I ACCEPTED THE WHITE WOLF'S COMMISSION TO DELIVER YOU INTO THE HANDS OF UNWORTHY CRETINS.
HAD YOU NOT ESCAPED, I WOULD HAVE KILLED THEM MYSELF.
HAD YOU NOT ESCAPED, I'D HAVE KNOWN YOU WERE NOT THE WORTHY FOE I ASSUMED YOU TO BE!
WHAM

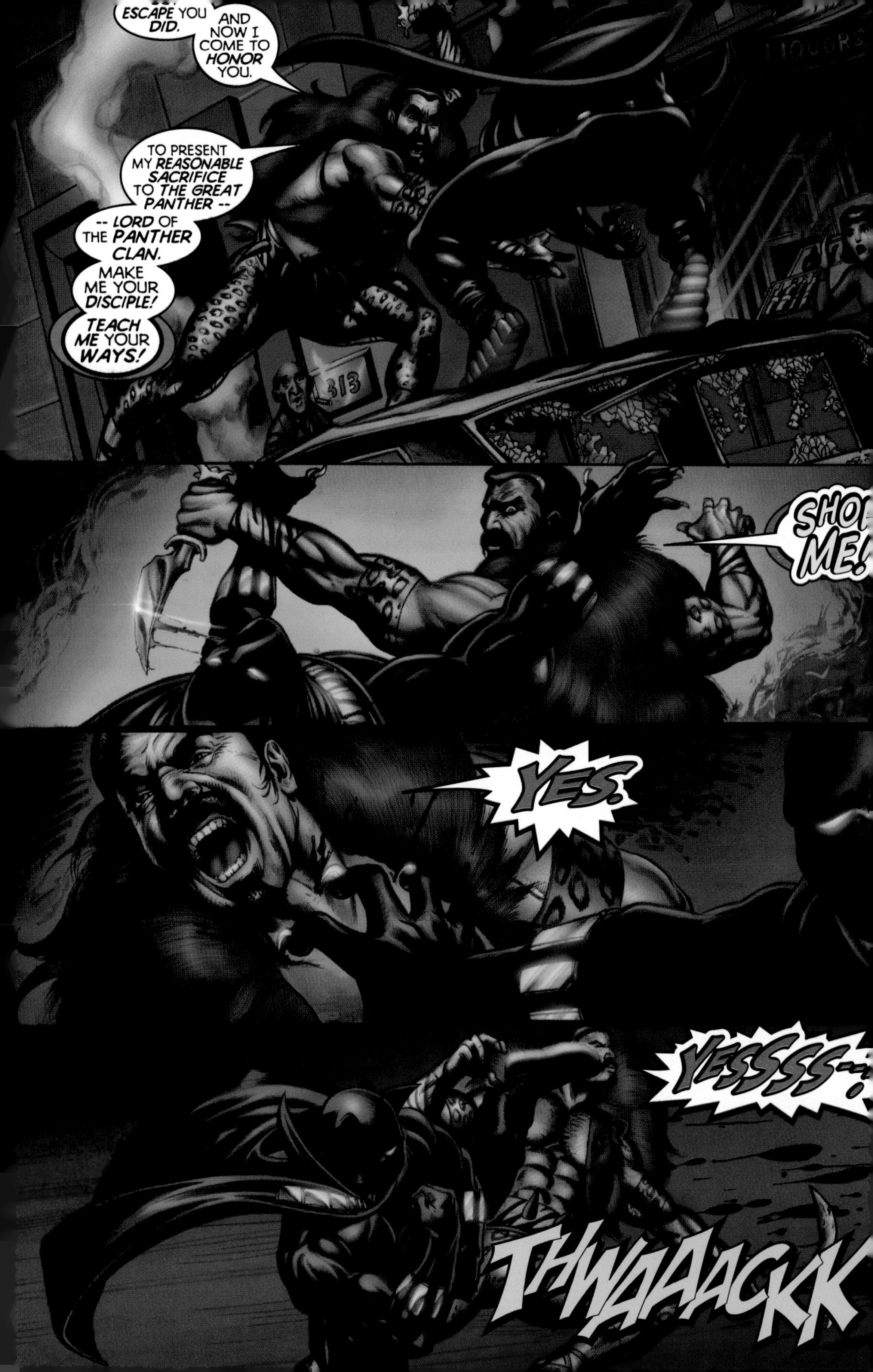
ESCAPE YOU DID.
AND NOW I COME TO HONOR YOU.
TO PRESENT MY REASONABLE SACRIFICE TO THE GREAT PANTHER --
-- LORD OF THE PANTHER CLAN.
MAKE ME YOUR DISCIPLE!
TEACH ME YOUR WAYS!
LIQUORS
313
ME!
YES.
YESSSS--
THWAAACKK

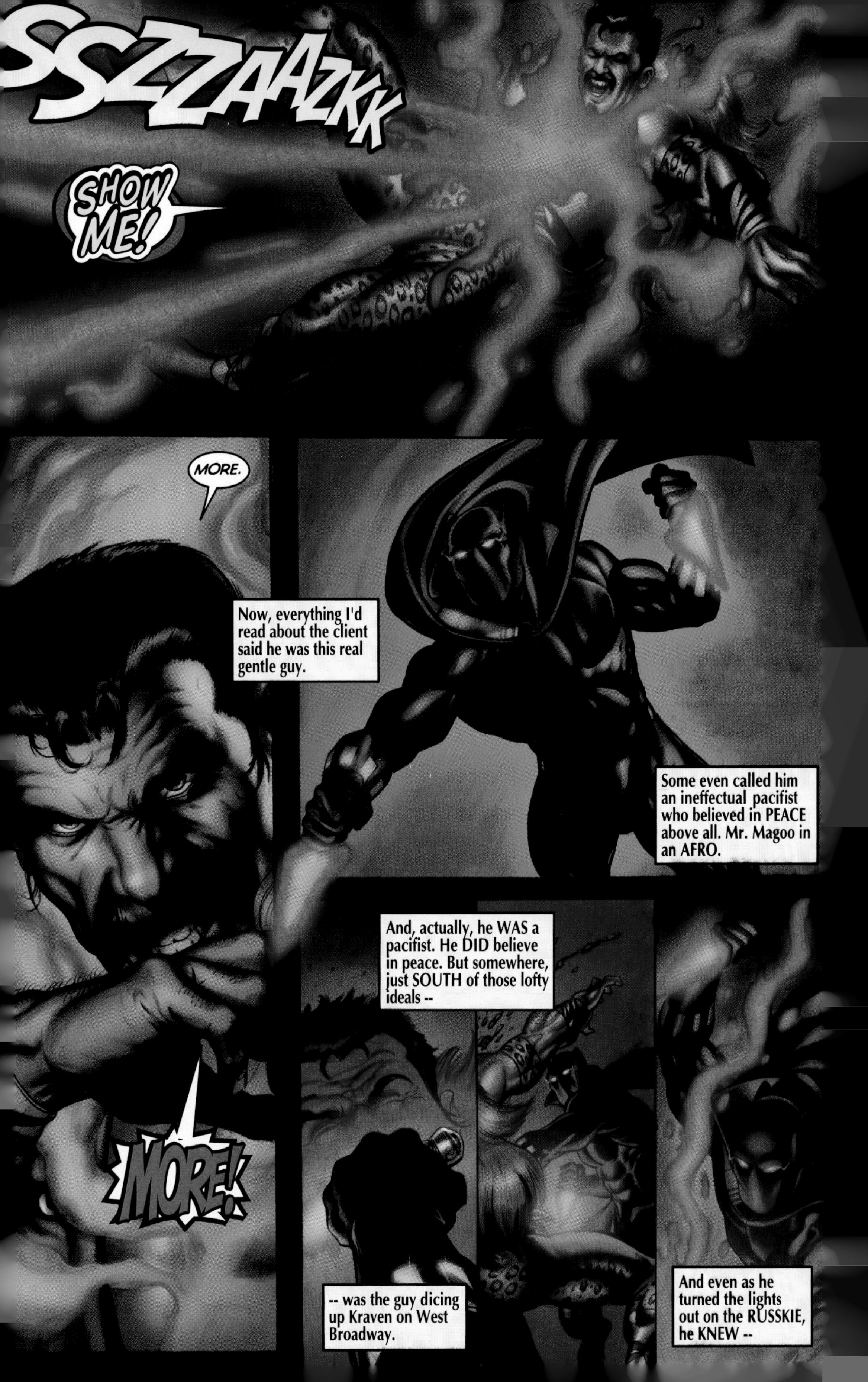
SSZZZAAZKK
SHOW ME!
MORE.
Now, everything I'd read about the client said he was this real gentle guy.
Some even called him an ineffectual pacifist who believed in PEACE above all. Mr. Magoo in an AFRO.
MORE!
And, actually, he WAS a pacifist. He DID believe in peace. But somewhere, just SOUTH of those lofty ideals --
-- was the guy dicing up Kraven on West Broadway.
And even as he turned the lights out on the RUSSKIE, he KNEW --

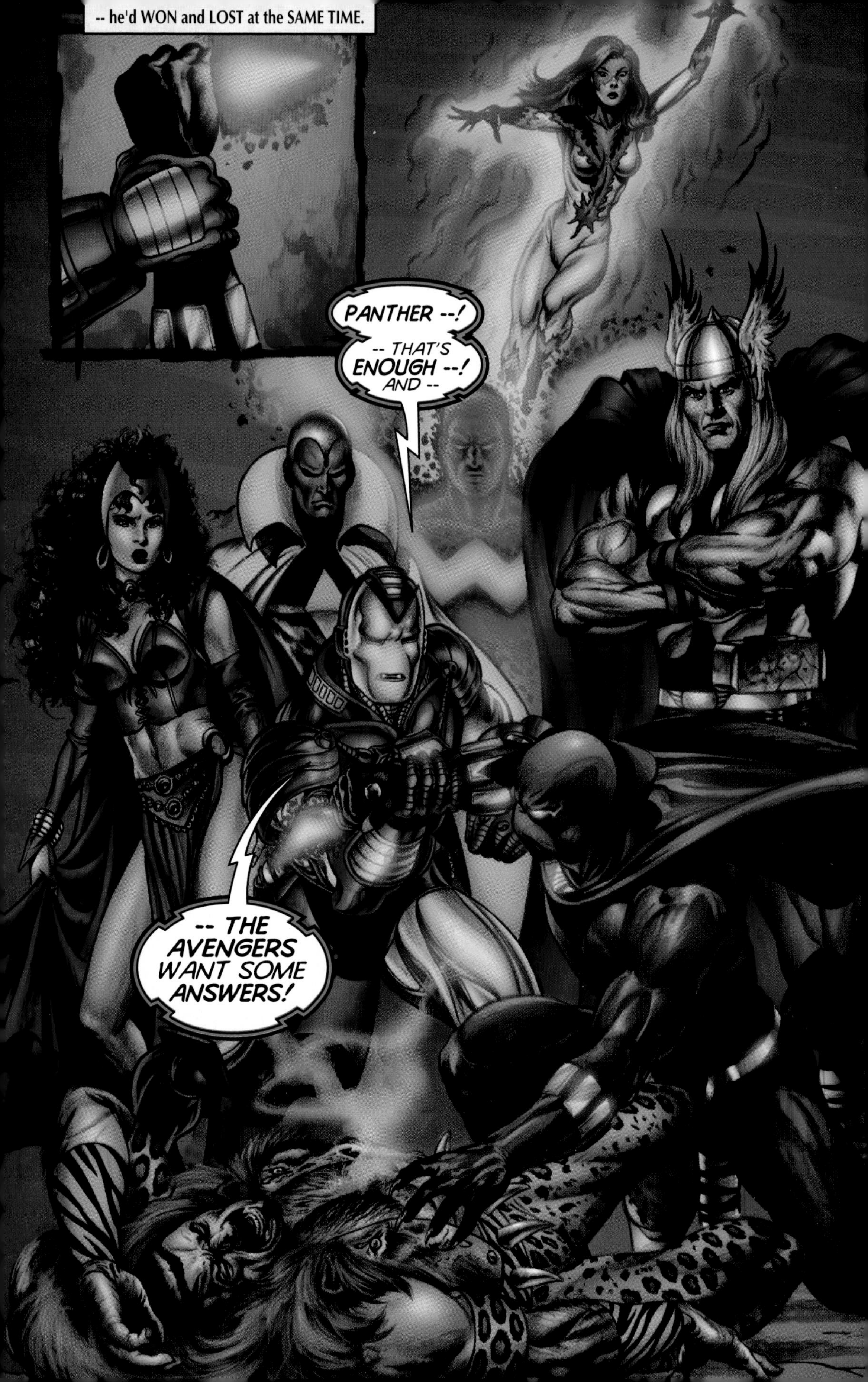
-- he'd WON and LOST at the SAME TIME.
PANTHER --! -- THAT'S ENOUGH --! AND --
-- THE AVENGERS WANT SOME ANSWERS!

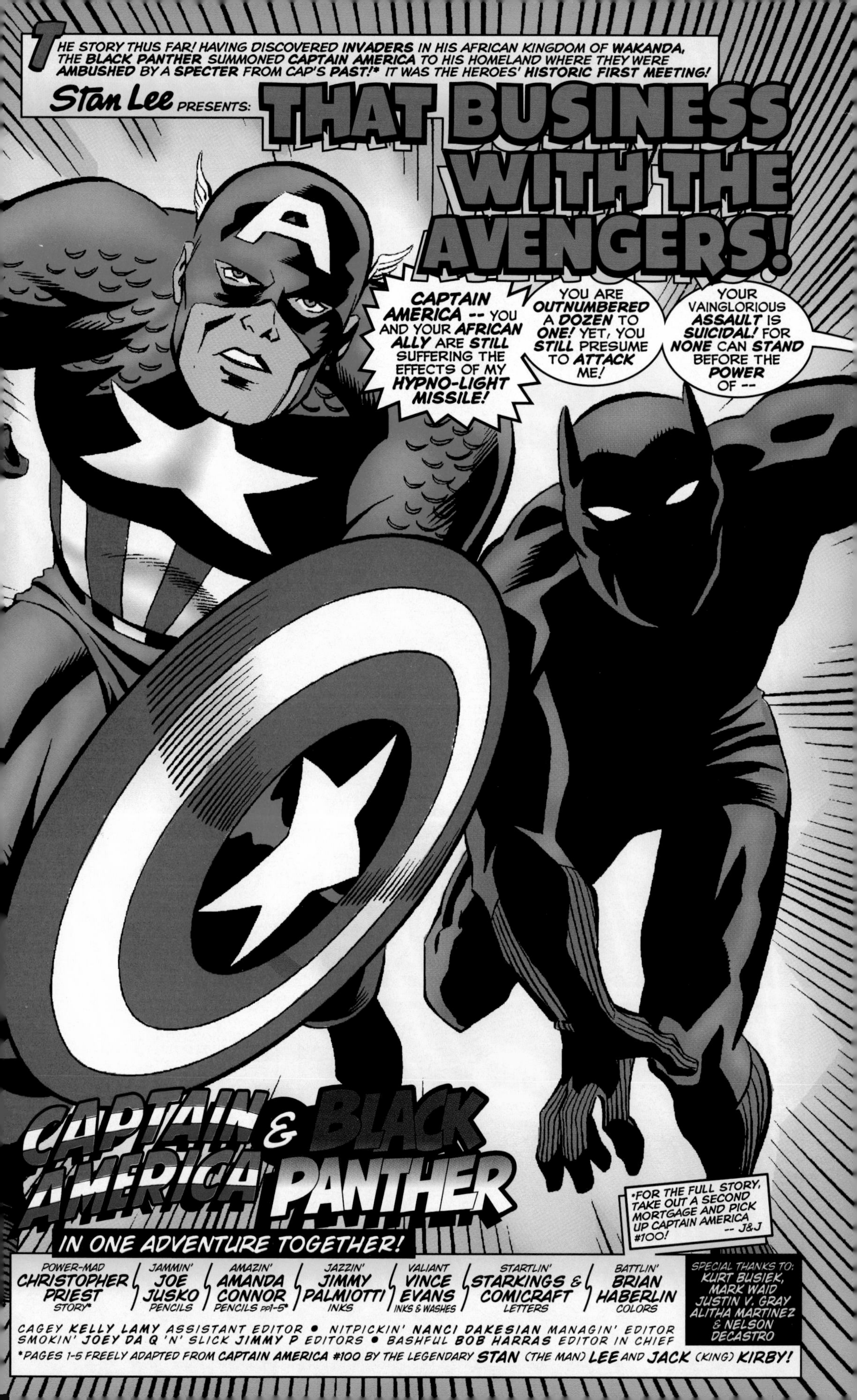
THE STORY THUS FAR! HAVING DISCOVERED INVADERS IN HIS AFRICAN KINGDOM OF WAKANDA, THE BLACK PANTHER SUMMONED CAPTAIN AMERICA TO HIS HOMELAND WHERE THEY WERE AMBUSHED BY A SPECTER FROM CAP'S PAST!* IT WAS THE HEROES' HISTORIC FIRST MEETING!
Stan Lee PRESENTS:
THAT BUSINESS WITH THE AVENGERS!
CAPTAIN AMERICA -- YOU AND YOUR AFRICAN ALLY ARE STILL SUFFERING THE EFFECTS OF MY HYPNO-LIGHT MISSILE!
YOU ARE OUTNUMBERED A DOZEN TO ONE! YET, YOU STILL PRESUME TO ATTACK ME!
YOUR VAINGLORIOUS ASSAULT IS SUICIDAL! FOR NONE CAN STAND BEFORE THE POWER OF --
CAPTAIN AMERICA & BLACK PANTHER
IN ONE ADVENTURE TOGETHER!
*FOR THE FULL STORY, TAKE OUT A SECOND MORTGAGE AND PICK UP CAPTAIN AMERICA #100! -- J&J
POWER-MAD CHRISTOPHER PRIEST STORY*
JAMMIN' JOE JUSKO PENCILS
AMAZIN' AMANDA CONNOR PENCILS pp1-5*
JAZZIN' JIMMY PALMIOTTI INKS
VALIANT VINCE EVANS INKS & WASHES
STARTLIN' STARKINGS & COMICRAFT LETTERS
BATTLIN' BRIAN HABERLIN COLORS
SPECIAL THANKS TO: KURT BUSIEK, MARK WAID, JUSTIN V. GRAY, ALITHA MARTINEZ & NELSON DECASTRO
CAGEY KELLY LAMY ASSISTANT EDITOR • NITPICKIN' NANCI DAKESIAN MANAGIN' EDITOR
SMOKIN' JOEY DA Q 'N' SLICK JIMMY P EDITORS • BASHFUL BOB HARRAS EDITOR IN CHIEF
*PAGES 1-5 FREELY ADAPTED FROM CAPTAIN AMERICA #100 BY THE LEGENDARY STAN (THE MAN) LEE AND JACK (KING) KIRBY!

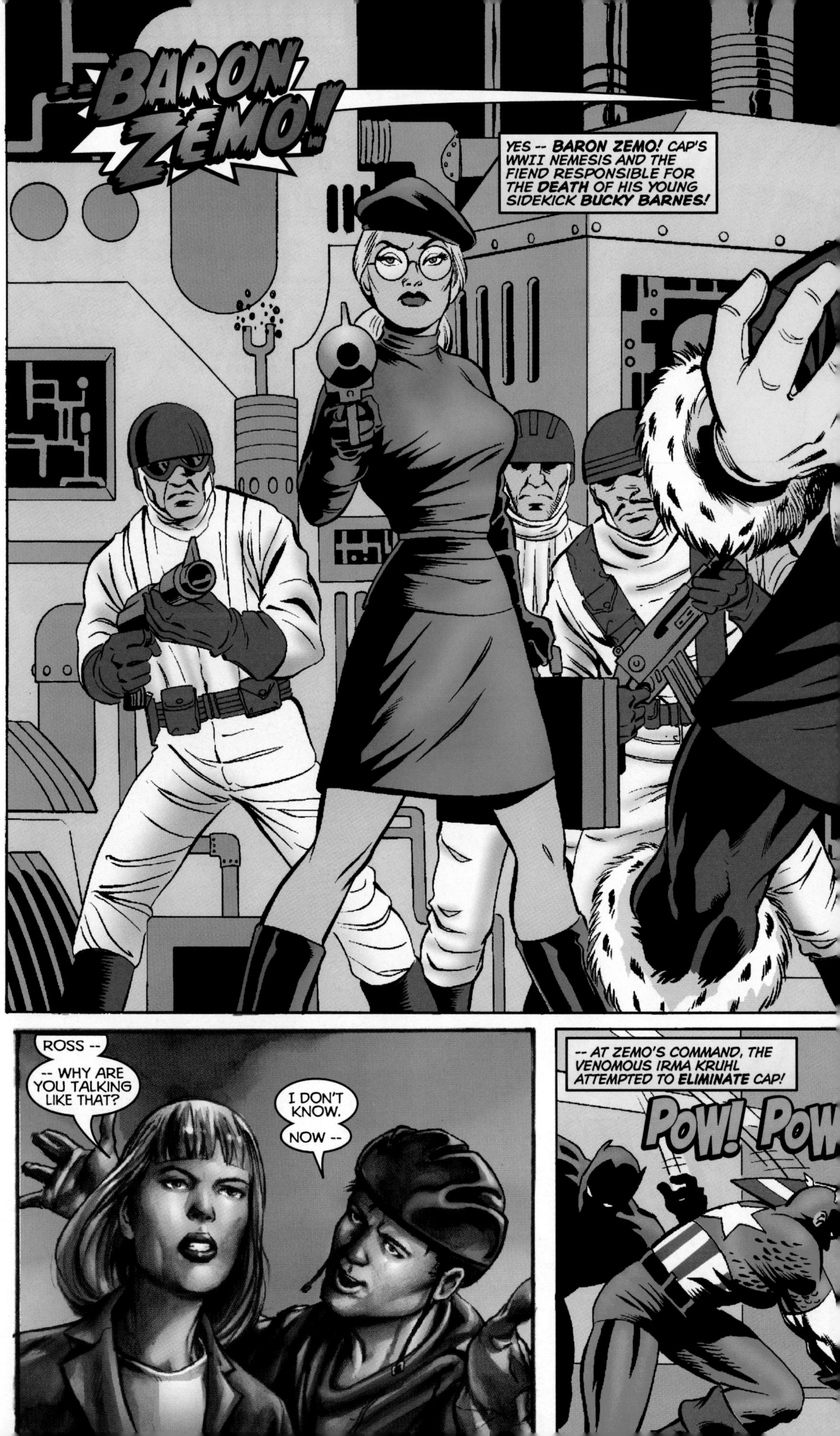
-- BARON ZEMO!
YES -- BARON ZEMO! CAP'S WWII NEMESIS AND THE FIEND RESPONSIBLE FOR THE DEATH OF HIS YOUNG SIDEKICK BUCKY BARNES!
ROSS --
-- WHY ARE YOU TALKING LIKE THAT?
I DON'T KNOW.
NOW --
-- AT ZEMO'S COMMAND, THE VENOMOUS IRMA KRUHL ATTEMPTED TO ELIMINATE CAP!
POW! POW

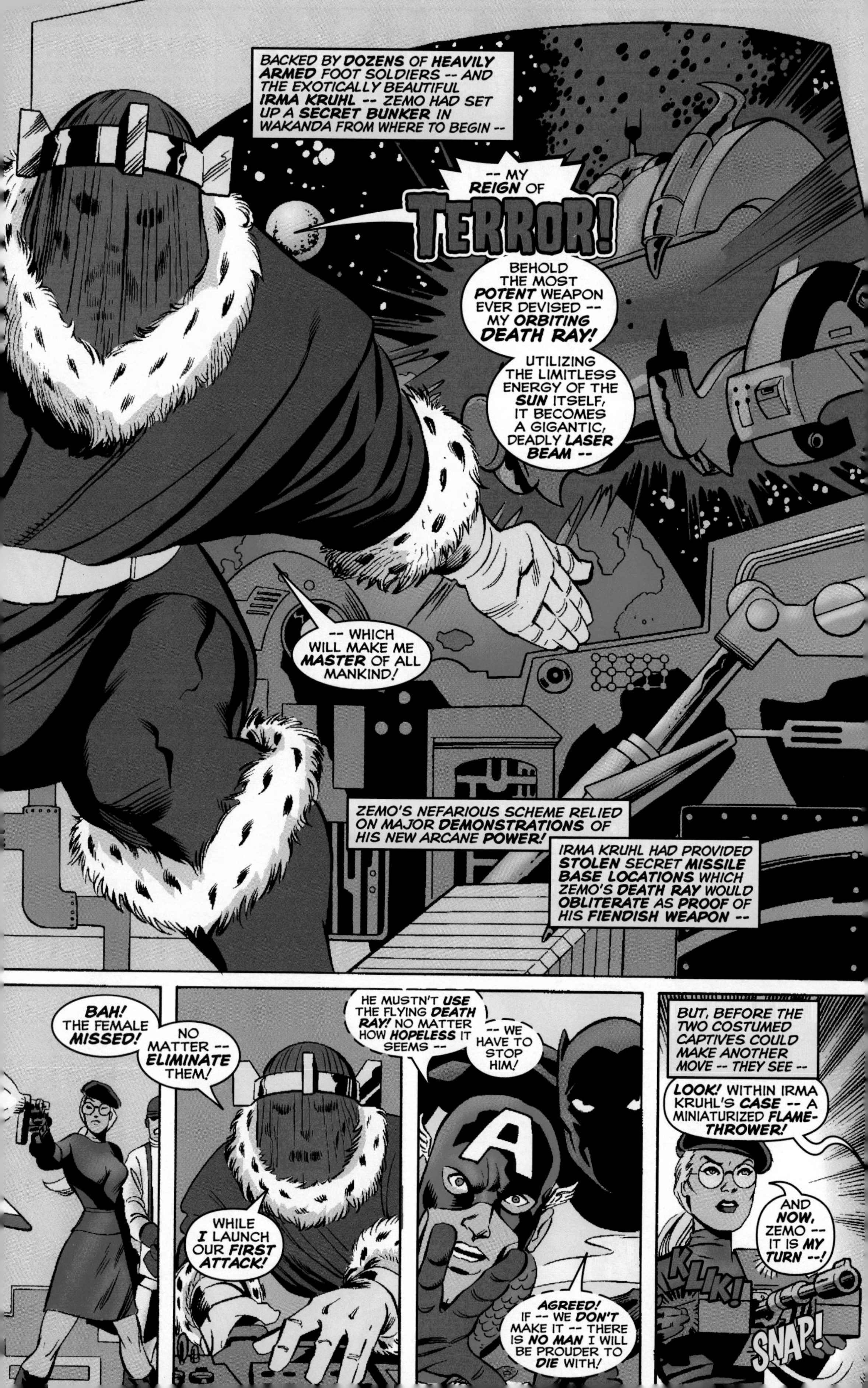
BACKED BY DOZENS OF HEAVILY ARMED FOOT SOLDIERS -- AND THE EXOTICALLY BEAUTIFUL IRMA KRUHL -- ZEMO HAD SET UP A SECRET BUNKER IN WAKANDA FROM WHERE TO BEGIN --
-- MY REIGN OF TERROR!
BEHOLD THE MOST POTENT WEAPON EVER DEVISED -- MY ORBITING DEATH RAY!
UTILIZING THE LIMITLESS ENERGY OF THE SUN ITSELF, IT BECOMES A GIGANTIC, DEADLY LASER BEAM --
-- WHICH WILL MAKE ME MASTER OF ALL MANKIND!
ZEMO'S NEFARIOUS SCHEME RELIED ON MAJOR DEMONSTRATIONS OF HIS NEW ARCANE POWER!
IRMA KRUHL HAD PROVIDED STOLEN SECRET MISSILE BASE LOCATIONS WHICH ZEMO'S DEATH RAY WOULD OBLITERATE AS PROOF OF HIS FIENDISH WEAPON --
BAH! THE FEMALE MISSED!
NO MATTER -- ELIMINATE THEM!
WHILE I LAUNCH OUR FIRST ATTACK!
HE MUSTN'T USE THE FLYING DEATH RAY! NO MATTER HOW HOPELESS IT SEEMS --
-- WE HAVE TO STOP HIM!
AGREED! IF -- WE DON'T MAKE IT -- THERE IS NO MAN I WILL BE PROUDER TO DIE WITH!
BUT, BEFORE THE TWO COSTUMED CAPTIVES COULD MAKE ANOTHER MOVE -- THEY SEE --
LOOK! WITHIN IRMA KRUHL'S CASE -- A MINIATURIZED FLAME-THROWER!
AND NOW, ZEMO -- IT IS MY TURN --!
KLIK!
SNAP!

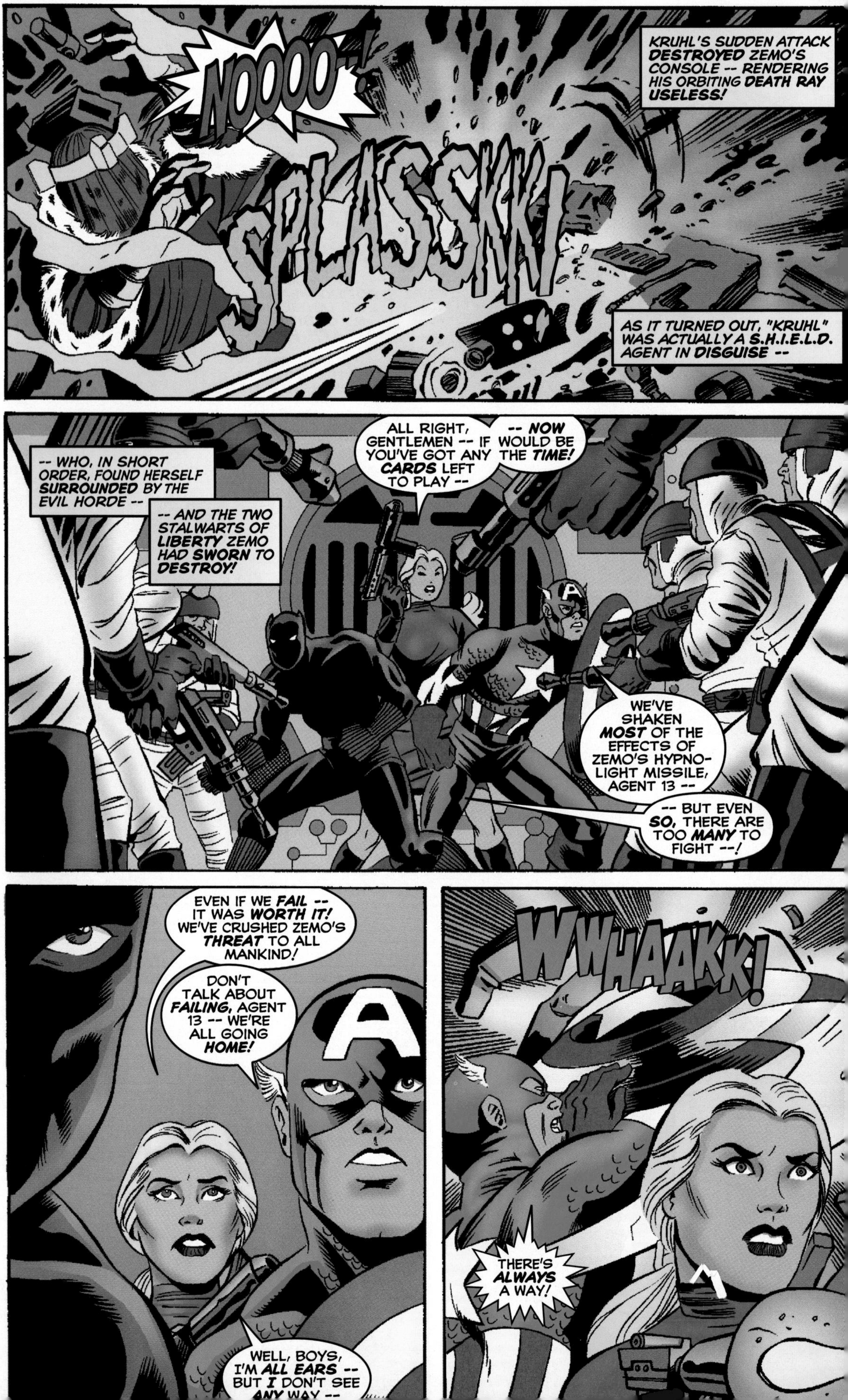
NOOOO--!
KRUHL'S SUDDEN ATTACK DESTROYED ZEMO'S CONSOLE -- RENDERING HIS ORBITING DEATH RAY USELESS!
SPLASSKK!
AS IT TURNED OUT, "KRUHL" WAS ACTUALLY A S.H.I.E.L.D. AGENT IN DISGUISE --
-- WHO, IN SHORT ORDER, FOUND HERSELF SURROUNDED BY THE EVIL HORDE --
-- AND THE TWO STALWARTS OF LIBERTY ZEMO HAD SWORN TO DESTROY!
ALL RIGHT, GENTLEMEN -- IF YOU'VE GOT ANY CARDS LEFT TO PLAY --
-- NOW WOULD BE THE TIME!
WE'VE SHAKEN MOST OF THE EFFECTS OF ZEMO'S HYPNO-LIGHT MISSILE, AGENT 13 --
-- BUT EVEN SO, THERE ARE TOO MANY TO FIGHT --!
EVEN IF WE FAIL -- IT WAS WORTH IT! WE'VE CRUSHED ZEMO'S THREAT TO ALL MANKIND!
DON'T TALK ABOUT FAILING, AGENT 13 -- WE'RE ALL GOING HOME!
WELL, BOYS, I'M ALL EARS -- BUT I DON'T SEE ANY WAY --
WWHAAKK!
THERE'S ALWAYS A WAY!

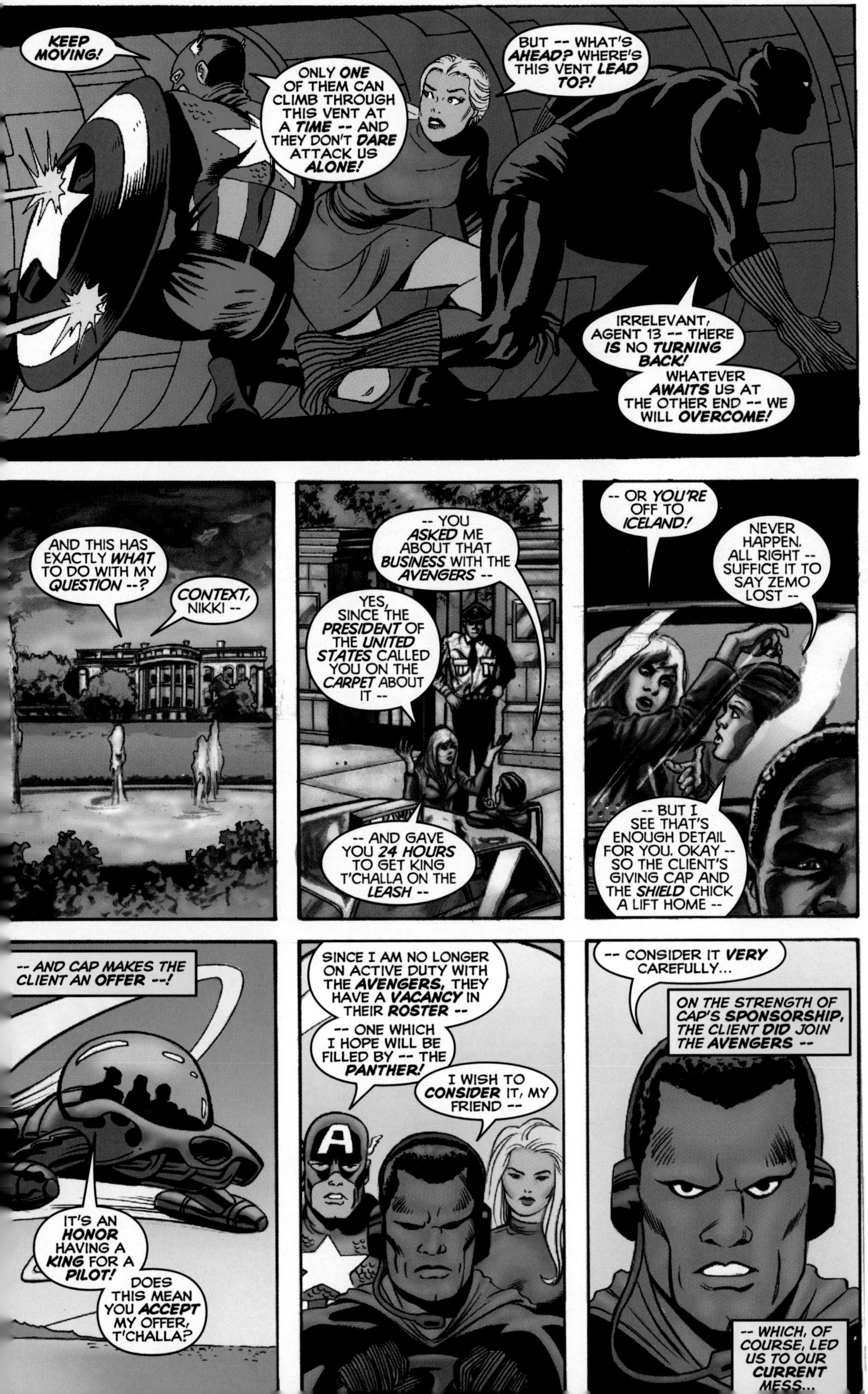
KEEP MOVING!
ONLY ONE OF THEM CAN CLIMB THROUGH THIS VENT AT A TIME -- AND THEY DON'T DARE ATTACK US ALONE!
BUT -- WHAT'S AHEAD? WHERE'S THIS VENT LEAD TO?!
IRRELEVANT, AGENT 13 -- THERE IS NO TURNING BACK!
WHATEVER AWAITS US AT THE OTHER END -- WE WILL OVERCOME!
AND THIS HAS EXACTLY WHAT TO DO WITH MY QUESTION --?
CONTEXT, NIKKI --
-- YOU ASKED ME ABOUT THAT BUSINESS WITH THE AVENGERS --
YES, SINCE THE PRESIDENT OF THE UNITED STATES CALLED YOU ON THE CARPET ABOUT IT --
-- AND GAVE YOU 24 HOURS TO GET KING T'CHALLA ON THE LEASH --
-- OR YOU'RE OFF TO ICELAND!
NEVER HAPPEN. ALL RIGHT -- SUFFICE IT TO SAY ZEMO LOST --
-- BUT I SEE THAT'S ENOUGH DETAIL FOR YOU. OKAY -- SO THE CLIENT'S GIVING CAP AND THE SHIELD CHICK A LIFT HOME --
-- AND CAP MAKES THE CLIENT AN OFFER --!
IT'S AN HONOR HAVING A KING FOR A PILOT!
DOES THIS MEAN YOU ACCEPT MY OFFER, T'CHALLA?
SINCE I AM NO LONGER ON ACTIVE DUTY WITH THE AVENGERS, THEY HAVE A VACANCY IN THEIR ROSTER --
-- ONE WHICH I HOPE WILL BE FILLED BY -- THE PANTHER!
I WISH TO CONSIDER IT, MY FRIEND --
-- CONSIDER IT VERY CAREFULLY...
ON THE STRENGTH OF CAP'S SPONSORSHIP, THE CLIENT DID JOIN THE AVENGERS --
-- WHICH, OF COURSE, LED US TO OUR CURRENT MESS...

LIZARD, LIZARD, LIZARD...

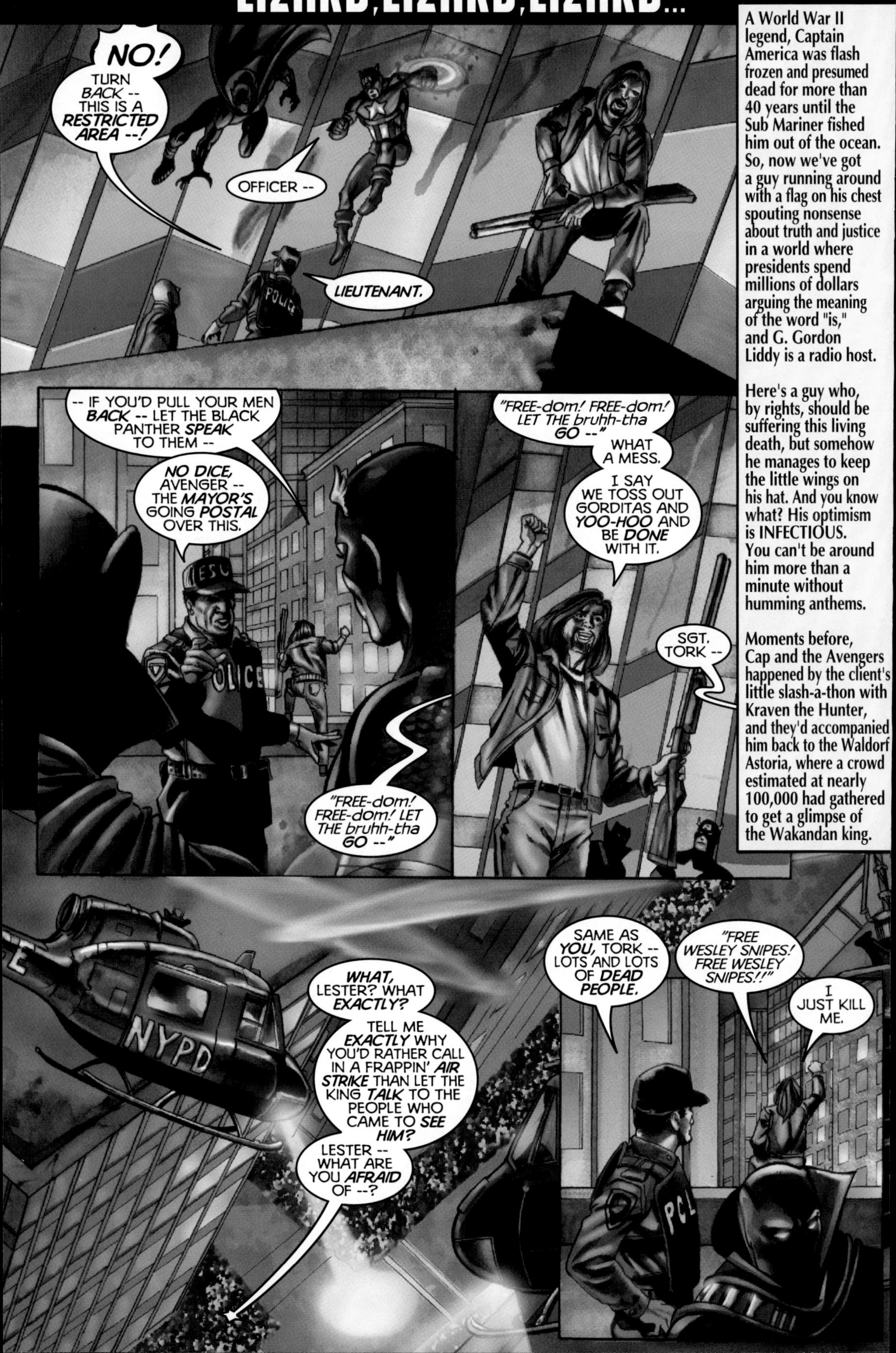
A World War II legend, Captain America was flash frozen and presumed dead for more than 40 years until the Sub Mariner fished him out of the ocean. So, now we've got a guy running around with a flag on his chest spouting nonsense about truth and justice in a world where presidents spend millions of dollars arguing the meaning of the word "is," and G. Gordon Liddy is a radio host.
Here's a guy who, by rights, should be suffering this living death, but somehow he manages to keep the little wings on his hat. And you know what? His optimism is INFECTIOUS. You can't be around him more than a minute without humming anthems.
Moments before, Cap and the Avengers happened by the client's little slash-a-thon with Kraven the Hunter, and they'd accompanied him back to the Waldorf Astoria, where a crowd estimated at nearly 100,000 had gathered to get a glimpse of the Wakandan king.
NO! TURN BACK -- THIS IS A RESTRICTED AREA --!
OFFICER --
LIEUTENANT.
-- IF YOU'D PULL YOUR MEN BACK -- LET THE BLACK PANTHER SPEAK TO THEM --
NO DICE, AVENGER -- THE MAYOR'S GOING POSTAL OVER THIS.
"FREE-dom! FREE-dom! LET THE bruhh-tha GO --"
"FREE-dom! FREE-dom! LET THE bruhh-tha GO --"
WHAT A MESS.
I SAY WE TOSS OUT GORDITAS AND YOO-HOO AND BE DONE WITH IT.
SGT. TORK --
WHAT, LESTER? WHAT EXACTLY?
TELL ME EXACTLY WHY YOU'D RATHER CALL IN A FRAPPIN' AIR STRIKE THAN LET THE KING TALK TO THE PEOPLE WHO CAME TO SEE HIM?
LESTER -- WHAT ARE YOU AFRAID OF --?
SAME AS YOU, TORK -- LOTS AND LOTS OF DEAD PEOPLE.
"FREE WESLEY SNIPES! FREE WESLEY SNIPES!!"
I JUST KILL ME.

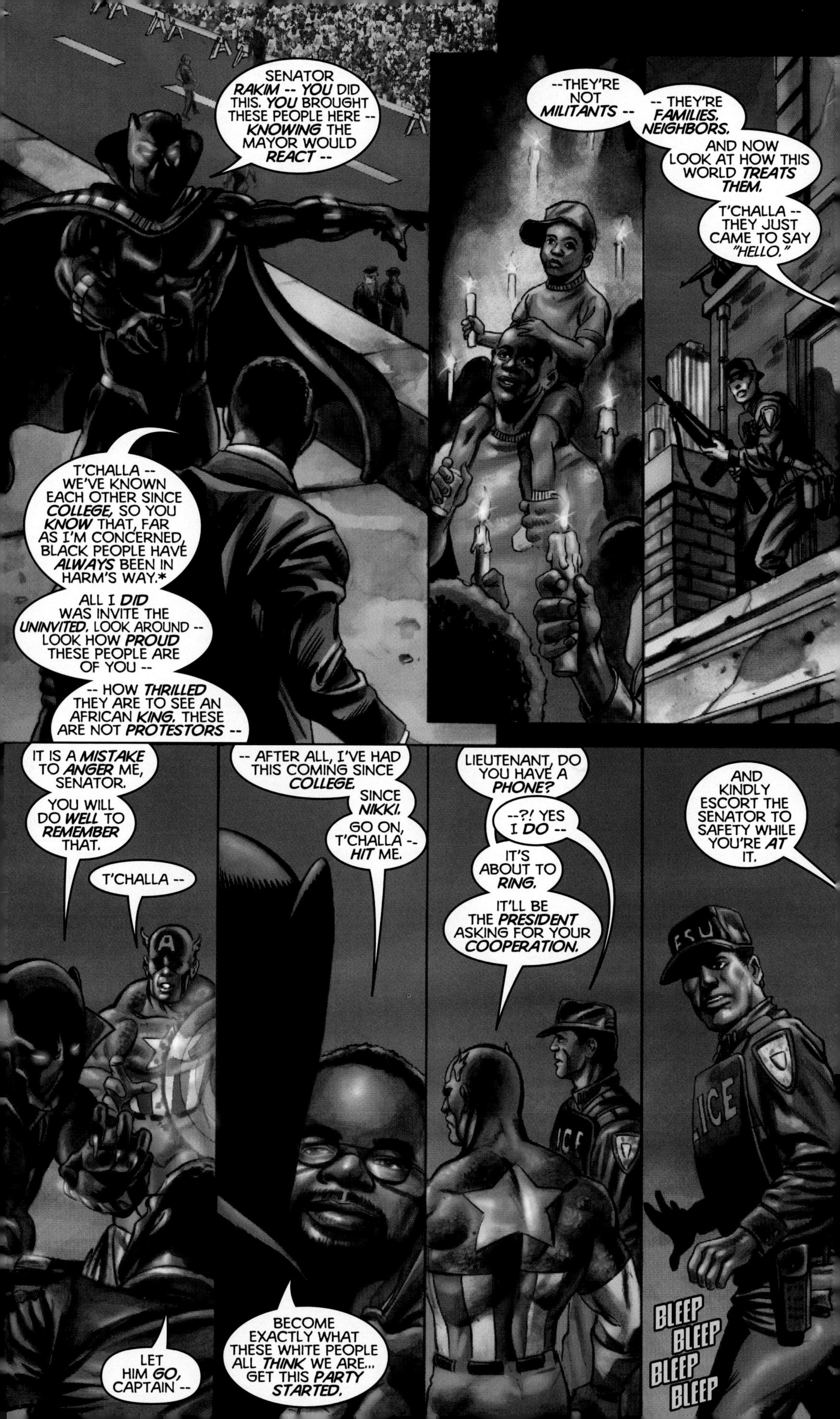
SENATOR RAKIM -- YOU DID THIS. YOU BROUGHT THESE PEOPLE HERE -- KNOWING THE MAYOR WOULD REACT --
T'CHALLA -- WE'VE KNOWN EACH OTHER SINCE COLLEGE, SO YOU KNOW THAT, FAR AS I'M CONCERNED, BLACK PEOPLE HAVE ALWAYS BEEN IN HARM'S WAY.*
ALL I DID WAS INVITE THE UNINVITED. LOOK AROUND -- LOOK HOW PROUD THESE PEOPLE ARE OF YOU --
-- HOW THRILLED THEY ARE TO SEE AN AFRICAN KING. THESE ARE NOT PROTESTORS --
--THEY'RE NOT MILITANTS --
-- THEY'RE FAMILIES. NEIGHBORS.
AND NOW LOOK AT HOW THIS WORLD TREATS THEM.
T'CHALLA -- THEY JUST CAME TO SAY "HELLO."
IT IS A MISTAKE TO ANGER ME, SENATOR.
YOU WILL DO WELL TO REMEMBER THAT.
T'CHALLA --
LET HIM GO, CAPTAIN --
-- AFTER ALL, I'VE HAD THIS COMING SINCE COLLEGE.
SINCE NIKKI.
GO ON, T'CHALLA -- HIT ME.
BECOME EXACTLY WHAT THESE WHITE PEOPLE ALL THINK WE ARE... GET THIS PARTY STARTED.
LIEUTENANT, DO YOU HAVE A PHONE?
--?! YES I DO --
IT'S ABOUT TO RING.
IT'LL BE THE PRESIDENT ASKING FOR YOUR COOPERATION.
AND KINDLY ESCORT THE SENATOR TO SAFETY WHILE YOU'RE AT IT.
BLEEP
BLEEP
BLEEP
BLEEP

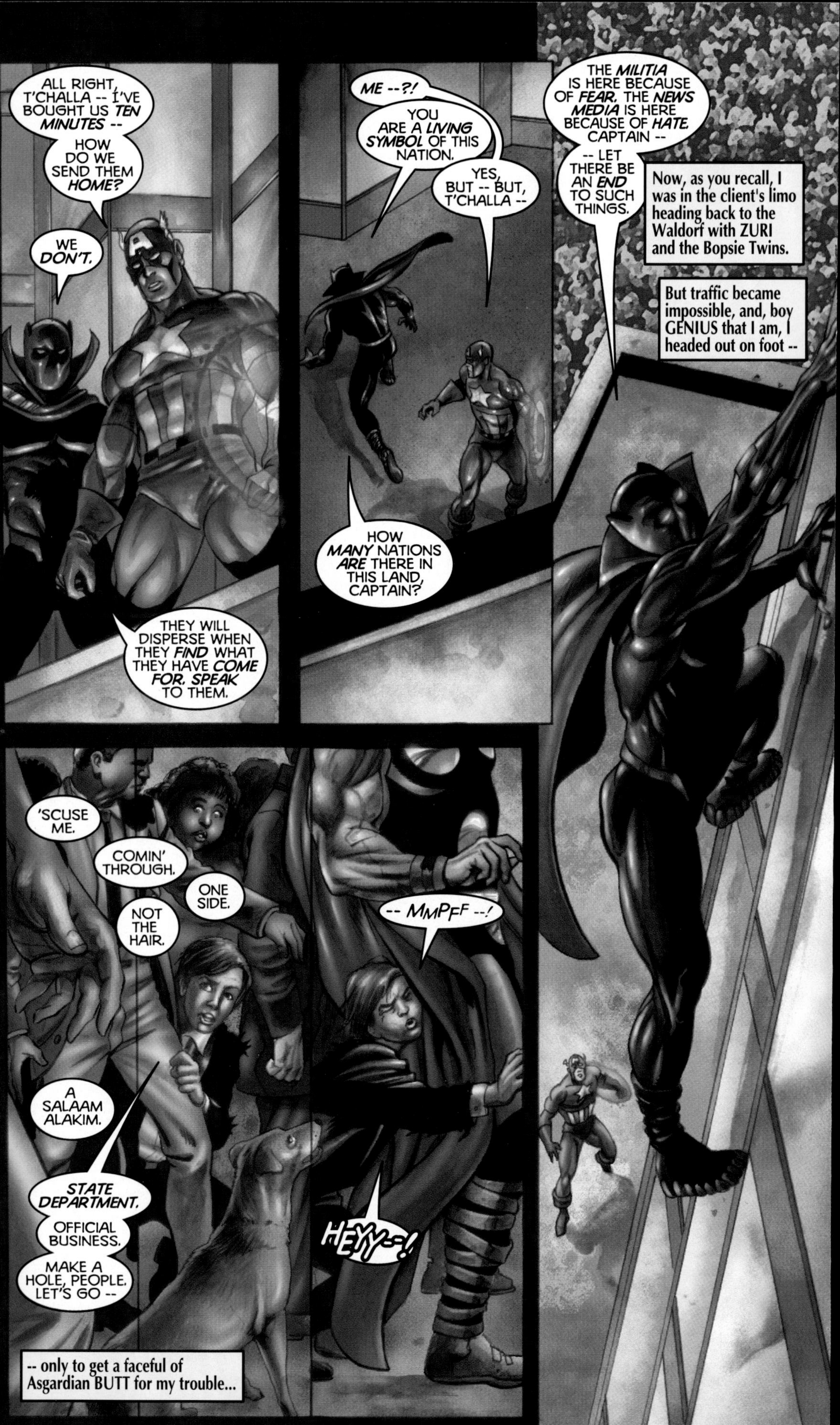
ALL RIGHT, T'CHALLA -- I'VE BOUGHT US TEN MINUTES --
HOW DO WE SEND THEM HOME?
WE DON'T.
THEY WILL DISPERSE WHEN THEY FIND WHAT THEY HAVE COME FOR. SPEAK TO THEM.
ME --?!
YOU ARE A LIVING SYMBOL OF THIS NATION.
YES, BUT -- BUT, T'CHALLA --
HOW MANY NATIONS ARE THERE IN THIS LAND, CAPTAIN?
THE MILITIA IS HERE BECAUSE OF FEAR. THE NEWS MEDIA IS HERE BECAUSE OF HATE. CAPTAIN --
-- LET THERE BE AN END TO SUCH THINGS.
Now, as you recall, I was in the client's limo heading back to the Waldorf with ZURI and the Bopsie Twins.
But traffic became impossible, and, boy GENIUS that I am, I headed out on foot --
'SCUSE ME.
COMIN' THROUGH.
ONE SIDE.
NOT THE HAIR.
A SALAAM ALAKIM.
STATE DEPARTMENT.
OFFICIAL BUSINESS.
MAKE A HOLE, PEOPLE. LET'S GO --
-- MMPFF --!
HEYY--!
-- only to get a faceful of Asgardian BUTT for my trouble...

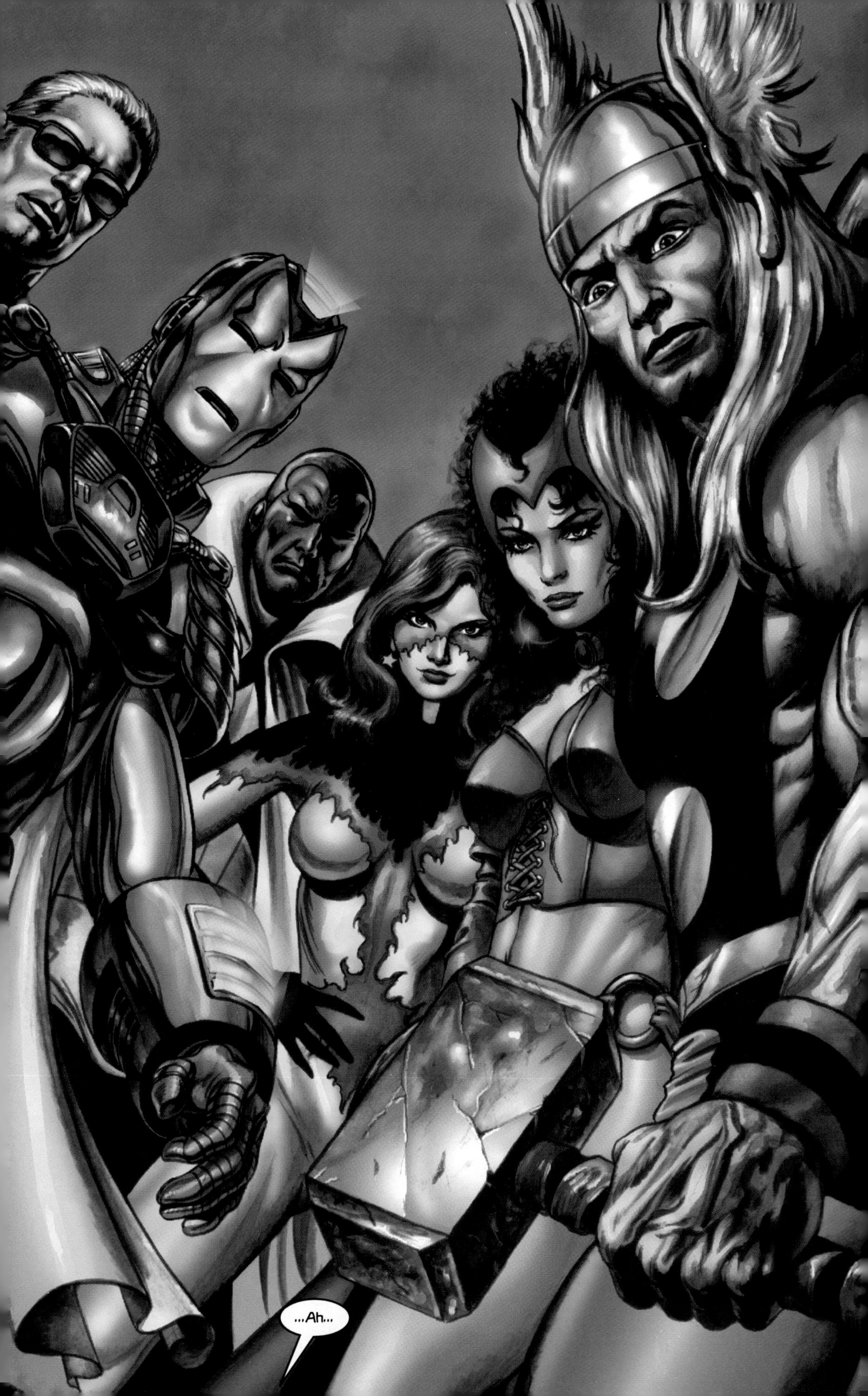
...Ah...

MEET THE FLINTSTONES

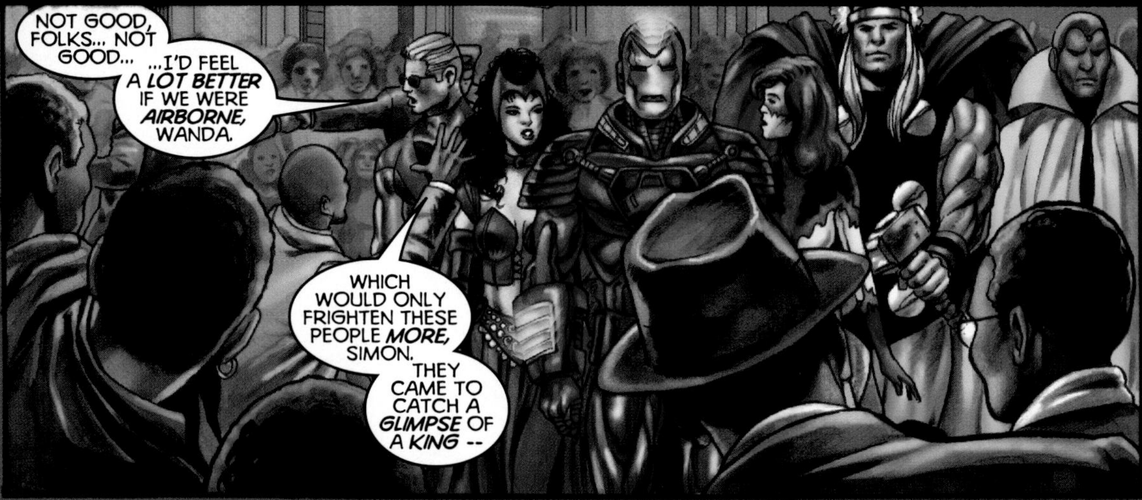
NOT GOOD, FOLKS... NOT GOOD...
...I'D FEEL A LOT BETTER IF WE WERE AIRBORNE, WANDA.
WHICH WOULD ONLY FRIGHTEN THESE PEOPLE MORE, SIMON.
THEY CAME TO CATCH A GLIMPSE OF A KING --

They called themselves the AVENGERS, which I had always assumed was Greek for "Gaudily Dressed Borderline Fascists." I always wondered who appointed THESE guys to "avenge" me: a group of people, unelected, unregulated, and powerful enough to level entire cities. The Village People with repulsor rays. If I could've figured out what made THESE people any different from any other radical militia group, black militant organization, rogue X-Mutants, or the moral right wing. I'd have probably had less problems with the obscenity of New York's mayor grinningly supporting THEM while aiming GUNS at his own citizens.

Years ago, the client was an active member of the Avengers and, having gotten to know the client a little over these past weeks, the question that came to mind was --

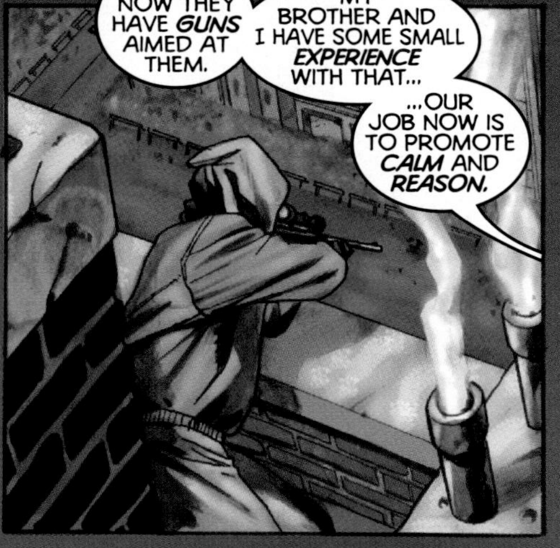
-- AND NOW THEY HAVE GUNS AIMED AT THEM.
MY BROTHER AND I HAVE SOME SMALL EXPERIENCE WITH THAT...
...OUR JOB NOW IS TO PROMOTE CALM AND REASON.

- why? I mean, why would a king leave his throne to pal around with Keptin Kourageous and Minit Moose?

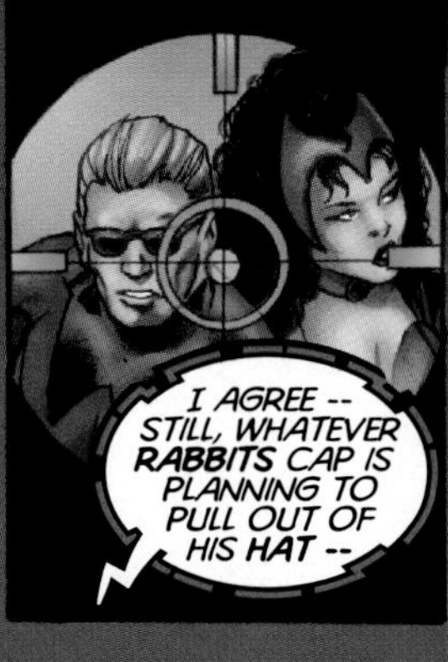
I AGREE -- STILL, WHATEVER RABBITS CAP IS PLANNING TO PULL OUT OF HIS HAT --

-- I mean, who could be SURE whose SIDE these people were on? And, remember, the client's cat suit was largely ceremonial. It was a badge of OFFICE --

-- not the expression of some chronic self-delusion. The client was never a "super" hero, and yet, for reasons known only to HIM, he joined these avenging types.

Of course, by the end of the day, I KNEW why.

Cap was the one who sponsored the client's membership, largely on the strength of their battle against Zemo. He and the client shared a bond of implicit, immutable trust that had never been broken --

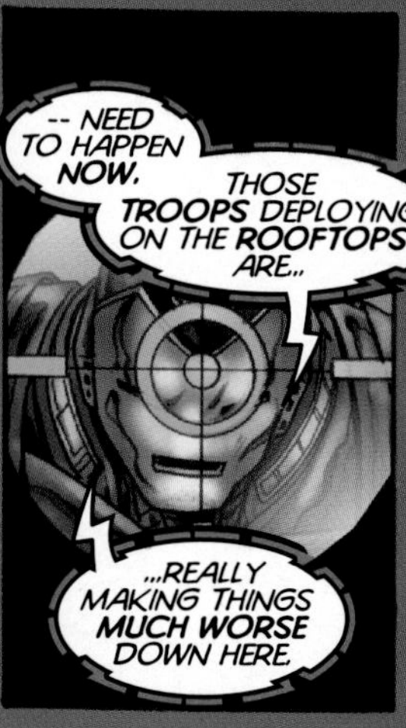
-- NEED TO HAPPEN NOW.
THOSE TROOPS DEPLOYING ON THE ROOFTOPS ARE...
...REALLY MAKING THINGS MUCH WORSE DOWN HERE.

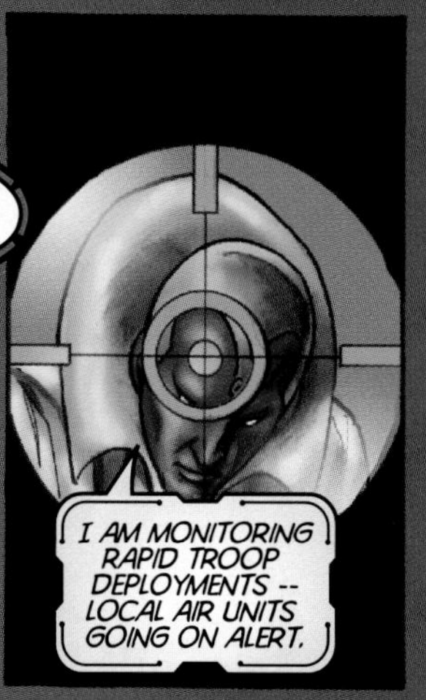
I AM MONITORING RAPID TROOP DEPLOYMENTS -- LOCAL AIR UNITS GOING ON ALERT.

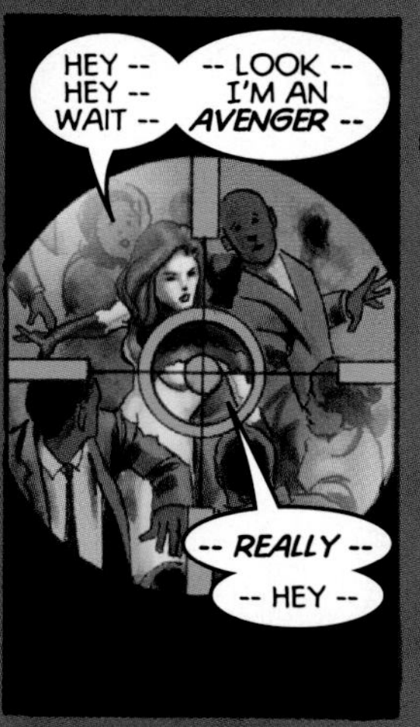
HEY -- HEY -- WAIT --
-- LOOK -- I'M AN AVENGER --
-- REALLY --
-- HEY --

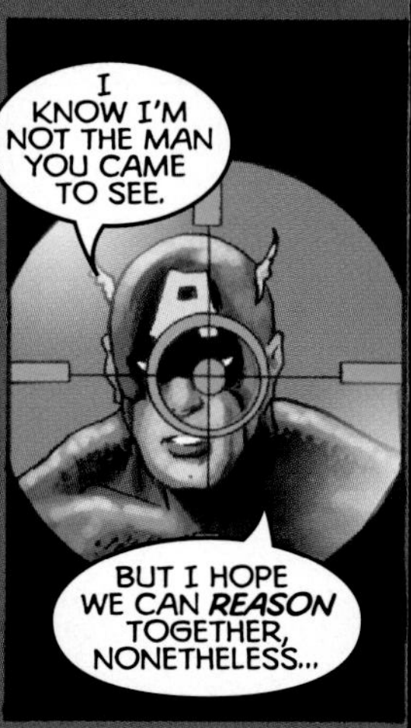
I KNOW I'M NOT THE MAN YOU CAME TO SEE.
BUT I HOPE WE CAN REASON TOGETHER, NONETHELESS...

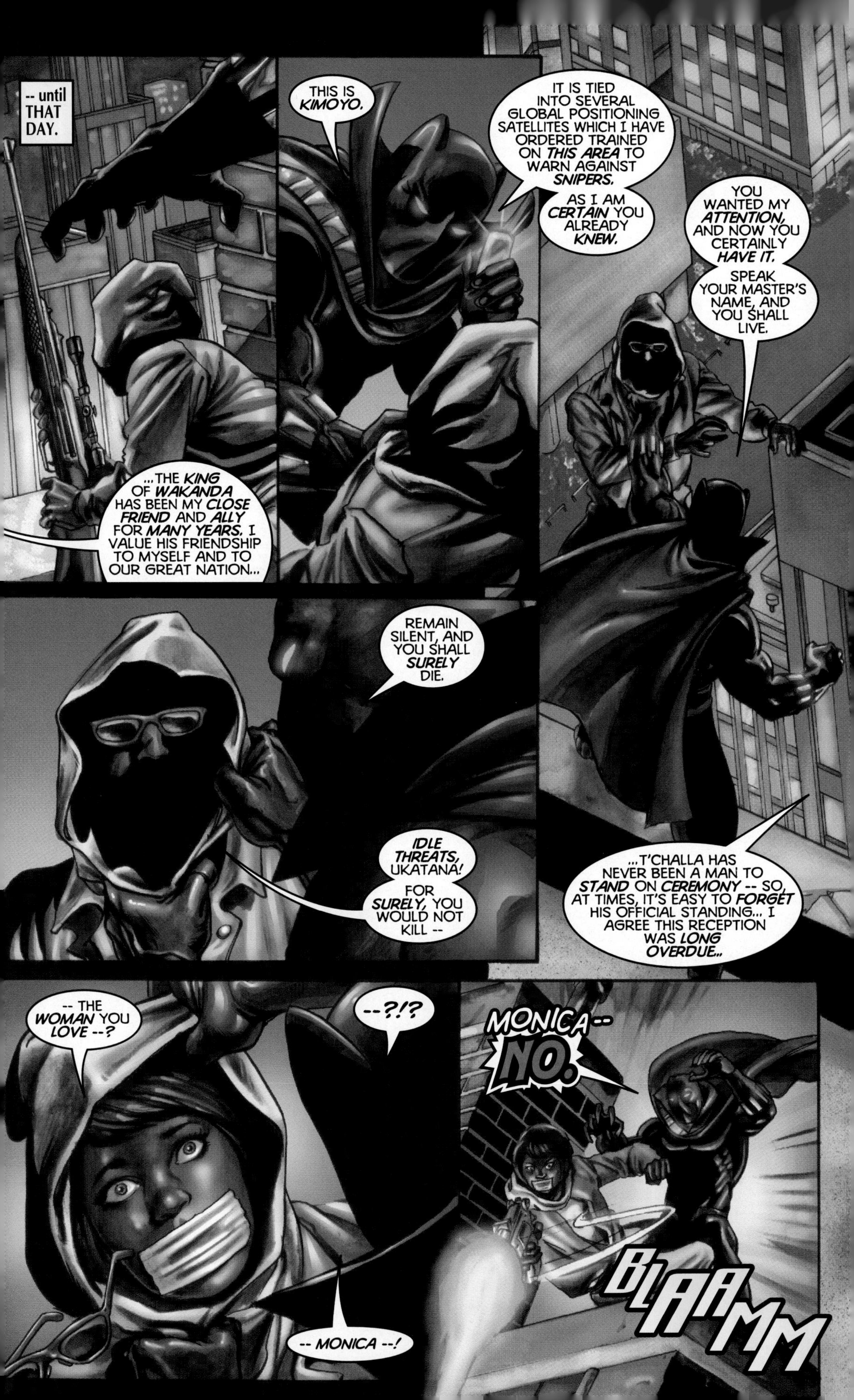
-- until THAT DAY.
...THE KING OF WAKANDA HAS BEEN MY CLOSE FRIEND AND ALLY FOR MANY YEARS. I VALUE HIS FRIENDSHIP TO MYSELF AND TO OUR GREAT NATION...
THIS IS KIMOYO.
IT IS TIED INTO SEVERAL GLOBAL POSITIONING SATELLITES WHICH I HAVE ORDERED TRAINED ON THIS AREA TO WARN AGAINST SNIPERS.
AS I AM CERTAIN YOU ALREADY KNEW.
YOU WANTED MY ATTENTION, AND NOW YOU CERTAINLY HAVE IT.
SPEAK YOUR MASTER'S NAME, AND YOU SHALL LIVE.
REMAIN SILENT, AND YOU SHALL SURELY DIE.
IDLE THREATS, UKATANA!
FOR SURELY, YOU WOULD NOT KILL --
...T'CHALLA HAS NEVER BEEN A MAN TO STAND ON CEREMONY -- SO, AT TIMES, IT'S EASY TO FORGET HIS OFFICIAL STANDING... I AGREE THIS RECEPTION WAS LONG OVERDUE...
-- THE WOMAN YOU LOVE --?
--?!?
-- MONICA --!
MONICA--
NO.
BLAAMM

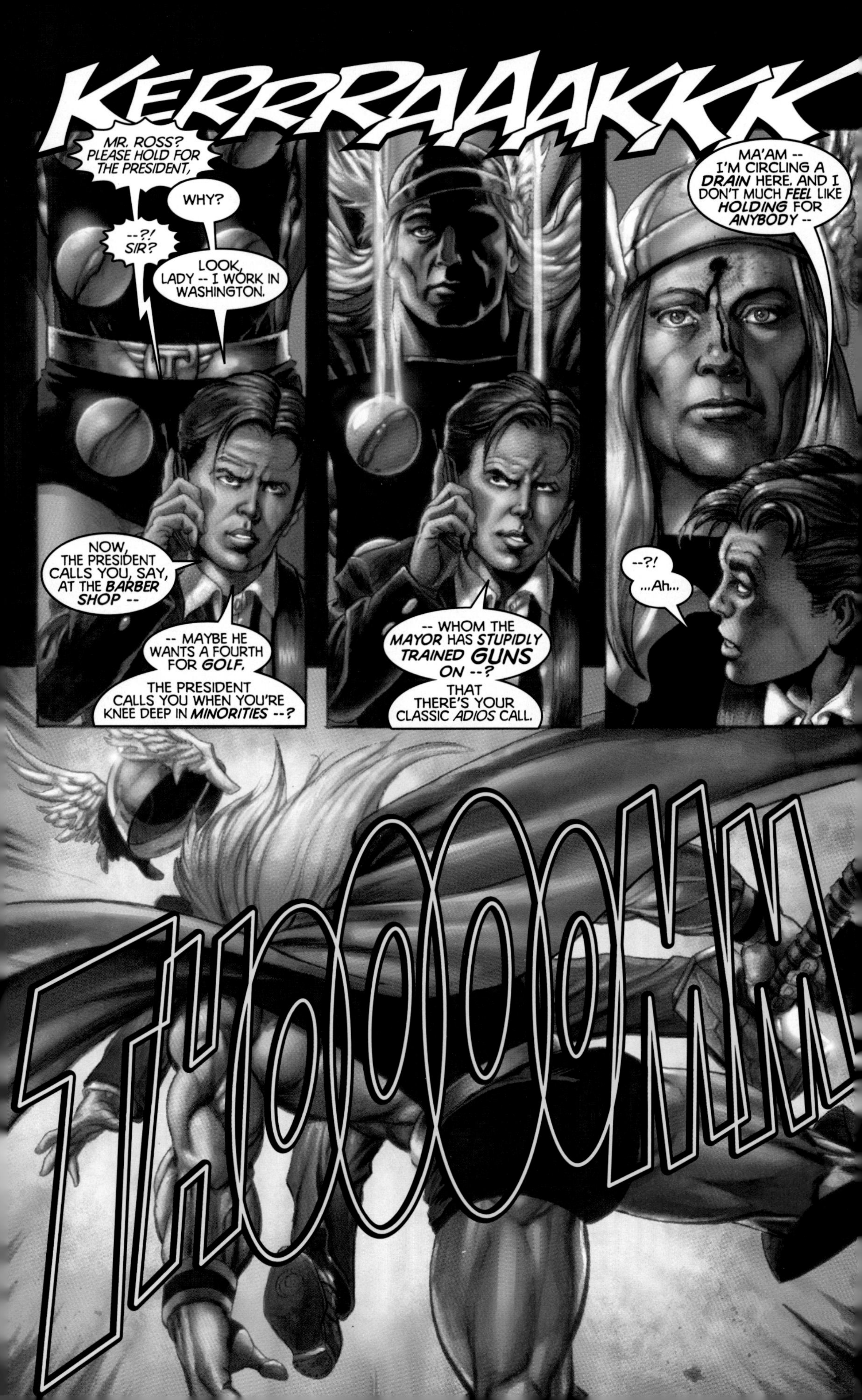
KERRRAAAKKK
MR. ROSS? PLEASE HOLD FOR THE PRESIDENT,
WHY?
--?! SIR?
LOOK, LADY -- I WORK IN WASHINGTON.
NOW, THE PRESIDENT CALLS YOU, SAY, AT THE BARBER SHOP --
-- MAYBE HE WANTS A FOURTH FOR GOLF.
THE PRESIDENT CALLS YOU WHEN YOU'RE KNEE DEEP IN MINORITIES --?
-- WHOM THE MAYOR HAS STUPIDLY TRAINED GUNS ON --?
THAT THERE'S YOUR CLASSIC ADIOS CALL.
MA'AM -- I'M CIRCLING A DRAIN HERE. AND I DON'T MUCH FEEL LIKE HOLDING FOR ANYBODY --
--?!
...Ah...
THOOOOMM

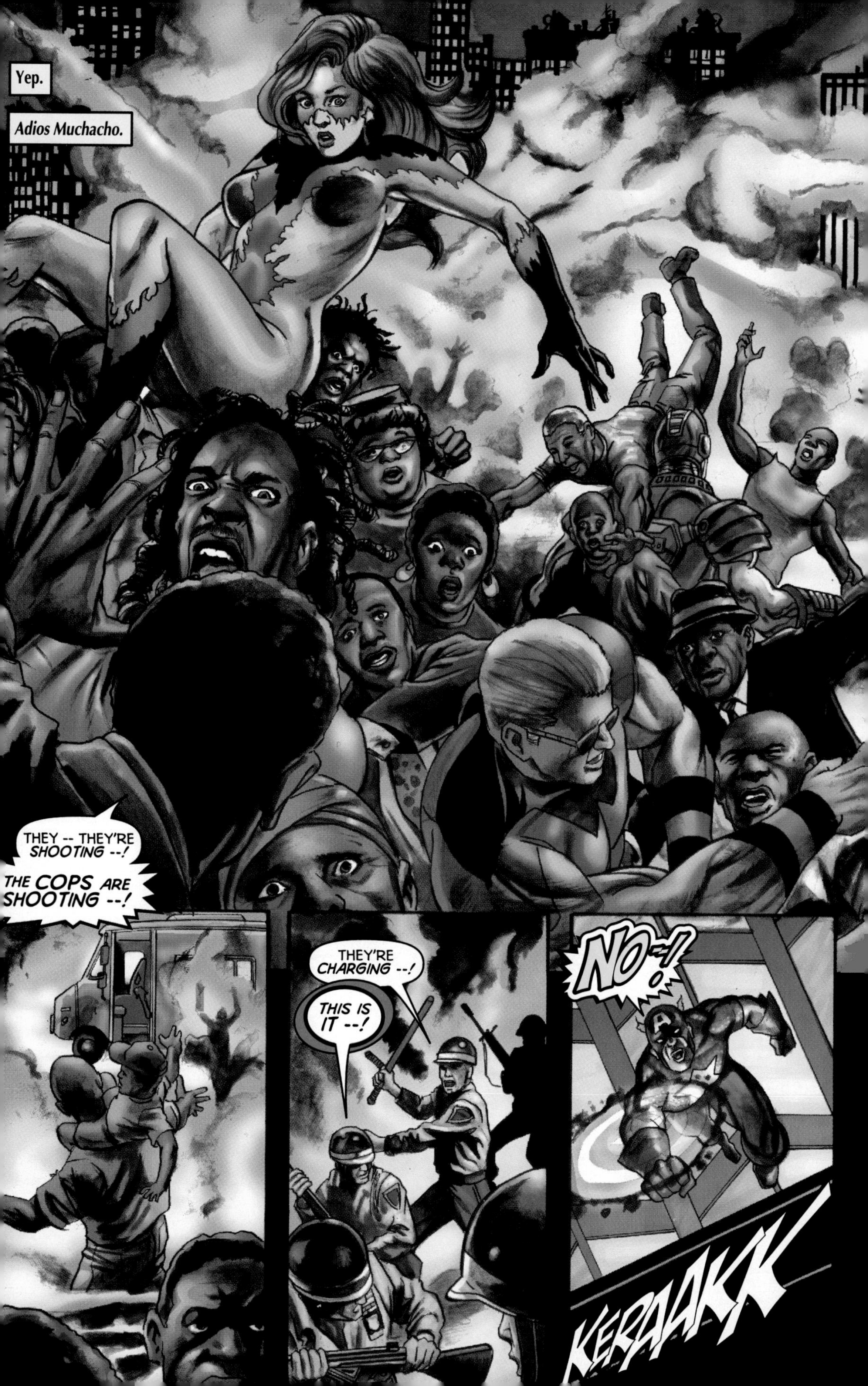
Yep.
Adios Muchacho.
THEY -- THEY'RE SHOOTING --!
THE COPS ARE SHOOTING --!
THEY'RE CHARGING --!
THIS IS IT --!
NO--!
KERAAKK

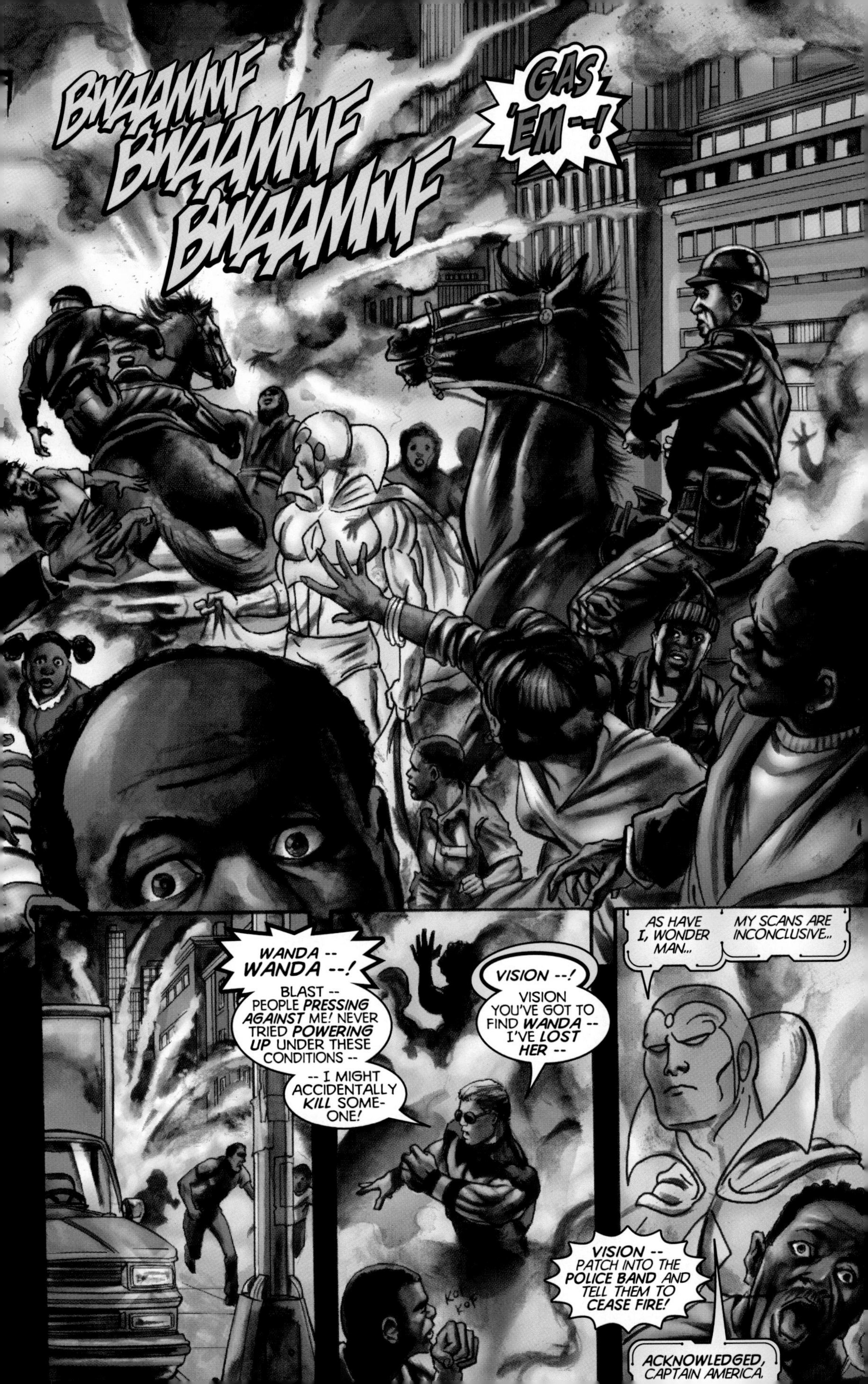

BWAAMMF BWAAMMF BWAAMMF
GAS 'EM --!
WANDA -- WANDA --!
BLAST -- PEOPLE PRESSING AGAINST ME! NEVER TRIED POWERING UP UNDER THESE CONDITIONS --
-- I MIGHT ACCIDENTALLY KILL SOME-ONE!
VISION --!
VISION YOU'VE GOT TO FIND WANDA -- I'VE LOST HER --
AS HAVE I, WONDER MAN...
MY SCANS ARE INCONCLUSIVE...
VISION -- PATCH INTO THE POLICE BAND AND TELL THEM TO CEASE FIRE!
ACKNOWLEDGED, CAPTAIN AMERICA.

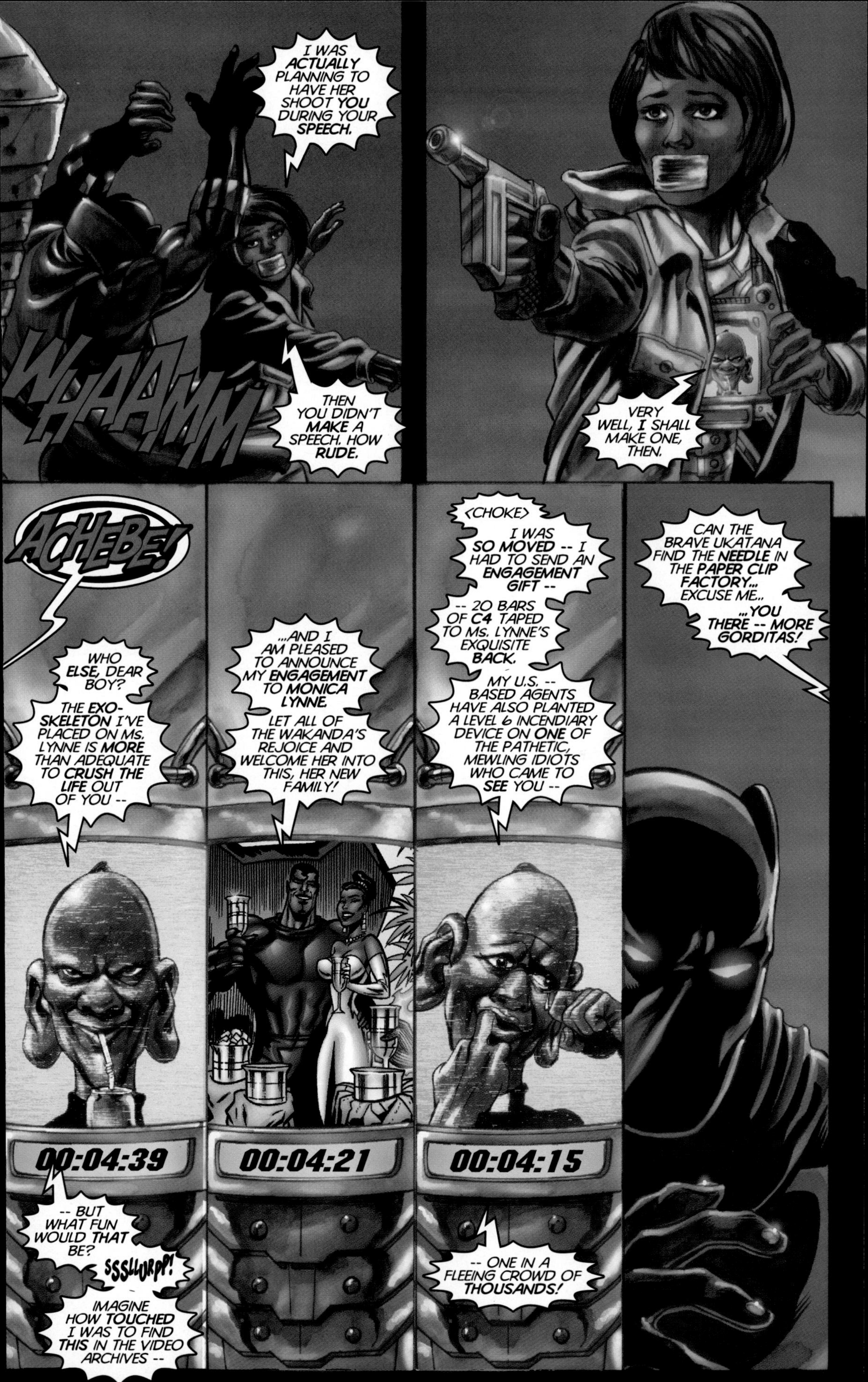
I WAS ACTUALLY PLANNING TO HAVE HER SHOOT YOU DURING YOUR SPEECH.
WHAAMM
THEN YOU DIDN'T MAKE A SPEECH. HOW RUDE.
VERY WELL, I SHALL MAKE ONE, THEN.
ACHEBE!
WHO ELSE, DEAR BOY?
THE EXO-SKELETON I'VE PLACED ON Ms. LYNNE IS MORE THAN ADEQUATE TO CRUSH THE LIFE OUT OF YOU --
00:04:39
-- BUT WHAT FUN WOULD THAT BE?
SSSLLURPP!
IMAGINE HOW TOUCHED I WAS TO FIND THIS IN THE VIDEO ARCHIVES --
...AND I AM PLEASED TO ANNOUNCE MY ENGAGEMENT TO MONICA LYNNE.
LET ALL OF THE WAKANDA'S REJOICE AND WELCOME HER INTO THIS, HER NEW FAMILY!
00:04:21
<CHOKE>
I WAS SO MOVED -- I HAD TO SEND AN ENGAGEMENT GIFT --
-- 20 BARS OF C4 TAPED TO Ms. LYNNE'S EXQUISITE BACK.
MY U.S. -- BASED AGENTS HAVE ALSO PLANTED A LEVEL 6 INCENDIARY DEVICE ON ONE OF THE PATHETIC, MEWLING IDIOTS WHO CAME TO SEE YOU --
00:04:15
-- ONE IN A FLEEING CROWD OF THOUSANDS!
CAN THE BRAVE UKATANA FIND THE NEEDLE IN THE PAPER CLIP FACTORY... EXCUSE ME...
...YOU THERE -- MORE GORDITAS!

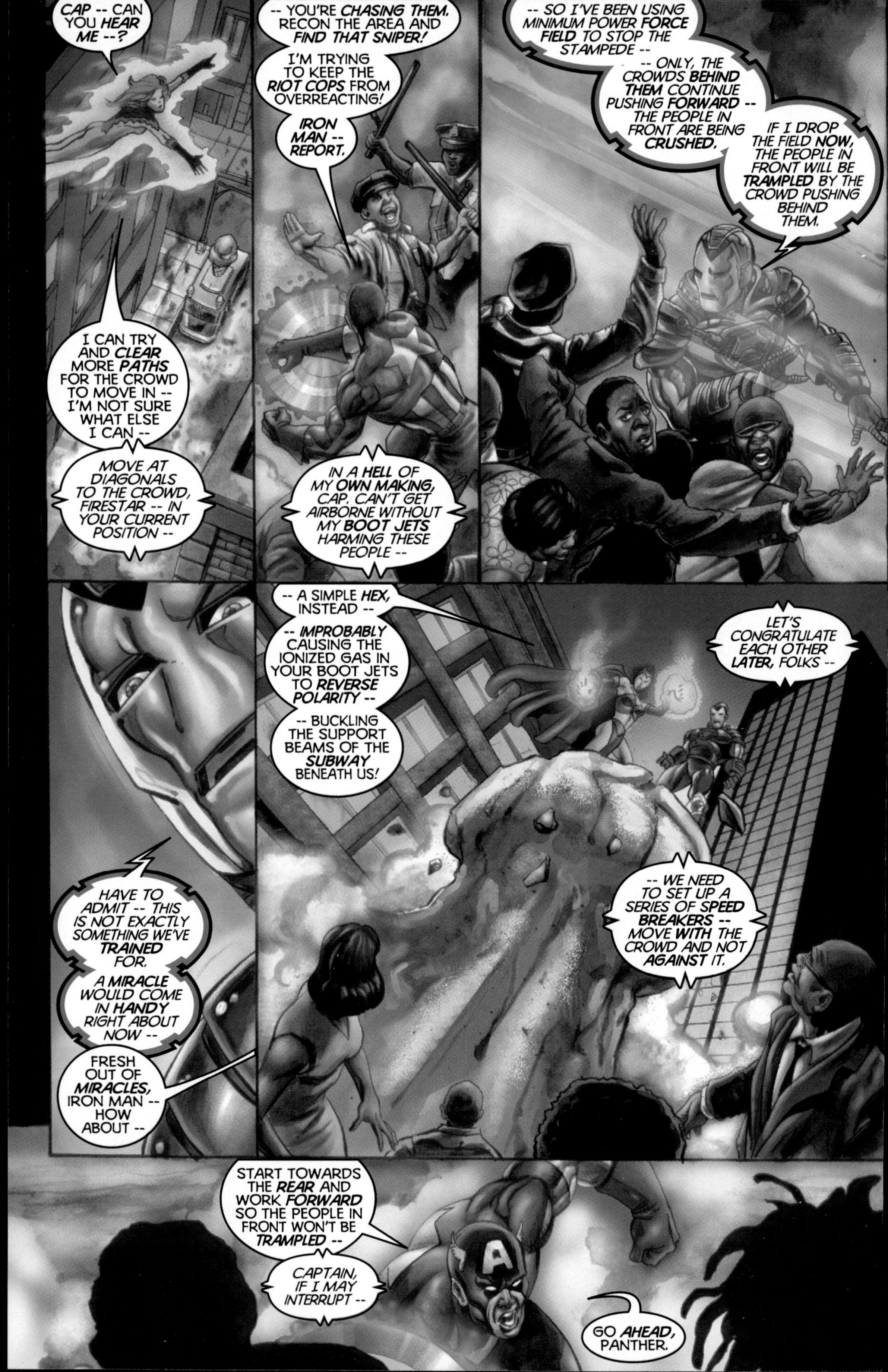
CAP -- CAN YOU HEAR ME --?
I CAN TRY AND CLEAR MORE PATHS FOR THE CROWD TO MOVE IN -- I'M NOT SURE WHAT ELSE I CAN --
MOVE AT DIAGONALS TO THE CROWD, FIRESTAR -- IN YOUR CURRENT POSITION --
-- YOU'RE CHASING THEM. RECON THE AREA AND FIND THAT SNIPER!
I'M TRYING TO KEEP THE RIOT COPS FROM OVERREACTING!
IRON MAN -- REPORT.
IN A HELL OF MY OWN MAKING, CAP. CAN'T GET AIRBORNE WITHOUT MY BOOT JETS HARMING THESE PEOPLE --
-- SO I'VE BEEN USING MINIMUM POWER FORCE FIELD TO STOP THE STAMPEDE --
-- ONLY, THE CROWDS BEHIND THEM CONTINUE PUSHING FORWARD -- THE PEOPLE IN FRONT ARE BEING CRUSHED.
IF I DROP THE FIELD NOW, THE PEOPLE IN FRONT WILL BE TRAMPLED BY THE CROWD PUSHING BEHIND THEM.
HAVE TO ADMIT -- THIS IS NOT EXACTLY SOMETHING WE'VE TRAINED FOR.
A MIRACLE WOULD COME IN HANDY RIGHT ABOUT NOW --
FRESH OUT OF MIRACLES, IRON MAN -- HOW ABOUT --
-- A SIMPLE HEX, INSTEAD --
-- IMPROBABLY CAUSING THE IONIZED GAS IN YOUR BOOT JETS TO REVERSE POLARITY --
-- BUCKLING THE SUPPORT BEAMS OF THE SUBWAY BENEATH US!
LET'S CONGRATULATE EACH OTHER LATER, FOLKS --
-- WE NEED TO SET UP A SERIES OF SPEED BREAKERS -- MOVE WITH THE CROWD AND NOT AGAINST IT.
START TOWARDS THE REAR AND WORK FORWARD SO THE PEOPLE IN FRONT WON'T BE TRAMPLED --
CAPTAIN, IF I MAY INTERRUPT --
GO AHEAD, PANTHER.

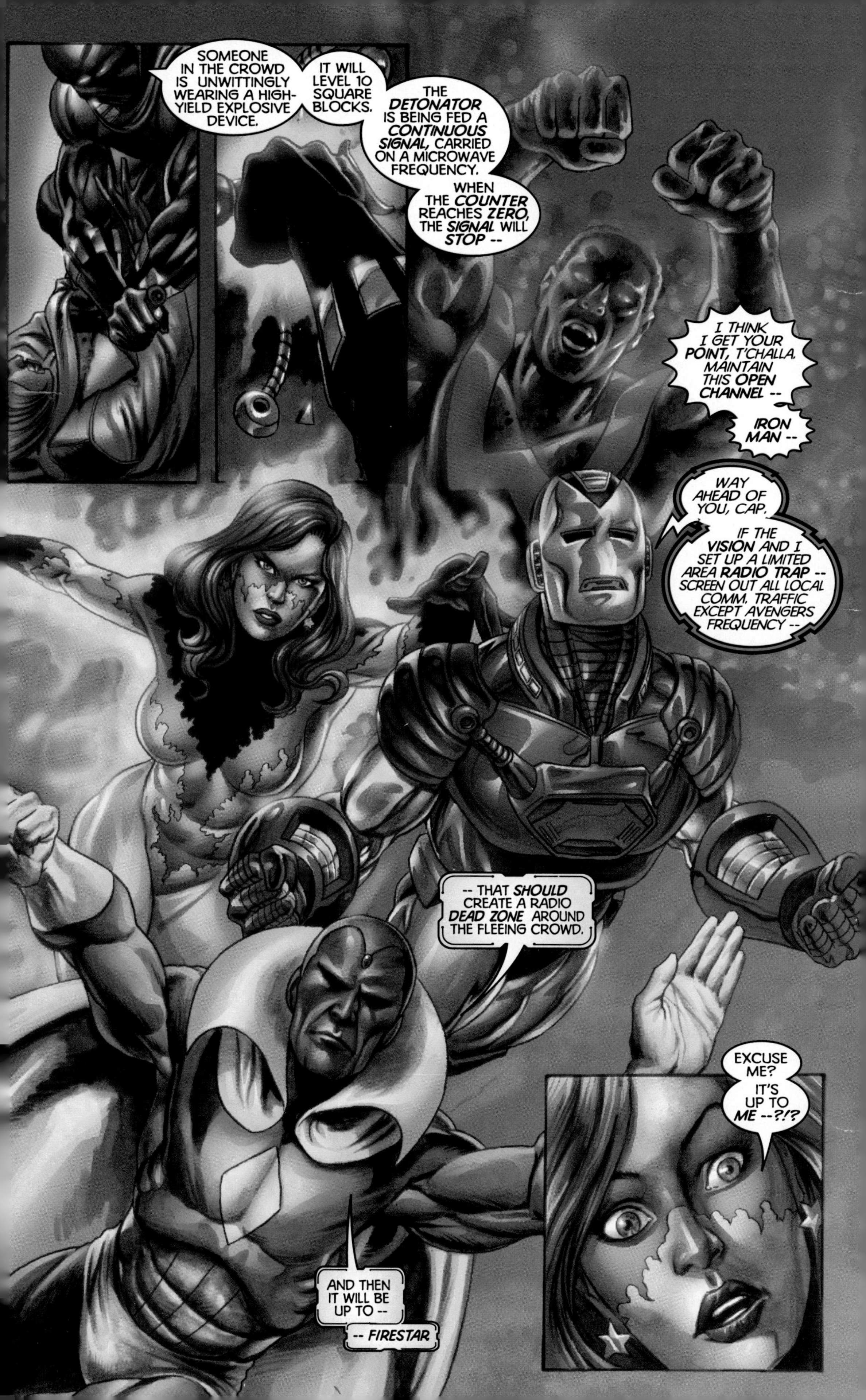
SOMEONE IN THE CROWD IS UNWITTINGLY WEARING A HIGH-YIELD EXPLOSIVE DEVICE.
IT WILL LEVEL 10 SQUARE BLOCKS.
THE DETONATOR IS BEING FED A CONTINUOUS SIGNAL, CARRIED ON A MICROWAVE FREQUENCY.
WHEN THE COUNTER REACHES ZERO, THE SIGNAL WILL STOP --
I THINK I GET YOUR POINT, T'CHALLA. MAINTAIN THIS OPEN CHANNEL --
IRON MAN --
WAY AHEAD OF YOU, CAP.
IF THE VISION AND I SET UP A LIMITED AREA RADIO TRAP -- SCREEN OUT ALL LOCAL COMM. TRAFFIC EXCEPT AVENGERS FREQUENCY --
-- THAT SHOULD CREATE A RADIO DEAD ZONE AROUND THE FLEEING CROWD.
AND THEN IT WILL BE UP TO --
-- FIRESTAR
EXCUSE ME?
IT'S UP TO ME --?!?

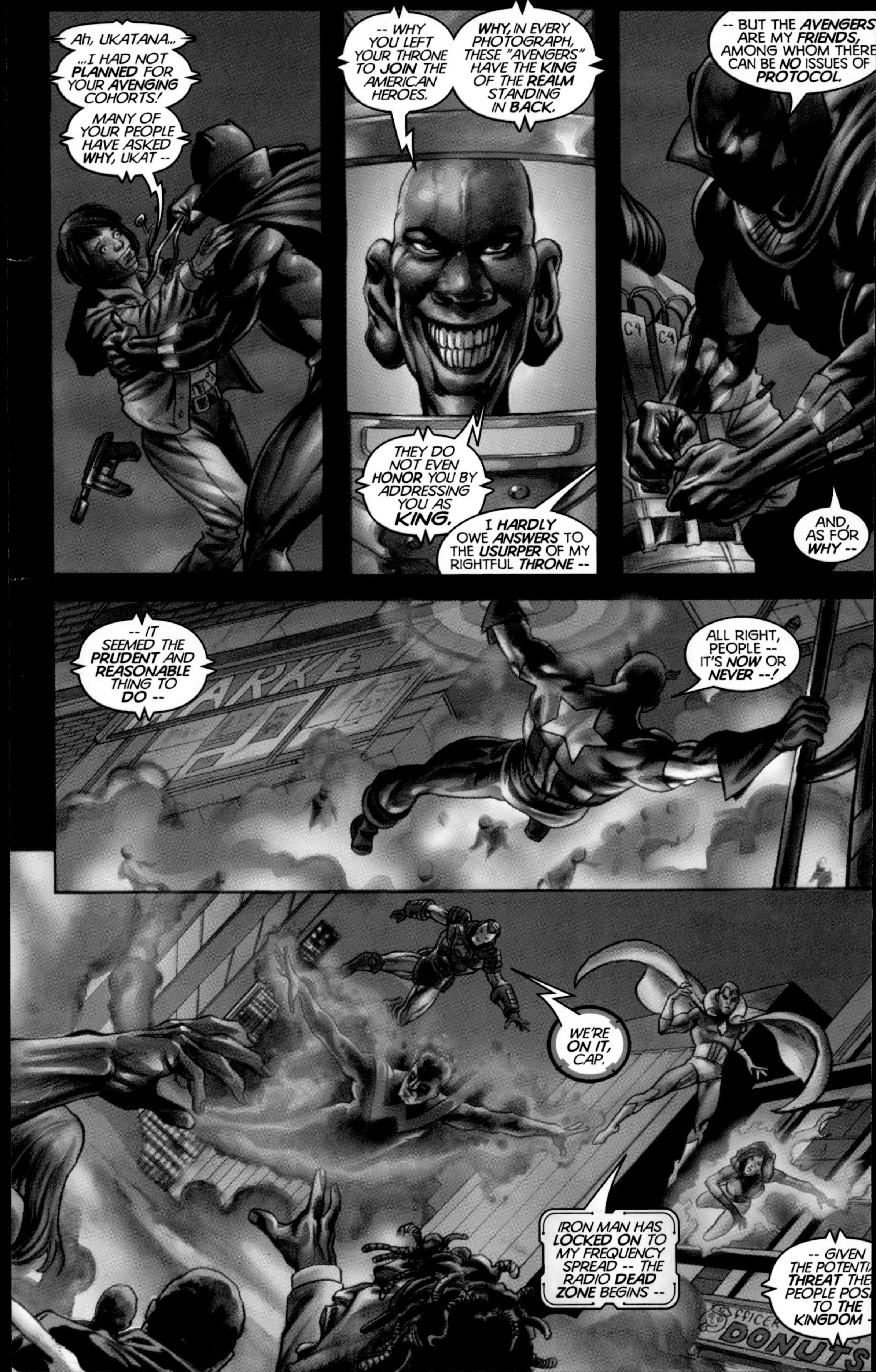
Ah, UKATANA...
...I HAD NOT PLANNED FOR YOUR AVENGING COHORTS!
MANY OF YOUR PEOPLE HAVE ASKED WHY, UKAT --
-- WHY YOU LEFT YOUR THRONE TO JOIN THE AMERICAN HEROES.
WHY, IN EVERY PHOTOGRAPH, THESE "AVENGERS" HAVE THE KING OF THE REALM STANDING IN BACK.
THEY DO NOT EVEN HONOR YOU BY ADDRESSING YOU AS KING.
I HARDLY OWE ANSWERS TO THE USURPER OF MY RIGHTFUL THRONE --
-- BUT THE AVENGERS ARE MY FRIENDS, AMONG WHOM THERE CAN BE NO ISSUES OF PROTOCOL.
C4
C4
AND, AS FOR WHY --
-- IT SEEMED THE PRUDENT AND REASONABLE THING TO DO --
ALL RIGHT, PEOPLE -- IT'S NOW OR NEVER --!
WE'RE ON IT, CAP.
IRON MAN HAS LOCKED ON TO MY FREQUENCY SPREAD -- THE RADIO DEAD ZONE BEGINS --
-- GIVEN THE POTENTI THREAT THE PEOPLE POS TO THE KINGDOM -
DONUTS

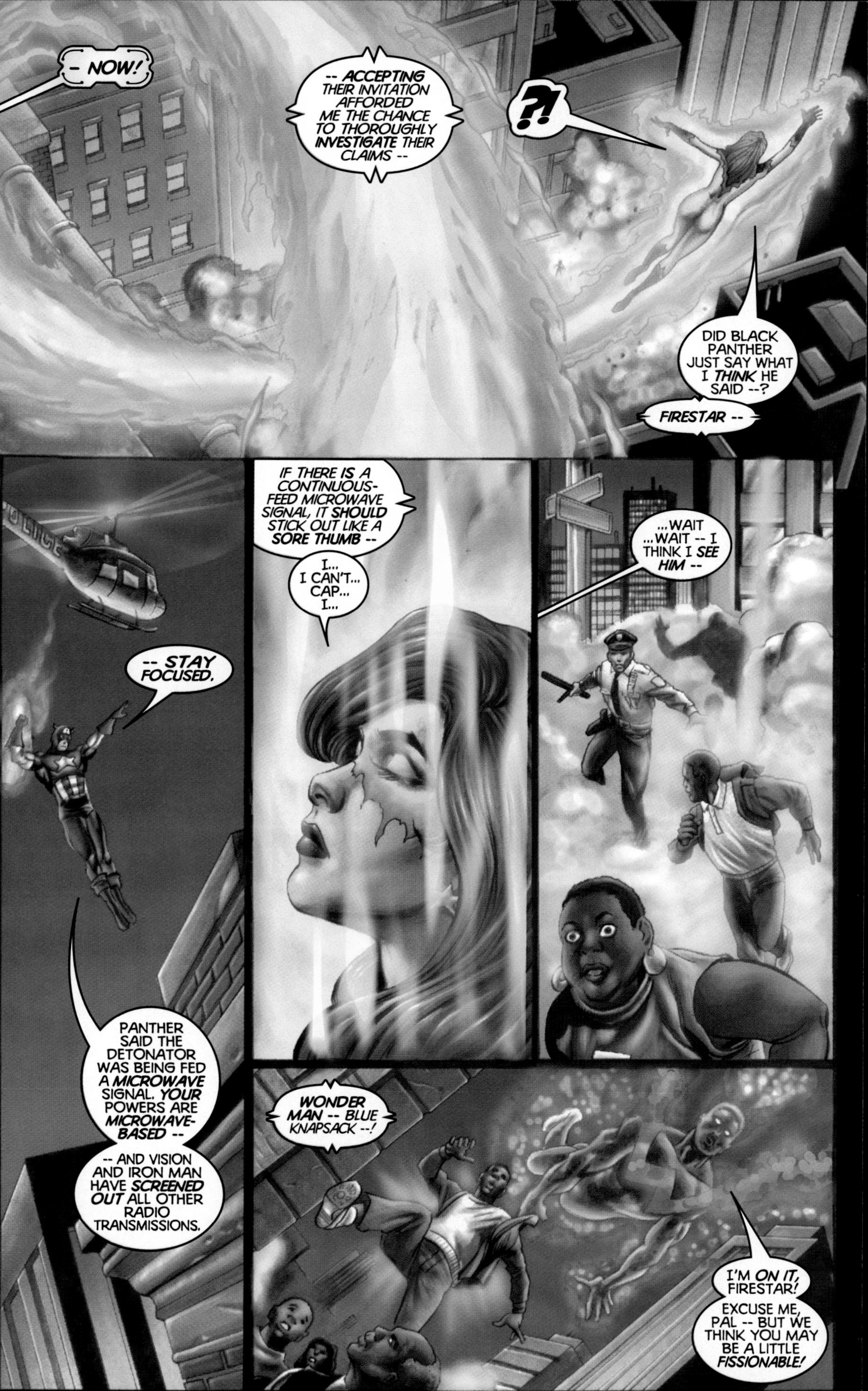
- NOW!
-- ACCEPTING THEIR INVITATION AFFORDED ME THE CHANCE TO THOROUGHLY INVESTIGATE THEIR CLAIMS --
?!
DID BLACK PANTHER JUST SAY WHAT I THINK HE SAID --?
FIRESTAR --
-- STAY FOCUSED.
PANTHER SAID THE DETONATOR WAS BEING FED A MICROWAVE SIGNAL. YOUR POWERS ARE MICROWAVE-BASED --
-- AND VISION AND IRON MAN HAVE SCREENED OUT ALL OTHER RADIO TRANSMISSIONS.
IF THERE IS A CONTINUOUS-FEED MICROWAVE SIGNAL, IT SHOULD STICK OUT LIKE A SORE THUMB --
I... I CAN'T... CAP... I...
...WAIT ...WAIT -- I THINK I SEE HIM --
WONDER MAN -- BLUE KNAPSACK --!
I'M ON IT, FIRESTAR!
EXCUSE ME, PAL -- BUT WE THINK YOU MAY BE A LITTLE FISSIONABLE!

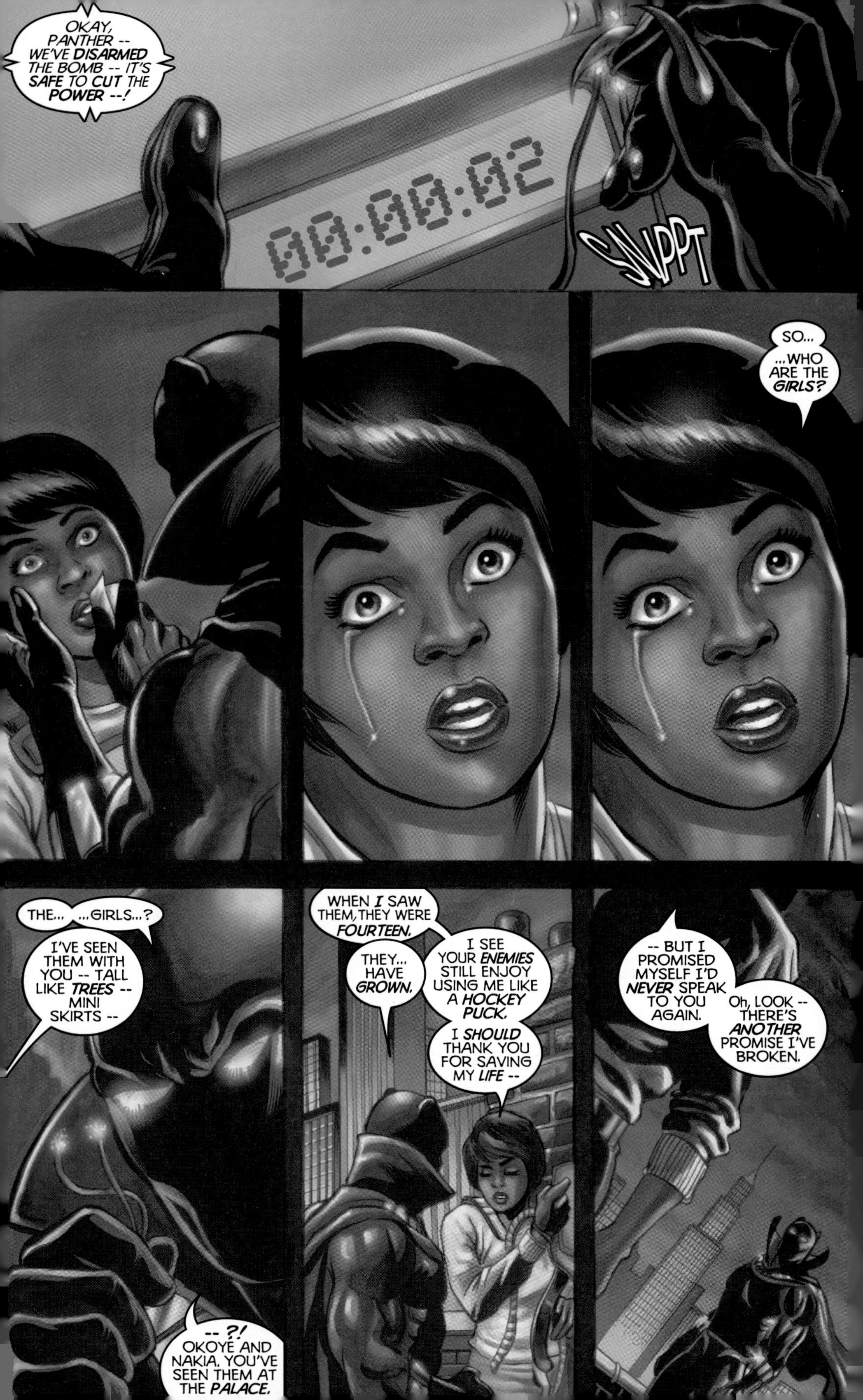
OKAY, PANTHER -- WE'VE DISARMED THE BOMB -- IT'S SAFE TO CUT THE POWER --!
00:00:02
SNPPT
SO...
...WHO ARE THE GIRLS?
THE...
...GIRLS...?
I'VE SEEN THEM WITH YOU -- TALL LIKE TREES -- MINI SKIRTS --
-- ?! OKOYE AND NAKIA, YOU'VE SEEN THEM AT THE PALACE.
WHEN I SAW THEM, THEY WERE FOURTEEN.
THEY... HAVE GROWN.
I SEE YOUR ENEMIES STILL ENJOY USING ME LIKE A HOCKEY PUCK.
I SHOULD THANK YOU FOR SAVING MY LIFE --
-- BUT I PROMISED MYSELF I'D NEVER SPEAK TO YOU AGAIN.
Oh, LOOK -- THERE'S ANOTHER PROMISE I'VE BROKEN.

JAIL HOUSE ROCK

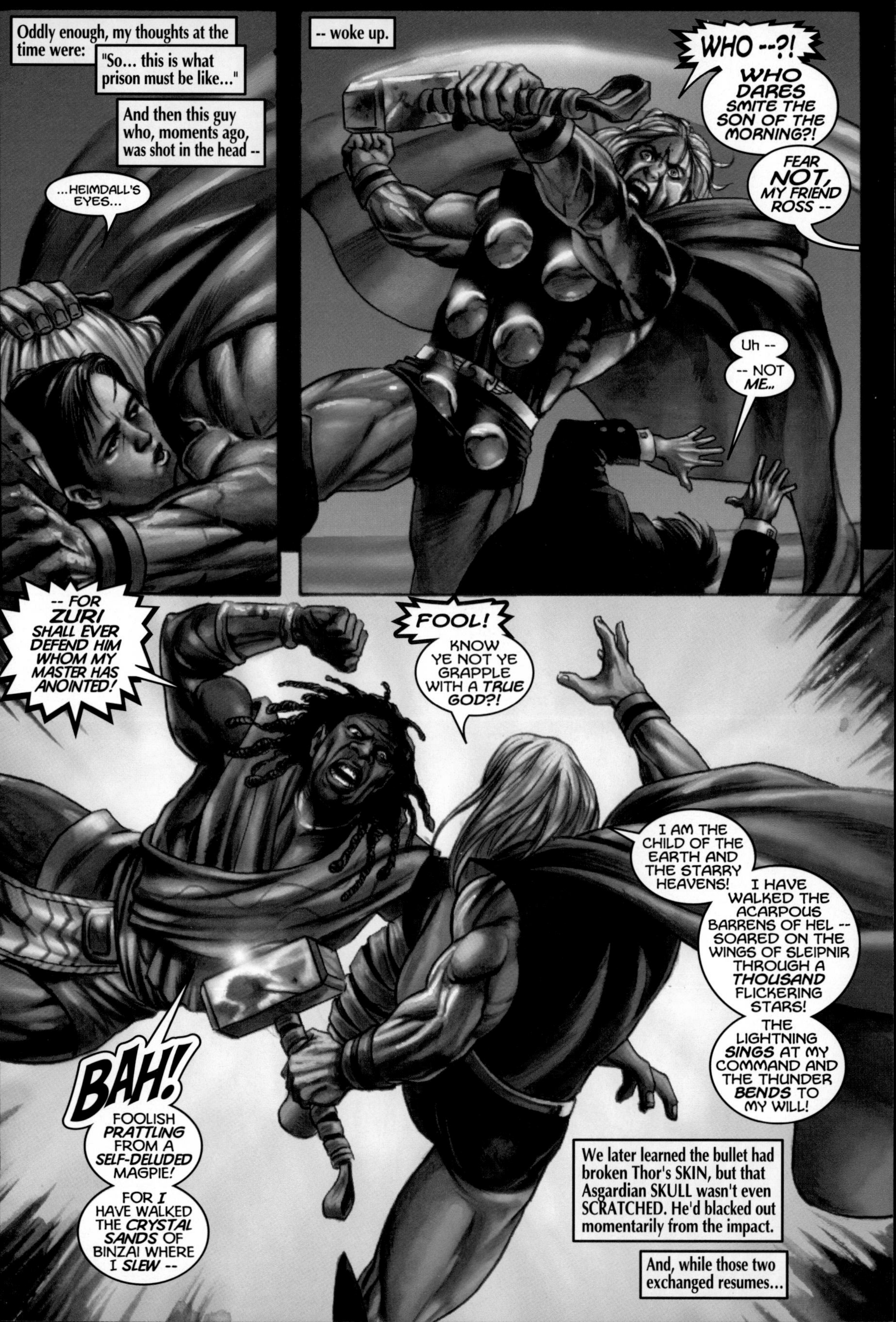

Oddly enough, my thoughts at the time were:
"So... this is what prison must be like..."
And then this guy who, moments ago, was shot in the head --
...HEIMDALL'S EYES...
-- woke up.
WHO --?!
WHO DARES SMITE THE SON OF THE MORNING?!
FEAR NOT, MY FRIEND ROSS --
Uh --
-- NOT ME...
-- FOR ZURI SHALL EVER DEFEND HIM WHOM MY MASTER HAS ANOINTED!
FOOL!
KNOW YE NOT YE GRAPPLE WITH A TRUE GOD?!
I AM THE CHILD OF THE EARTH AND THE STARRY HEAVENS!
I HAVE WALKED THE ACARPOUS BARRENS OF HEL -- SOARED ON THE WINGS OF SLEIPNIR THROUGH A THOUSAND FLICKERING STARS!
THE LIGHTNING SINGS AT MY COMMAND AND THE THUNDER BENDS TO MY WILL!
BAH!
FOOLISH PRATTLING FROM A SELF-DELUDED MAGPIE!
FOR I HAVE WALKED THE CRYSTAL SANDS OF BINZAI WHERE I SLEW --
We later learned the bullet had broken Thor's SKIN, but that Asgardian SKULL wasn't even SCRATCHED. He'd blacked out momentarily from the impact.
And, while those two exchanged resumes...

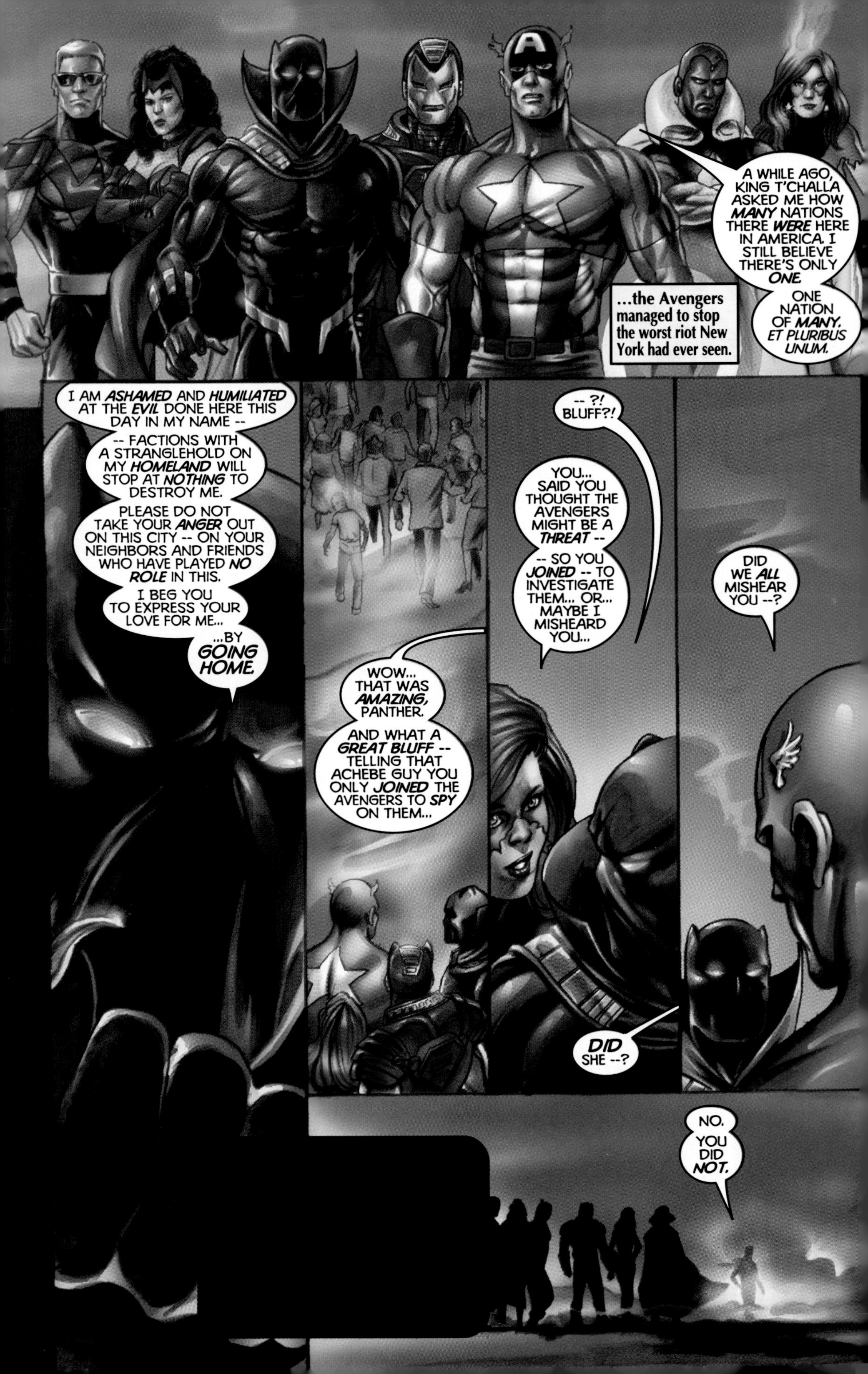
A WHILE AGO, KING T'CHALLA ASKED ME HOW MANY NATIONS THERE WERE HERE IN AMERICA. I STILL BELIEVE THERE'S ONLY ONE.
ONE NATION OF MANY. ET PLURIBUS UNUM.
...the Avengers managed to stop the worst riot New York had ever seen.
I AM ASHAMED AND HUMILIATED AT THE EVIL DONE HERE THIS DAY IN MY NAME --
-- FACTIONS WITH A STRANGLEHOLD ON MY HOMELAND WILL STOP AT NOTHING TO DESTROY ME.
PLEASE DO NOT TAKE YOUR ANGER OUT ON THIS CITY -- ON YOUR NEIGHBORS AND FRIENDS WHO HAVE PLAYED NO ROLE IN THIS.
I BEG YOU TO EXPRESS YOUR LOVE FOR ME...
...BY GOING HOME.
WOW... THAT WAS AMAZING, PANTHER.
AND WHAT A GREAT BLUFF -- TELLING THAT ACHEBE GUY YOU ONLY JOINED THE AVENGERS TO SPY ON THEM...
-- ?! BLUFF?!
YOU... SAID YOU THOUGHT THE AVENGERS MIGHT BE A THREAT --
-- SO YOU JOINED -- TO INVESTIGATE THEM... OR... MAYBE I MISHEARD YOU...
DID SHE --?
DID WE ALL MISHEAR YOU --?
NO. YOU DID NOT.

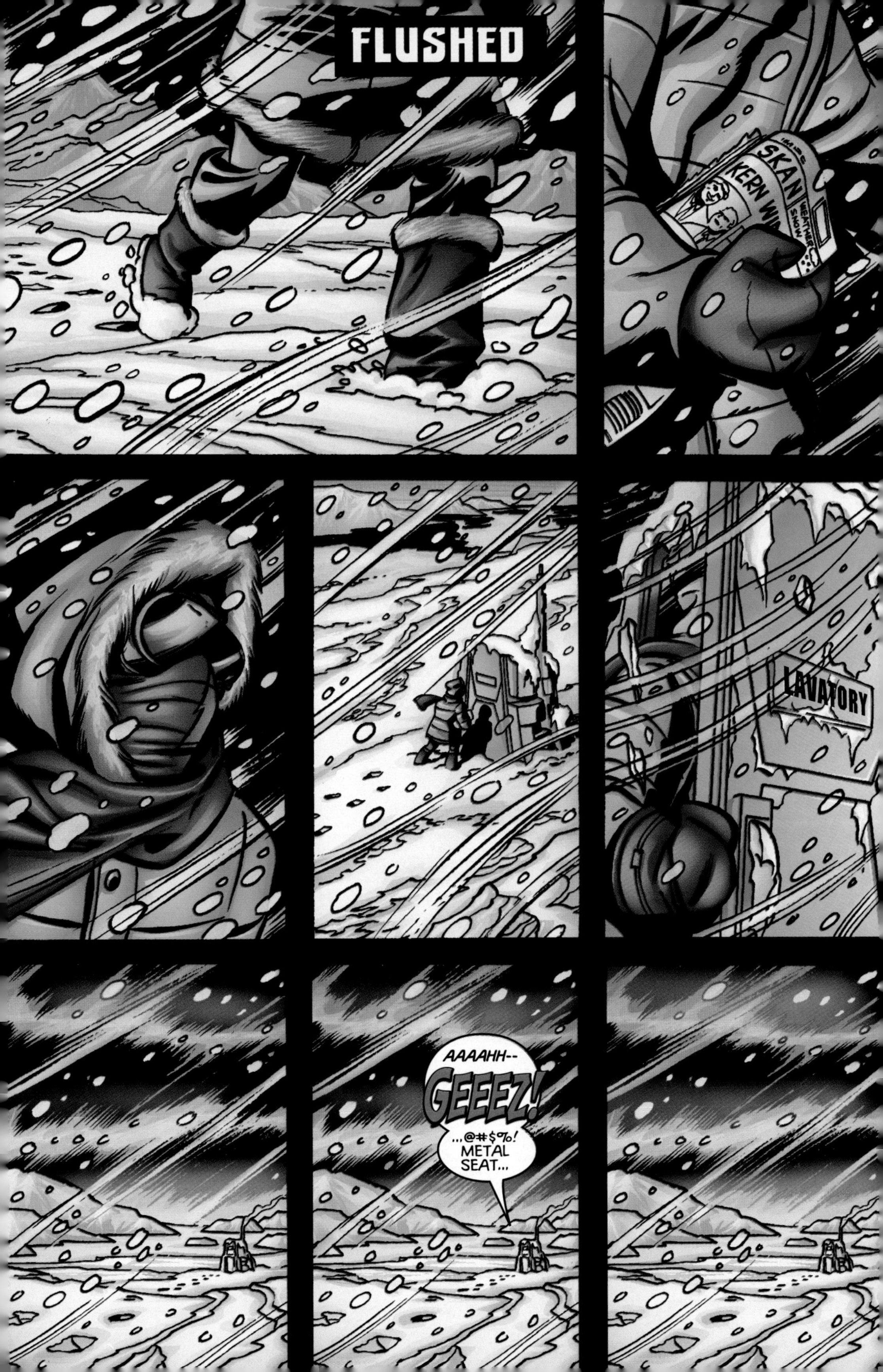
FLUSHED
SKAN
WEATHER SHOW
LAVATORY
AAAAHH--
GEEEZ!
...,@#$%! METAL SEAT...

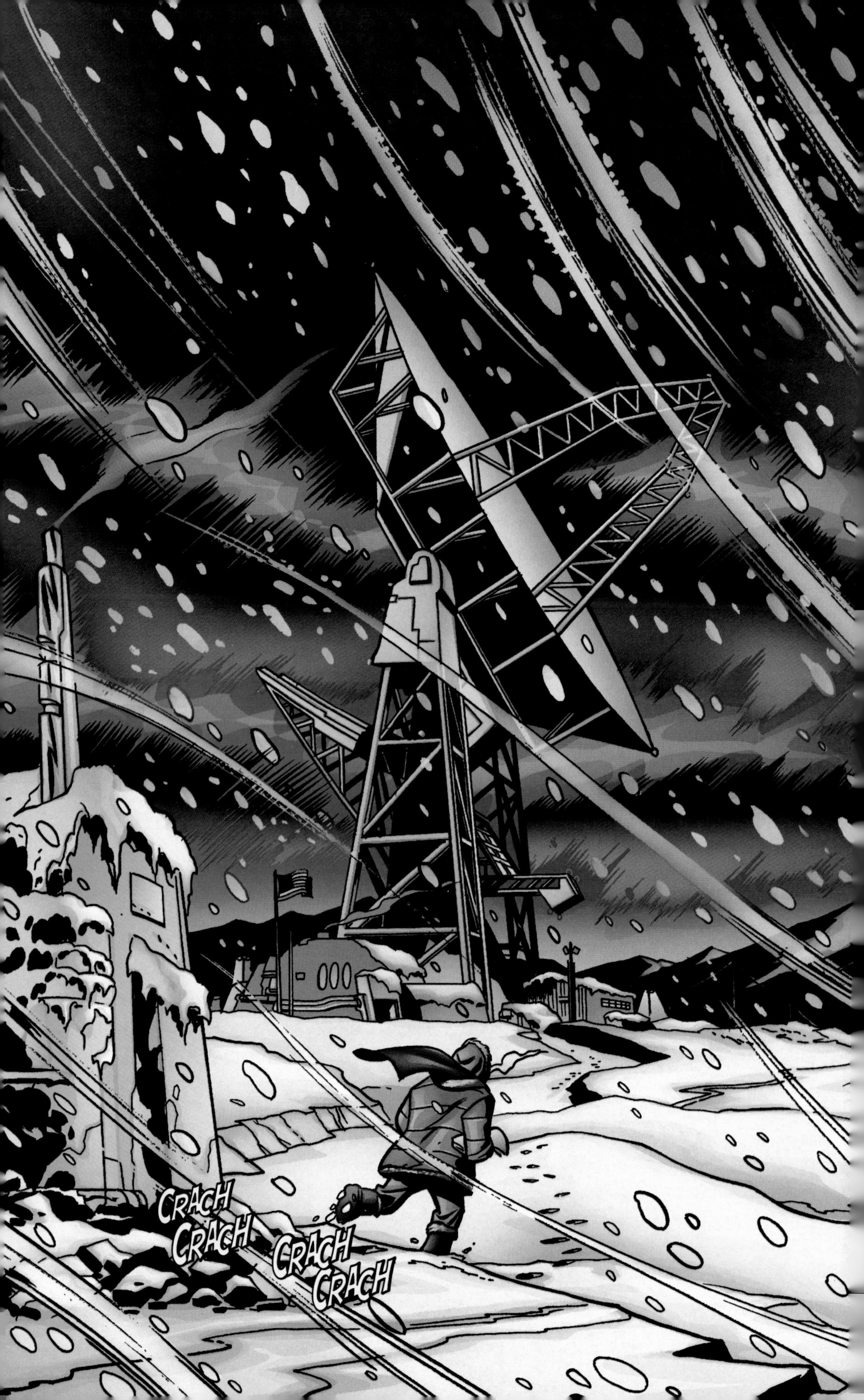
CRACH
CRACH
CRACH
CRACH

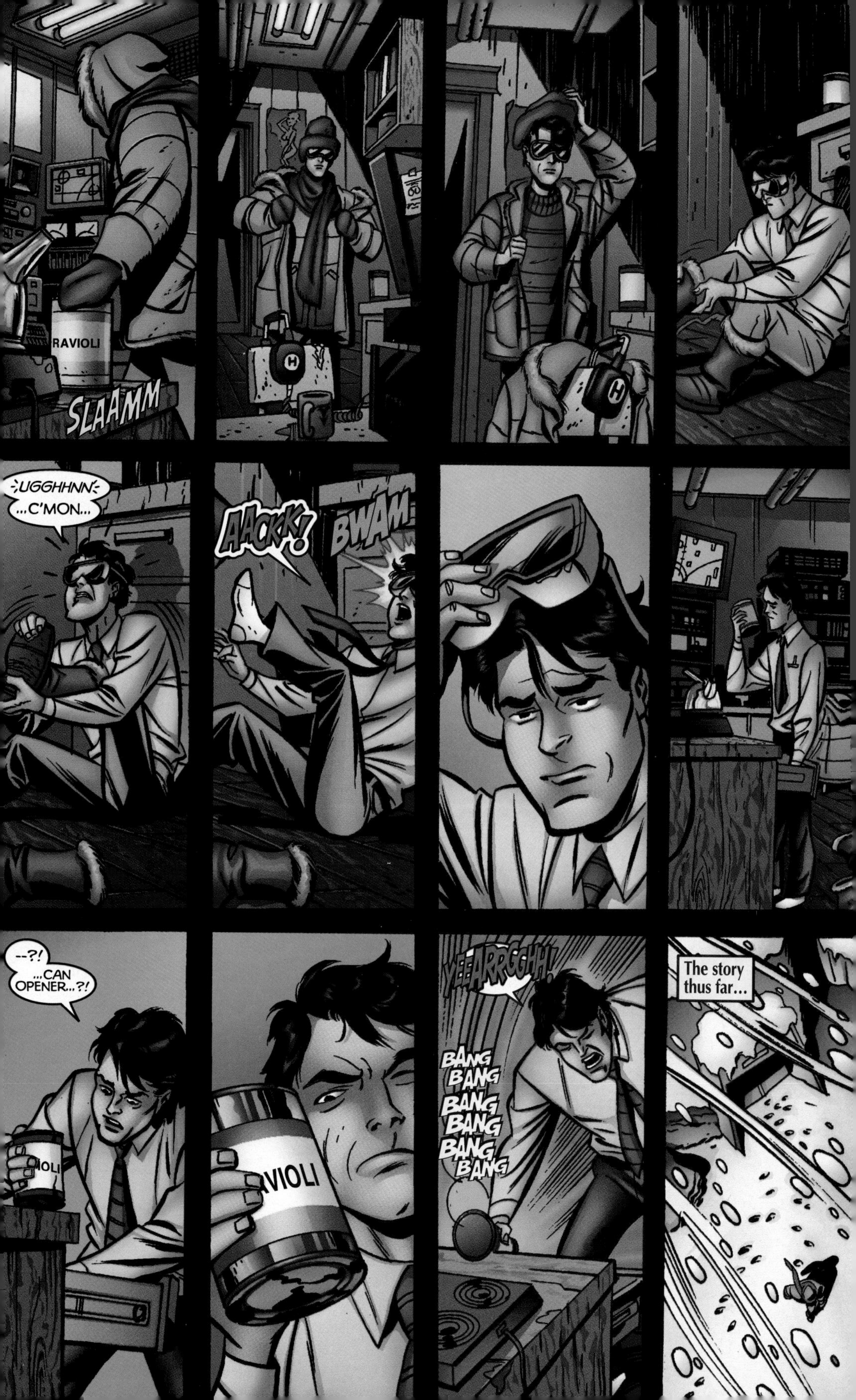
RAVIOLI
SLAAMM
UGGHHNN
...C'MON...
AACKK!
BWAM
--?!
...CAN
OPENER...?!
RAVIOLI
YEEARRGGHH!
BANG
BANG
BANG
BANG
BANG
BANG
The story thus far...

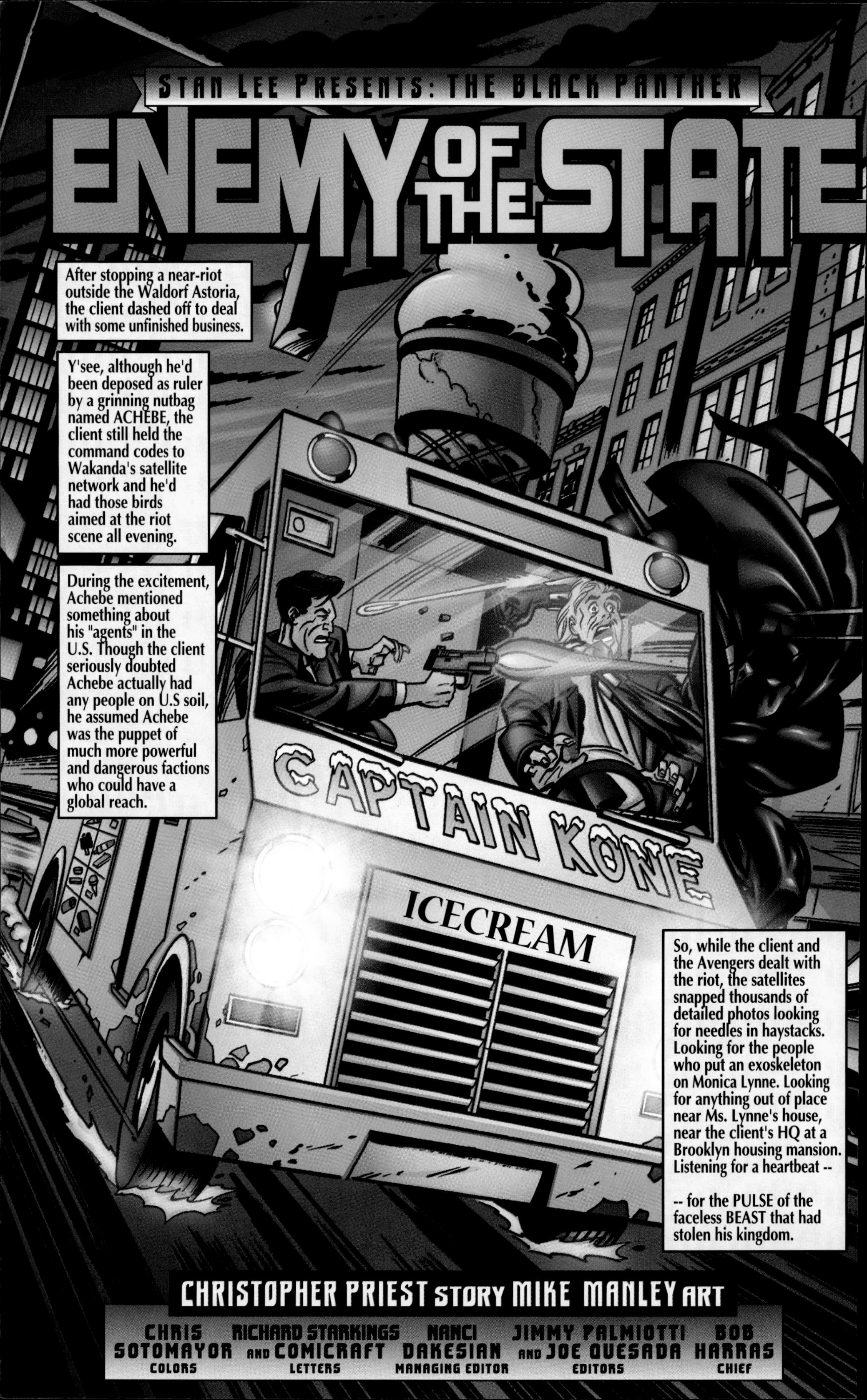
STAN LEE PRESENTS: THE BLACK PANTHER
ENEMY OF THE STATE
After stopping a near-riot outside the Waldorf Astoria, the client dashed off to deal with some unfinished business.
Y'see, although he'd been deposed as ruler by a grinning nutbag named ACHEBE, the client still held the command codes to Wakanda's satellite network and he'd had those birds aimed at the riot scene all evening.
During the excitement, Achebe mentioned something about his "agents" in the U.S. Though the client seriously doubted Achebe actually had any people on U.S soil, he assumed Achebe was the puppet of much more powerful and dangerous factions who could have a global reach.
CAPTAIN KONE
ICECREAM
So, while the client and the Avengers dealt with the riot, the satellites snapped thousands of detailed photos looking for needles in haystacks. Looking for the people who put an exoskeleton on Monica Lynne. Looking for anything out of place near Ms. Lynne's house, near the client's HQ at a Brooklyn housing mansion. Listening for a heartbeat --
-- for the PULSE of the faceless BEAST that had stolen his kingdom.
CHRISTOPHER PRIEST STORY MIKE MANLEY ART
CHRIS SOTOMAYOR COLORS
RICHARD STARKINGS AND COMICRAFT LETTERS
NANCI DAKESIAN MANAGING EDITOR
JIMMY PALMIOTTI AND JOE QUESADA EDITORS
BOB HARRAS CHIEF

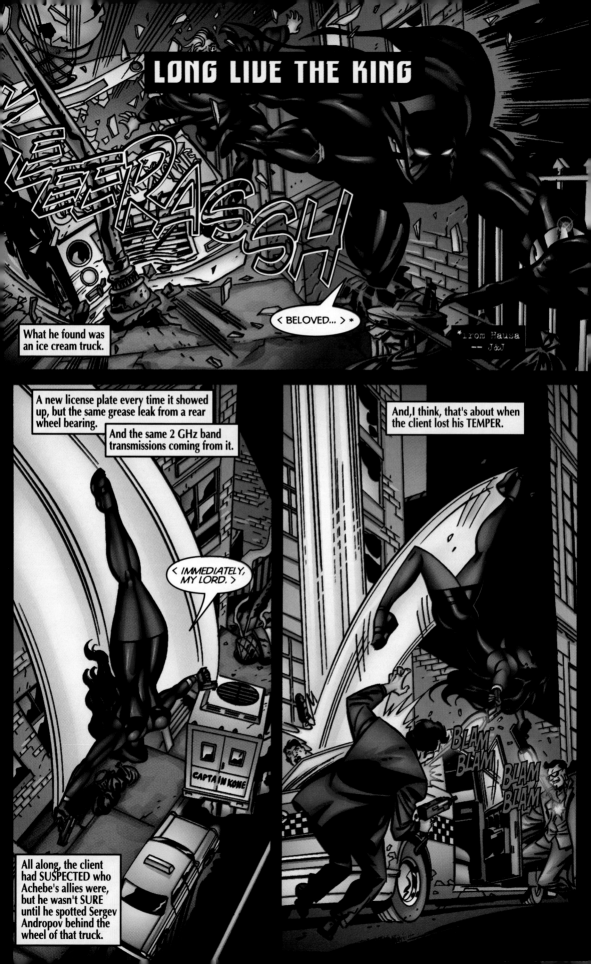

LONG LIVE THE KING

VEEERASSH

< BELOVED... > *

*from Hausa
-- J&J

What he found was an ice cream truck.

A new license plate every time it showed up, but the same grease leak from a rear wheel bearing.

And the same 2 GHz band transmissions coming from it.

< IMMEDIATELY, MY LORD. >

CAPTAIN KONE

All along, the client had SUSPECTED who Achebe's allies were, but he wasn't SURE until he spotted Sergev Andropov behind the wheel of that truck.

And, I think, that's about when the client lost his TEMPER.

BLAM BLAM

BLAM BLAM

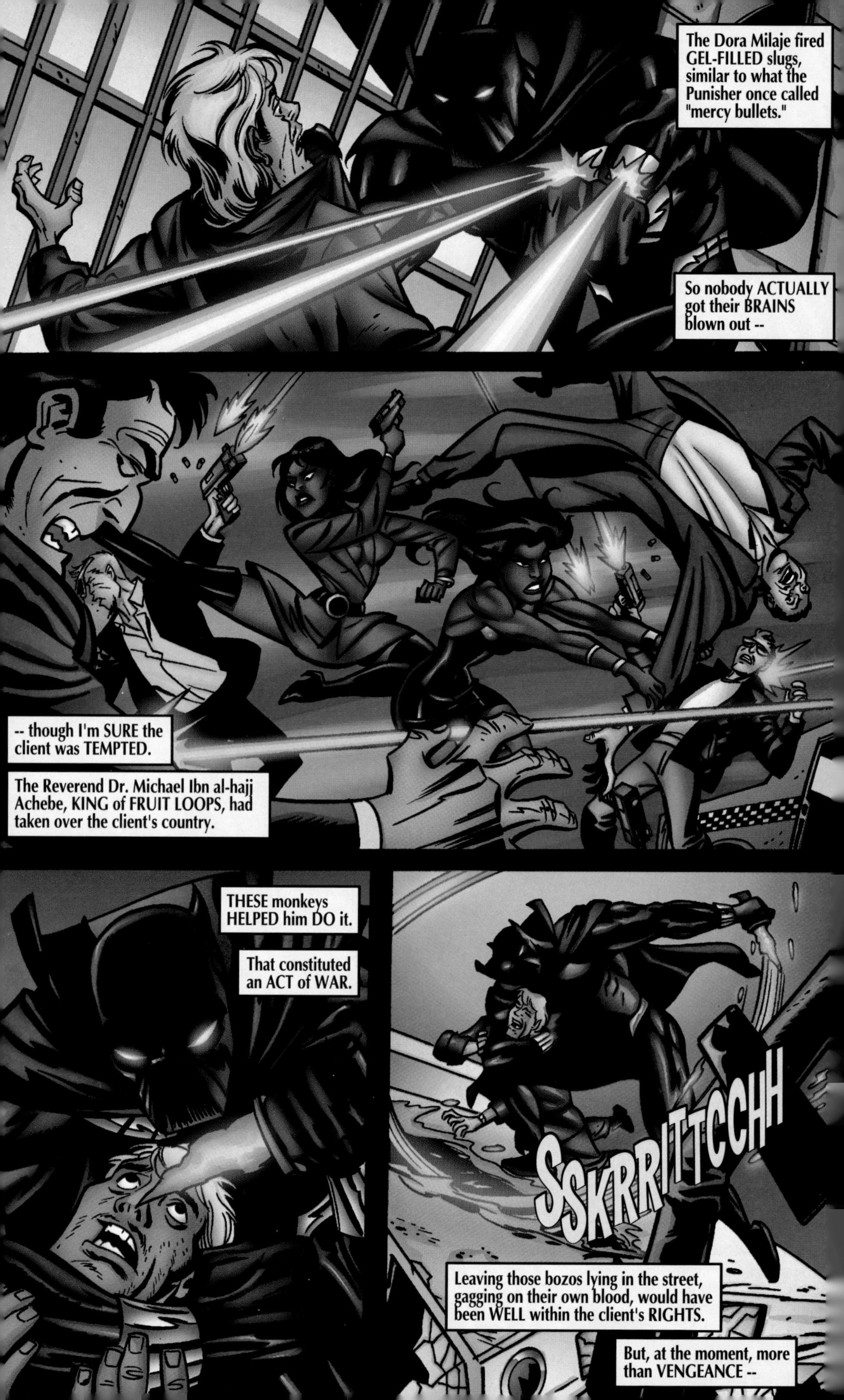

The Dora Milaje fired GEL-FILLED slugs, similar to what the Punisher once called "mercy bullets."
So nobody ACTUALLY got their BRAINS blown out --
-- though I'm SURE the client was TEMPTED.
The Reverend Dr. Michael Ibn al-hajj Achebe, KING of FRUIT LOOPS, had taken over the client's country.
THESE monkeys HELPED him DO it.
That constituted an ACT of WAR.
SSKRRITTCCHH
Leaving those bozos lying in the street, gagging on their own blood, would have been WELL within the client's RIGHTS.
But, at the moment, more than VENGEANCE --

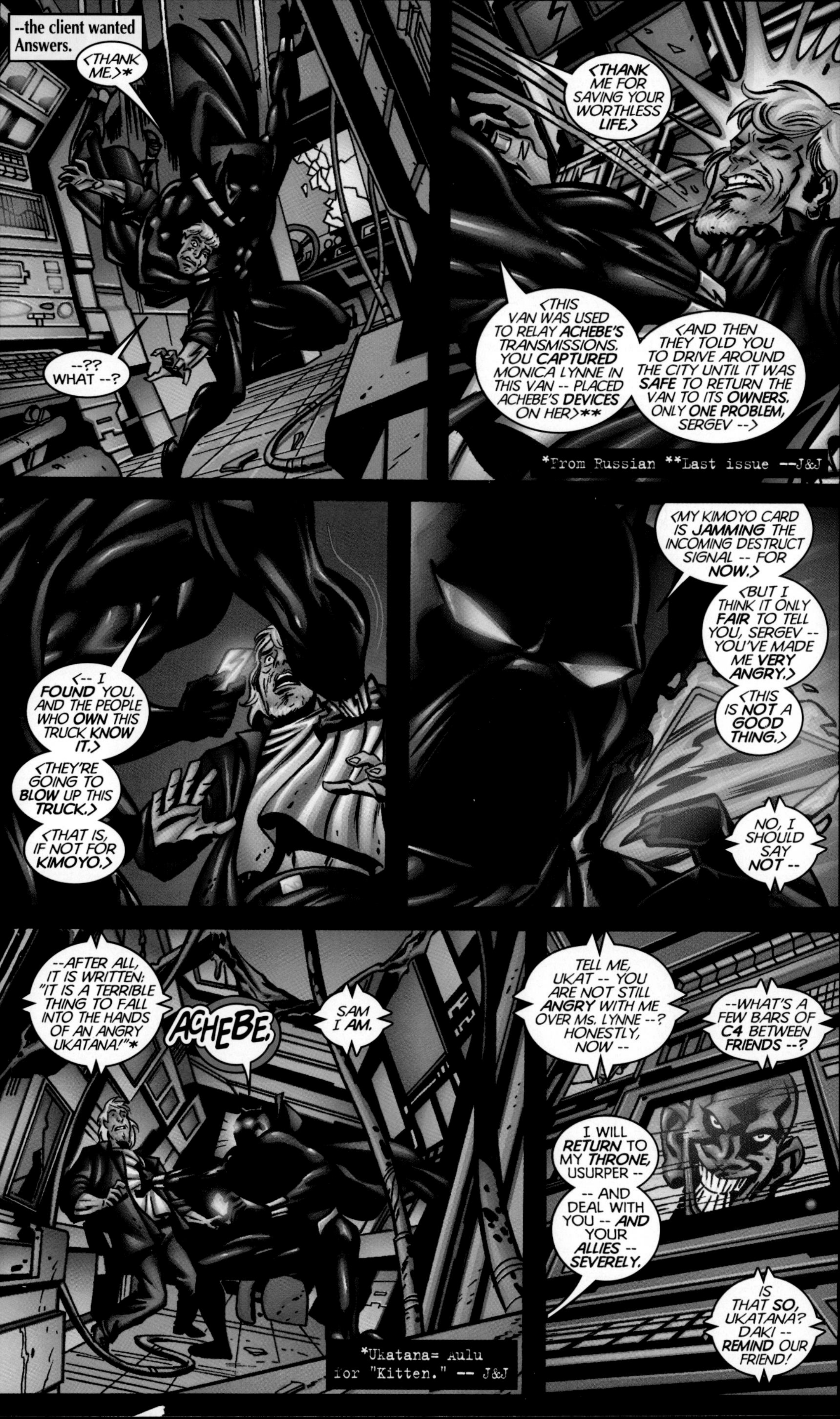
--the client wanted Answers.
<THANK ME.>*
--?? WHAT --?
<THANK ME FOR SAVING YOUR WORTHLESS LIFE.>
<THIS VAN WAS USED TO RELAY ACHEBE'S TRANSMISSIONS. YOU CAPTURED MONICA LYNNE IN THIS VAN -- PLACED ACHEBE'S DEVICES ON HER>**
<AND THEN THEY TOLD YOU TO DRIVE AROUND THE CITY UNTIL IT WAS SAFE TO RETURN THE VAN TO ITS OWNERS. ONLY ONE PROBLEM, SERGEV -->
*From Russian **Last issue --J&J
<-- I FOUND YOU. AND THE PEOPLE WHO OWN THIS TRUCK KNOW IT.>
<THEY'RE GOING TO BLOW UP THIS TRUCK.>
<THAT IS, IF NOT FOR KIMOYO.>
<MY KIMOYO CARD IS JAMMING THE INCOMING DESTRUCT SIGNAL -- FOR NOW.>
<BUT I THINK IT ONLY FAIR TO TELL YOU, SERGEV -- YOU'VE MADE ME VERY ANGRY.>
<THIS IS NOT A GOOD THING.>
NO, I SHOULD SAY NOT --
--AFTER ALL, IT IS WRITTEN: "IT IS A TERRIBLE THING TO FALL INTO THE HANDS OF AN ANGRY UKATANA!"*
ACHEBE.
SAM I AM.
*Ukatana= Aulu for "Kitten." -- J&J
TELL ME, UKAT -- YOU ARE NOT STILL ANGRY WITH ME OVER Ms. LYNNE --? HONESTLY, NOW --
--WHAT'S A FEW BARS OF C4 BETWEEN FRIENDS --?
I WILL RETURN TO MY THRONE, USURPER --
-- AND DEAL WITH YOU -- AND YOUR ALLIES -- SEVERELY.
IS THAT SO, UKATANA? DAKI -- REMIND OUR FRIEND!

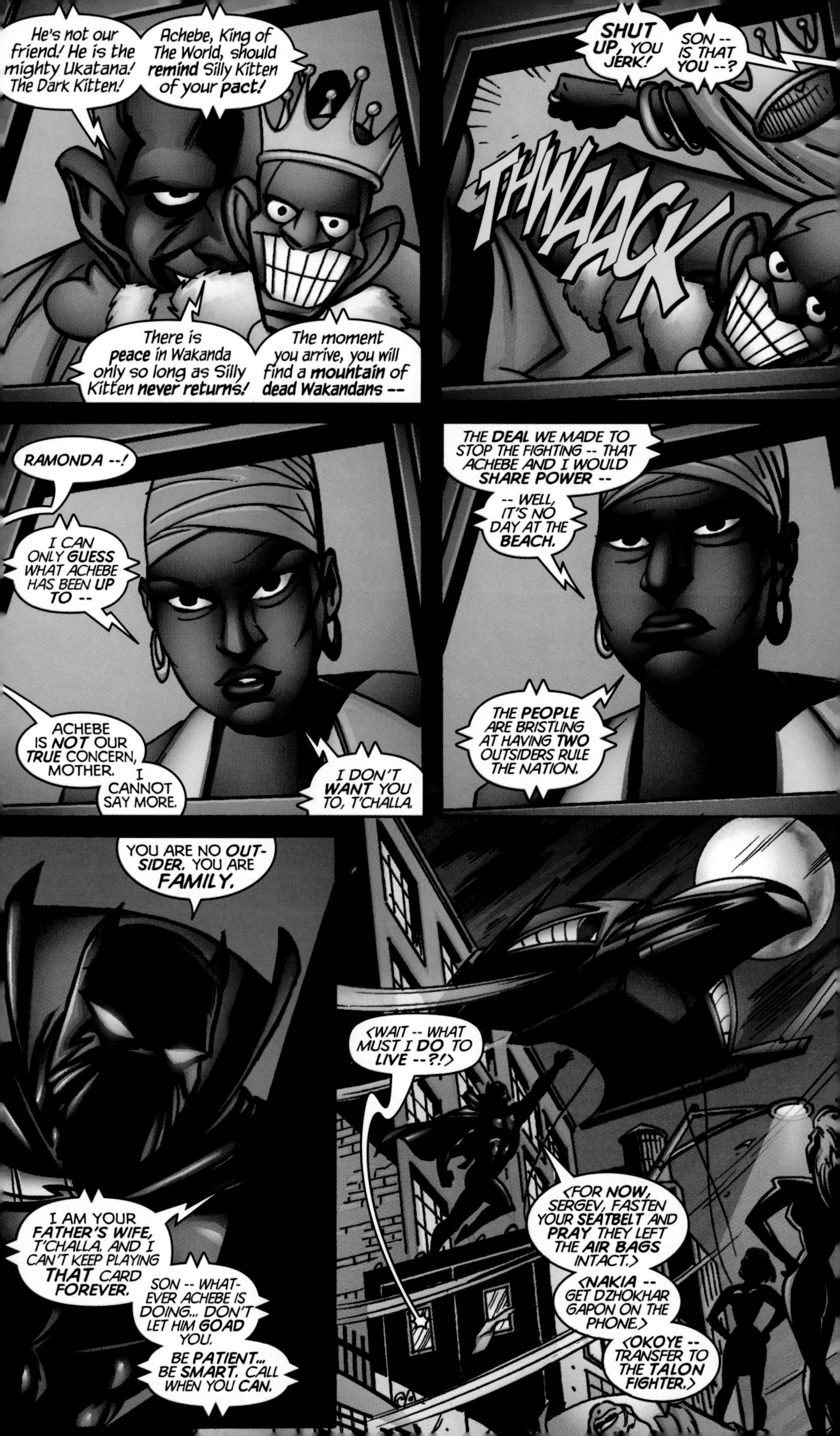
He's not our friend! He is the mighty Ukatana! The Dark Kitten!
Achebe, King of The World, should remind Silly Kitten of your pact!
There is peace in Wakanda only so long as Silly Kitten never returns!
The moment you arrive, you will find a mountain of dead Wakandans --
SHUT UP, YOU JERK!
SON -- IS THAT YOU --?
THWAACK
RAMONDA --!
I CAN ONLY GUESS WHAT ACHEBE HAS BEEN UP TO --
ACHEBE IS NOT OUR TRUE CONCERN, MOTHER.
I CANNOT SAY MORE.
I DON'T WANT YOU TO, T'CHALLA.
THE DEAL WE MADE TO STOP THE FIGHTING -- THAT ACHEBE AND I WOULD SHARE POWER --
-- WELL, IT'S NO DAY AT THE BEACH.
THE PEOPLE ARE BRISTLING AT HAVING TWO OUTSIDERS RULE THE NATION.
YOU ARE NO OUTSIDER. YOU ARE FAMILY.
I AM YOUR FATHER'S WIFE, T'CHALLA. AND I CAN'T KEEP PLAYING THAT CARD FOREVER.
SON -- WHATEVER ACHEBE IS DOING... DON'T LET HIM GOAD YOU.
BE PATIENT... BE SMART. CALL WHEN YOU CAN.
<WAIT -- WHAT MUST I DO TO LIVE --?!>
<FOR NOW, SERGEV, FASTEN YOUR SEATBELT AND PRAY THEY LEFT THE AIR BAGS INTACT.>
<NAKIA -- GET DZHOKHAR GAPON ON THE PHONE.>
<OKOYE -- TRANSFER TO THE TALON FIGHTER.>

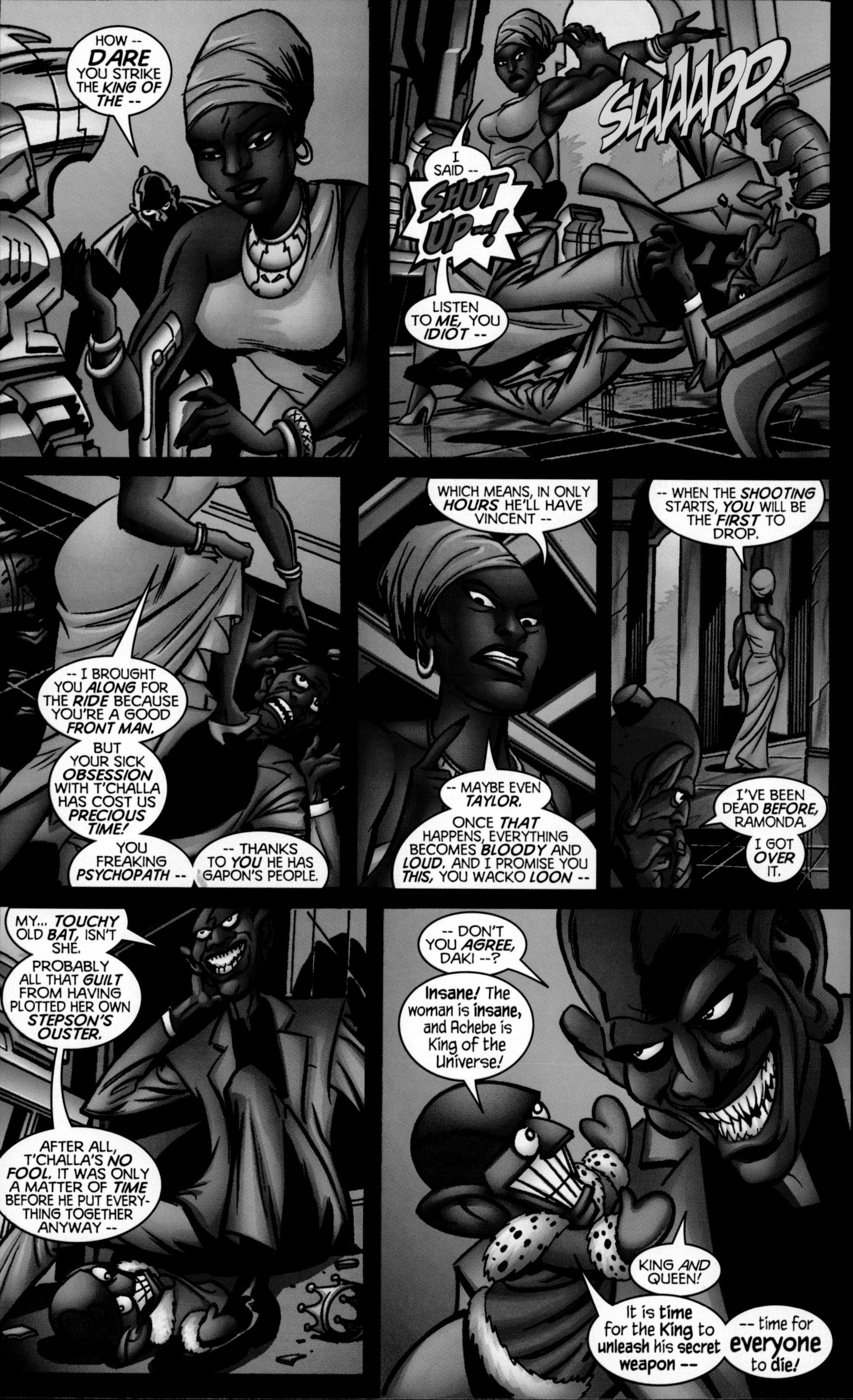

HOW -- DARE YOU STRIKE THE KING OF THE --
I SAID -- SHUT UP--!
SLAAAPP
LISTEN TO ME, YOU IDIOT --
-- I BROUGHT YOU ALONG FOR THE RIDE BECAUSE YOU'RE A GOOD FRONT MAN.
BUT YOUR SICK OBSESSION WITH T'CHALLA HAS COST US PRECIOUS TIME!
YOU FREAKING PSYCHOPATH --
-- THANKS TO YOU HE HAS GAPON'S PEOPLE.
WHICH MEANS, IN ONLY HOURS HE'LL HAVE VINCENT --
-- MAYBE EVEN TAYLOR.
ONCE THAT HAPPENS, EVERYTHING BECOMES BLOODY AND LOUD. AND I PROMISE YOU THIS, YOU WACKO LOON --
-- WHEN THE SHOOTING STARTS, YOU WILL BE THE FIRST TO DROP.
I'VE BEEN DEAD BEFORE, RAMONDA.
I GOT OVER IT.
MY... TOUCHY OLD BAT, ISN'T SHE.
PROBABLY ALL THAT GUILT FROM HAVING PLOTTED HER OWN STEPSON'S OUSTER.
AFTER ALL, T'CHALLA'S NO FOOL. IT WAS ONLY A MATTER OF TIME BEFORE HE PUT EVERYTHING TOGETHER ANYWAY --
-- DON'T YOU AGREE, DAKI --?
Insane! The woman is insane, and Achebe is King of the Universe!
KING AND QUEEN!
It is time for the King to unleash his secret weapon --
-- time for everyone to die!

MYSTERY DATE

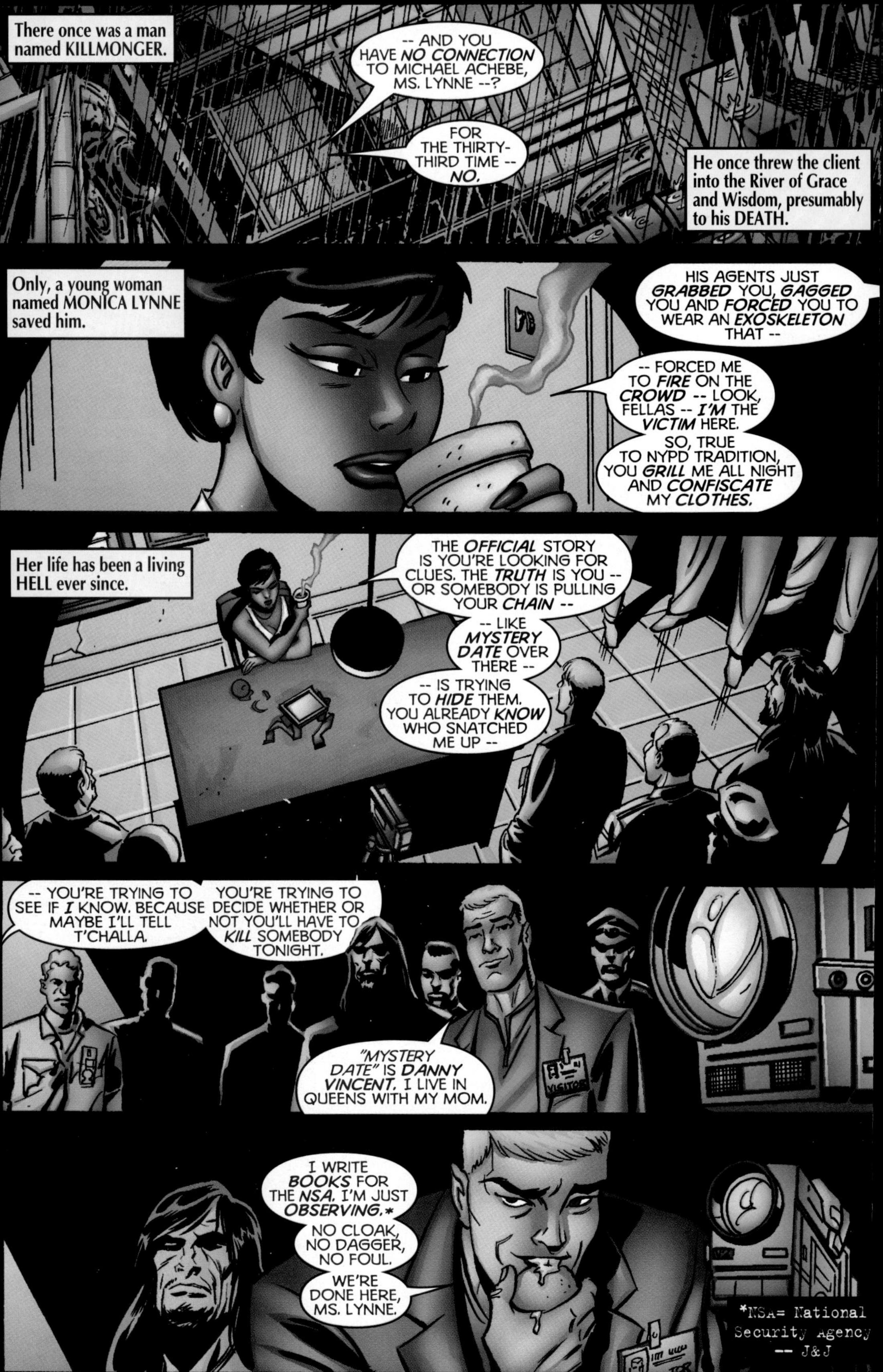

There once was a man named KILLMONGER.
-- AND YOU HAVE NO CONNECTION TO MICHAEL ACHEBE, MS. LYNNE --?
FOR THE THIRTY-THIRD TIME -- NO.
He once threw the client into the River of Grace and Wisdom, presumably to his DEATH.
Only, a young woman named MONICA LYNNE saved him.
HIS AGENTS JUST GRABBED YOU, GAGGED YOU AND FORCED YOU TO WEAR AN EXOSKELETON THAT --
-- FORCED ME TO FIRE ON THE CROWD -- LOOK, FELLAS -- I'M THE VICTIM HERE.
SO, TRUE TO NYPD TRADITION, YOU GRILL ME ALL NIGHT AND CONFISCATE MY CLOTHES.
Her life has been a living HELL ever since.
THE OFFICIAL STORY IS YOU'RE LOOKING FOR CLUES. THE TRUTH IS YOU -- OR SOMEBODY IS PULLING YOUR CHAIN --
-- LIKE MYSTERY DATE OVER THERE --
-- IS TRYING TO HIDE THEM. YOU ALREADY KNOW WHO SNATCHED ME UP --
-- YOU'RE TRYING TO SEE IF I KNOW. BECAUSE MAYBE I'LL TELL T'CHALLA.
YOU'RE TRYING TO DECIDE WHETHER OR NOT YOU'LL HAVE TO KILL SOMEBODY TONIGHT.
"MYSTERY DATE" IS DANNY VINCENT. I LIVE IN QUEENS WITH MY MOM.
I WRITE BOOKS FOR THE NSA. I'M JUST OBSERVING.*
NO CLOAK, NO DAGGER, NO FOUL.
WE'RE DONE HERE, MS. LYNNE.
*NSA= National Security Agency -- J&J

TRUCK MAN

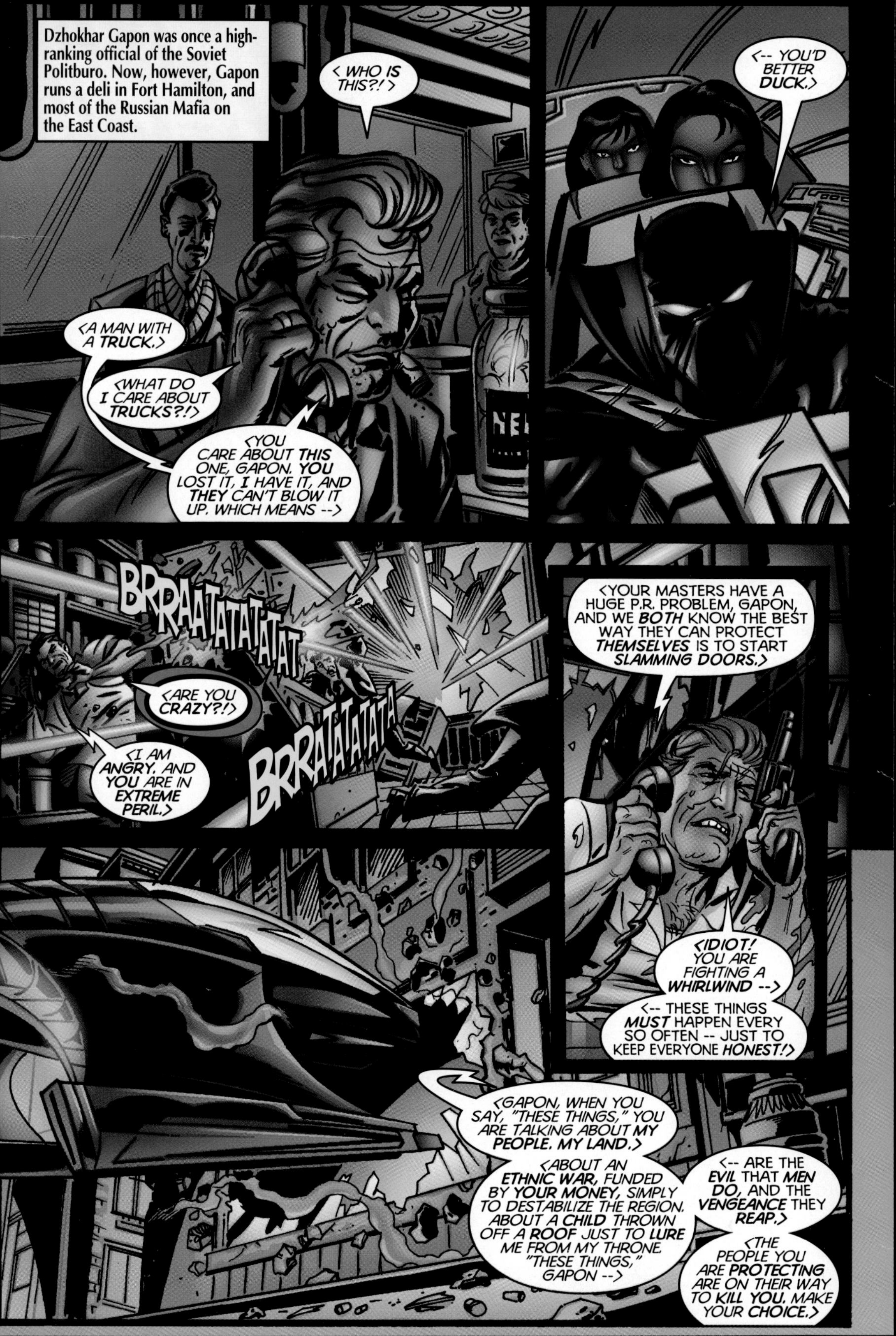

Dzhokhar Gapon was once a high-ranking official of the Soviet Politburo. Now, however, Gapon runs a deli in Fort Hamilton, and most of the Russian Mafia on the East Coast.
<WHO IS THIS?!>
<A MAN WITH A TRUCK.>
<WHAT DO I CARE ABOUT TRUCKS?!>
<YOU CARE ABOUT THIS ONE, GAPON. YOU LOST IT, I HAVE IT, AND THEY CAN'T BLOW IT UP. WHICH MEANS -->
<-- YOU'D BETTER DUCK.>
BRRAATATATATATAT
<ARE YOU CRAZY?!>
<I AM ANGRY. AND YOU ARE IN EXTREME PERIL.>
BRRATATATATA
<YOUR MASTERS HAVE A HUGE P.R. PROBLEM, GAPON, AND WE BOTH KNOW THE BEST WAY THEY CAN PROTECT THEMSELVES IS TO START SLAMMING DOORS.>
<IDIOT! YOU ARE FIGHTING A WHIRLWIND -->
<-- THESE THINGS MUST HAPPEN EVERY SO OFTEN -- JUST TO KEEP EVERYONE HONEST!>
<GAPON, WHEN YOU SAY, "THESE THINGS," YOU ARE TALKING ABOUT MY PEOPLE. MY LAND.>
<ABOUT AN ETHNIC WAR, FUNDED BY YOUR MONEY, SIMPLY TO DESTABILIZE THE REGION. ABOUT A CHILD THROWN OFF A ROOF JUST TO LURE ME FROM MY THRONE. "THESE THINGS," GAPON -->
<-- ARE THE EVIL THAT MEN DO, AND THE VENGEANCE THEY REAP.>
<THE PEOPLE YOU ARE PROTECTING ARE ON THEIR WAY TO KILL YOU. MAKE YOUR CHOICE.>

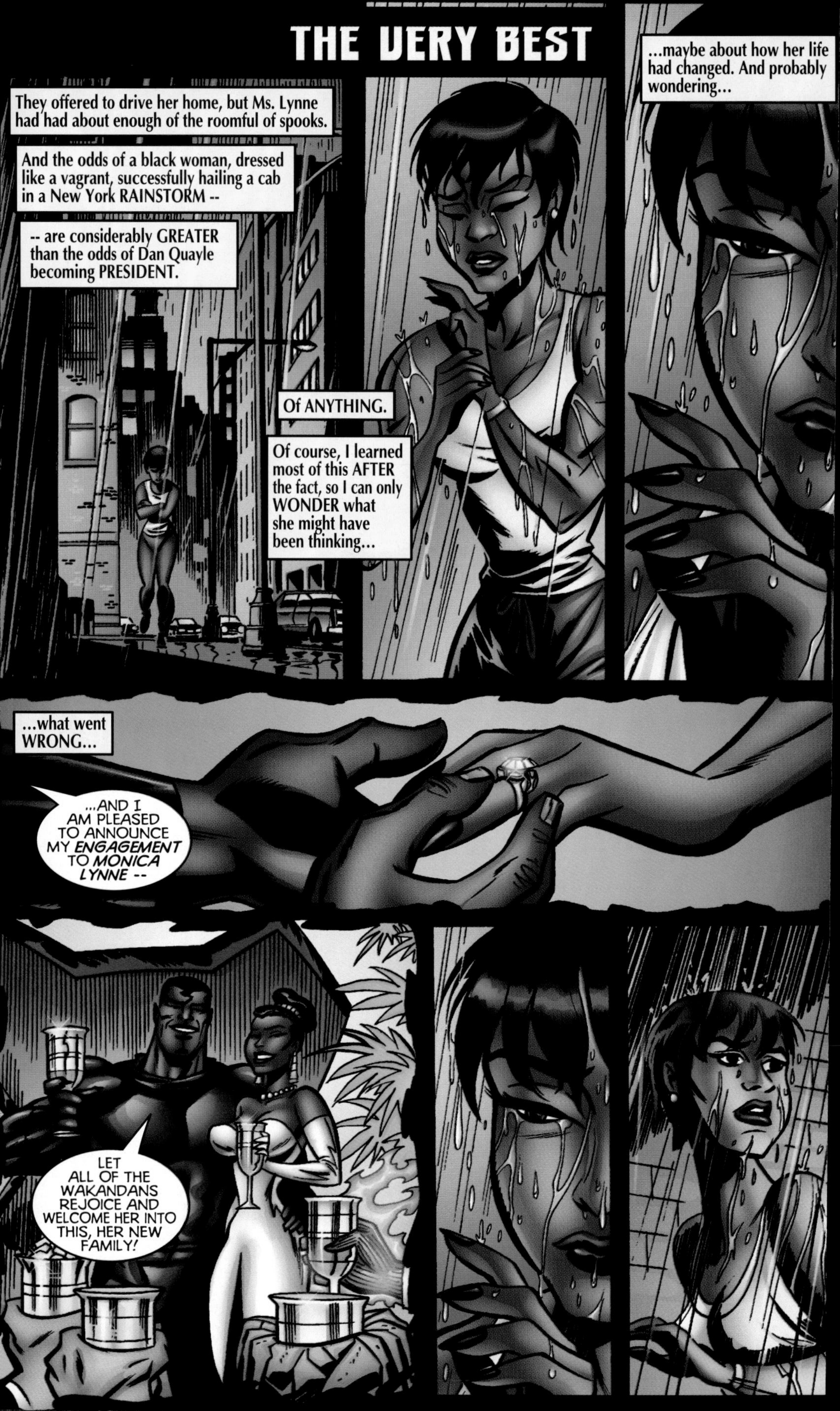

THE VERY BEST
They offered to drive her home, but Ms. Lynne had had about enough of the roomful of spooks.
And the odds of a black woman, dressed like a vagrant, successfully hailing a cab in a New York RAINSTORM --
-- are considerably GREATER than the odds of Dan Quayle becoming PRESIDENT.
Of ANYTHING.
Of course, I learned most of this AFTER the fact, so I can only WONDER what she might have been thinking...
...maybe about how her life had changed. And probably wondering...
...what went WRONG...
...AND I AM PLEASED TO ANNOUNCE MY ENGAGEMENT TO MONICA LYNNE --
LET ALL OF THE WAKANDANS REJOICE AND WELCOME HER INTO THIS, HER NEW FAMILY!

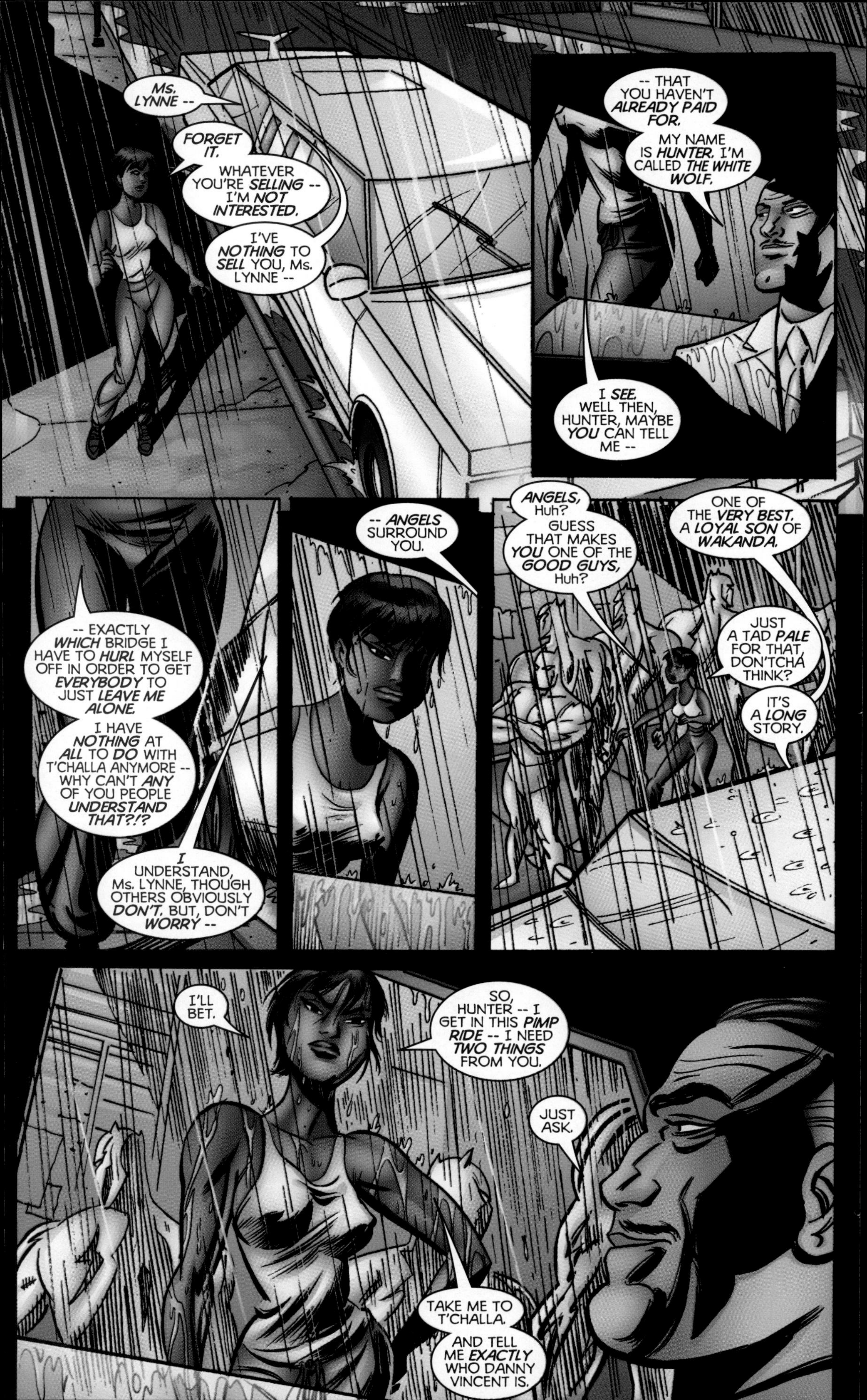

Ms. LYNNE --
FORGET IT. WHATEVER YOU'RE SELLING -- I'M NOT INTERESTED.
I'VE NOTHING TO SELL YOU, Ms. LYNNE --
-- THAT YOU HAVEN'T ALREADY PAID FOR.
MY NAME IS HUNTER. I'M CALLED THE WHITE WOLF.
I SEE. WELL THEN, HUNTER, MAYBE YOU CAN TELL ME --
-- EXACTLY WHICH BRIDGE I HAVE TO HURL MYSELF OFF IN ORDER TO GET EVERYBODY TO JUST LEAVE ME ALONE.
I HAVE NOTHING AT ALL TO DO WITH T'CHALLA ANYMORE -- WHY CAN'T ANY OF YOU PEOPLE UNDERSTAND THAT?!?
I UNDERSTAND, Ms. LYNNE, THOUGH OTHERS OBVIOUSLY DON'T. BUT, DON'T WORRY --
-- ANGELS SURROUND YOU.
ANGELS, Huh? GUESS THAT MAKES YOU ONE OF THE GOOD GUYS, Huh?
ONE OF THE VERY BEST. A LOYAL SON OF WAKANDA.
JUST A TAD PALE FOR THAT, DON'TCHA THINK?
IT'S A LONG STORY.
I'LL BET.
SO, HUNTER -- I GET IN THIS PIMP RIDE -- I NEED TWO THINGS FROM YOU.
JUST ASK.
TAKE ME TO T'CHALLA.
AND TELL ME EXACTLY WHO DANNY VINCENT IS.

JACK BE QUICK

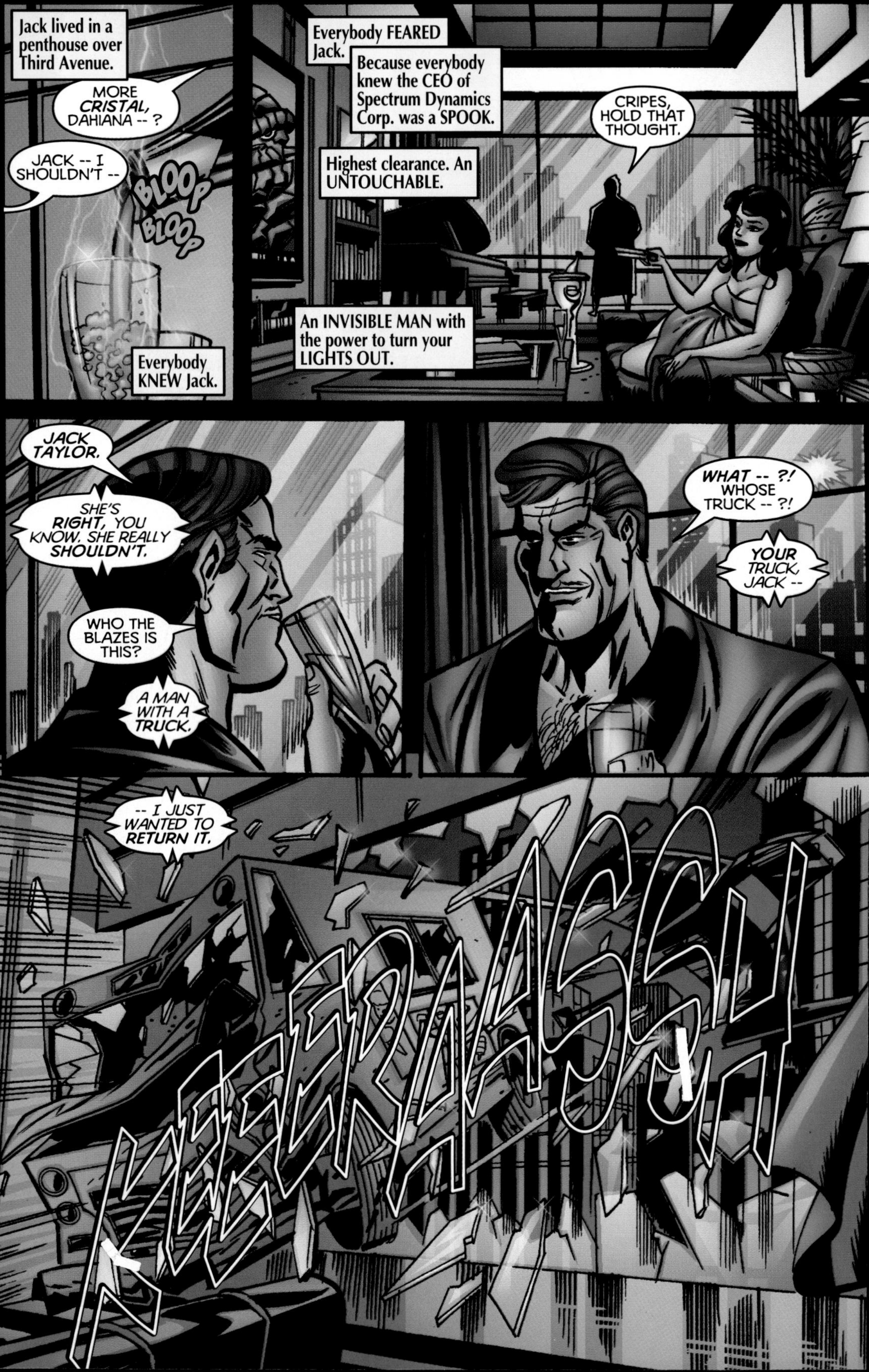

Jack lived in a penthouse over Third Avenue.
MORE CRISTAL, DAHIANA -- ?
JACK -- I SHOULDN'T --
BLOOP BLOOP
Everybody KNEW Jack.
Everybody FEARED Jack.
Because everybody knew the CEO of Spectrum Dynamics Corp. was a SPOOK.
Highest clearance. An UNTOUCHABLE.
An INVISIBLE MAN with the power to turn your LIGHTS OUT.
CRIPES, HOLD THAT THOUGHT.
JACK TAYLOR.
SHE'S RIGHT, YOU KNOW. SHE REALLY SHOULDN'T.
WHO THE BLAZES IS THIS?
A MAN WITH A TRUCK.
WHAT -- ?! WHOSE TRUCK -- ?!
YOUR TRUCK, JACK --
-- I JUST WANTED TO RETURN IT.

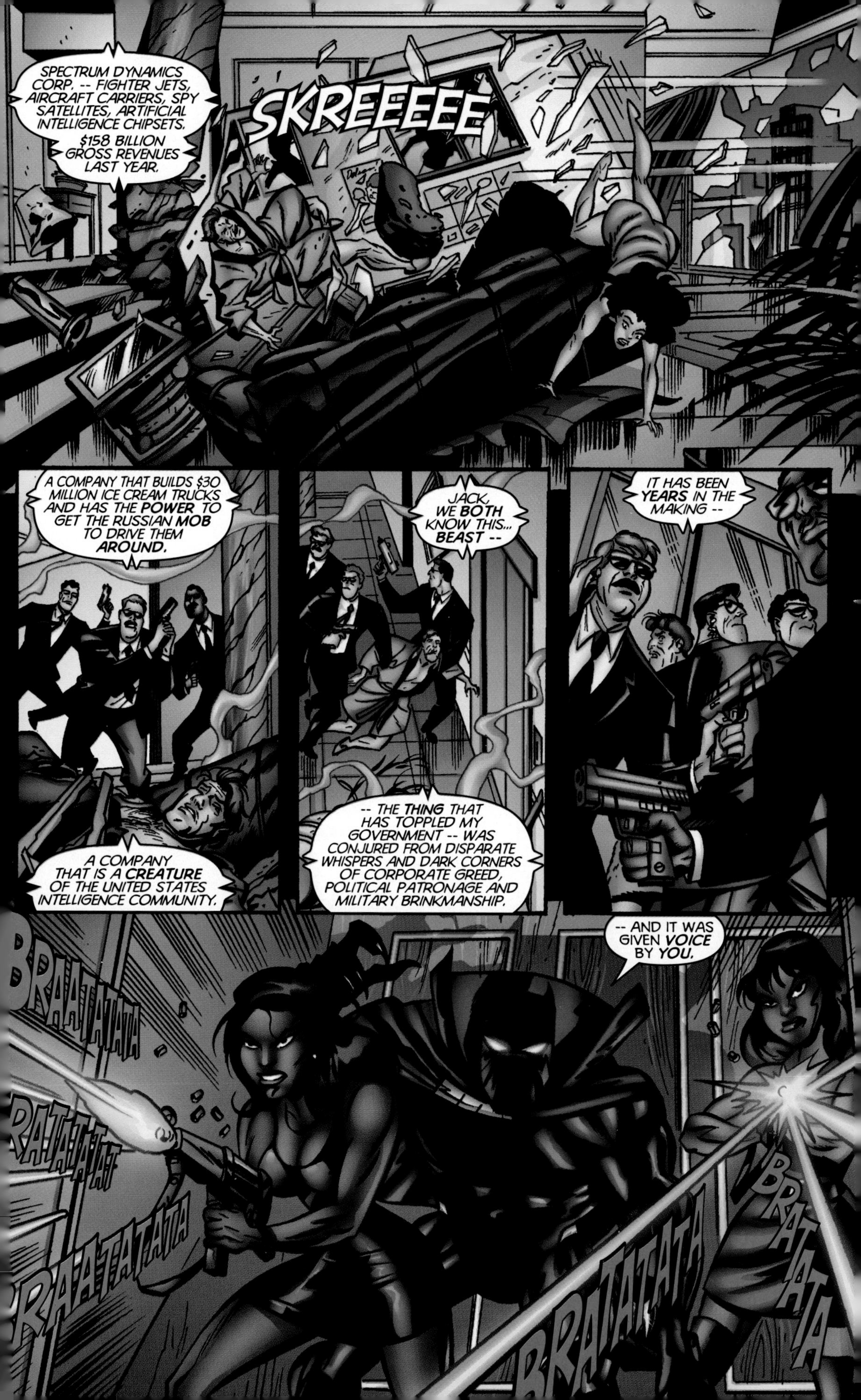
SPECTRUM DYNAMICS CORP. -- FIGHTER JETS, AIRCRAFT CARRIERS, SPY SATELLITES, ARTIFICIAL INTELLIGENCE CHIPSETS.
$158 BILLION GROSS REVENUES LAST YEAR.
SKREEEEEE
A COMPANY THAT BUILDS $30 MILLION ICE CREAM TRUCKS AND HAS THE POWER TO GET THE RUSSIAN MOB TO DRIVE THEM AROUND.
A COMPANY THAT IS A CREATURE OF THE UNITED STATES INTELLIGENCE COMMUNITY.
JACK, WE BOTH KNOW THIS... BEAST --
-- THE THING THAT HAS TOPPLED MY GOVERNMENT -- WAS CONJURED FROM DISPARATE WHISPERS AND DARK CORNERS OF CORPORATE GREED, POLITICAL PATRONAGE AND MILITARY BRINKMANSHIP.
IT HAS BEEN YEARS IN THE MAKING --
-- AND IT WAS GIVEN VOICE BY YOU.
BRAATATATA
RATATATAT
RAATATATA
BRATATATA
BRATATA

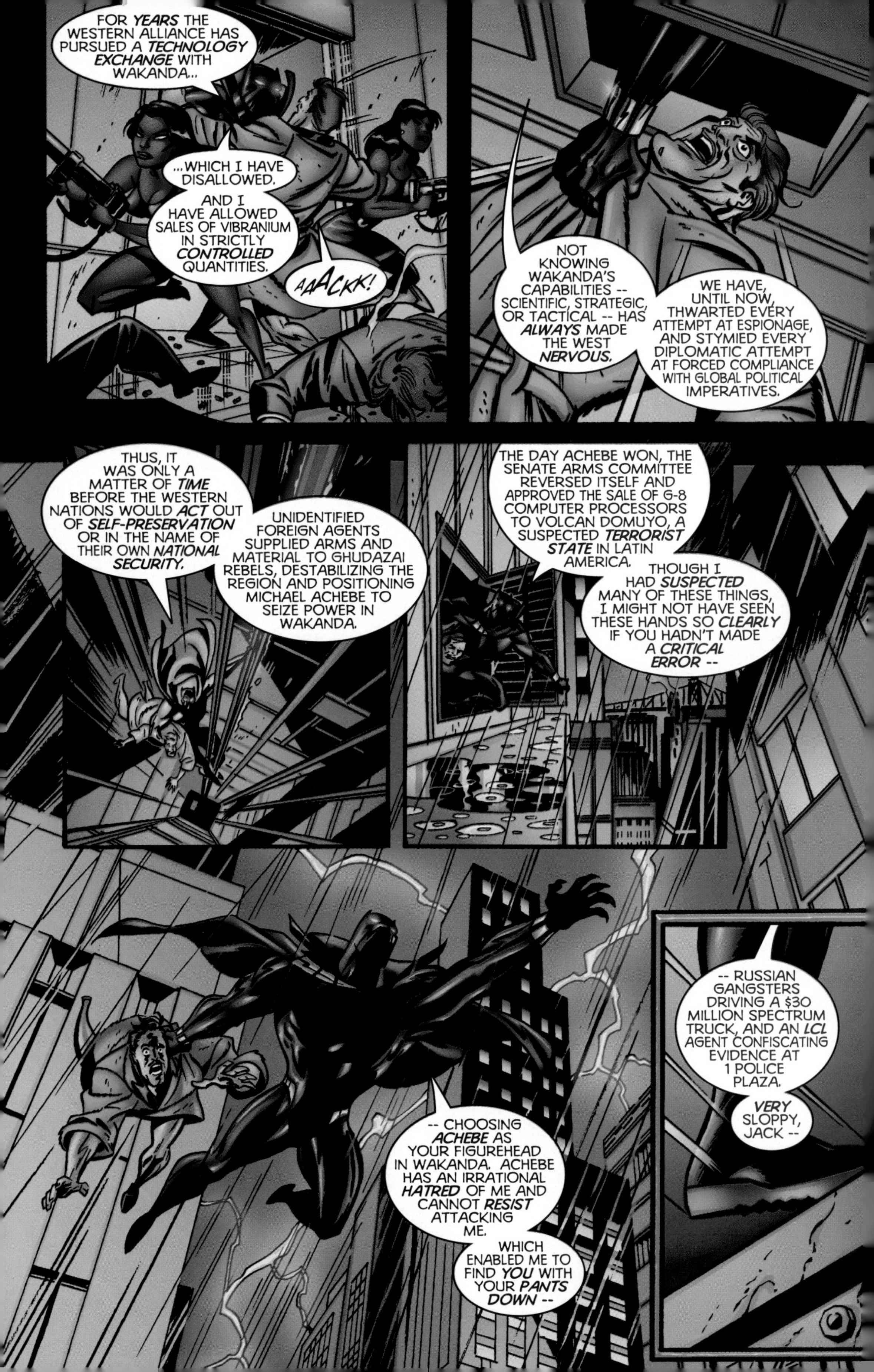
FOR YEARS THE WESTERN ALLIANCE HAS PURSUED A TECHNOLOGY EXCHANGE WITH WAKANDA...
...WHICH I HAVE DISALLOWED.
AND I HAVE ALLOWED SALES OF VIBRANIUM IN STRICTLY CONTROLLED QUANTITIES.
AAACKK!
NOT KNOWING WAKANDA'S CAPABILITIES -- SCIENTIFIC, STRATEGIC, OR TACTICAL -- HAS ALWAYS MADE THE WEST NERVOUS.
WE HAVE, UNTIL NOW, THWARTED EVERY ATTEMPT AT ESPIONAGE, AND STYMIED EVERY DIPLOMATIC ATTEMPT AT FORCED COMPLIANCE WITH GLOBAL POLITICAL IMPERATIVES.
THUS, IT WAS ONLY A MATTER OF TIME BEFORE THE WESTERN NATIONS WOULD ACT OUT OF SELF-PRESERVATION OR IN THE NAME OF THEIR OWN NATIONAL SECURITY.
UNIDENTIFIED FOREIGN AGENTS SUPPLIED ARMS AND MATERIAL TO GHUDAZAI REBELS, DESTABILIZING THE REGION AND POSITIONING MICHAEL ACHEBE TO SEIZE POWER IN WAKANDA.
THE DAY ACHEBE WON, THE SENATE ARMS COMMITTEE REVERSED ITSELF AND APPROVED THE SALE OF G-8 COMPUTER PROCESSORS TO VOLCAN DOMUYO, A SUSPECTED TERRORIST STATE IN LATIN AMERICA.
THOUGH I HAD SUSPECTED MANY OF THESE THINGS, I MIGHT NOT HAVE SEEN THESE HANDS SO CLEARLY IF YOU HADN'T MADE A CRITICAL ERROR --
-- CHOOSING ACHEBE AS YOUR FIGUREHEAD IN WAKANDA. ACHEBE HAS AN IRRATIONAL HATRED OF ME AND CANNOT RESIST ATTACKING ME.
WHICH ENABLED ME TO FIND YOU WITH YOUR PANTS DOWN --
-- RUSSIAN GANGSTERS DRIVING A $30 MILLION SPECTRUM TRUCK, AND AN LCL AGENT CONFISCATING EVIDENCE AT 1 POLICE PLAZA.
VERY SLOPPY, JACK --

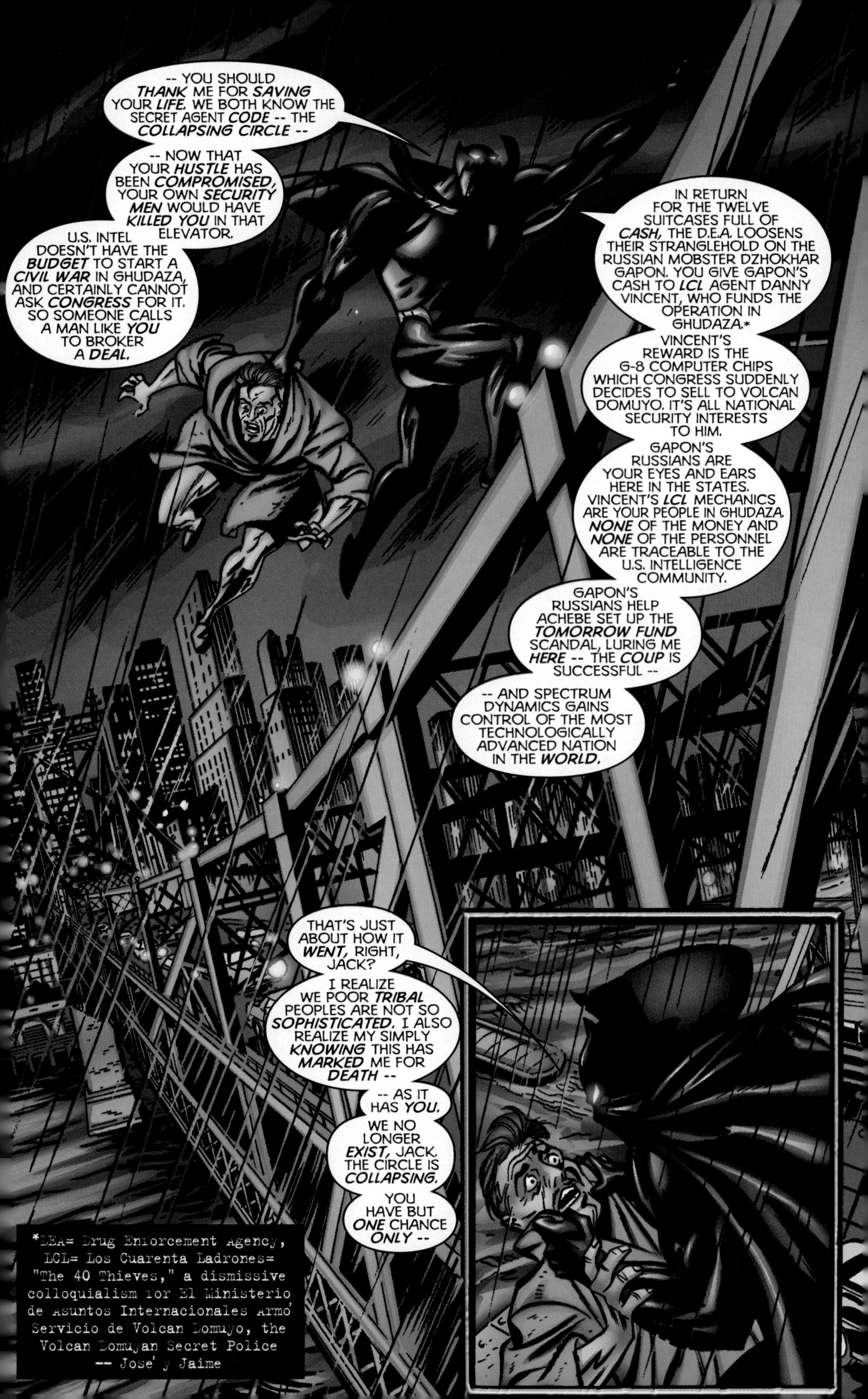
-- YOU SHOULD THANK ME FOR SAVING YOUR LIFE. WE BOTH KNOW THE SECRET AGENT CODE -- THE COLLAPSING CIRCLE --
-- NOW THAT YOUR HUSTLE HAS BEEN COMPROMISED, YOUR OWN SECURITY MEN WOULD HAVE KILLED YOU IN THAT ELEVATOR.
U.S. INTEL DOESN'T HAVE THE BUDGET TO START A CIVIL WAR IN GHUDAZA, AND CERTAINLY CANNOT ASK CONGRESS FOR IT. SO SOMEONE CALLS A MAN LIKE YOU TO BROKER A DEAL.
IN RETURN FOR THE TWELVE SUITCASES FULL OF CASH, THE D.E.A. LOOSENS THEIR STRANGLEHOLD ON THE RUSSIAN MOBSTER DZHOKHAR GAPON. YOU GIVE GAPON'S CASH TO LCL AGENT DANNY VINCENT, WHO FUNDS THE OPERATION IN GHUDAZA.*
VINCENT'S REWARD IS THE G-8 COMPUTER CHIPS WHICH CONGRESS SUDDENLY DECIDES TO SELL TO VOLCAN DOMUYO. IT'S ALL NATIONAL SECURITY INTERESTS TO HIM.
GAPON'S RUSSIANS ARE YOUR EYES AND EARS HERE IN THE STATES. VINCENT'S LCL MECHANICS ARE YOUR PEOPLE IN GHUDAZA. NONE OF THE MONEY AND NONE OF THE PERSONNEL ARE TRACEABLE TO THE U.S. INTELLIGENCE COMMUNITY.
GAPON'S RUSSIANS HELP ACHEBE SET UP THE TOMORROW FUND SCANDAL, LURING ME HERE -- THE COUP IS SUCCESSFUL --
-- AND SPECTRUM DYNAMICS GAINS CONTROL OF THE MOST TECHNOLOGICALLY ADVANCED NATION IN THE WORLD.
THAT'S JUST ABOUT HOW IT WENT, RIGHT, JACK?
I REALIZE WE POOR TRIBAL PEOPLES ARE NOT SO SOPHISTICATED. I ALSO REALIZE MY SIMPLY KNOWING THIS HAS MARKED ME FOR DEATH --
-- AS IT HAS YOU.
WE NO LONGER EXIST, JACK. THE CIRCLE IS COLLAPSING.
YOU HAVE BUT ONE CHANCE ONLY --
*DEA= Drug Enforcement Agency, LCL= Los Cuarenta Ladrones= "The 40 Thieves," a dismissive colloquialism for El Ministerio de Asuntos Internacionales Armó Servicio de Volcan Domuyo, the Volcan Domuyan Secret Police -- José y Jaime

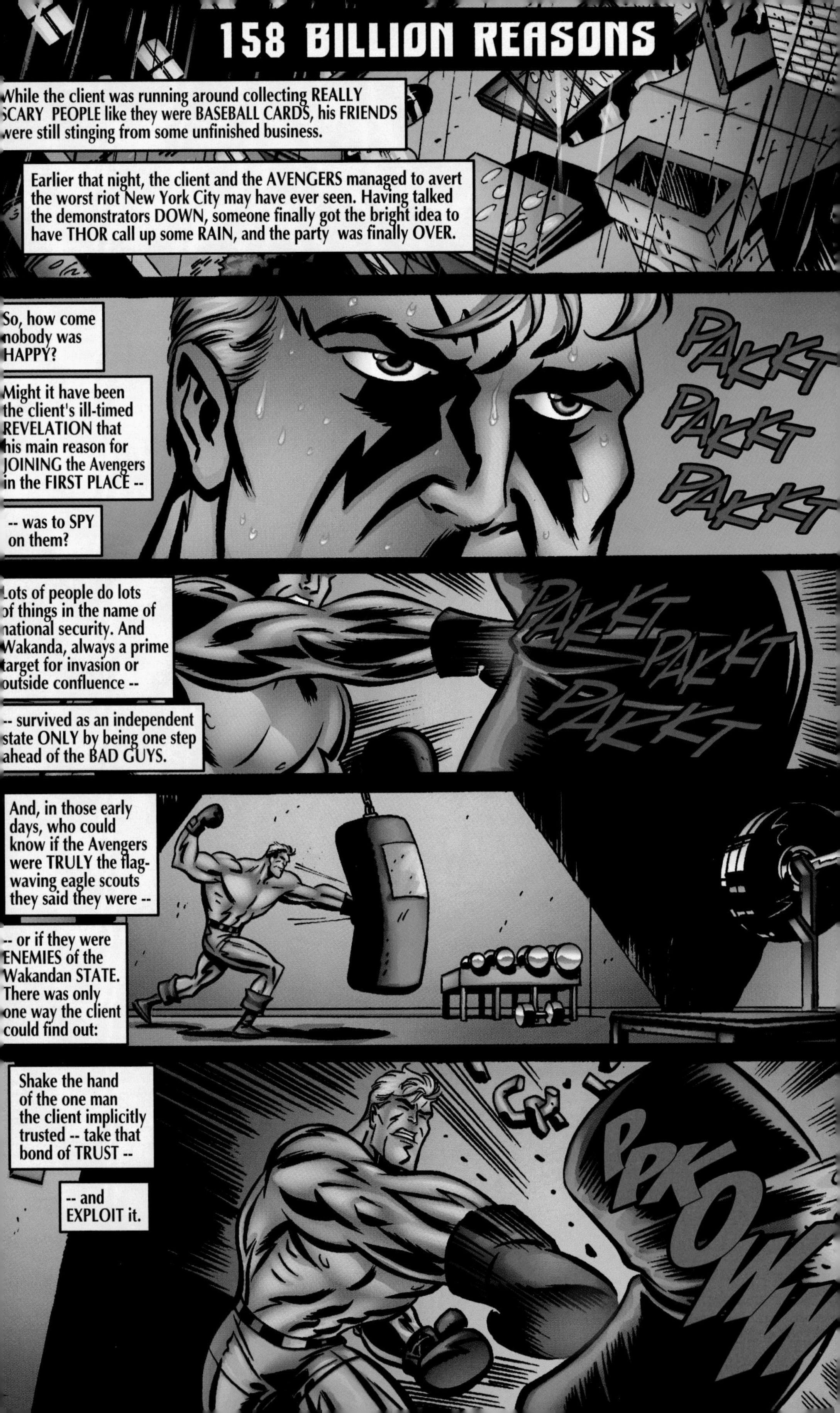

158 BILLION REASONS
While the client was running around collecting REALLY SCARY PEOPLE like they were BASEBALL CARDS, his FRIENDS were still stinging from some unfinished business.
Earlier that night, the client and the AVENGERS managed to avert the worst riot New York City may have ever seen. Having talked the demonstrators DOWN, someone finally got the bright idea to have THOR call up some RAIN, and the party was finally OVER.
So, how come nobody was HAPPY?
Might it have been the client's ill-timed REVELATION that his main reason for JOINING the Avengers in the FIRST PLACE --
-- was to SPY on them?
PAKKT PAKKT PAKKT
Lots of people do lots of things in the name of national security. And Wakanda, always a prime target for invasion or outside confluence --
-- survived as an independent state ONLY by being one step ahead of the BAD GUYS.
PAKKT PAKKT PAKKT
And, in those early days, who could know if the Avengers were TRULY the flag-waving eagle scouts they said they were --
-- or if they were ENEMIES of the Wakandan STATE. There was only one way the client could find out:
Shake the hand of the one man the client implicitly trusted -- take that bond of TRUST --
-- and EXPLOIT it.
PPKOWW

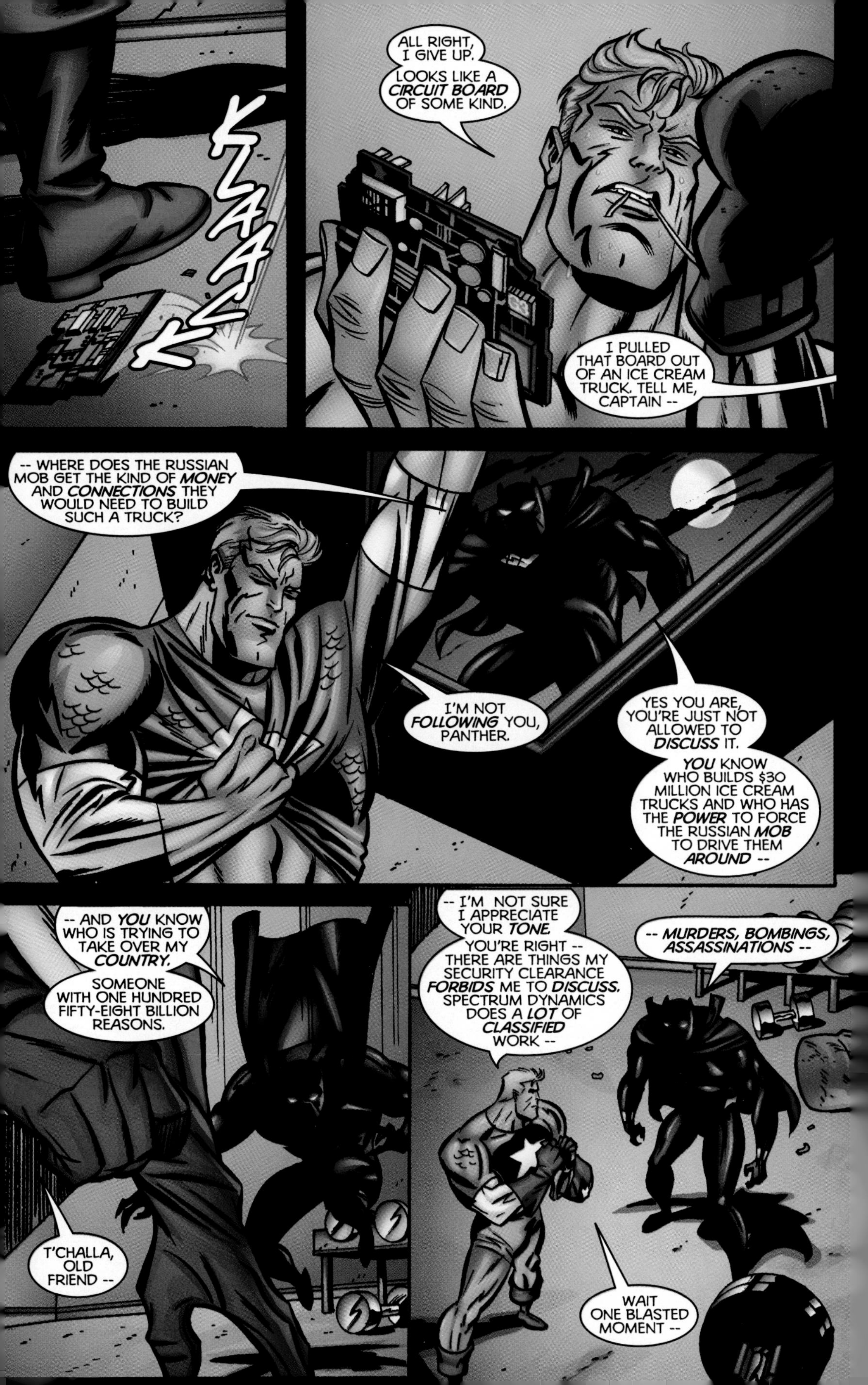
KLAACK
ALL RIGHT, I GIVE UP.
LOOKS LIKE A CIRCUIT BOARD OF SOME KIND.
I PULLED THAT BOARD OUT OF AN ICE CREAM TRUCK. TELL ME, CAPTAIN --
-- WHERE DOES THE RUSSIAN MOB GET THE KIND OF MONEY AND CONNECTIONS THEY WOULD NEED TO BUILD SUCH A TRUCK?
I'M NOT FOLLOWING YOU, PANTHER.
YES YOU ARE, YOU'RE JUST NOT ALLOWED TO DISCUSS IT.
YOU KNOW WHO BUILDS $30 MILLION ICE CREAM TRUCKS AND WHO HAS THE POWER TO FORCE THE RUSSIAN MOB TO DRIVE THEM AROUND --
-- AND YOU KNOW WHO IS TRYING TO TAKE OVER MY COUNTRY.
SOMEONE WITH ONE HUNDRED FIFTY-EIGHT BILLION REASONS.
T'CHALLA, OLD FRIEND --
-- I'M NOT SURE I APPRECIATE YOUR TONE.
YOU'RE RIGHT -- THERE ARE THINGS MY SECURITY CLEARANCE FORBIDS ME TO DISCUSS. SPECTRUM DYNAMICS DOES A LOT OF CLASSIFIED WORK --
-- MURDERS, BOMBINGS, ASSASSINATIONS --
WAIT ONE BLASTED MOMENT --

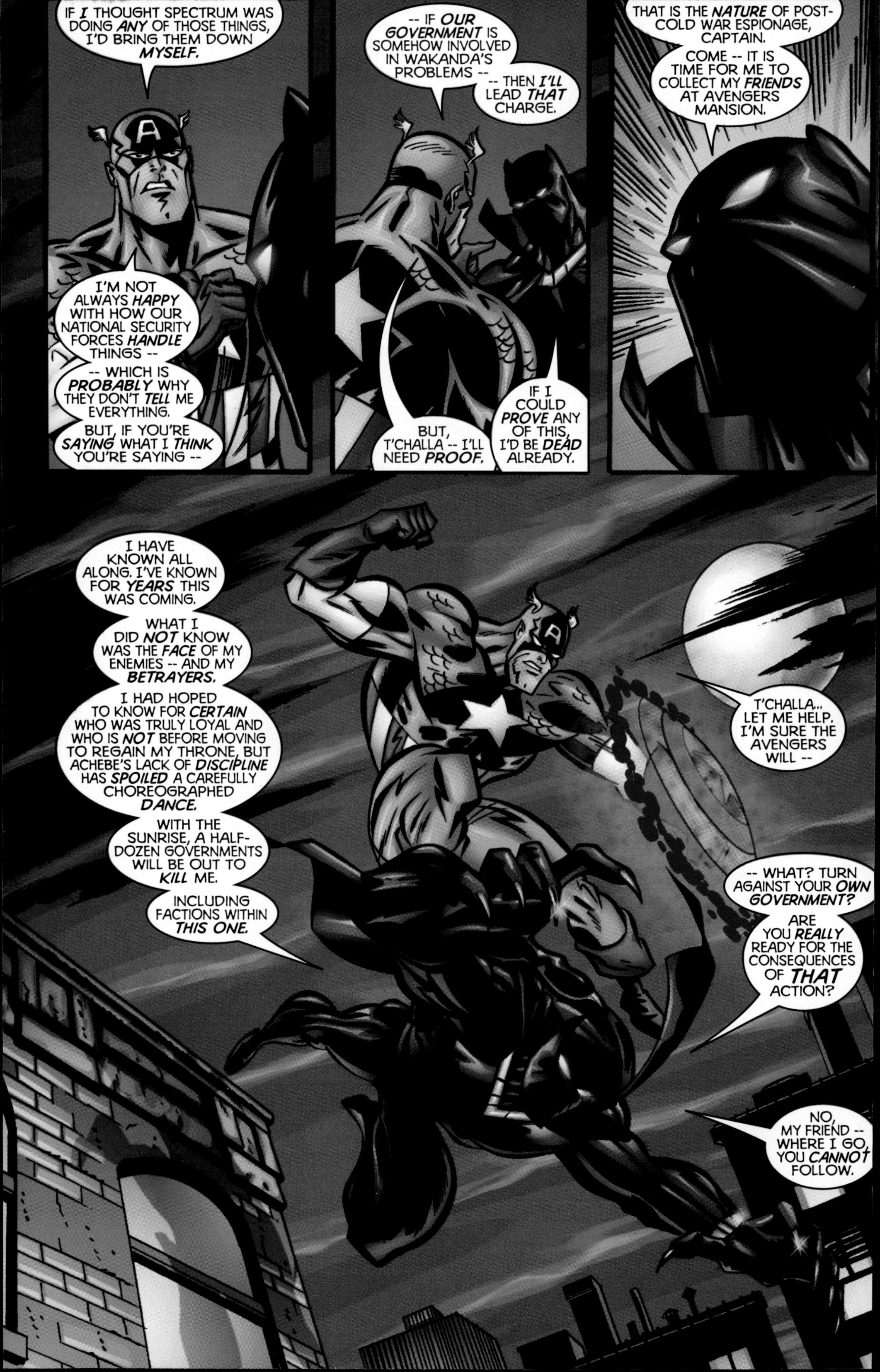

IF I THOUGHT SPECTRUM WAS DOING ANY OF THOSE THINGS, I'D BRING THEM DOWN MYSELF.
I'M NOT ALWAYS HAPPY WITH HOW OUR NATIONAL SECURITY FORCES HANDLE THINGS --
-- WHICH IS PROBABLY WHY THEY DON'T TELL ME EVERYTHING.
BUT, IF YOU'RE SAYING WHAT I THINK YOU'RE SAYING --
-- IF OUR GOVERNMENT IS SOMEHOW INVOLVED IN WAKANDA'S PROBLEMS --
-- THEN I'LL LEAD THAT CHARGE.
BUT, T'CHALLA -- I'LL NEED PROOF.
IF I COULD PROVE ANY OF THIS, I'D BE DEAD ALREADY.
THAT IS THE NATURE OF POST-COLD WAR ESPIONAGE, CAPTAIN.
COME -- IT IS TIME FOR ME TO COLLECT MY FRIENDS AT AVENGERS MANSION.
I HAVE KNOWN ALL ALONG. I'VE KNOWN FOR YEARS THIS WAS COMING.
WHAT I DID NOT KNOW WAS THE FACE OF MY ENEMIES -- AND MY BETRAYERS.
I HAD HOPED TO KNOW FOR CERTAIN WHO WAS TRULY LOYAL AND WHO IS NOT BEFORE MOVING TO REGAIN MY THRONE, BUT ACHEBE'S LACK OF DISCIPLINE HAS SPOILED A CAREFULLY CHOREOGRAPHED DANCE.
WITH THE SUNRISE, A HALF-DOZEN GOVERNMENTS WILL BE OUT TO KILL ME.
INCLUDING FACTIONS WITHIN THIS ONE.
T'CHALLA... LET ME HELP. I'M SURE THE AVENGERS WILL --
-- WHAT? TURN AGAINST YOUR OWN GOVERNMENT?
ARE YOU REALLY READY FOR THE CONSEQUENCES OF THAT ACTION?
NO, MY FRIEND -- WHERE I GO, YOU CANNOT FOLLOW.

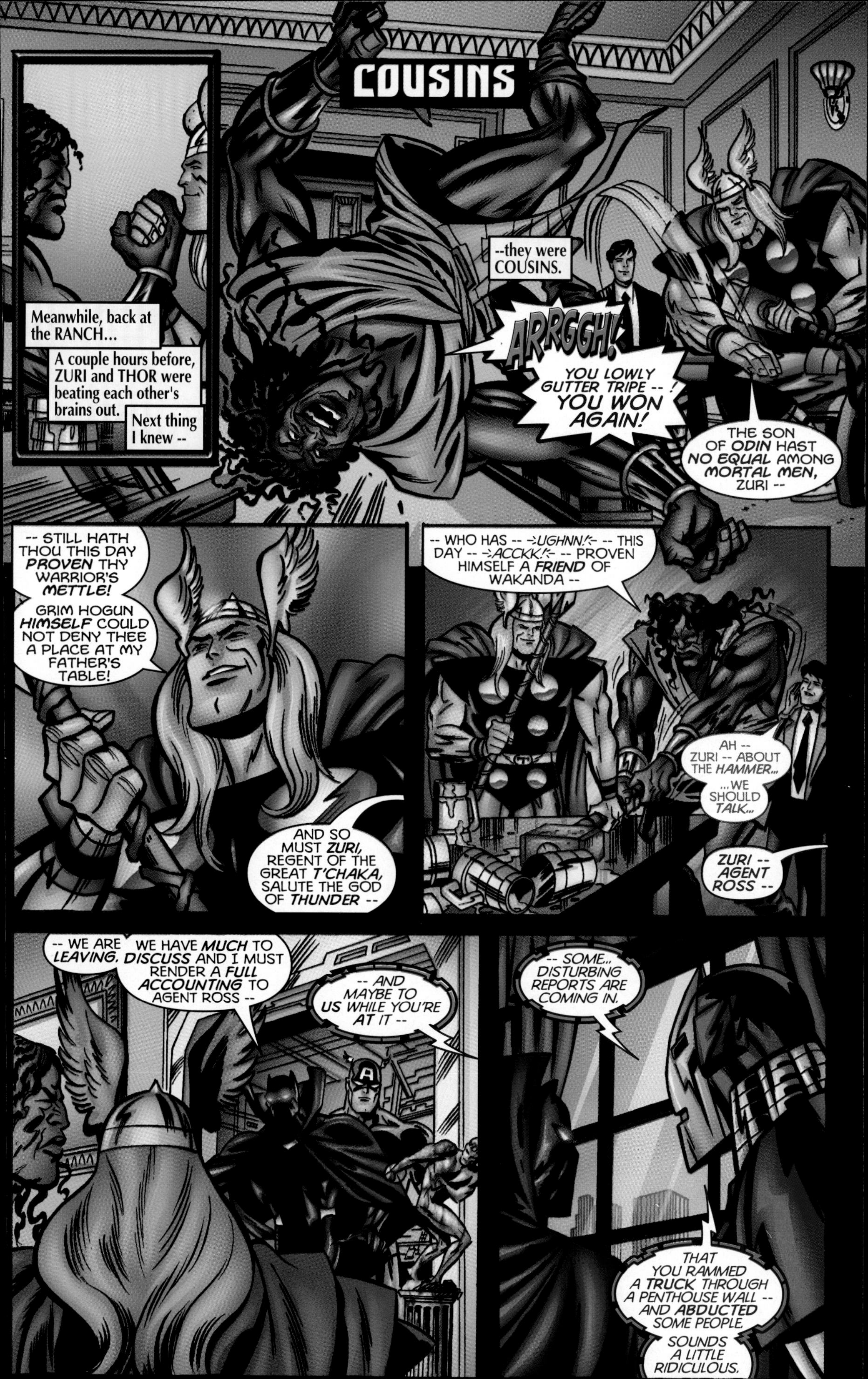
COUSINS
Meanwhile, back at the RANCH...
A couple hours before, ZURI and THOR were beating each other's brains out.
Next thing I knew --
--they were COUSINS.
ARRGGH!
YOU LOWLY GUTTER TRIPE -- ! YOU WON AGAIN!
THE SON OF ODIN HAST NO EQUAL AMONG MORTAL MEN, ZURI --
-- STILL HATH THOU THIS DAY PROVEN THY WARRIOR'S METTLE!
GRIM HOGUN HIMSELF COULD NOT DENY THEE A PLACE AT MY FATHER'S TABLE!
AND SO MUST ZURI, REGENT OF THE GREAT T'CHAKA, SALUTE THE GOD OF THUNDER --
-- WHO HAS -- UGHNN! -- THIS DAY -- ACCKK! -- PROVEN HIMSELF A FRIEND OF WAKANDA --
AH -- ZURI -- ABOUT THE HAMMER... ...WE SHOULD TALK...
ZURI -- AGENT ROSS --
-- WE ARE LEAVING.
WE HAVE MUCH TO DISCUSS AND I MUST RENDER A FULL ACCOUNTING TO AGENT ROSS --
-- AND MAYBE TO US WHILE YOU'RE AT IT --
-- SOME... DISTURBING REPORTS ARE COMING IN.
THAT YOU RAMMED A TRUCK THROUGH A PENTHOUSE WALL -- AND ABDUCTED SOME PEOPLE.
SOUNDS A LITTLE RIDICULOUS.

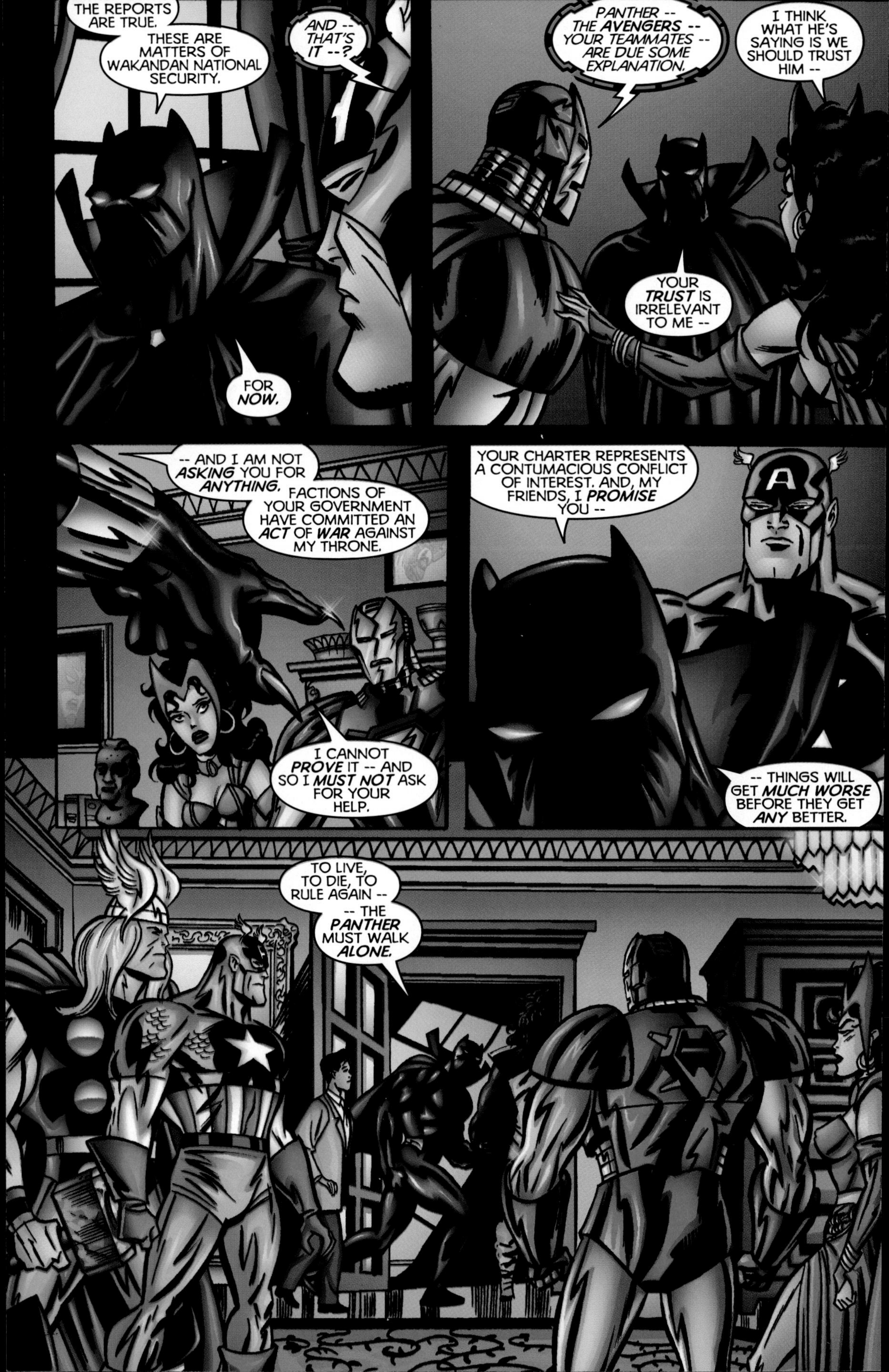

THE REPORTS ARE TRUE.
THESE ARE MATTERS OF WAKANDAN NATIONAL SECURITY.
AND -- THAT'S IT --?
FOR NOW.
PANTHER -- THE AVENGERS -- YOUR TEAMMATES -- ARE DUE SOME EXPLANATION.
I THINK WHAT HE'S SAYING IS WE SHOULD TRUST HIM --
YOUR TRUST IS IRRELEVANT TO ME --
-- AND I AM NOT ASKING YOU FOR ANYTHING.
FACTIONS OF YOUR GOVERNMENT HAVE COMMITTED AN ACT OF WAR AGAINST MY THRONE.
I CANNOT PROVE IT -- AND SO I MUST NOT ASK FOR YOUR HELP.
YOUR CHARTER REPRESENTS A CONTUMACIOUS CONFLICT OF INTEREST. AND, MY FRIENDS, I PROMISE YOU --
-- THINGS WILL GET MUCH WORSE BEFORE THEY GET ANY BETTER.
TO LIVE, TO DIE, TO RULE AGAIN --
-- THE PANTHER MUST WALK ALONE.

YOU MUST BE *ABSOLUTELY CERTAIN* OF THIS.

I am.

MY *CORONATION* AS *KING* OF WAKANDA *MUST* COME TO PASS.

It shall.

NOTHING MUST *JEOPARDIZE* MY GREAT *PLANS.*

Nothing shall →sigh← Achebe --

-- You must learn to trust me.

I DO, DAKI, I DO. BUT THESE ARE *PERILOUS* TIMES.

All the more reason for you to let me do the thinking.

The *access codes* for the prowlers are hidden in an encrypted file. But guess *who* has the crypto key? Three guesses.

Ah... W'KABI --?

Wrong!

KANTU --?

Wrong again! You *really* are an idiot, Achebe!

Here -- I'll give you a hint --

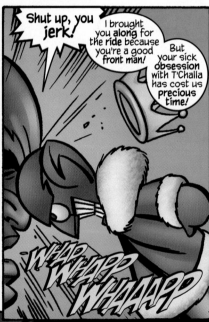

Shut up, you *jerk!*

I brought you along for the ride because you're a good front man!

But your sick obsession with T'Challa has cost us precious time!

WHAP WHAPP WHAAAPP

Ah, YES. *RAMONDA.*

Rah-monnnnnn-DAH!

YES. RAMONDA...

Rrrramonda!

...RAMONDA...

Rahhhh-monda!

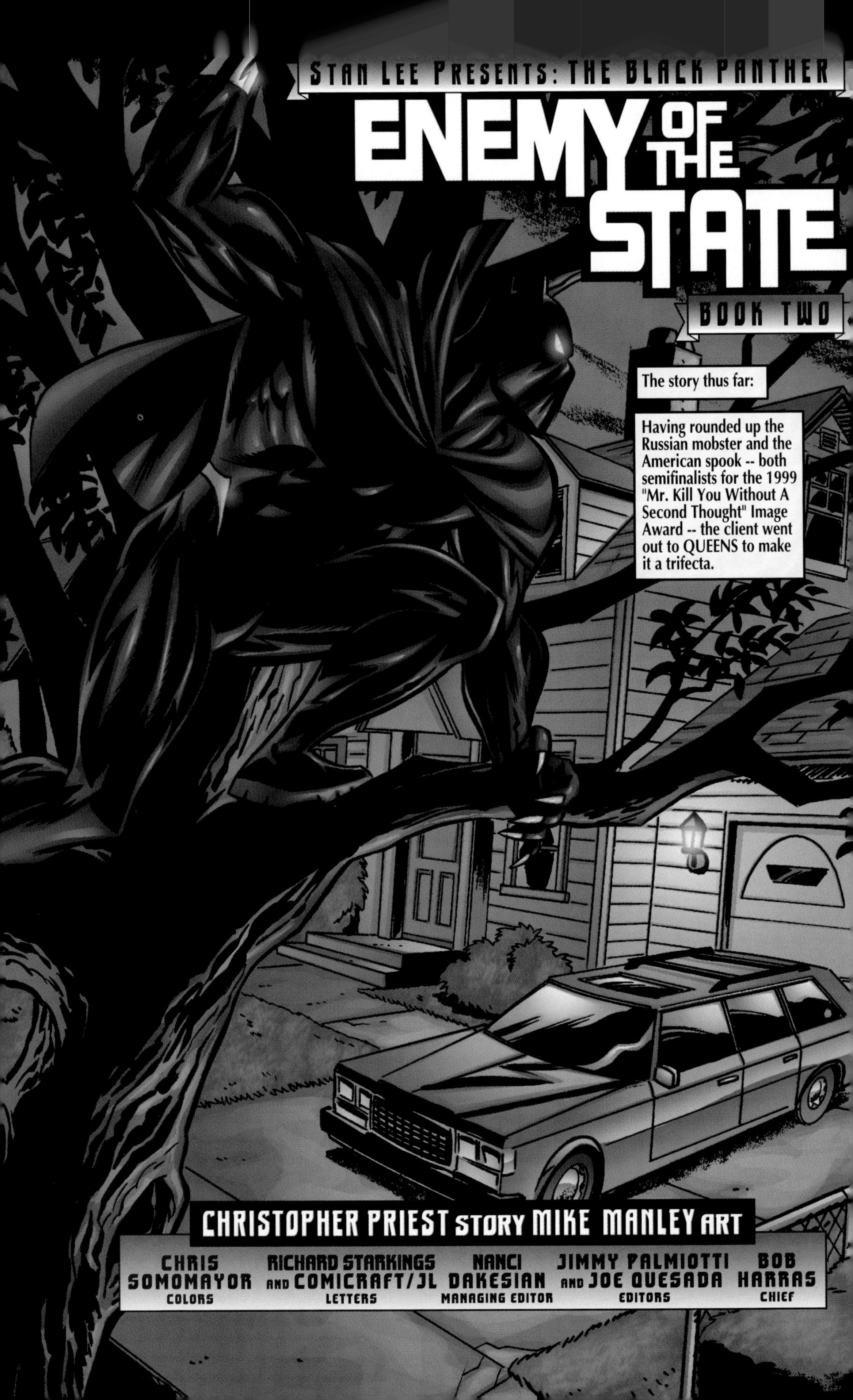
STAN LEE PRESENTS: THE BLACK PANTHER
ENEMY OF THE STATE
BOOK TWO
The story thus far:
Having rounded up the Russian mobster and the American spook -- both semifinalists for the 1999 "Mr. Kill You Without A Second Thought" Image Award -- the client went out to QUEENS to make it a trifecta.
CHRISTOPHER PRIEST STORY MIKE MANLEY ART
CHRIS SOMOMAYOR COLORS
RICHARD STARKINGS AND COMICRAFT/JL LETTERS
NANCI DAKESIAN MANAGING EDITOR
JIMMY PALMIOTTI AND JOE QUESADA EDITORS
BOB HARRAS CHIEF

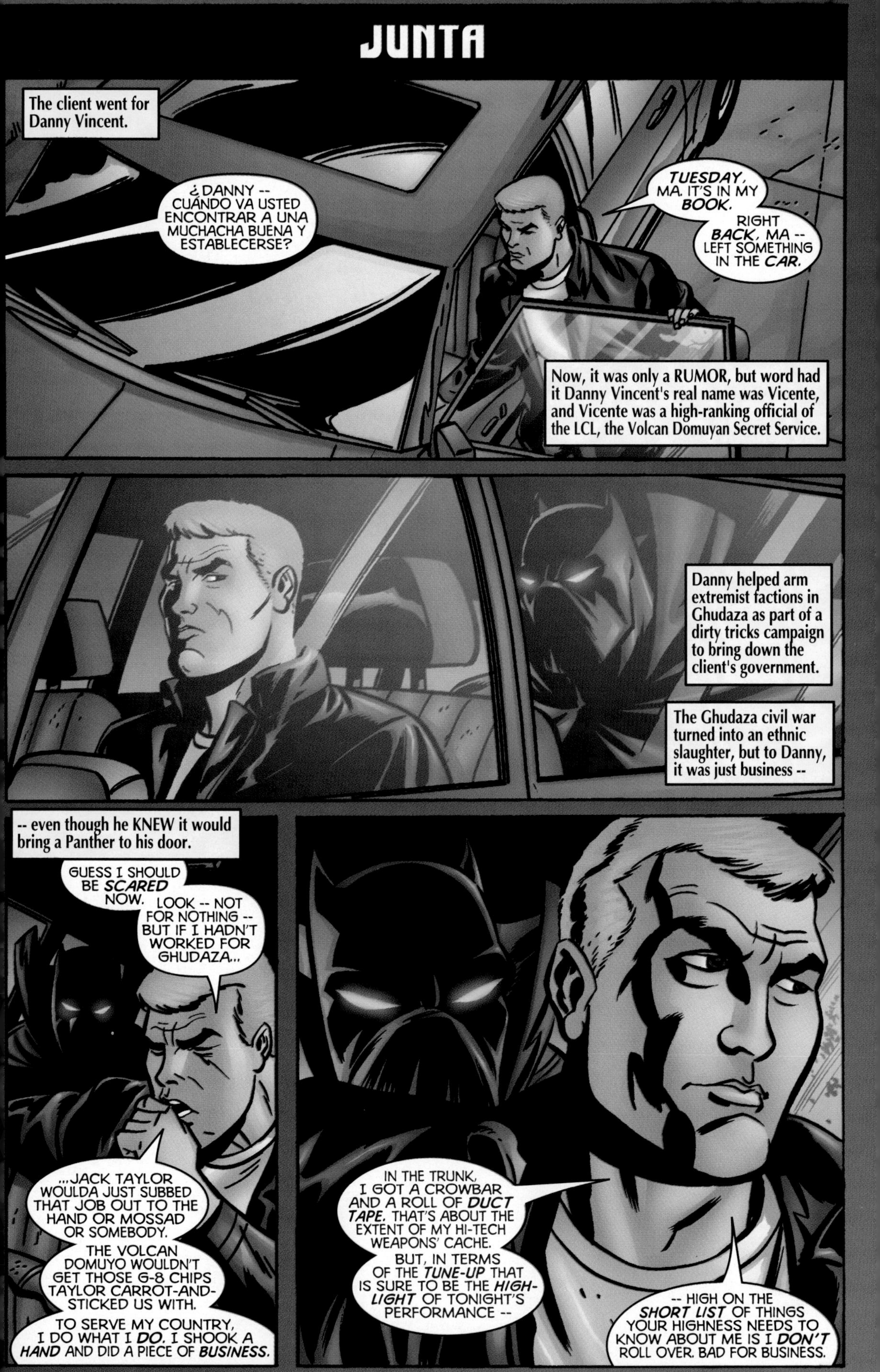

JUNTA
The client went for Danny Vincent.
¿DANNY -- CUÁNDO VA USTED ENCONTRAR A UNA MUCHACHA BUENA Y ESTABLECERSE?
TUESDAY, MA. IT'S IN MY BOOK.
RIGHT BACK, MA -- LEFT SOMETHING IN THE CAR.
Now, it was only a RUMOR, but word had it Danny Vincent's real name was Vicente, and Vicente was a high-ranking official of the LCL, the Volcan Domuyan Secret Service.
Danny helped arm extremist factions in Ghudaza as part of a dirty tricks campaign to bring down the client's government.
The Ghudaza civil war turned into an ethnic slaughter, but to Danny, it was just business --
-- even though he KNEW it would bring a Panther to his door.
GUESS I SHOULD BE SCARED NOW.
LOOK -- NOT FOR NOTHING -- BUT IF I HADN'T WORKED FOR GHUDAZA...
...JACK TAYLOR WOULDA JUST SUBBED THAT JOB OUT TO THE HAND OR MOSSAD OR SOMEBODY.
THE VOLCAN DOMUYO WOULDN'T GET THOSE G-8 CHIPS TAYLOR CARROT-AND-STICKED US WITH.
TO SERVE MY COUNTRY, I DO WHAT I DO. I SHOOK A HAND AND DID A PIECE OF BUSINESS.
IN THE TRUNK, I GOT A CROWBAR AND A ROLL OF DUCT TAPE. THAT'S ABOUT THE EXTENT OF MY HI-TECH WEAPONS' CACHE.
BUT, IN TERMS OF THE TUNE-UP THAT IS SURE TO BE THE HIGHLIGHT OF TONIGHT'S PERFORMANCE --
-- HIGH ON THE SHORT LIST OF THINGS YOUR HIGHNESS NEEDS TO KNOW ABOUT ME IS I DON'T ROLL OVER. BAD FOR BUSINESS.

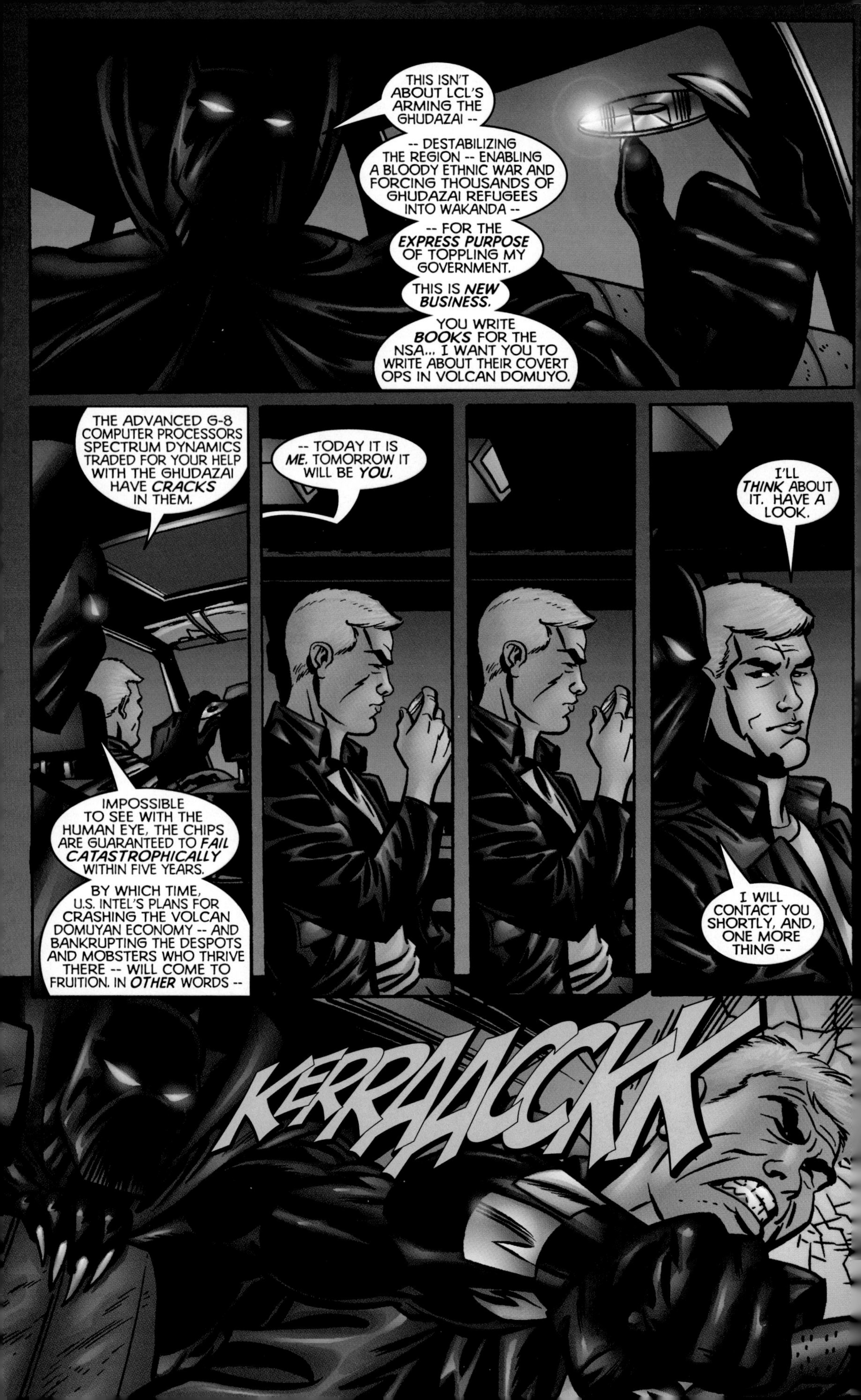

THIS ISN'T ABOUT LCL'S ARMING THE GHUDAZAI --
-- DESTABILIZING THE REGION -- ENABLING A BLOODY ETHNIC WAR AND FORCING THOUSANDS OF GHUDAZAI REFUGEES INTO WAKANDA --
-- FOR THE *EXPRESS PURPOSE* OF TOPPLING MY GOVERNMENT.
THIS IS ***NEW BUSINESS.***
YOU WRITE ***BOOKS*** FOR THE NSA... I WANT YOU TO WRITE ABOUT THEIR COVERT OPS IN VOLCAN DOMUYO.
THE ADVANCED G-8 COMPUTER PROCESSORS SPECTRUM DYNAMICS TRADED FOR YOUR HELP WITH THE GHUDAZAI HAVE ***CRACKS*** IN THEM.
IMPOSSIBLE TO SEE WITH THE HUMAN EYE, THE CHIPS ARE GUARANTEED TO ***FAIL CATASTROPHICALLY*** WITHIN FIVE YEARS.
BY WHICH TIME, U.S. INTEL'S PLANS FOR CRASHING THE VOLCAN DOMUYAN ECONOMY -- AND BANKRUPTING THE DESPOTS AND MOBSTERS WHO THRIVE THERE -- WILL COME TO FRUITION. IN ***OTHER*** WORDS --
-- TODAY IT IS ***ME.*** TOMORROW IT WILL BE ***YOU.***
I'LL ***THINK*** ABOUT IT. HAVE A LOOK.
I WILL CONTACT YOU SHORTLY, AND, ONE MORE THING --
KERRAACCKK

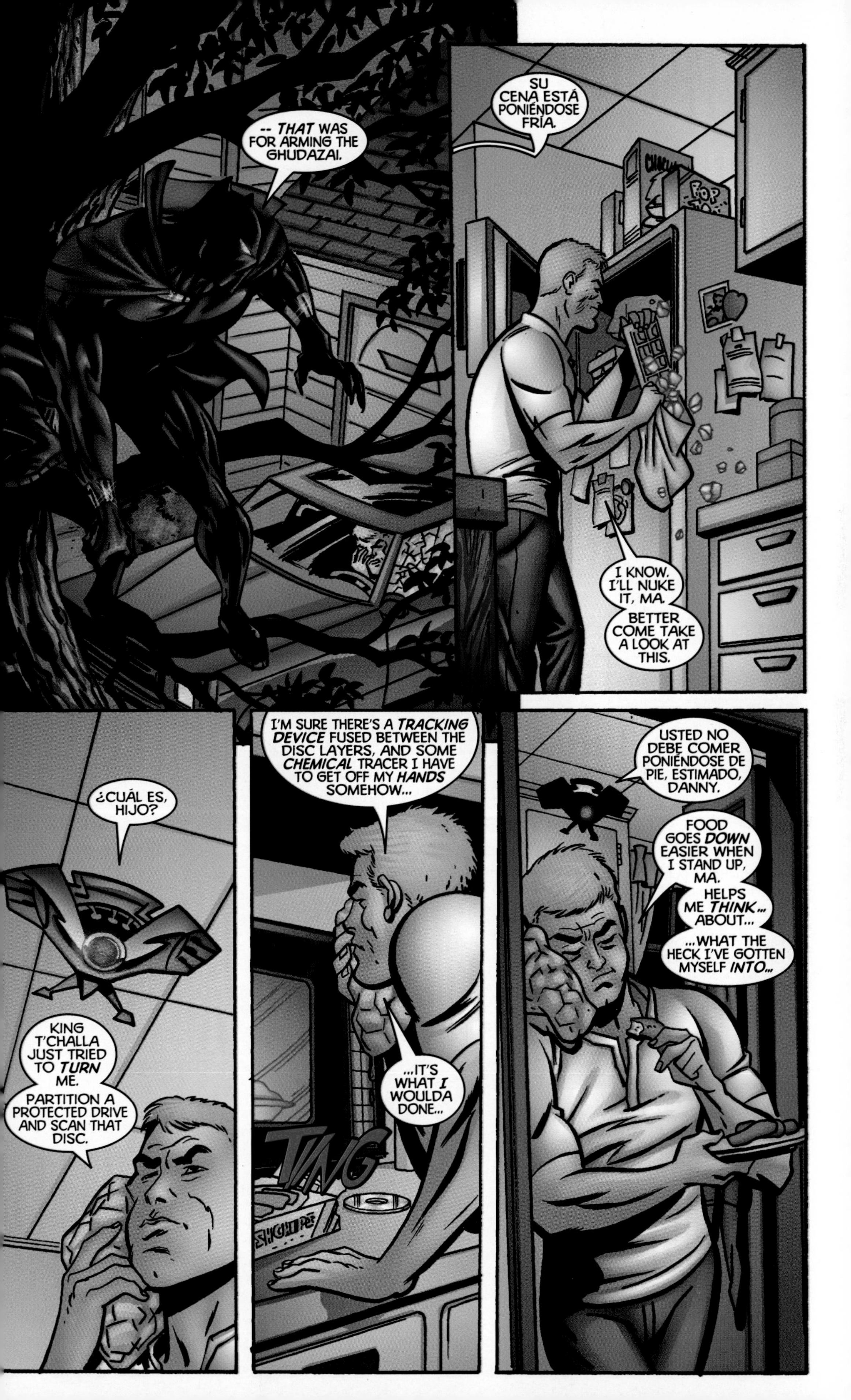
-- *THAT* WAS FOR ARMING THE GHUDAZAI.
SU CENA ESTÁ PONIÉNDOSE FRÍA.
I KNOW. I'LL NUKE IT, MA.
BETTER COME TAKE A LOOK AT THIS.
¿CUÁL ES, HIJO?
KING T'CHALLA JUST TRIED TO *TURN* ME.
PARTITION A PROTECTED DRIVE AND SCAN THAT DISC.
I'M SURE THERE'S A *TRACKING DEVICE* FUSED BETWEEN THE DISC LAYERS, AND SOME *CHEMICAL* TRACER I HAVE TO GET OFF MY *HANDS* SOMEHOW...
...IT'S WHAT *I* WOULDA DONE...
TING
USTED NO DEBE COMER PONIÉNDOSE DE PIE, ESTIMADO, DANNY.
FOOD GOES *DOWN* EASIER WHEN I STAND UP, MA.
HELPS ME *THINK*... ABOUT...
...WHAT THE HECK I'VE GOTTEN MYSELF *INTO*...

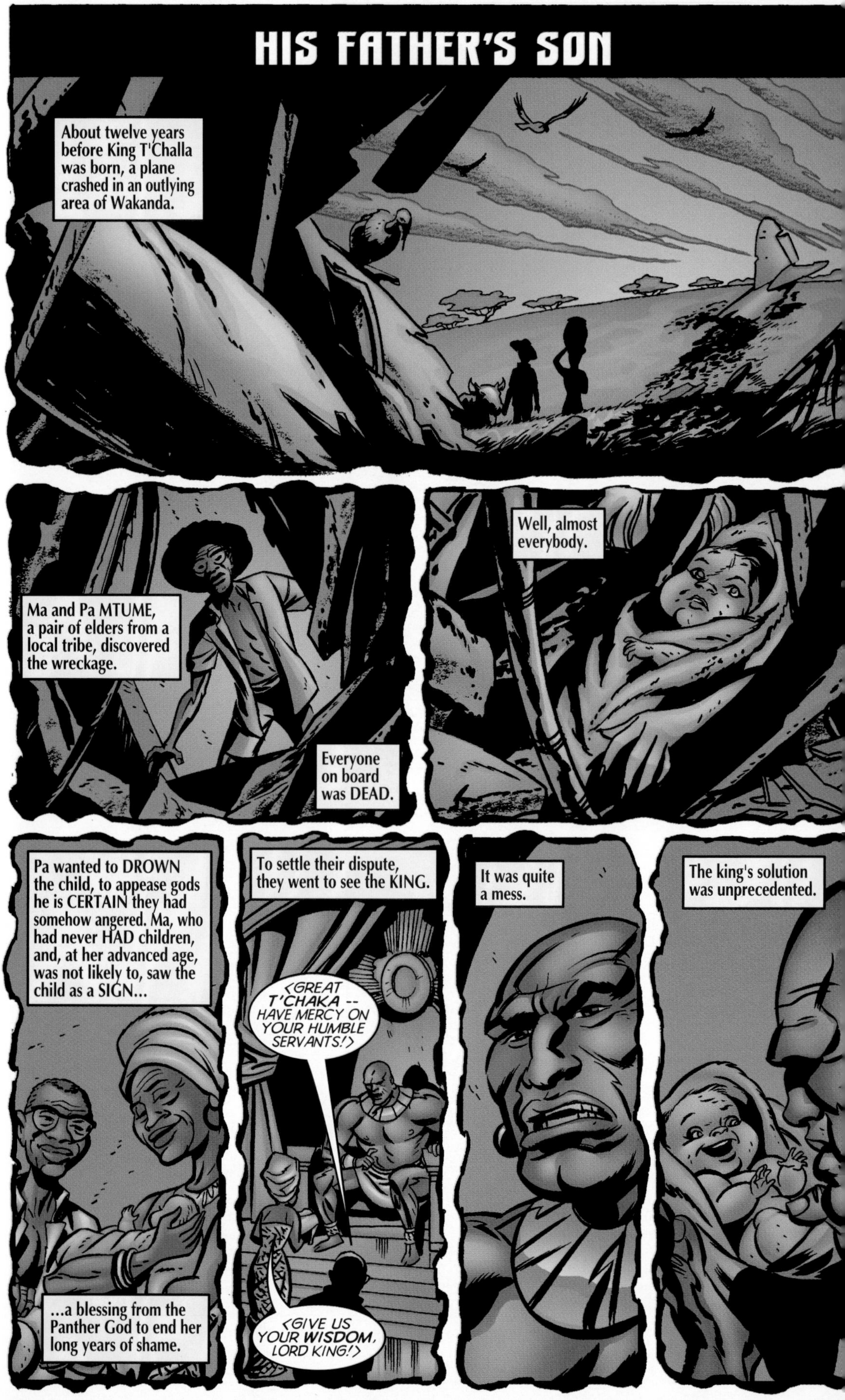
HIS FATHER'S SON
About twelve years before King T'Challa was born, a plane crashed in an outlying area of Wakanda.
Ma and Pa MTUME, a pair of elders from a local tribe, discovered the wreckage.
Everyone on board was DEAD.
Well, almost everybody.
Pa wanted to DROWN the child, to appease gods he is CERTAIN they had somehow angered. Ma, who had never HAD children, and, at her advanced age, was not likely to, saw the child as a SIGN...
...a blessing from the Panther God to end her long years of shame.
To settle their dispute, they went to see the KING.
<GREAT T'CHAKA -- HAVE MERCY ON YOUR HUMBLE SERVANTS!>
<GIVE US YOUR WISDOM, LORD KING!>
It was quite a mess.
The king's solution was unprecedented.

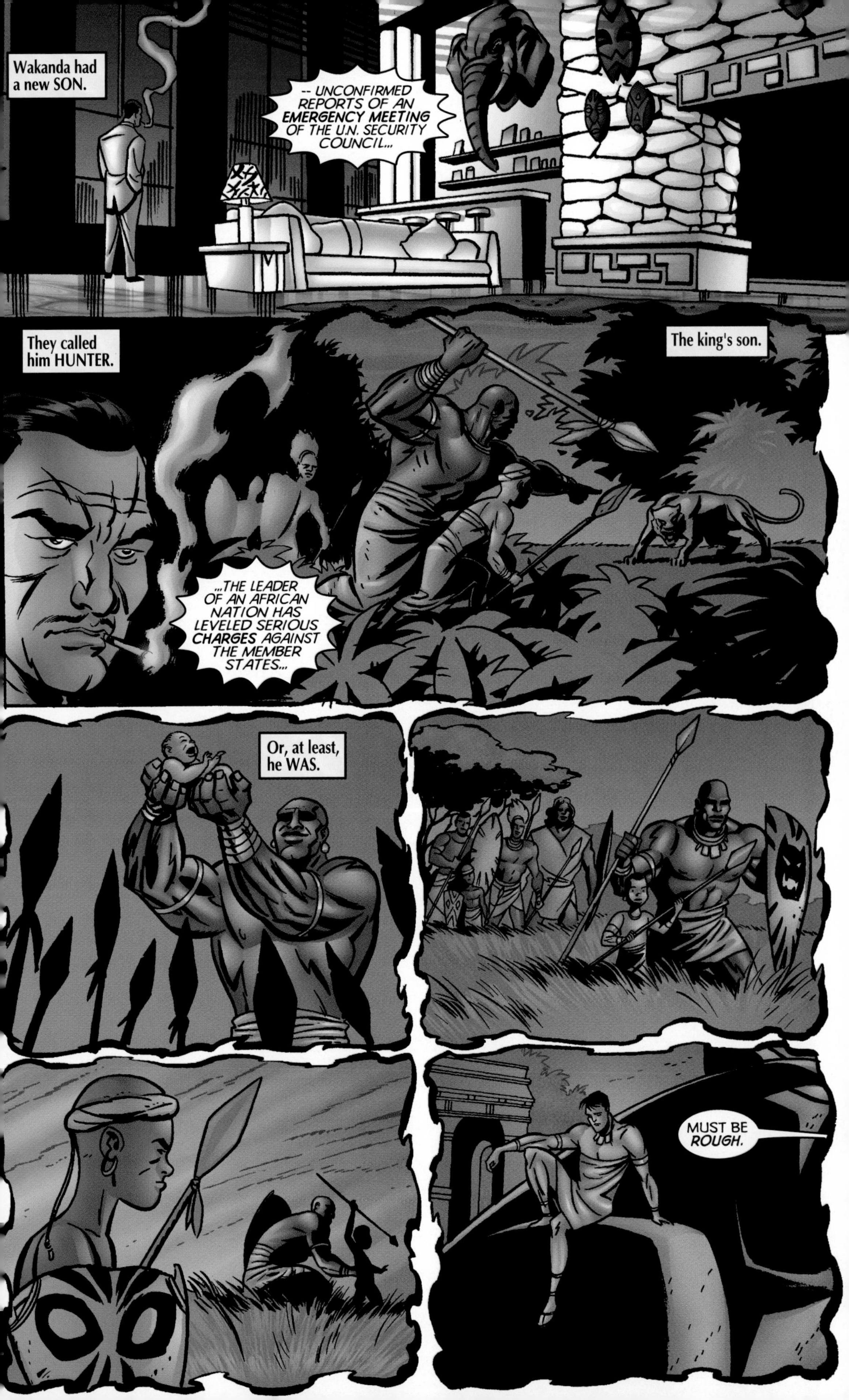
Wakanda had a new SON.
-- UNCONFIRMED REPORTS OF AN EMERGENCY MEETING OF THE U.N. SECURITY COUNCIL...
They called him HUNTER.
The king's son.
...THE LEADER OF AN AFRICAN NATION HAS LEVELED SERIOUS CHARGES AGAINST THE MEMBER STATES...
Or, at least, he WAS.
MUST BE ROUGH.

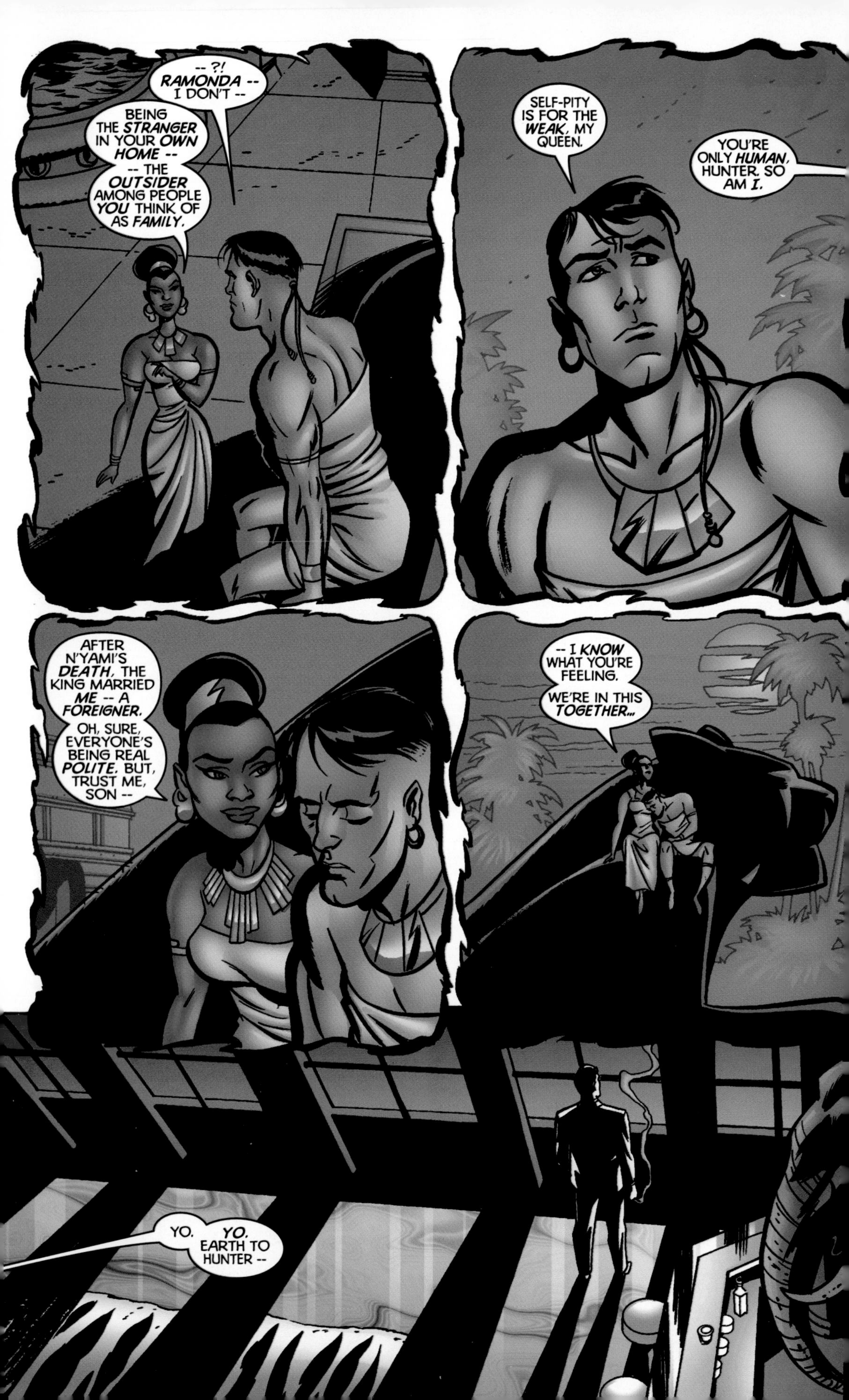
-- ?! RAMONDA -- I DON'T --
BEING THE STRANGER IN YOUR OWN HOME --
-- THE OUTSIDER AMONG PEOPLE YOU THINK OF AS FAMILY.
SELF-PITY IS FOR THE WEAK, MY QUEEN.
YOU'RE ONLY HUMAN, HUNTER. SO AM I.
AFTER N'YAMI'S DEATH, THE KING MARRIED ME -- A FOREIGNER.
OH, SURE, EVERYONE'S BEING REAL POLITE. BUT, TRUST ME, SON --
-- I KNOW WHAT YOU'RE FEELING.
WE'RE IN THIS TOGETHER...
YO. YO. EARTH TO HUNTER --

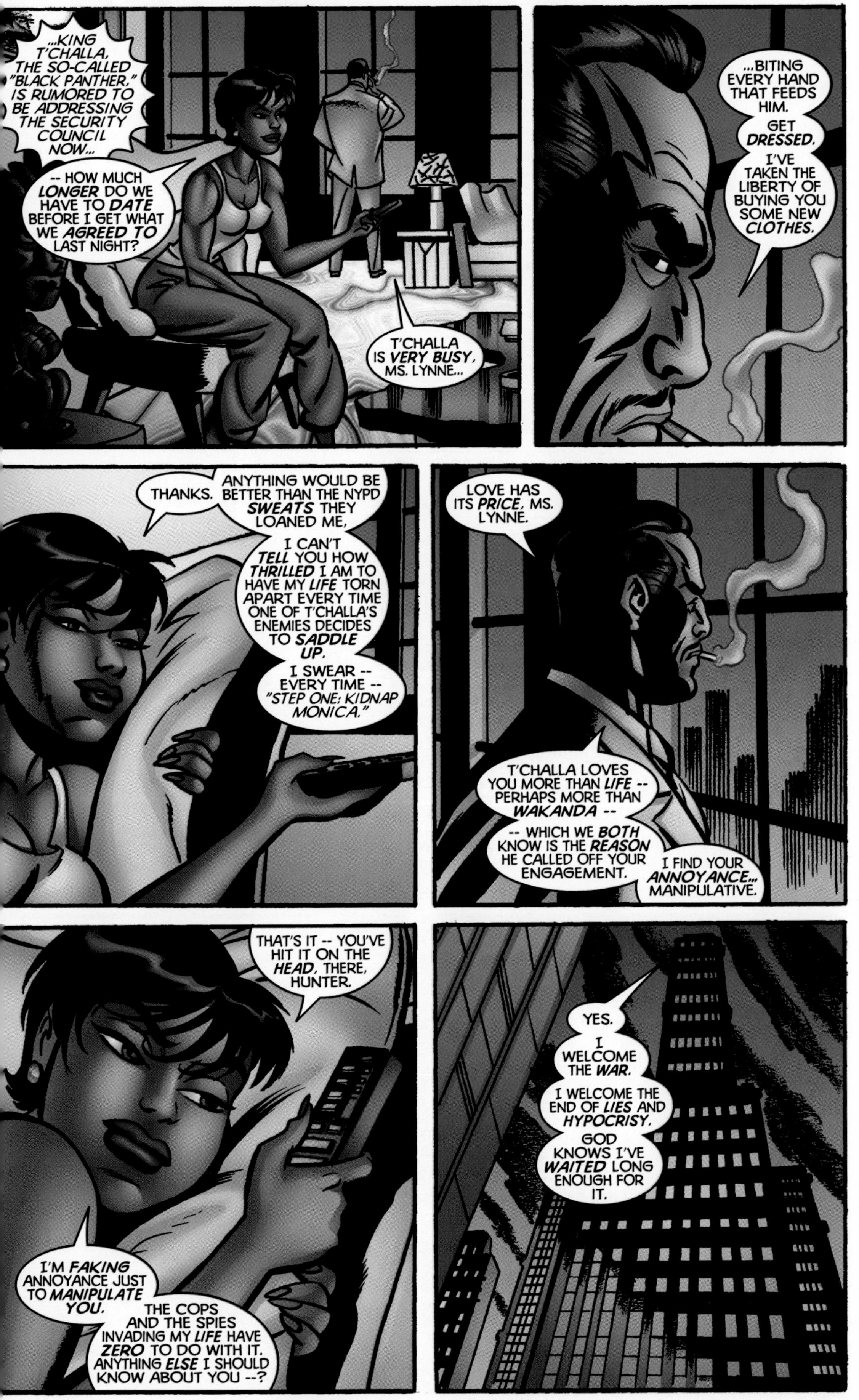
...KING T'CHALLA, THE SO-CALLED "BLACK PANTHER," IS RUMORED TO BE ADDRESSING THE SECURITY COUNCIL NOW...
-- HOW MUCH LONGER DO WE HAVE TO DATE BEFORE I GET WHAT WE AGREED TO LAST NIGHT?
T'CHALLA IS VERY BUSY, MS. LYNNE...
...BITING EVERY HAND THAT FEEDS HIM.
GET DRESSED.
I'VE TAKEN THE LIBERTY OF BUYING YOU SOME NEW CLOTHES.
THANKS.
ANYTHING WOULD BE BETTER THAN THE NYPD SWEATS THEY LOANED ME,
I CAN'T TELL YOU HOW THRILLED I AM TO HAVE MY LIFE TORN APART EVERY TIME ONE OF T'CHALLA'S ENEMIES DECIDES TO SADDLE UP.
I SWEAR -- EVERY TIME -- "STEP ONE: KIDNAP MONICA."
LOVE HAS ITS PRICE, MS. LYNNE.
T'CHALLA LOVES YOU MORE THAN LIFE -- PERHAPS MORE THAN WAKANDA --
-- WHICH WE BOTH KNOW IS THE REASON HE CALLED OFF YOUR ENGAGEMENT.
I FIND YOUR ANNOYANCE... MANIPULATIVE.
THAT'S IT -- YOU'VE HIT IT ON THE HEAD, THERE, HUNTER.
I'M FAKING ANNOYANCE JUST TO MANIPULATE YOU.
THE COPS AND THE SPIES INVADING MY LIFE HAVE ZERO TO DO WITH IT. ANYTHING ELSE I SHOULD KNOW ABOUT YOU --?
YES.
I WELCOME THE WAR.
I WELCOME THE END OF LIES AND HYPOCRISY.
GOD KNOWS I'VE WAITED LONG ENOUGH FOR IT.

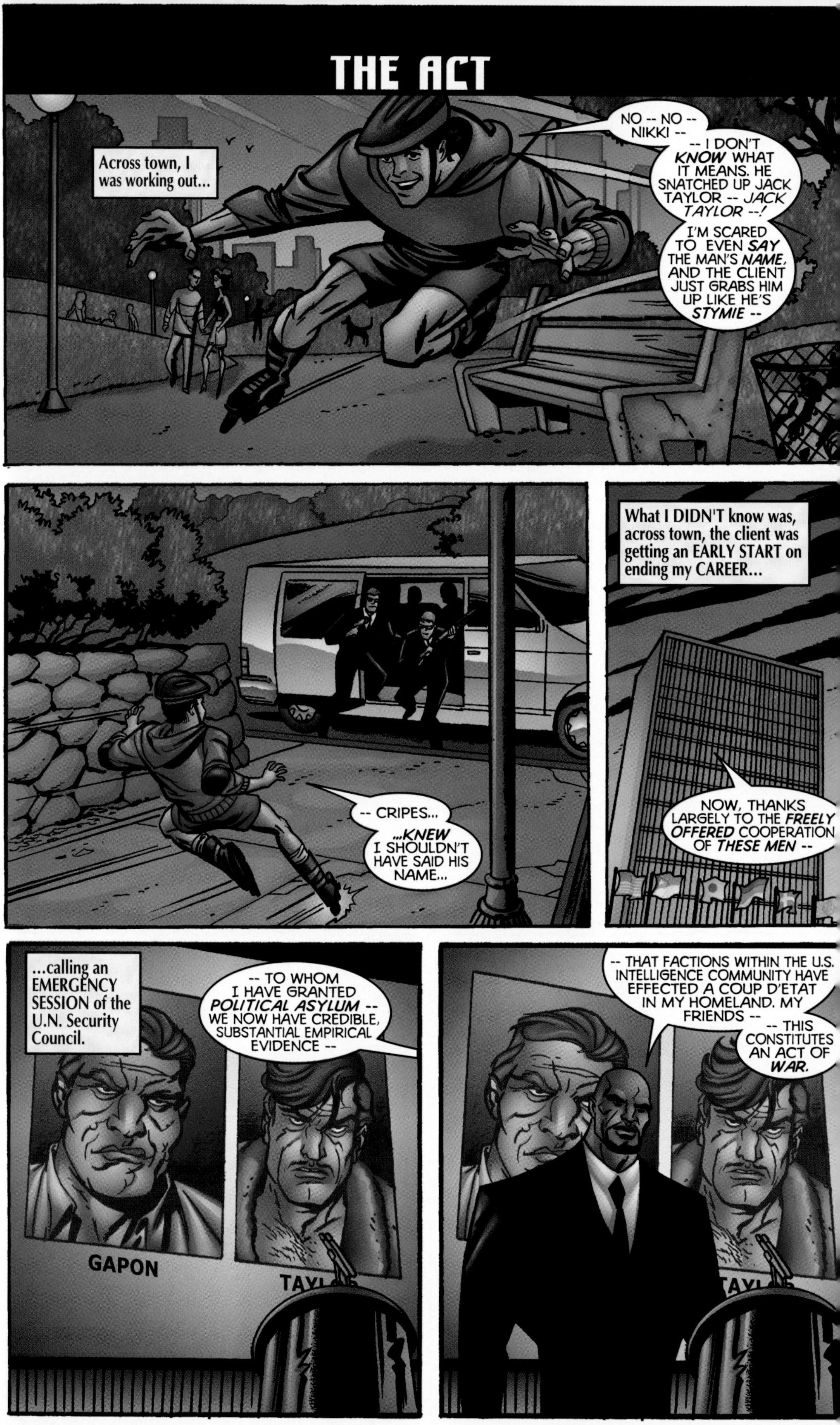
THE ACT
Across town, I was working out...
NO -- NO -- NIKKI --
-- I DON'T KNOW WHAT IT MEANS. HE SNATCHED UP JACK TAYLOR -- JACK TAYLOR --!
I'M SCARED TO EVEN SAY THE MAN'S NAME, AND THE CLIENT JUST GRABS HIM UP LIKE HE'S STYMIE --
-- CRIPES...
...KNEW I SHOULDN'T HAVE SAID HIS NAME...
What I DIDN'T know was, across town, the client was getting an EARLY START on ending my CAREER...
NOW, THANKS LARGELY TO THE FREELY OFFERED COOPERATION OF THESE MEN --
...calling an EMERGENCY SESSION of the U.N. Security Council.
-- TO WHOM I HAVE GRANTED POLITICAL ASYLUM -- WE NOW HAVE CREDIBLE, SUBSTANTIAL EMPIRICAL EVIDENCE --
GAPON
-- THAT FACTIONS WITHIN THE U.S. INTELLIGENCE COMMUNITY HAVE EFFECTED A COUP D'ETAT IN MY HOMELAND. MY FRIENDS --
-- THIS CONSTITUTES AN ACT OF WAR.

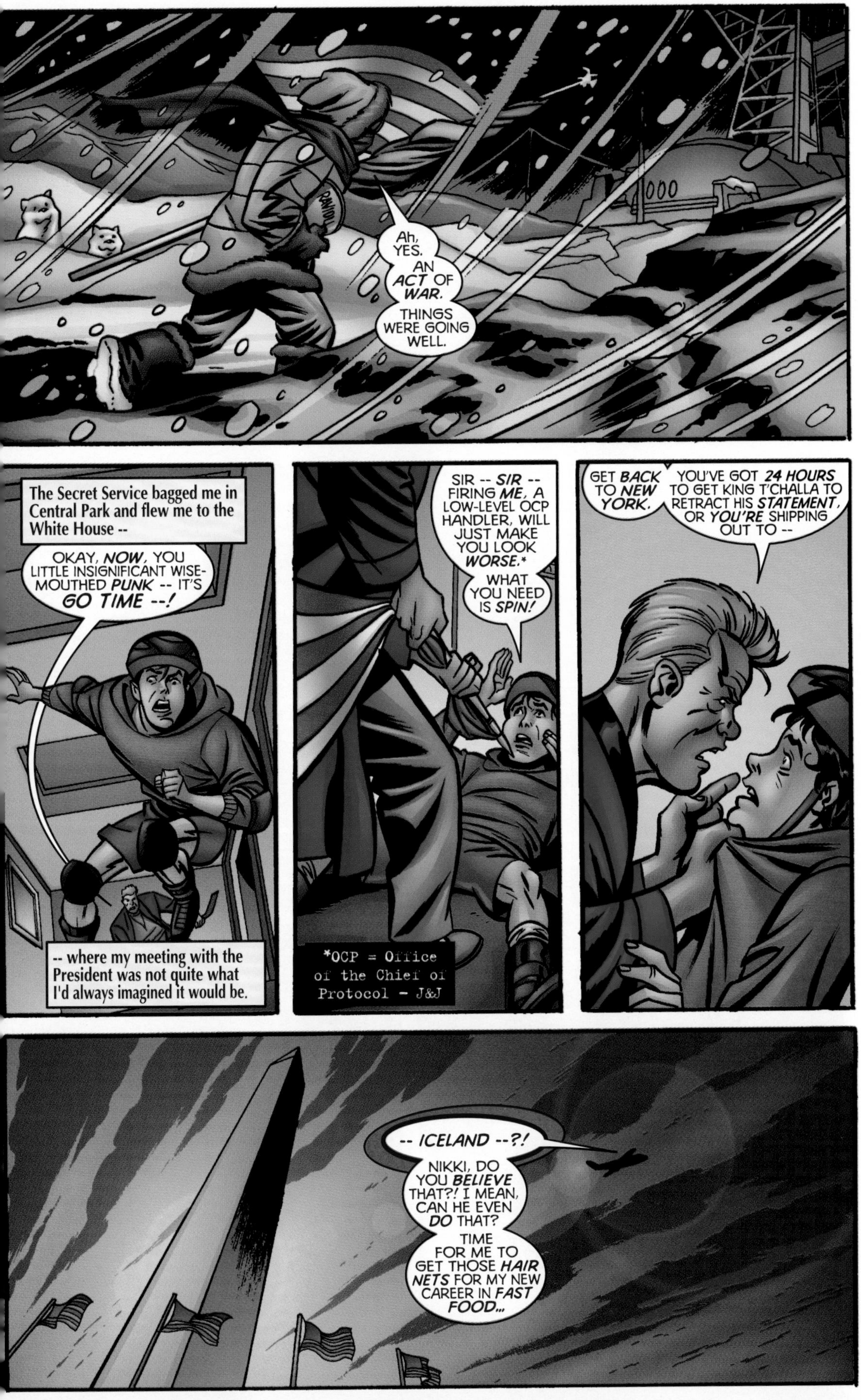
Ah, YES. AN ACT OF WAR.
THINGS WERE GOING WELL.
The Secret Service bagged me in Central Park and flew me to the White House --
OKAY, NOW, YOU LITTLE INSIGNIFICANT WISE-MOUTHED PUNK -- IT'S GO TIME --!
-- where my meeting with the President was not quite what I'd always imagined it would be.
SIR -- SIR -- FIRING ME, A LOW-LEVEL OCP HANDLER, WILL JUST MAKE YOU LOOK WORSE.*
WHAT YOU NEED IS SPIN!
*OCP = Office of the Chief of Protocol - J&J
GET BACK TO NEW YORK.
YOU'VE GOT 24 HOURS TO GET KING T'CHALLA TO RETRACT HIS STATEMENT, OR YOU'RE SHIPPING OUT TO --
-- ICELAND --?!
NIKKI, DO YOU BELIEVE THAT?! I MEAN, CAN HE EVEN DO THAT?
TIME FOR ME TO GET THOSE HAIR NETS FOR MY NEW CAREER IN FAST FOOD...

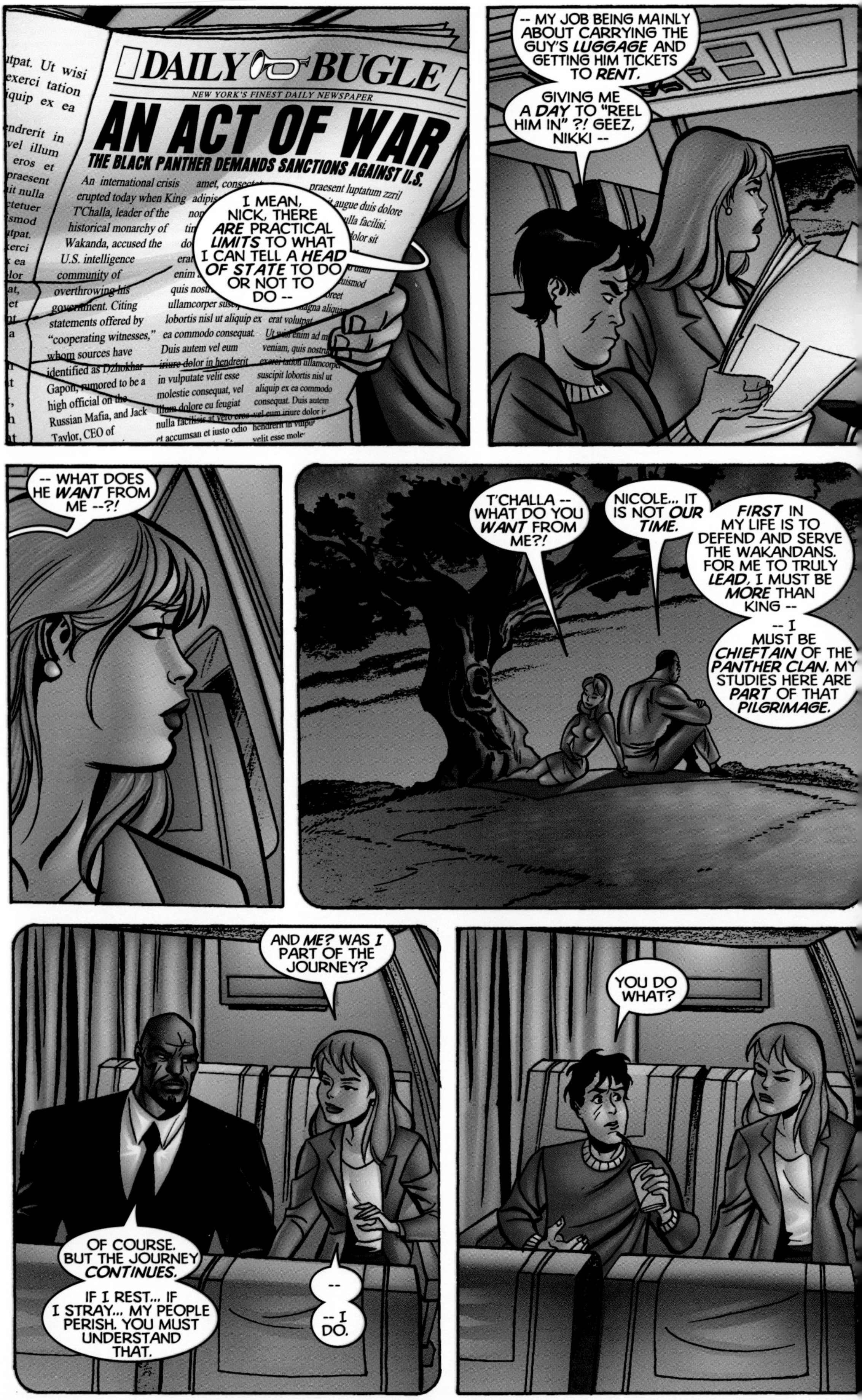
DAILY BUGLE
NEW YORK'S FINEST DAILY NEWSPAPER
AN ACT OF WAR
THE BLACK PANTHER DEMANDS SANCTIONS AGAINST U.S.
An international crisis erupted today when King T'Challa, leader of the historical monarchy of Wakanda, accused the U.S. intelligence community of overthrowing his government. Citing statements offered by "cooperating witnesses," whom sources have identified as Dzhokhar Gapon, rumored to be a high official on the Russian Mafia, and Jack Taylor, CEO of
I MEAN, NICK, THERE *ARE* PRACTICAL *LIMITS* TO WHAT I CAN TELL A *HEAD OF STATE* TO DO OR NOT TO DO --
-- MY JOB BEING MAINLY ABOUT CARRYING THE GUY'S *LUGGAGE* AND GETTING HIM TICKETS TO *RENT.*
GIVING ME A *DAY* TO "REEL HIM IN" ?! GEEZ, NIKKI --
-- WHAT DOES HE *WANT* FROM ME --?!
T'CHALLA -- WHAT DO YOU *WANT* FROM ME?!
NICOLE... IT IS NOT *OUR TIME.*
FIRST IN MY LIFE IS TO DEFEND AND SERVE THE WAKANDANS. FOR ME TO TRULY *LEAD,* I MUST BE *MORE* THAN KING --
-- I MUST BE *CHIEFTAIN* OF THE *PANTHER CLAN.* MY STUDIES HERE ARE *PART* OF THAT *PILGRIMAGE.*
AND *ME?* WAS *I* PART OF THE JOURNEY?
OF COURSE. BUT THE JOURNEY *CONTINUES.*
IF I REST... IF I STRAY... MY PEOPLE PERISH. YOU MUST UNDERSTAND THAT.
--
-- I DO.
YOU DO WHAT?

ARE YOU EVEN *LISTENING* TO ME?

LOOK -- I THINK *YOU* NEED TO RUN WITH THE BALL FOR AWHILE.

TOSS ME WHATEVER'S ON YOUR DESK AND *YOU* HANDLE KING T'CHALLA.

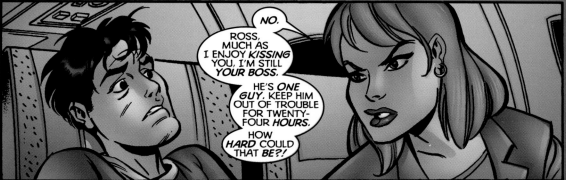

NO.

ROSS, MUCH AS I ENJOY *KISSING* YOU, I'M STILL *YOUR BOSS.*

HE'S *ONE GUY.* KEEP HIM OUT OF TROUBLE FOR TWENTY-FOUR *HOURS.*

HOW *HARD* COULD THAT *BE?!*

LESS THAN AN HOUR LATER

YYYEEEEAAAAHHH!

BOOM BOOM BOOOM

SEVENTEEN HOURS AFTER THAT

-- WHICH, OF COURSE, BROUGHT ME *HERE.*

BUT, I'M GETTING *AHEAD* OF MYSELF AGAIN.

STAY WITH ME... THIS GETS A LITTLE COMPLICATED...

BRAAAATATATATATATAT

WHITE GUYS

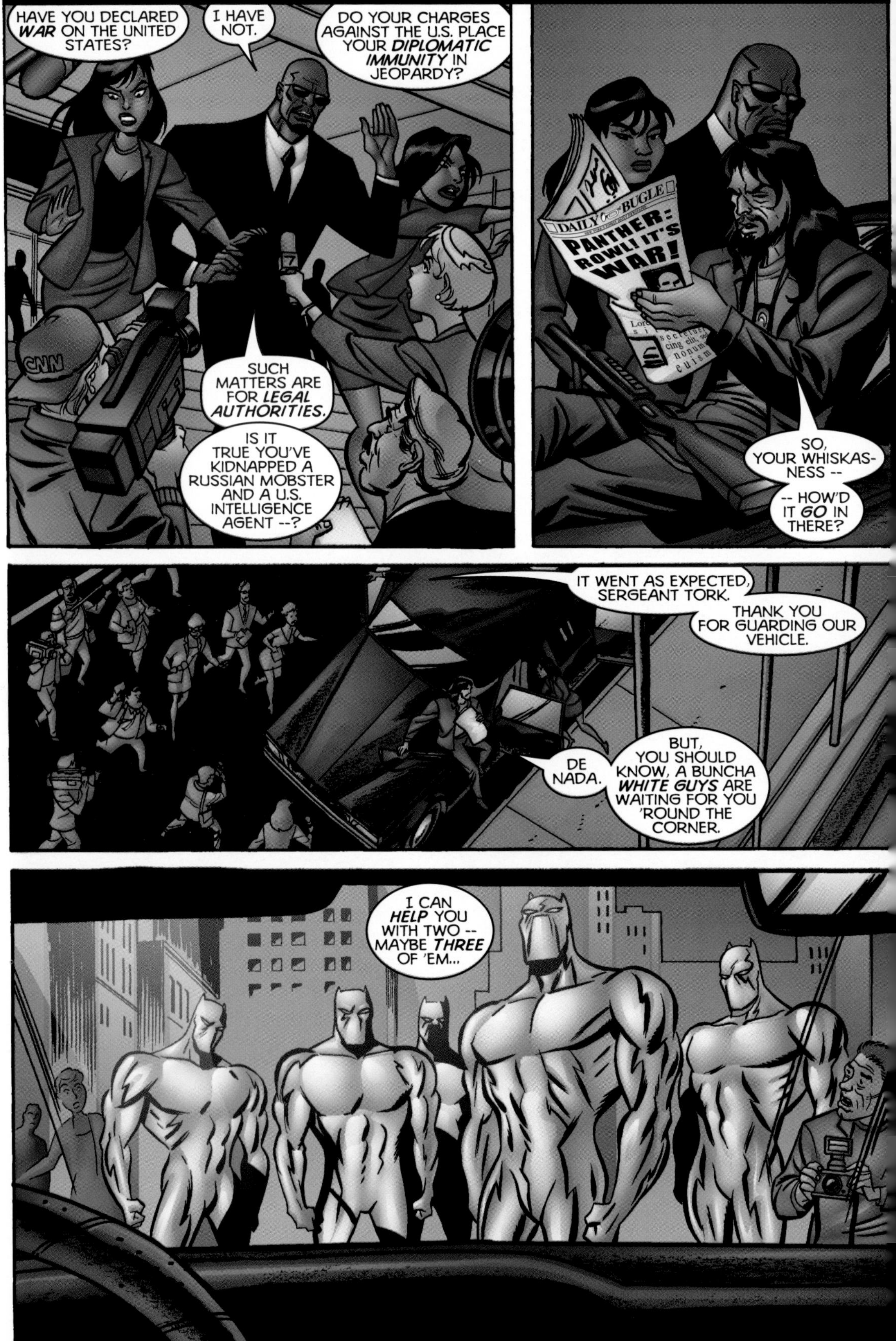
HAVE YOU DECLARED WAR ON THE UNITED STATES?
I HAVE NOT.
DO YOUR CHARGES AGAINST THE U.S. PLACE YOUR DIPLOMATIC IMMUNITY IN JEOPARDY?
SUCH MATTERS ARE FOR LEGAL AUTHORITIES.
IS IT TRUE YOU'VE KIDNAPPED A RUSSIAN MOBSTER AND A U.S. INTELLIGENCE AGENT --?
CNN
DAILY BUGLE
PANTHER: ROWL! IT'S WAR!
SO, YOUR WHISKAS-NESS --
-- HOW'D IT GO IN THERE?
IT WENT AS EXPECTED, SERGEANT TORK.
THANK YOU FOR GUARDING OUR VEHICLE.
DE NADA.
BUT, YOU SHOULD KNOW, A BUNCHA WHITE GUYS ARE WAITING FOR YOU 'ROUND THE CORNER.
I CAN HELP YOU WITH TWO -- MAYBE THREE OF 'EM...

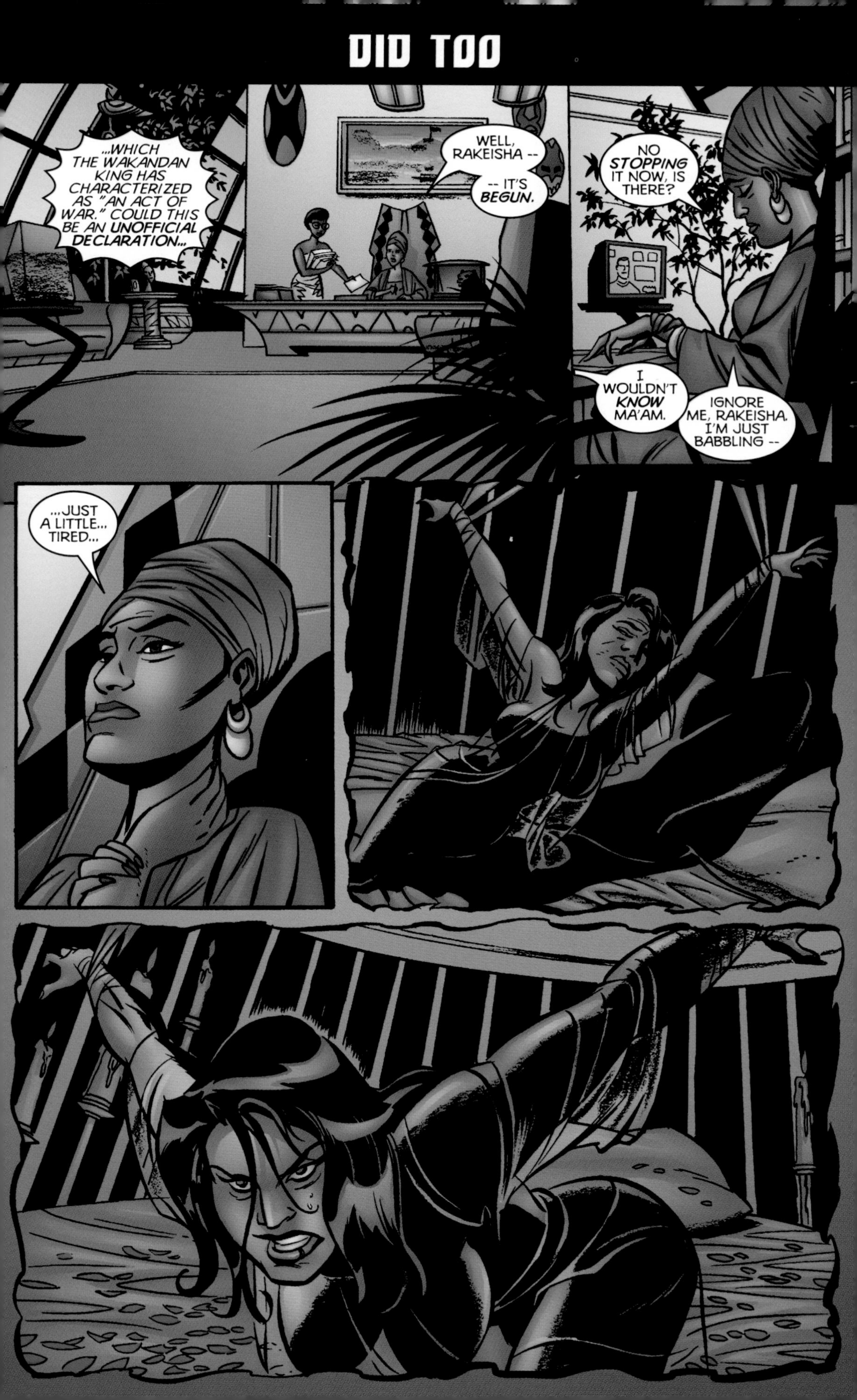
DID TOO
...WHICH THE WAKANDAN KING HAS CHARACTERIZED AS "AN ACT OF WAR." COULD THIS BE AN UNOFFICIAL DECLARATION...
WELL, RAKEISHA --
-- IT'S BEGUN.
NO STOPPING IT NOW, IS THERE?
I WOULDN'T KNOW MA'AM.
IGNORE ME, RAKEISHA. I'M JUST BABBLING --
...JUST A LITTLE... TIRED...

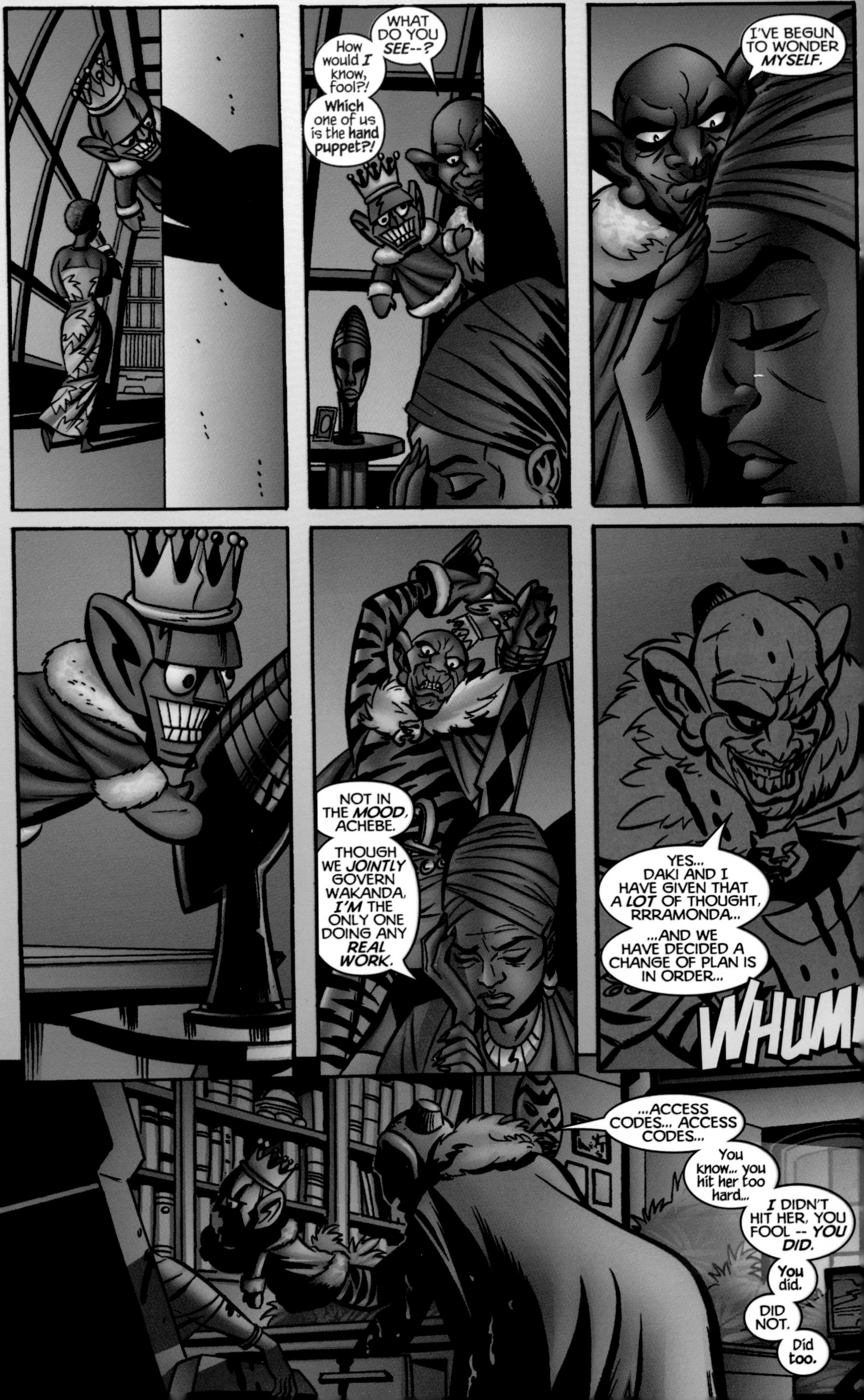
WHAT DO YOU SEE--?
How would I know, fool?!
Which one of us is the hand puppet?!
I'VE BEGUN TO WONDER MYSELF.
NOT IN THE MOOD, ACHEBE.
THOUGH WE JOINTLY GOVERN WAKANDA, I'M THE ONLY ONE DOING ANY REAL WORK.
YES... DAKI AND I HAVE GIVEN THAT A LOT OF THOUGHT, RRRAMONDA...
...AND WE HAVE DECIDED A CHANGE OF PLAN IS IN ORDER...
WHUM
...ACCESS CODES... ACCESS CODES...
You know... you hit her too hard...
I DIDN'T HIT HER, YOU FOOL -- YOU DID.
You did.
DID NOT.
Did too.

THE HOCKEY PUCK

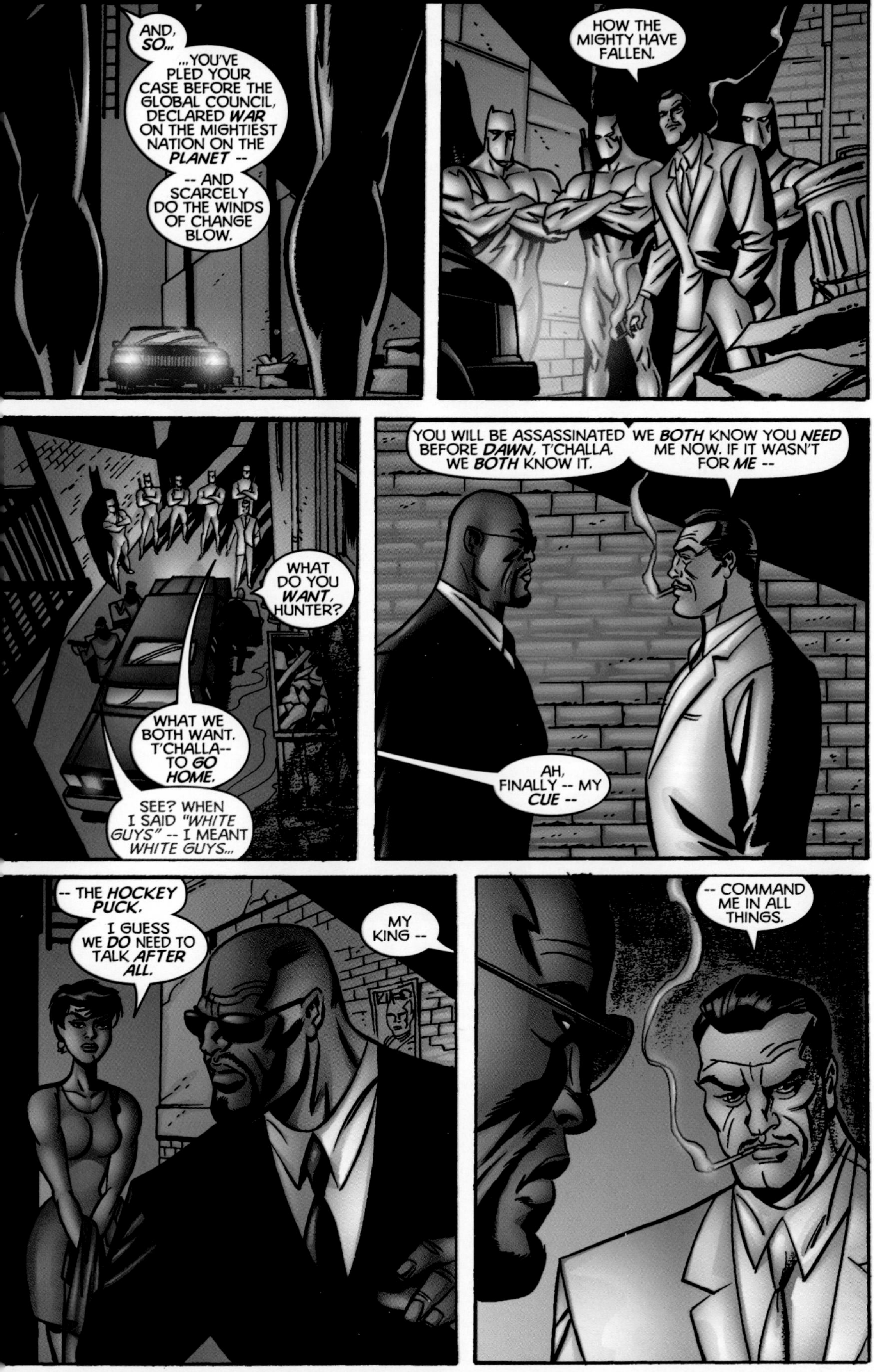
AND, SO...
...YOU'VE PLED YOUR CASE BEFORE THE GLOBAL COUNCIL, DECLARED WAR ON THE MIGHTIEST NATION ON THE PLANET --
-- AND SCARCELY DO THE WINDS OF CHANGE BLOW.
HOW THE MIGHTY HAVE FALLEN.
WHAT DO YOU WANT, HUNTER?
WHAT WE BOTH WANT. T'CHALLA-- TO GO HOME.
SEE? WHEN I SAID "WHITE GUYS" -- I MEANT WHITE GUYS...
YOU WILL BE ASSASSINATED BEFORE DAWN, T'CHALLA. WE BOTH KNOW IT.
WE BOTH KNOW YOU NEED ME NOW. IF IT WASN'T FOR ME --
AH, FINALLY -- MY CUE --
-- THE HOCKEY PUCK.
I GUESS WE DO NEED TO TALK AFTER ALL.
MY KING --
-- COMMAND ME IN ALL THINGS.

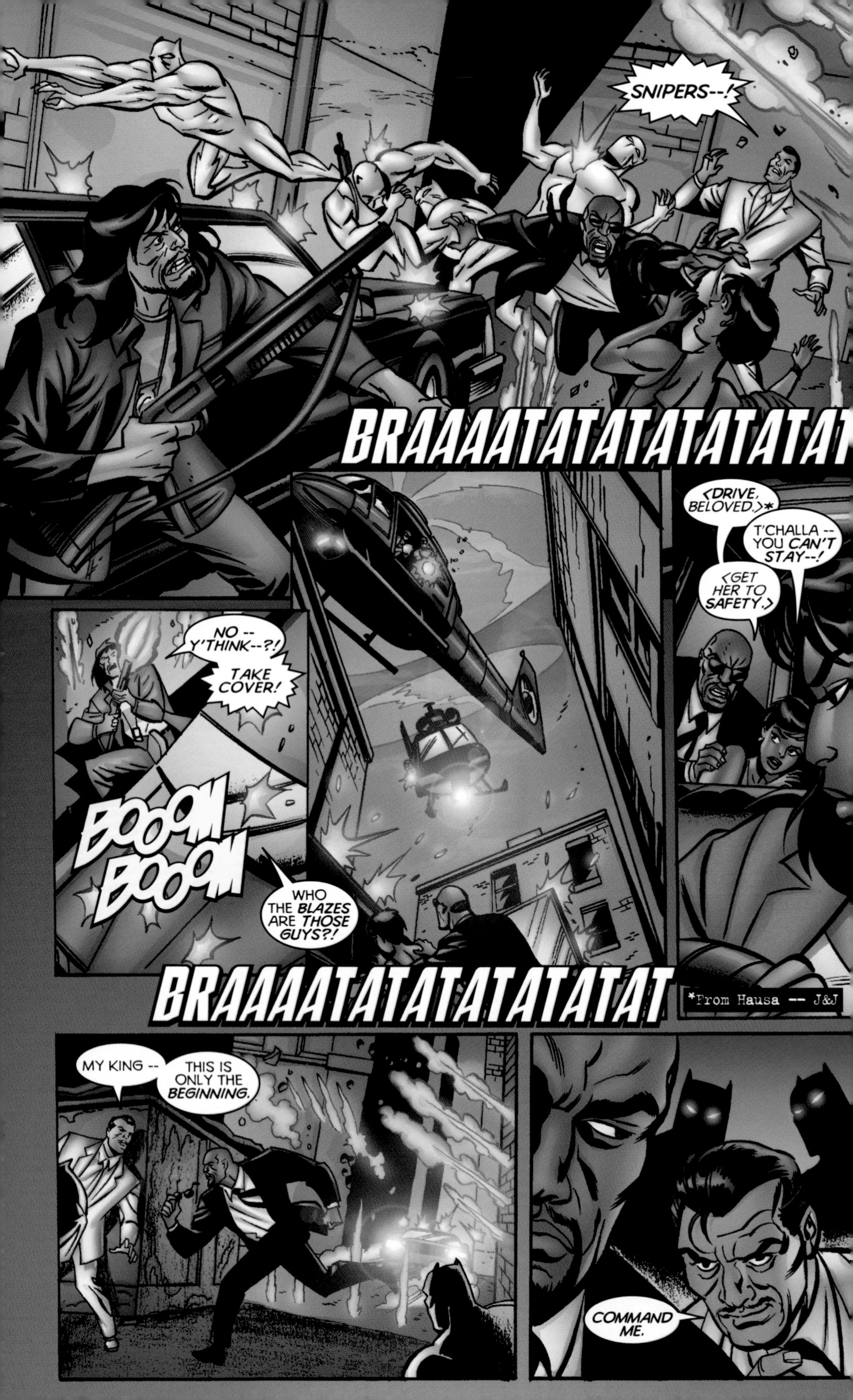
SNIPERS--!
BRAAAATATATATATATAT
<DRIVE, BELOVED.>*
T'CHALLA -- YOU CAN'T STAY--!
<GET HER TO SAFETY.>
NO -- Y'THINK--?!
TAKE COVER!
BOOOM BOOOM
WHO THE BLAZES ARE THOSE GUYS?!
BRAAAATATATATATATAT
*From Hausa -- J&J
MY KING --
THIS IS ONLY THE BEGINNING.
COMMAND ME.

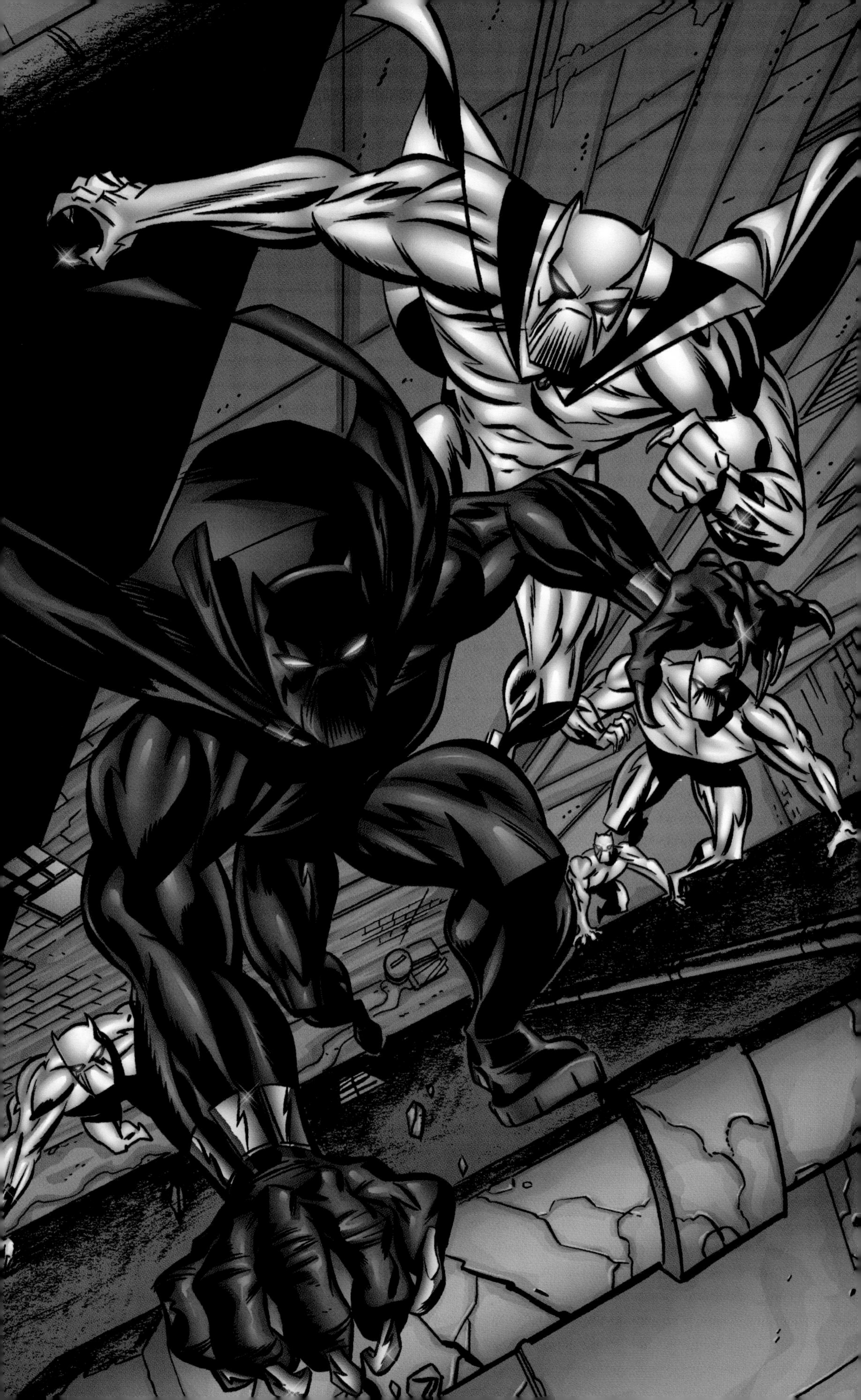

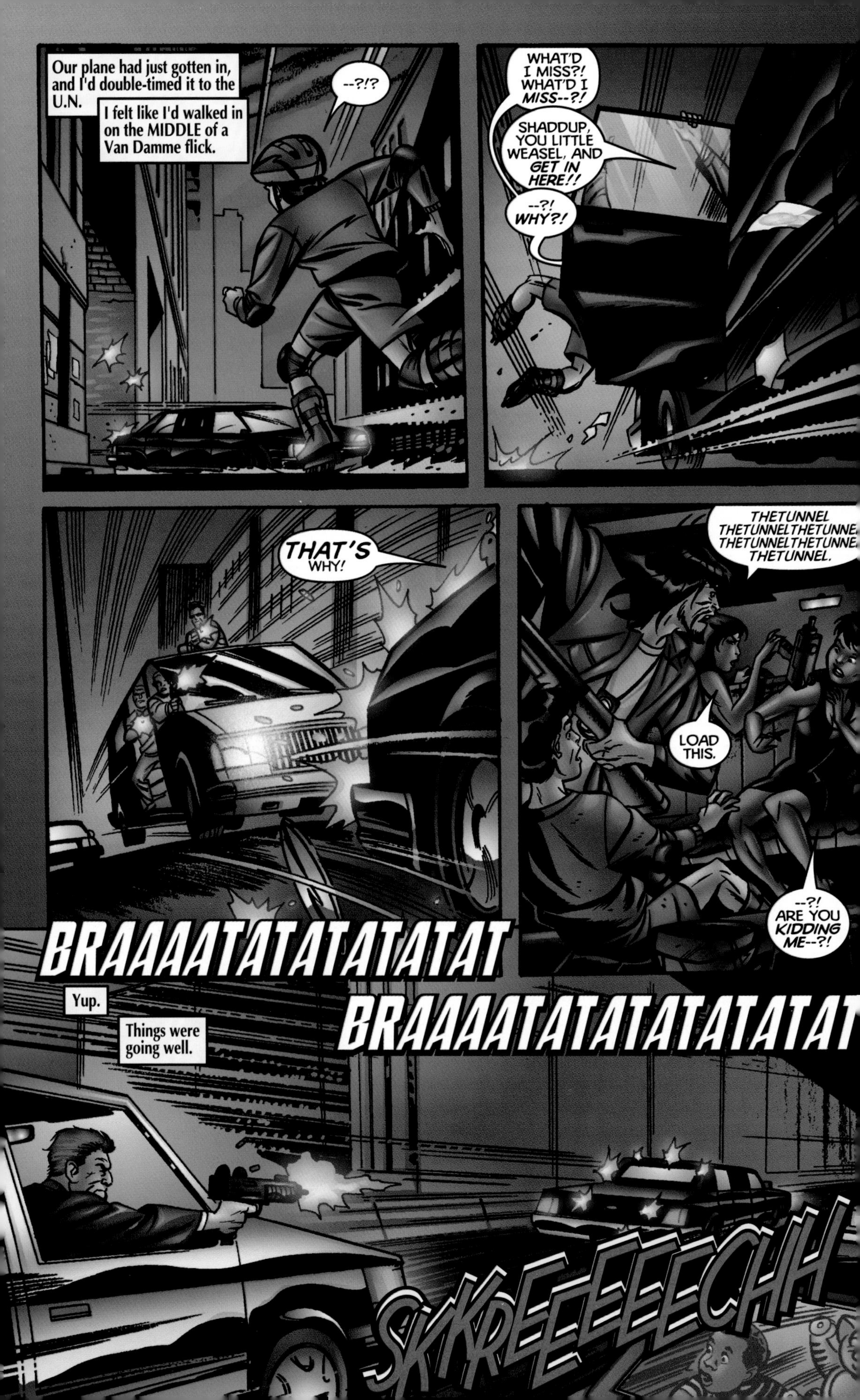

Our plane had just gotten in, and I'd double-timed it to the U.N.
I felt like I'd walked in on the MIDDLE of a Van Damme flick.
--?!?
WHAT'D I MISS?! WHAT'D I MISS--?!
SHADDUP, YOU LITTLE WEASEL, AND GET IN HERE!!
--?! WHY?!
THAT'S WHY!
THETUNNEL THETUNNELTHETUNNE THETUNNELTHETUNNE THETUNNEL.
LOAD THIS.
--?! ARE YOU KIDDING ME--?!
BRAAAATATATATATAT
Yup.
BRAAAATATATATATATAT
Things were going well.
SKKREEEEEECHH

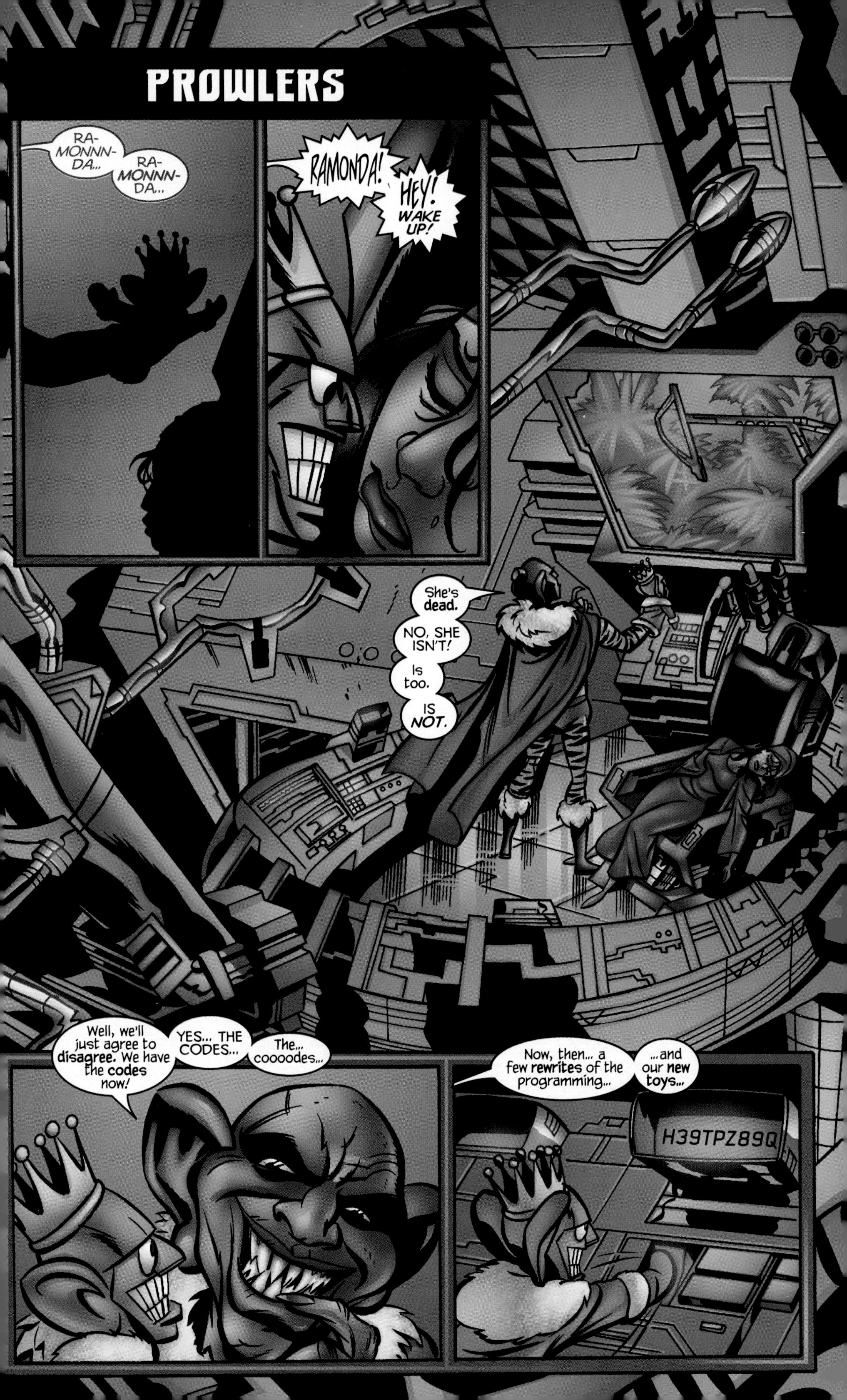
PROWLERS
RA-MONNN-DA...
RA-MONNN-DA...
RAMONDA!
HEY! WAKE UP!
She's dead.
NO, SHE ISN'T!
Is too.
IS NOT.
Well, we'll just agree to disagree. We have the codes now!
YES... THE CODES...
The... cooooodes...
Now, then... a few rewrites of the programming...
...and our new toys...
H39TPZ89Q

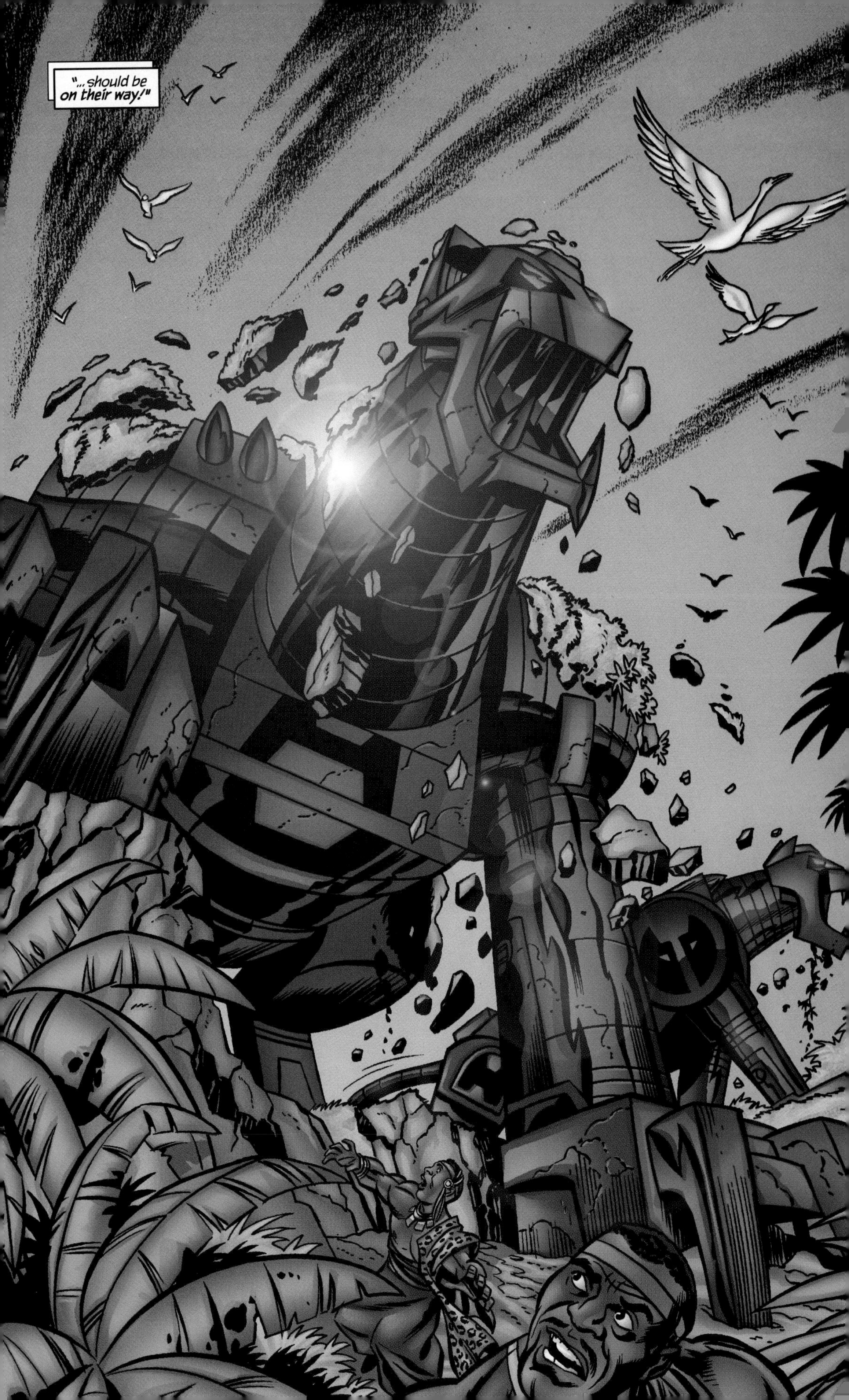
"...should be on their way!"

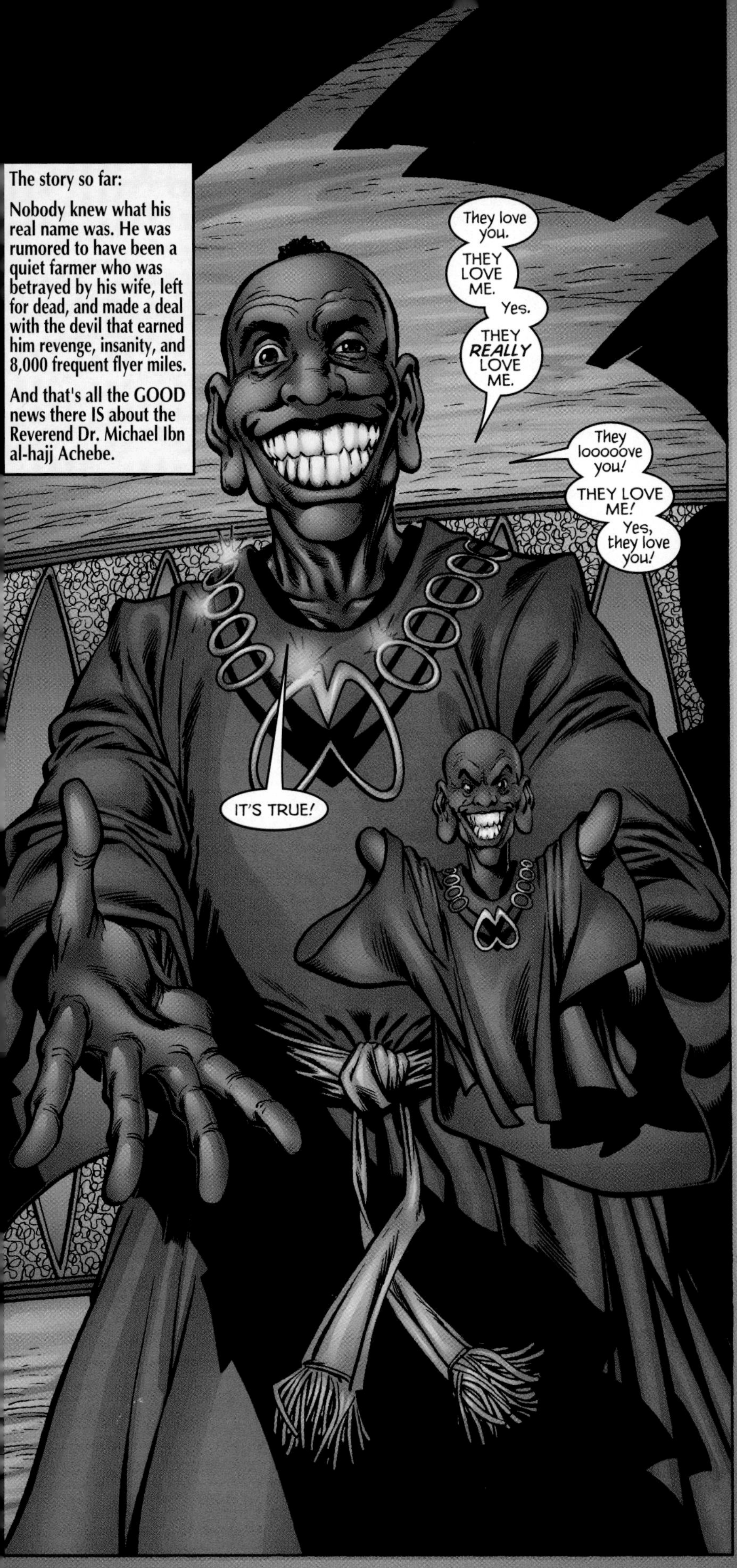
The story so far:
Nobody knew what his real name was. He was rumored to have been a quiet farmer who was betrayed by his wife, left for dead, and made a deal with the devil that earned him revenge, insanity, and 8,000 frequent flyer miles.
And that's all the GOOD news there IS about the Reverend Dr. Michael Ibn al-hajj Achebe.
They love you.
THEY LOVE ME.
Yes.
THEY *REALLY* LOVE ME.
They looooove you!
THEY LOVE ME!
Yes, they love you!
IT'S TRUE!

Months before, Achebe had been one of thousands of ragged refugees from a bloody, ethnic war in Ghudaza. A war instigated by Latin American terrorists who were financed by Russian mob money -- all of this courtesy of rogue factions within the U.S. Intelligence community. The idea was to destabilize the region and flood Wakanda -- a remote African nation roughly the size of New Jersey -- with fleeing Ghudazai, the Reverend Achebe chief among them.

And after luring the Wakandan king -- my client -- away from home, the U.S. Intelligence rogues triggered a palace coup, exiling my client to the U.S. and landing the good reverend in the Big Chair. Thing is, Achebe's nutbag-osity, which I'm sure the spooks originally saw as a plus, got amped to the Nth degree after he was forcibly separated from his original benefactor, a guy named Mephisto. *

Add to that the fact my client, the Wakandan king, wasn't nearly as naive as everyone hoped he'd be, and you have the potential for a real mess.

Luckily, Achebe was not one to disappoint.

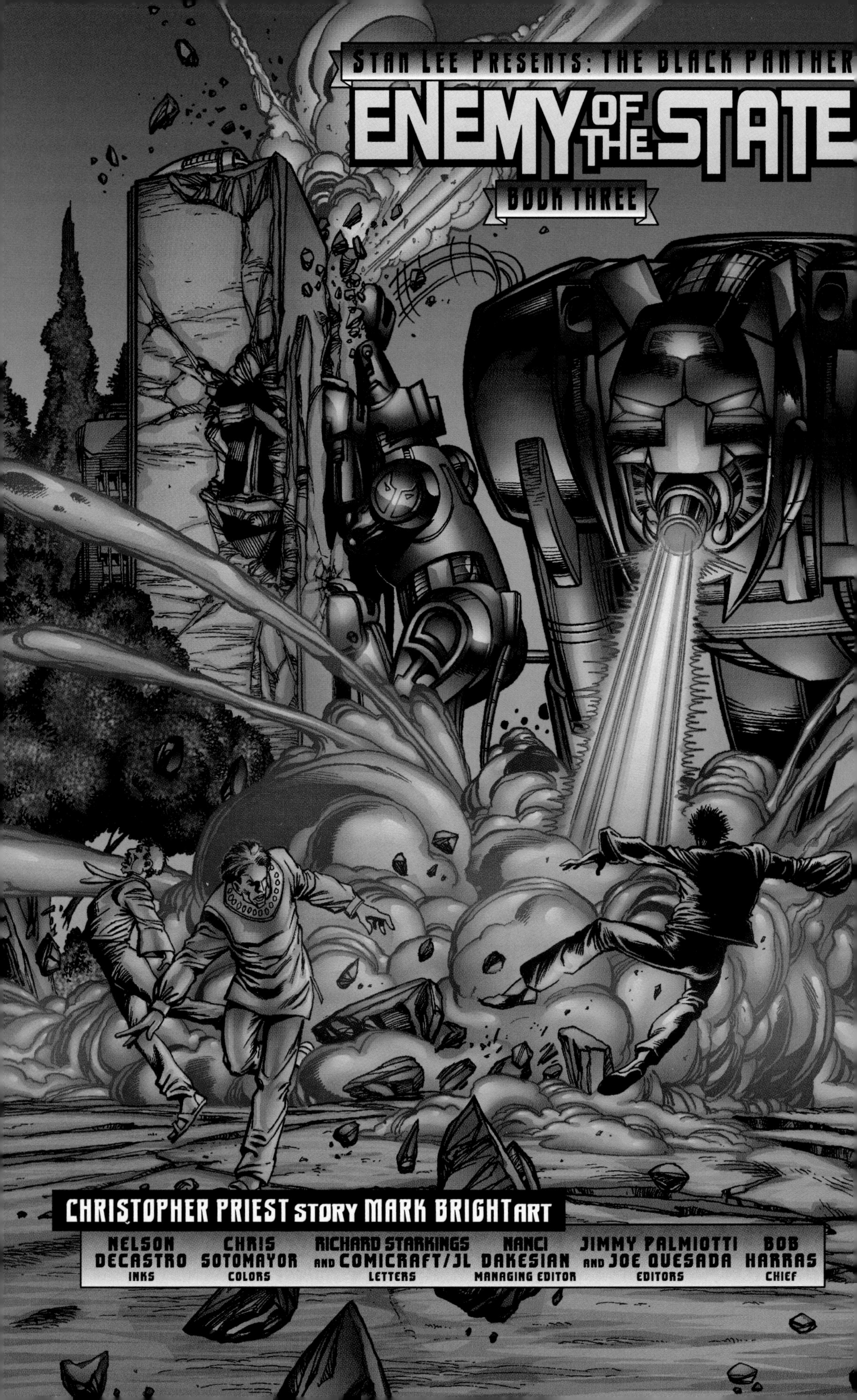
STAN LEE PRESENTS: THE BLACK PANTHER
ENEMY OF THE STATE
BOOK THREE
CHRISTOPHER PRIEST STORY MARK BRIGHT ART
NELSON DECASTRO INKS
CHRIS SOTOMAYOR COLORS
RICHARD STARKINGS AND COMICRAFT/JL LETTERS
NANCI DAKESIAN MANAGING EDITOR
JIMMY PALMIOTTI AND JOE QUESADA EDITORS
BOB HARRAS CHIEF

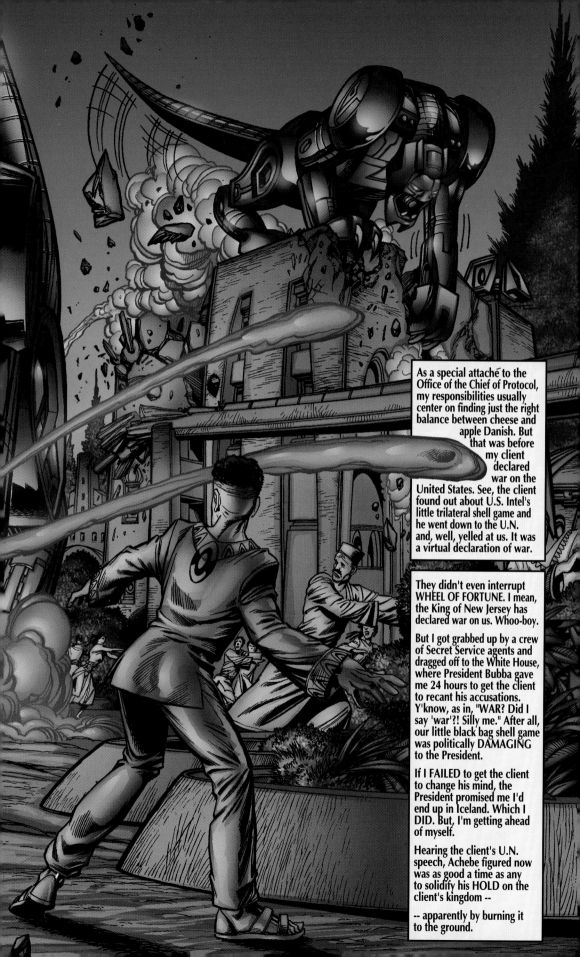

As a special attaché to the Office of the Chief of Protocol, my responsibilities usually center on finding just the right balance between cheese and apple Danish. But that was before my client declared war on the United States. See, the client found out about U.S. Intel's little trilateral shell game and he went down to the U.N. and, well, yelled at us. It was a virtual declaration of war.

They didn't even interrupt WHEEL OF FORTUNE. I mean, the King of New Jersey has declared war on us. Whoo-boy.

But I got grabbed up by a crew of Secret Service agents and dragged off to the White House, where President Bubba gave me 24 hours to get the client to recant his accusations. Y'know, as in, "WAR? Did I say 'war'?! Silly me." After all, our little black bag shell game was politically DAMAGING to the President.

If I FAILED to get the client to change his mind, the President promised me I'd end up in Iceland. Which I DID. But, I'm getting ahead of myself.

Hearing the client's U.N. speech, Achebe figured now was as good a time as any to solidify his HOLD on the client's kingdom --

-- apparently by burning it to the ground.

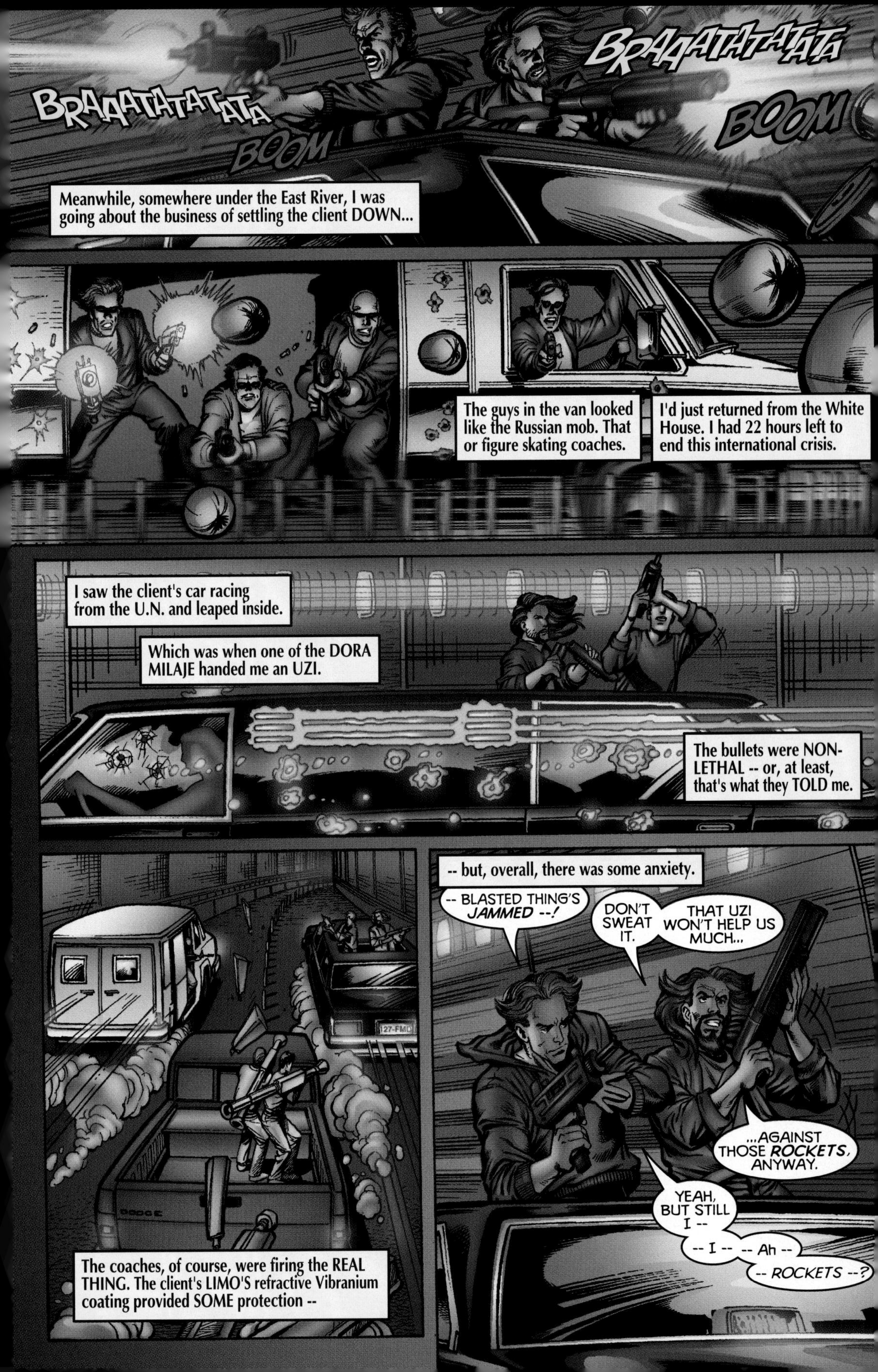
BRAAATATATATA
BOOM
BRAAATATATATATA
BOOM
Meanwhile, somewhere under the East River, I was going about the business of settling the client DOWN...
The guys in the van looked like the Russian mob. That or figure skating coaches.
I'd just returned from the White House. I had 22 hours left to end this international crisis.
I saw the client's car racing from the U.N. and leaped inside.
Which was when one of the DORA MILAJE handed me an UZI.
The bullets were NON-LETHAL -- or, at least, that's what they TOLD me.
The coaches, of course, were firing the REAL THING. The client's LIMO'S refractive Vibranium coating provided SOME protection --
-- but, overall, there was some anxiety.
-- BLASTED THING'S *JAMMED* --!
DON'T SWEAT IT.
THAT UZI WON'T HELP US MUCH...
...AGAINST THOSE *ROCKETS*, ANYWAY.
YEAH, BUT STILL I --
-- I --
-- Ah --
-- *ROCKETS* --?

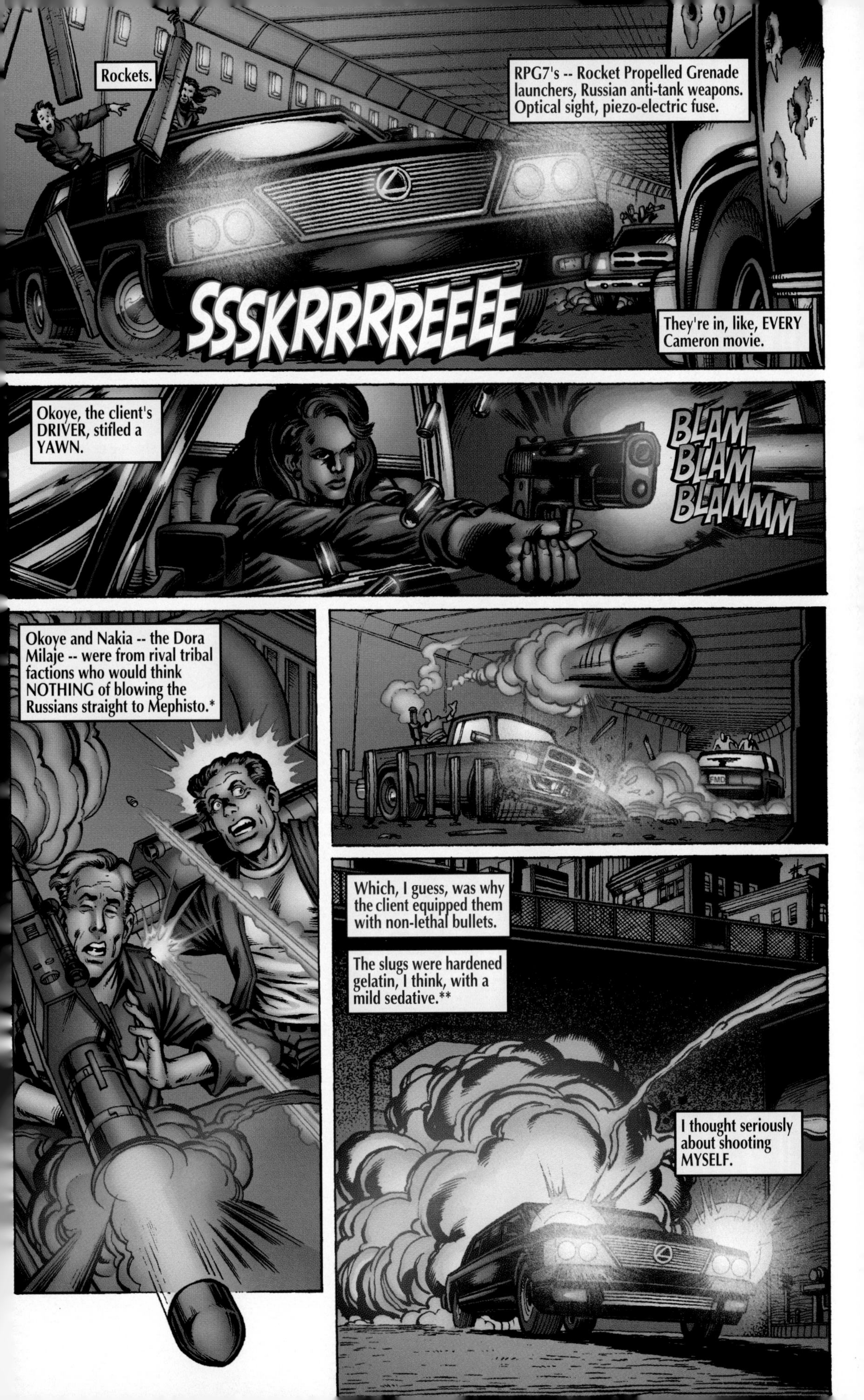
Rockets.
RPG7's -- Rocket Propelled Grenade launchers, Russian anti-tank weapons. Optical sight, piezo-electric fuse.
SSSKRRRRREEEEE
They're in, like, EVERY Cameron movie.
Okoye, the client's DRIVER, stifled a YAWN.
BLAM BLAM BLAMMM
Okoye and Nakia -- the Dora Milaje -- were from rival tribal factions who would think NOTHING of blowing the Russians straight to Mephisto.*
Which, I guess, was why the client equipped them with non-lethal bullets.
The slugs were hardened gelatin, I think, with a mild sedative.**
I thought seriously about shooting MYSELF.

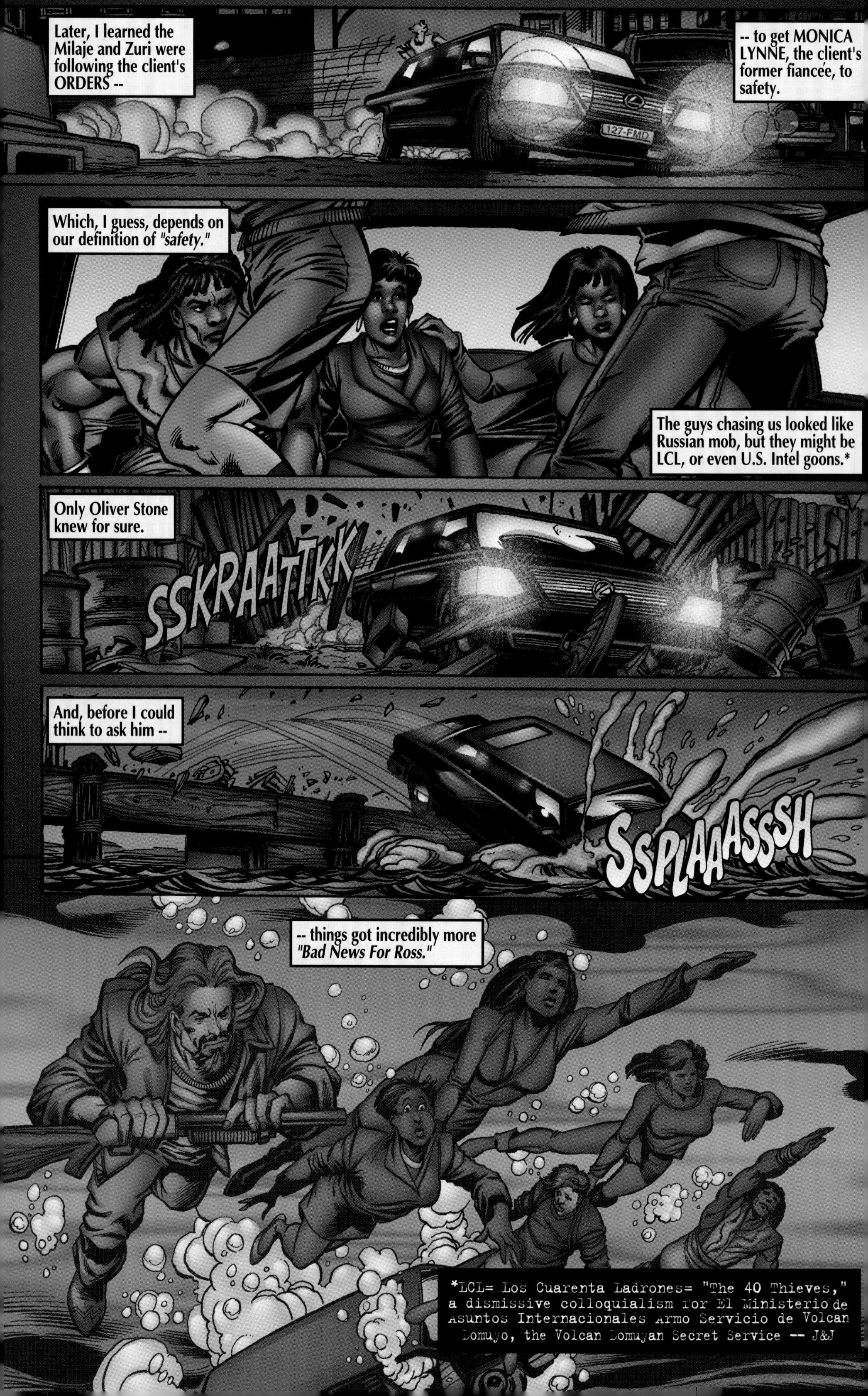
Later, I learned the Milaje and Zuri were following the client's ORDERS --
-- to get MONICA LYNNE, the client's former fiancée, to safety.
127-FMD
Which, I guess, depends on our definition of "safety."
The guys chasing us looked like Russian mob, but they might be LCL, or even U.S. Intel goons.*
Only Oliver Stone knew for sure.
SSKRAATTKK
And, before I could think to ask him --
SSPLAAASSSH
-- things got incredibly more "Bad News For Ross."
*LCL= Los Cuarenta Ladrones= "The 40 Thieves," a dismissive colloquialism for El Ministerio de Asuntos Internacionales Armo Servicio de Volcan Domuyo, the Volcan Domuyan Secret Service -- J&J

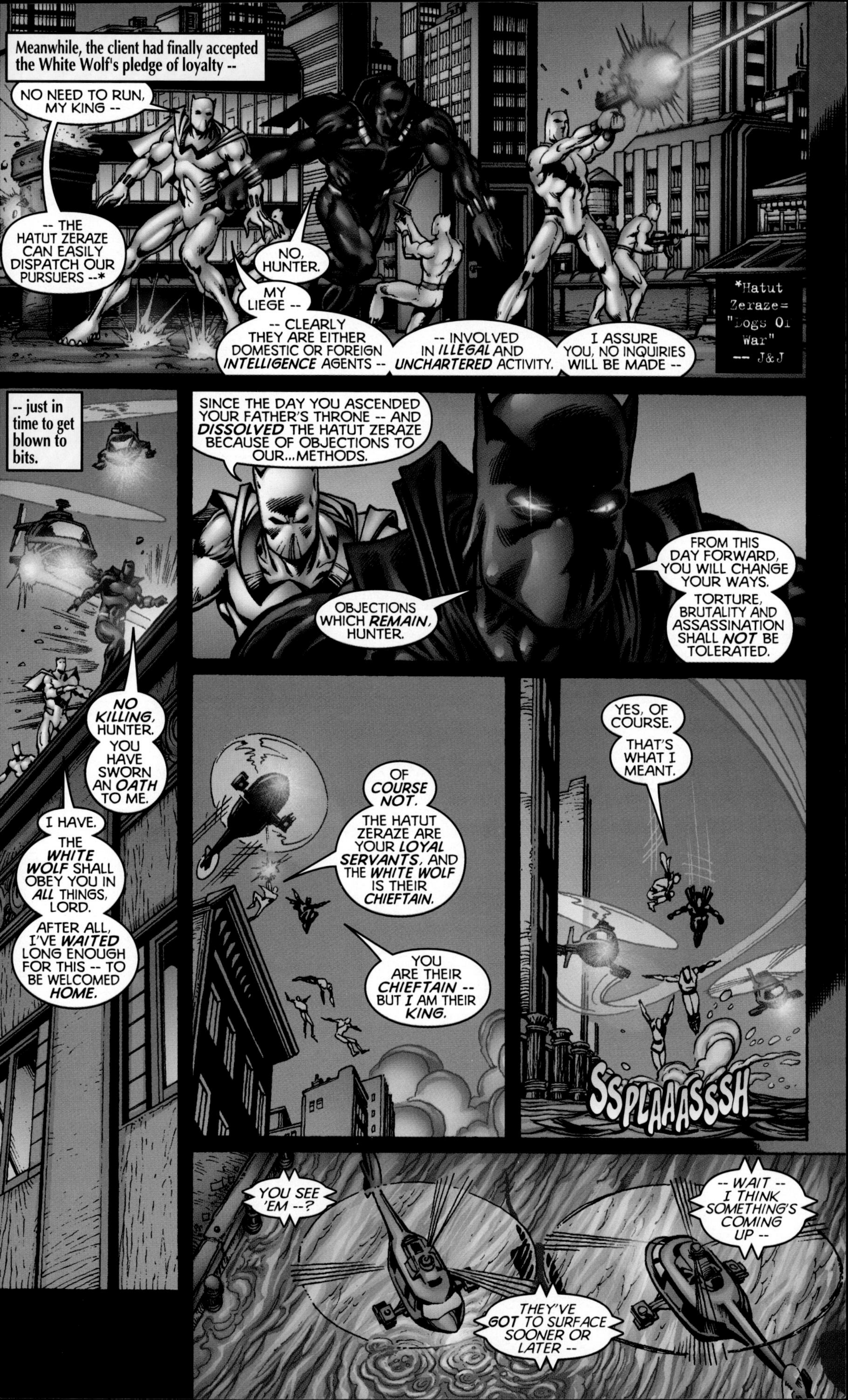

Meanwhile, the client had finally accepted the White Wolf's pledge of loyalty --
NO NEED TO RUN, MY KING --
-- THE HATUT ZERAZE CAN EASILY DISPATCH OUR PURSUERS --*
NO, HUNTER.
MY LIEGE --
-- CLEARLY THEY ARE EITHER DOMESTIC OR FOREIGN INTELLIGENCE AGENTS --
-- INVOLVED IN ILLEGAL AND UNCHARTERED ACTIVITY.
I ASSURE YOU, NO INQUIRIES WILL BE MADE --
*Hatut Zeraze= "Dogs Of War" -- J&J
-- just in time to get blown to bits.
SINCE THE DAY YOU ASCENDED YOUR FATHER'S THRONE -- AND DISSOLVED THE HATUT ZERAZE BECAUSE OF OBJECTIONS TO OUR...METHODS.
OBJECTIONS WHICH REMAIN, HUNTER.
FROM THIS DAY FORWARD, YOU WILL CHANGE YOUR WAYS.
TORTURE, BRUTALITY AND ASSASSINATION SHALL NOT BE TOLERATED.
NO KILLING, HUNTER. YOU HAVE SWORN AN OATH TO ME.
I HAVE.
THE WHITE WOLF SHALL OBEY YOU IN ALL THINGS, LORD.
AFTER ALL, I'VE WAITED LONG ENOUGH FOR THIS -- TO BE WELCOMED HOME.
OF COURSE NOT.
THE HATUT ZERAZE ARE YOUR LOYAL SERVANTS, AND THE WHITE WOLF IS THEIR CHIEFTAIN.
YOU ARE THEIR CHIEFTAIN -- BUT I AM THEIR KING.
YES, OF COURSE.
THAT'S WHAT I MEANT.
SSPLAAASSSH
YOU SEE 'EM --?
-- WAIT -- I THINK SOMETHING'S COMING UP --
THEY'VE GOT TO SURFACE SOONER OR LATER --

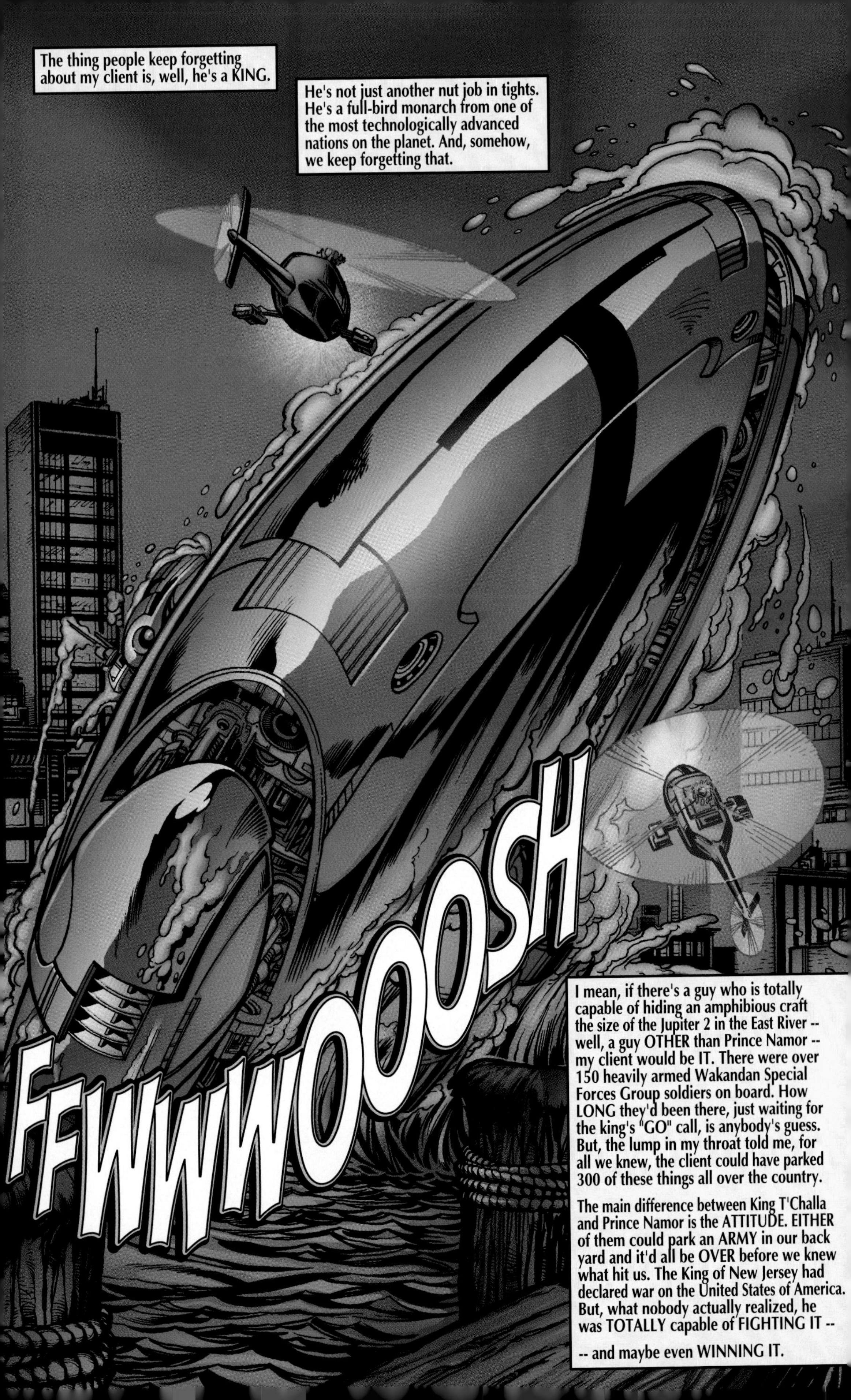

The thing people keep forgetting about my client is, well, he's a KING.
He's not just another nut job in tights. He's a full-bird monarch from one of the most technologically advanced nations on the planet. And, somehow, we keep forgetting that.
FFWWWOOOOSH
I mean, if there's a guy who is totally capable of hiding an amphibious craft the size of the Jupiter 2 in the East River -- well, a guy OTHER than Prince Namor -- my client would be IT. There were over 150 heavily armed Wakandan Special Forces Group soldiers on board. How LONG they'd been there, just waiting for the king's "GO" call, is anybody's guess. But, the lump in my throat told me, for all we knew, the client could have parked 300 of these things all over the country.
The main difference between King T'Challa and Prince Namor is the ATTITUDE. EITHER of them could park an ARMY in our back yard and it'd all be OVER before we knew what hit us. The King of New Jersey had declared war on the United States of America. But, what nobody actually realized, he was TOTALLY capable of FIGHTING IT --
-- and maybe even WINNING IT.

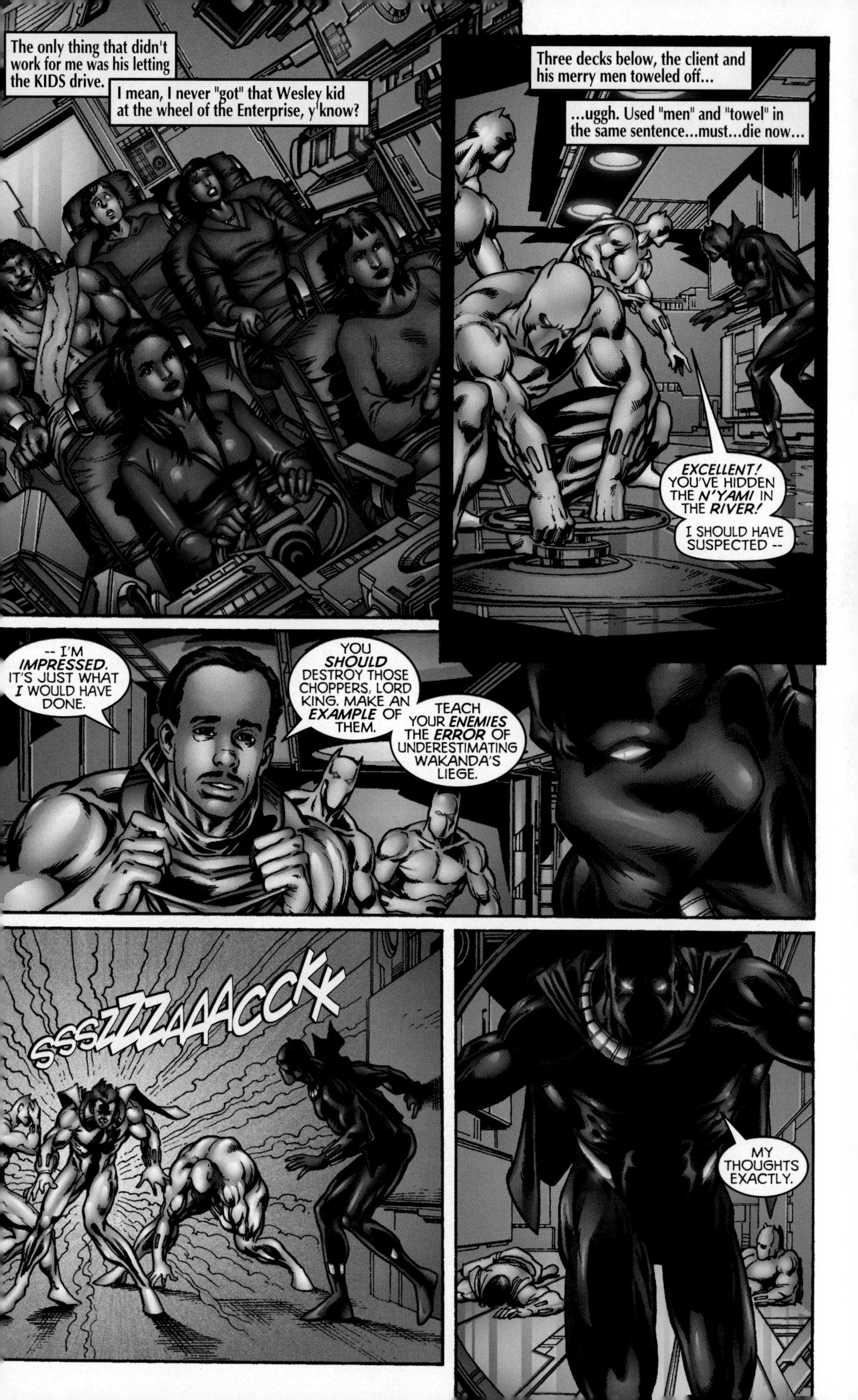
The only thing that didn't work for me was his letting the KIDS drive.
I mean, I never "got" that Wesley kid at the wheel of the Enterprise, y'know?
Three decks below, the client and his merry men toweled off...
...uggh. Used "men" and "towel" in the same sentence...must...die now...
EXCELLENT! YOU'VE HIDDEN THE N'YAMI IN THE RIVER!
I SHOULD HAVE SUSPECTED --
-- I'M IMPRESSED. IT'S JUST WHAT I WOULD HAVE DONE.
YOU SHOULD DESTROY THOSE CHOPPERS, LORD KING. MAKE AN EXAMPLE OF THEM.
TEACH YOUR ENEMIES THE ERROR OF UNDERESTIMATING WAKANDA'S LIEGE.
SSSZZZAAAACCKK
MY THOUGHTS EXACTLY.

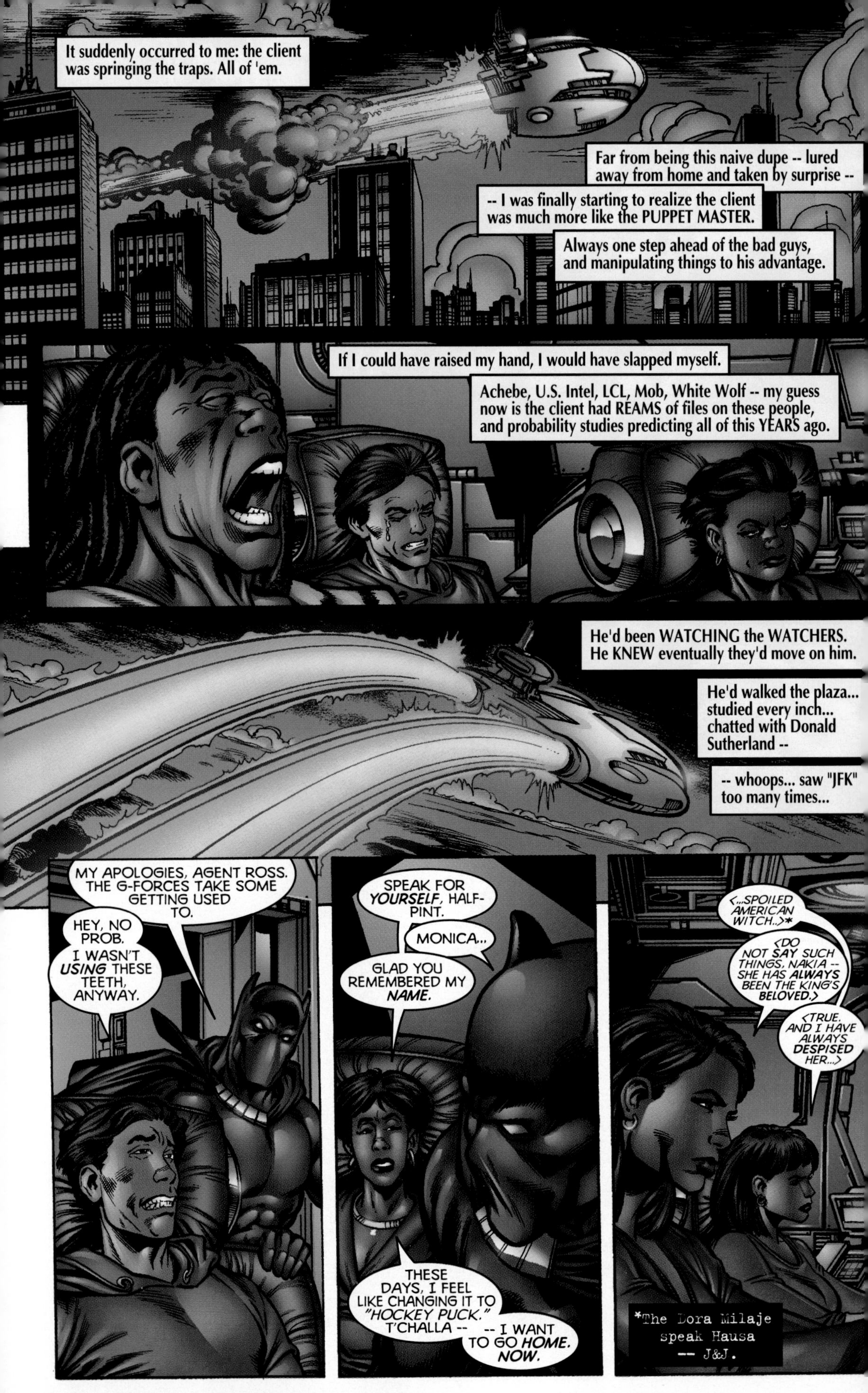

It suddenly occurred to me: the client was springing the traps. All of 'em.
Far from being this naive dupe -- lured away from home and taken by surprise --
-- I was finally starting to realize the client was much more like the PUPPET MASTER.
Always one step ahead of the bad guys, and manipulating things to his advantage.
If I could have raised my hand, I would have slapped myself.
Achebe, U.S. Intel, LCL, Mob, White Wolf -- my guess now is the client had REAMS of files on these people, and probability studies predicting all of this YEARS ago.
He'd been WATCHING the WATCHERS. He KNEW eventually they'd move on him.
He'd walked the plaza... studied every inch... chatted with Donald Sutherland --
-- whoops... saw "JFK" too many times...
MY APOLOGIES, AGENT ROSS. THE G-FORCES TAKE SOME GETTING USED TO.
HEY, NO PROB. I WASN'T *USING* THESE TEETH, ANYWAY.
SPEAK FOR *YOURSELF*, HALF-PINT.
MONICA...
GLAD YOU REMEMBERED MY *NAME.*
THESE DAYS, I FEEL LIKE CHANGING IT TO *"HOCKEY PUCK."* T'CHALLA --
-- I WANT TO GO *HOME. NOW.*
<...SPOILED AMERICAN WITCH...>*
<DO NOT *SAY* SUCH THINGS, NAKIA -- SHE HAS *ALWAYS* BEEN THE KING'S *BELOVED.*>
<TRUE. AND I HAVE *ALWAYS* *DESPISED* HER...>
*The Dora Milaje speak Hausa -- J&J.

FEAR AND LOATHING

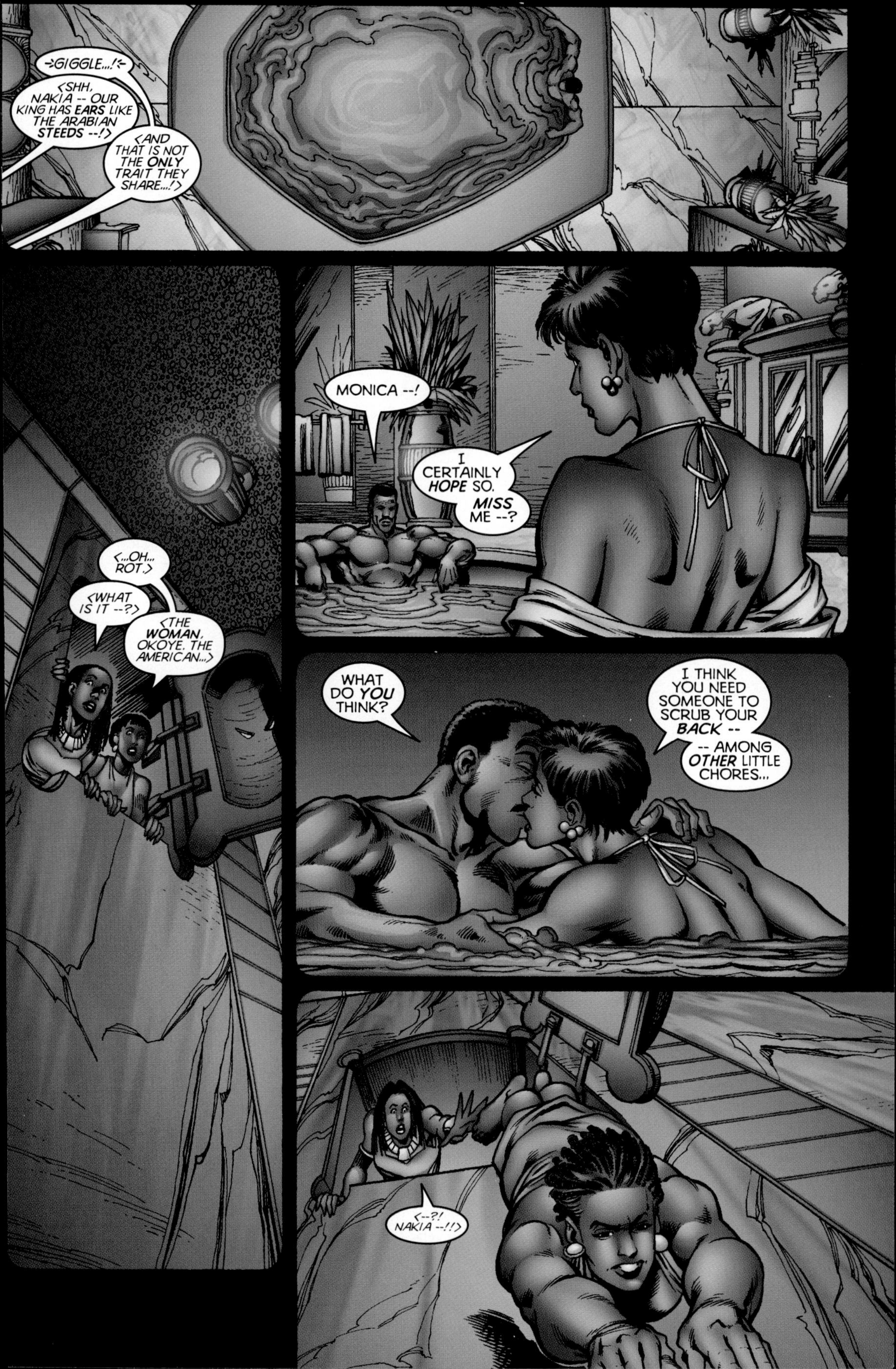

-GIGGLE...!-
<SHH, NAKIA -- OUR KING HAS EARS LIKE THE ARABIAN STEEDS --!>
<AND THAT IS NOT THE ONLY TRAIT THEY SHARE...!>
<...OH... ROT.>
<WHAT IS IT --?>
<THE WOMAN, OKOYE. THE AMERICAN...>
MONICA --!
I CERTAINLY HOPE SO. MISS ME --?
WHAT DO YOU THINK?
I THINK YOU NEED SOMEONE TO SCRUB YOUR BACK --
-- AMONG OTHER LITTLE CHORES...
<--?! NAKIA --!!>

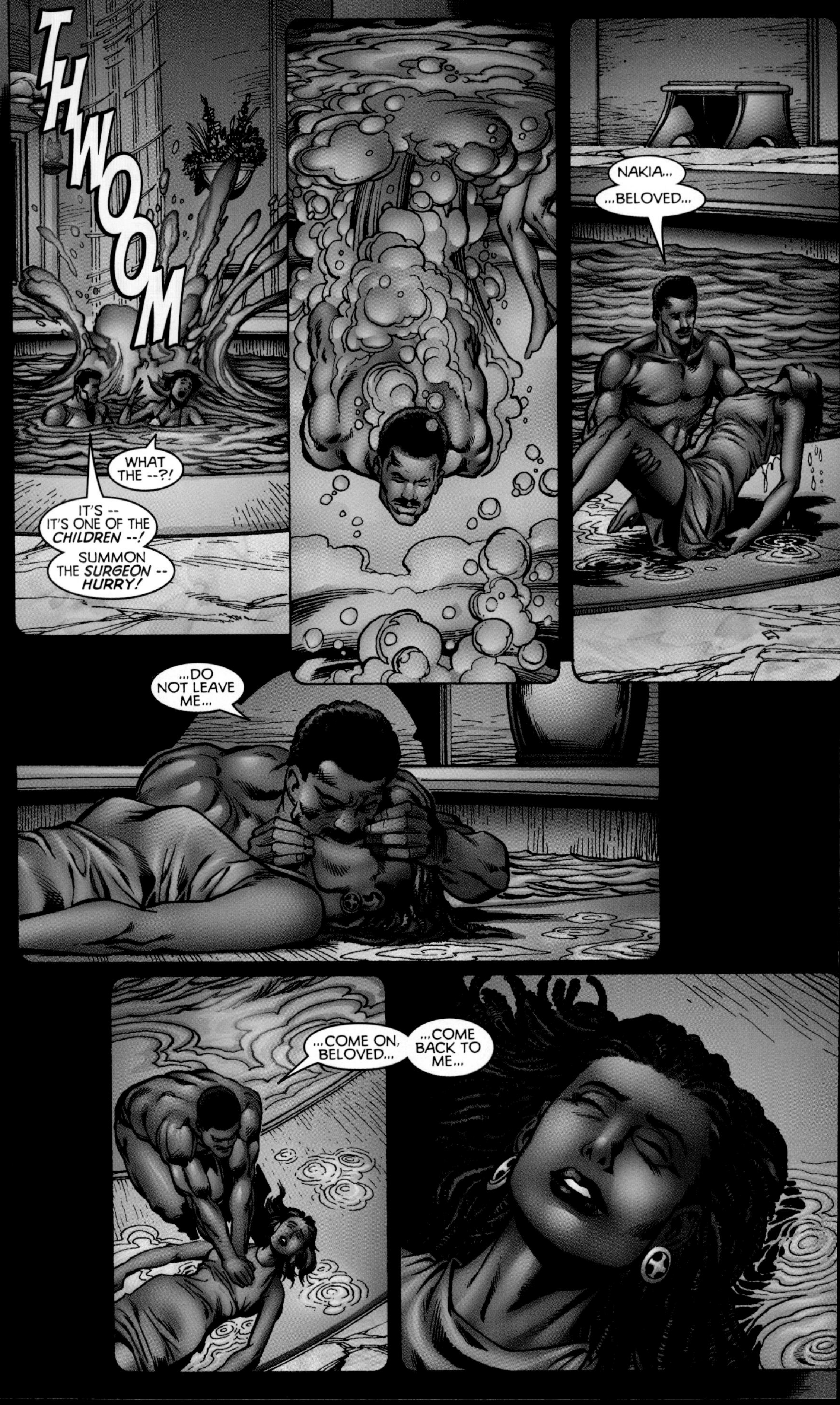
THWOOM
WHAT THE --?!
IT'S -- IT'S ONE OF THE CHILDREN --! SUMMON THE SURGEON -- HURRY!
NAKIA...
...BELOVED...
...DO NOT LEAVE ME...
...COME ON, BELOVED...
...COME BACK TO ME...

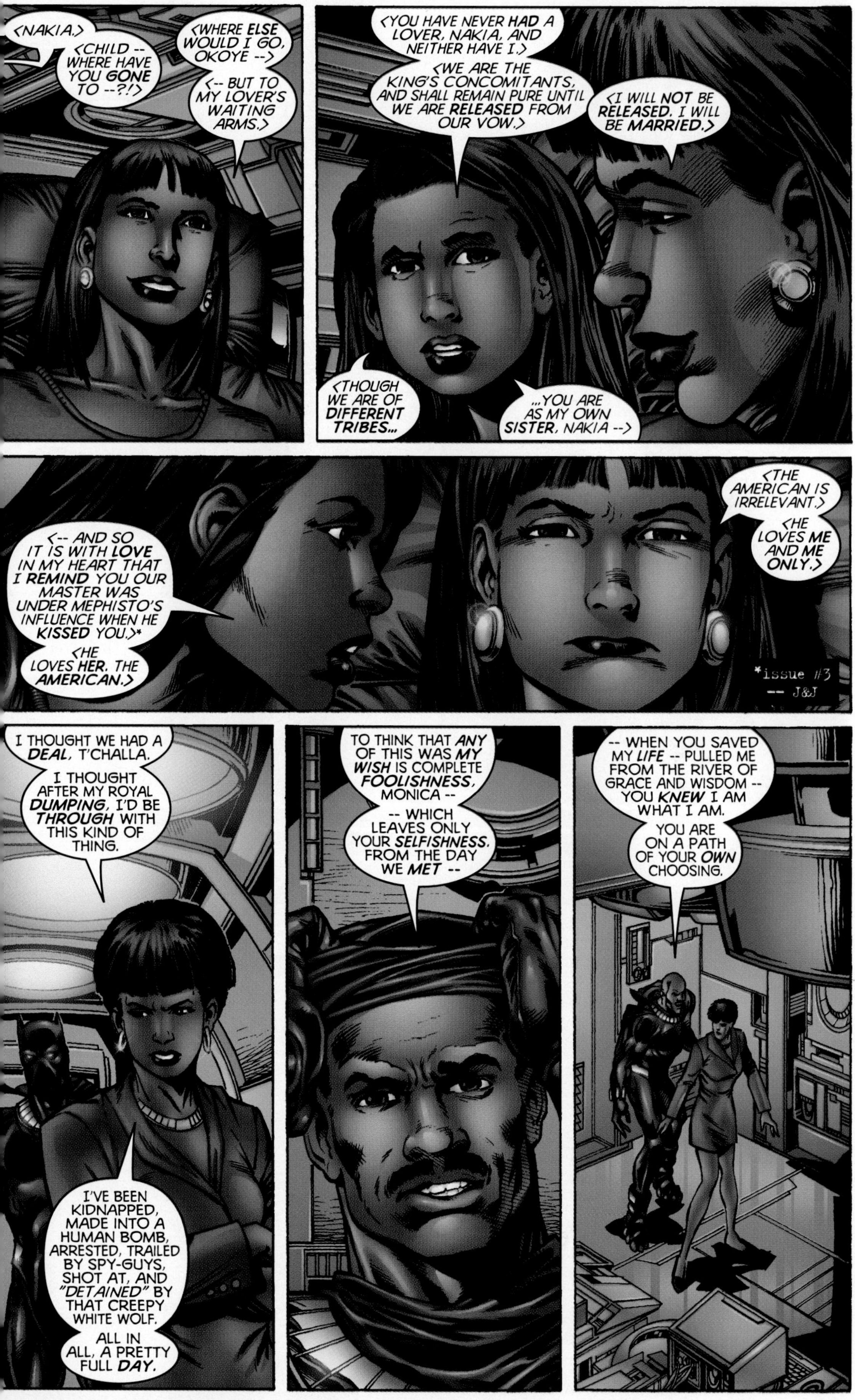
<NAKIA.>
<CHILD -- WHERE HAVE YOU GONE TO --?!>
<WHERE ELSE WOULD I GO, OKOYE -->
<-- BUT TO MY LOVER'S WAITING ARMS.>
<YOU HAVE NEVER HAD A LOVER, NAKIA, AND NEITHER HAVE I.>
<WE ARE THE KING'S CONCOMITANTS, AND SHALL REMAIN PURE UNTIL WE ARE RELEASED FROM OUR VOW.>
<I WILL NOT BE RELEASED. I WILL BE MARRIED.>
<THOUGH WE ARE OF DIFFERENT TRIBES...
...YOU ARE AS MY OWN SISTER, NAKIA -->
<-- AND SO IT IS WITH LOVE IN MY HEART THAT I REMIND YOU OUR MASTER WAS UNDER MEPHISTO'S INFLUENCE WHEN HE KISSED YOU.>*
<HE LOVES HER. THE AMERICAN.>
<THE AMERICAN IS IRRELEVANT.>
<HE LOVES ME AND ME ONLY.>
*issue #3 -- J&J
I THOUGHT WE HAD A DEAL, T'CHALLA.
I THOUGHT AFTER MY ROYAL DUMPING, I'D BE THROUGH WITH THIS KIND OF THING.
I'VE BEEN KIDNAPPED, MADE INTO A HUMAN BOMB, ARRESTED, TRAILED BY SPY-GUYS, SHOT AT, AND "DETAINED" BY THAT CREEPY WHITE WOLF.
ALL IN ALL, A PRETTY FULL DAY.
TO THINK THAT ANY OF THIS WAS MY WISH IS COMPLETE FOOLISHNESS, MONICA --
-- WHICH LEAVES ONLY YOUR SELFISHNESS, FROM THE DAY WE MET --
-- WHEN YOU SAVED MY LIFE -- PULLED ME FROM THE RIVER OF GRACE AND WISDOM -- YOU KNEW I AM WHAT I AM.
YOU ARE ON A PATH OF YOUR OWN CHOOSING.

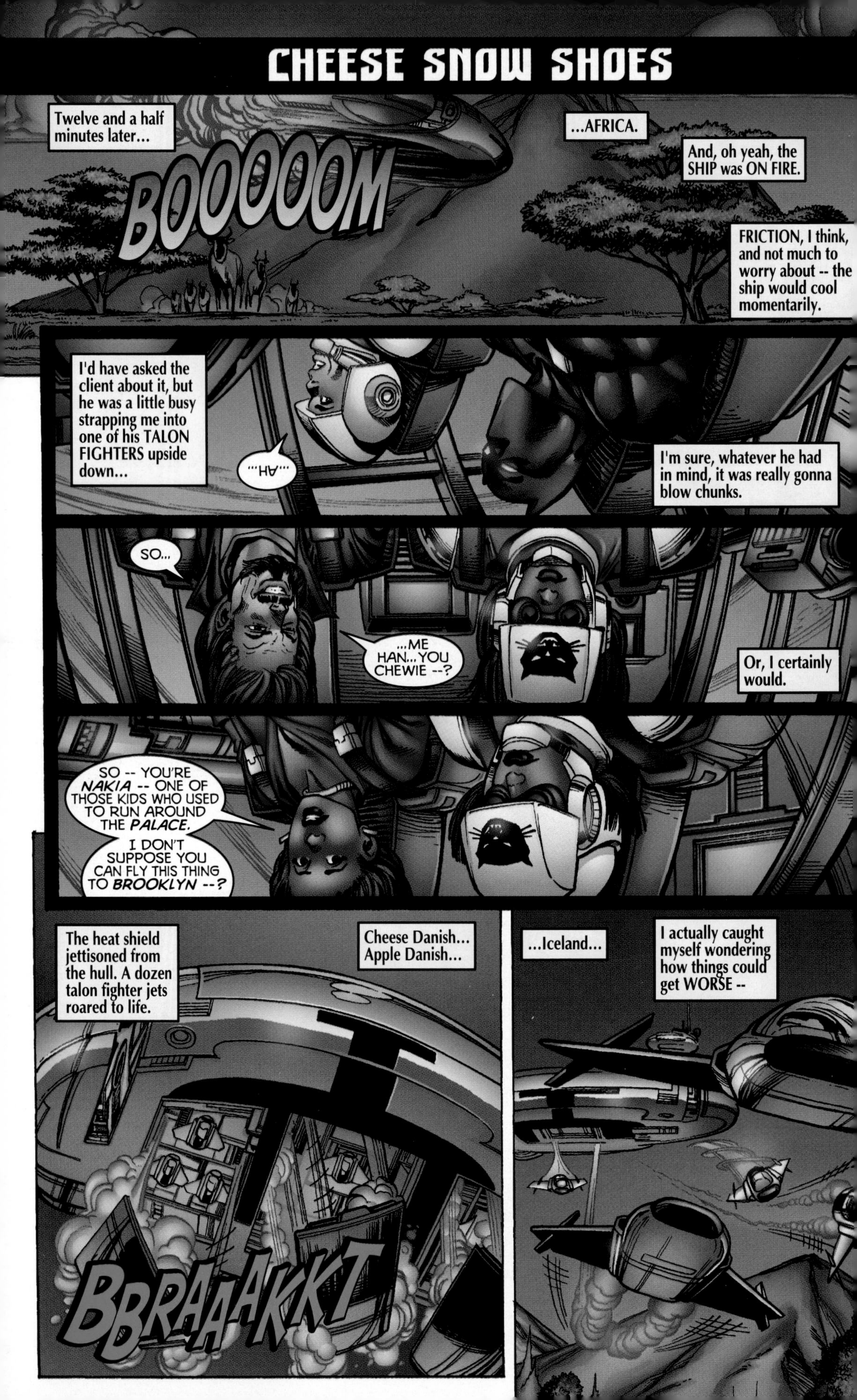
CHEESE SNOW SHOES
Twelve and a half minutes later...
BOOOOOM
...AFRICA.
And, oh yeah, the SHIP was ON FIRE.
FRICTION, I think, and not much to worry about -- the ship would cool momentarily.
I'd have asked the client about it, but he was a little busy strapping me into one of his TALON FIGHTERS upside down...
AH...
I'm sure, whatever he had in mind, it was really gonna blow chunks.
SO...
...ME HAN...YOU CHEWIE --?
Or, I certainly would.
SO -- YOU'RE NAKIA -- ONE OF THOSE KIDS WHO USED TO RUN AROUND THE PALACE.
I DON'T SUPPOSE YOU CAN FLY THIS THING TO BROOKLYN --?
The heat shield jettisoned from the hull. A dozen talon fighter jets roared to life.
Cheese Danish... Apple Danish...
BBRAAAKKT
...Iceland...
I actually caught myself wondering how things could get WORSE --

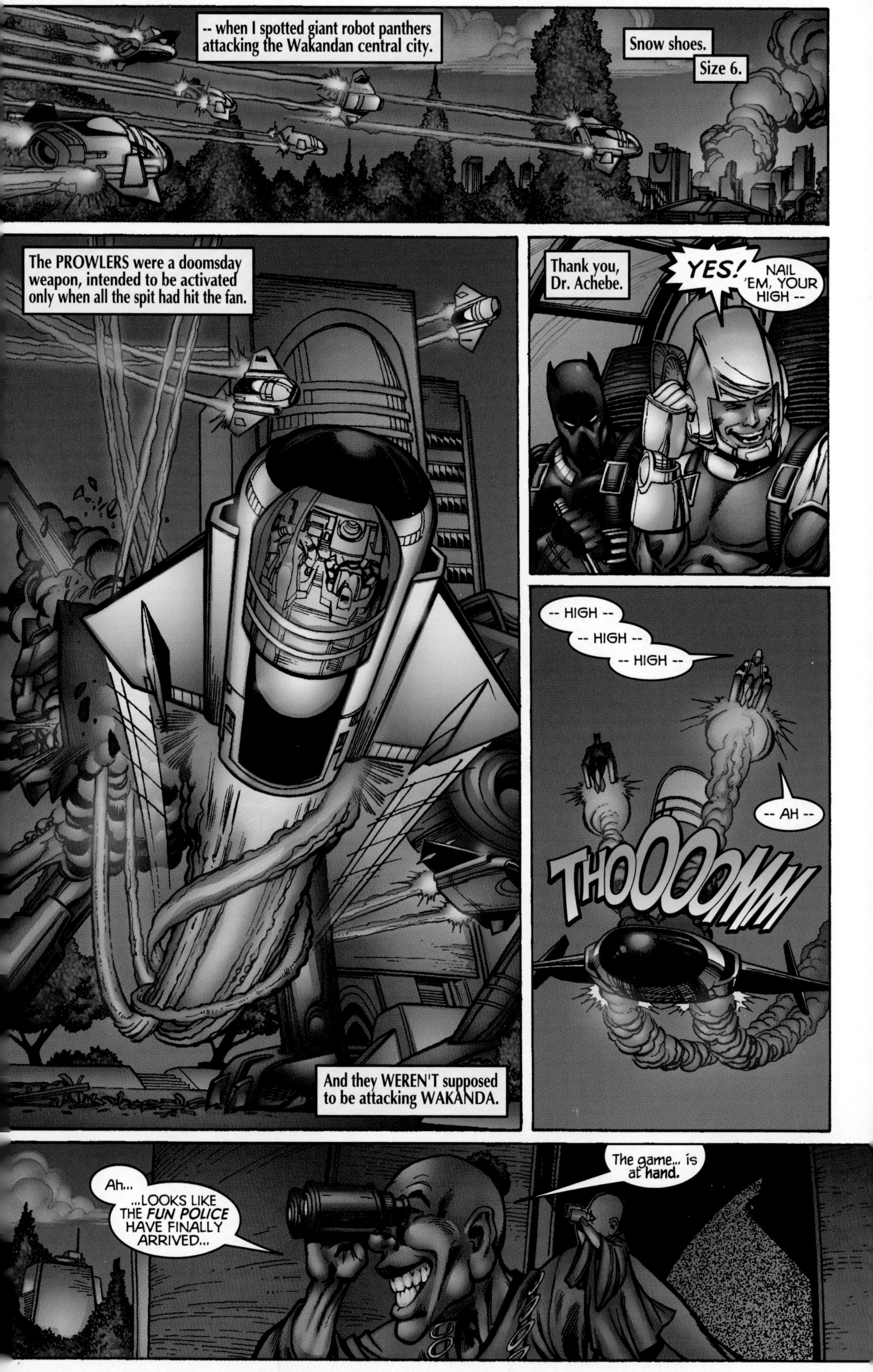
-- when I spotted giant robot panthers attacking the Wakandan central city.
Snow shoes.
Size 6.
The PROWLERS were a doomsday weapon, intended to be activated only when all the spit had hit the fan.
And they WEREN'T supposed to be attacking WAKANDA.
Thank you, Dr. Achebe.
YES!
NAIL 'EM, YOUR HIGH --
-- HIGH --
-- HIGH --
-- HIGH --
-- AH --
THOOOOMM
Ah...
...LOOKS LIKE THE FUN POLICE HAVE FINALLY ARRIVED...
The game... is at hand.

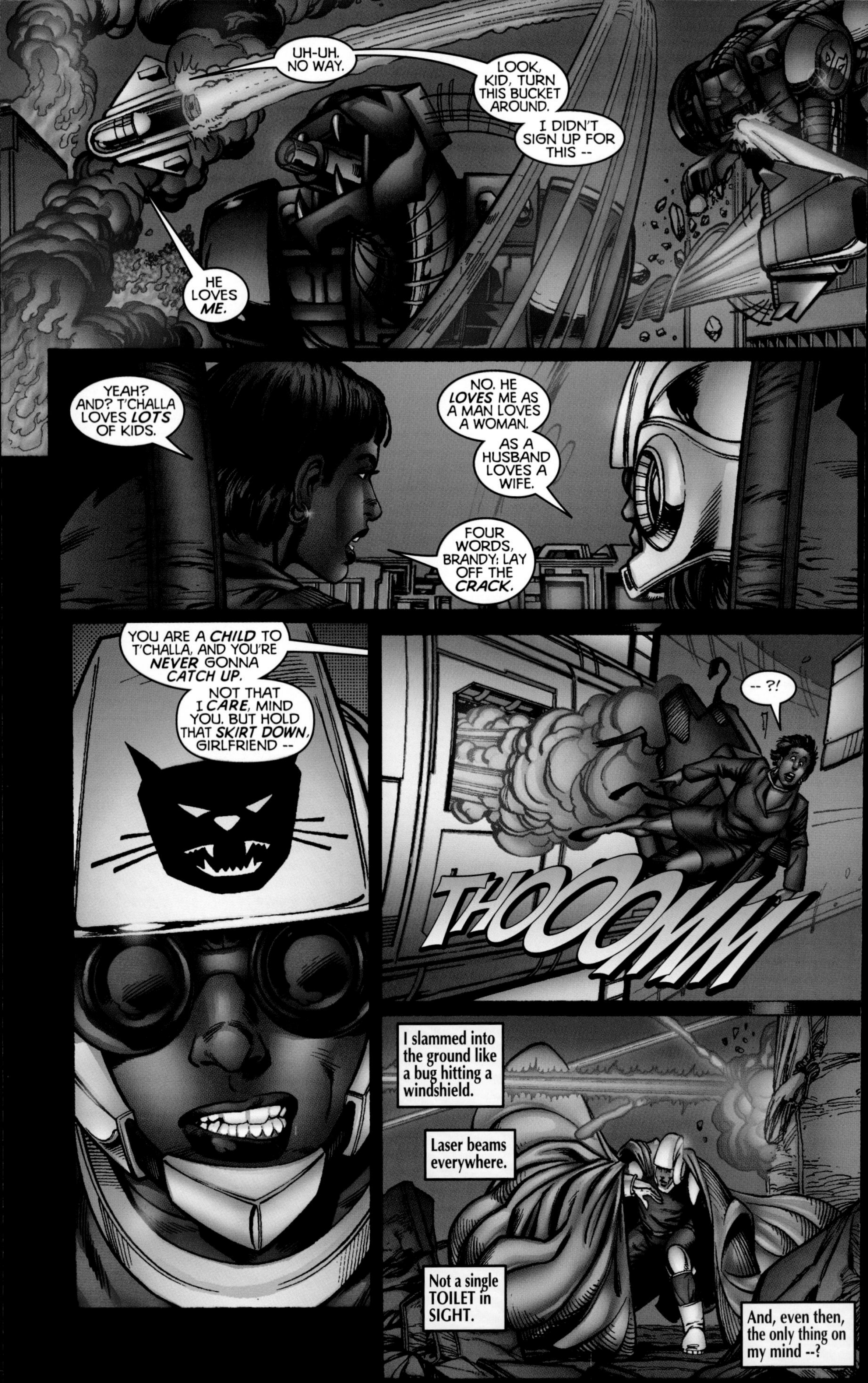

UH-UH. NO WAY.
LOOK, KID, TURN THIS BUCKET AROUND.
I DIDN'T SIGN UP FOR THIS --
HE LOVES ME.
YEAH? AND? T'CHALLA LOVES LOTS OF KIDS.
NO. HE LOVES ME AS A MAN LOVES A WOMAN.
AS A HUSBAND LOVES A WIFE.
FOUR WORDS, BRANDY: LAY OFF THE CRACK.
YOU ARE A CHILD TO T'CHALLA, AND YOU'RE NEVER GONNA CATCH UP.
NOT THAT I CARE, MIND YOU. BUT HOLD THAT SKIRT DOWN, GIRLFRIEND --
-- ?!
THOOOMM
I slammed into the ground like a bug hitting a windshield.
Laser beams everywhere.
Not a single TOILET in SIGHT.
And, even then, the only thing on my mind --?

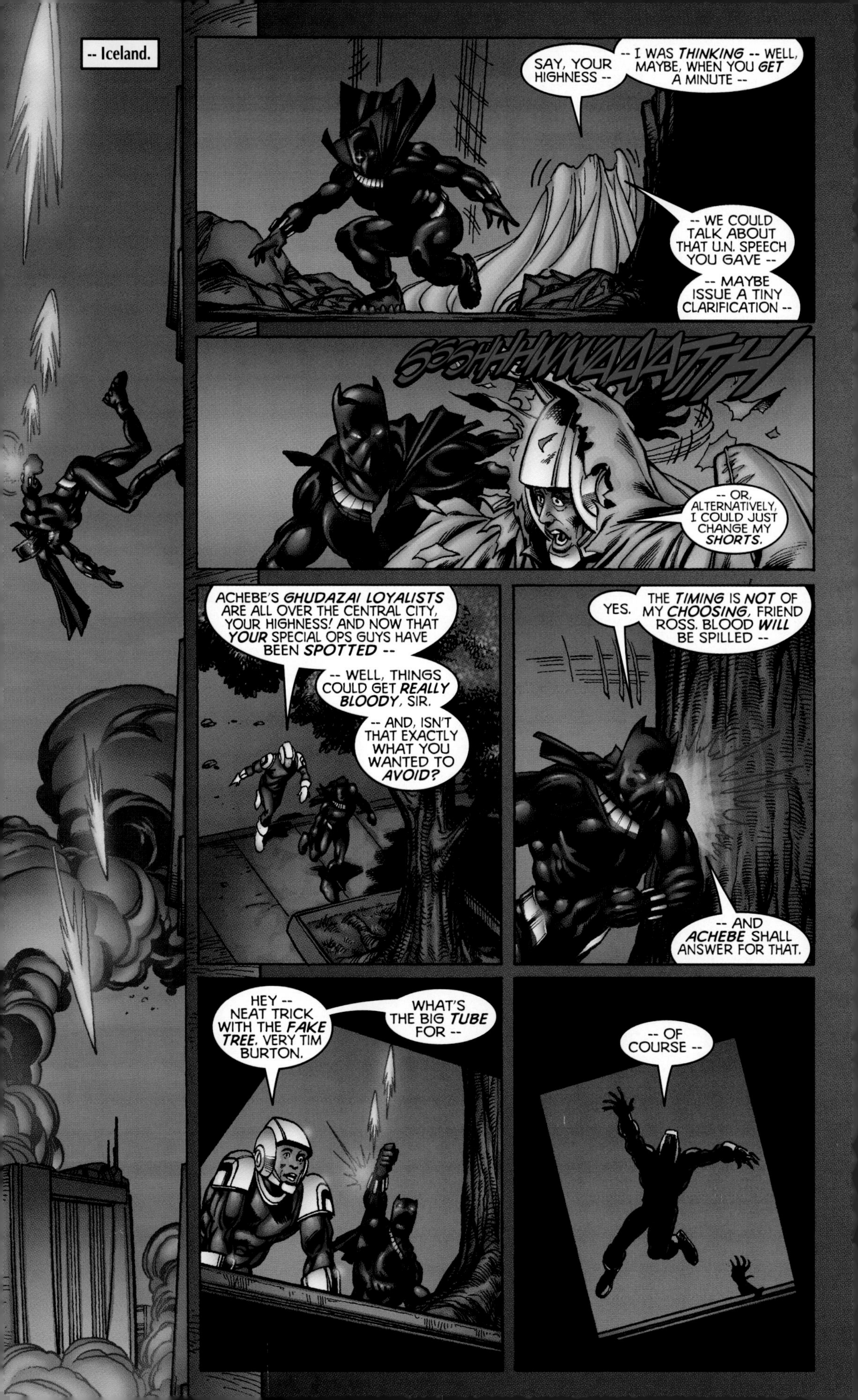
-- Iceland.
SAY, YOUR HIGHNESS --
-- I WAS THINKING -- WELL, MAYBE, WHEN YOU GET A MINUTE --
-- WE COULD TALK ABOUT THAT U.N. SPEECH YOU GAVE --
-- MAYBE ISSUE A TINY CLARIFICATION --
SSSHHHWWAAAATTH
-- OR, ALTERNATIVELY, I COULD JUST CHANGE MY SHORTS.
ACHEBE'S GHUDAZAI LOYALISTS ARE ALL OVER THE CENTRAL CITY, YOUR HIGHNESS! AND NOW THAT YOUR SPECIAL OPS GUYS HAVE BEEN SPOTTED --
-- WELL, THINGS COULD GET REALLY BLOODY, SIR.
-- AND, ISN'T THAT EXACTLY WHAT YOU WANTED TO AVOID?
YES.
THE TIMING IS NOT OF MY CHOOSING, FRIEND ROSS. BLOOD WILL BE SPILLED --
-- AND ACHEBE SHALL ANSWER FOR THAT.
HEY -- NEAT TRICK WITH THE FAKE TREE. VERY TIM BURTON.
WHAT'S THE BIG TUBE FOR --
-- OF COURSE --

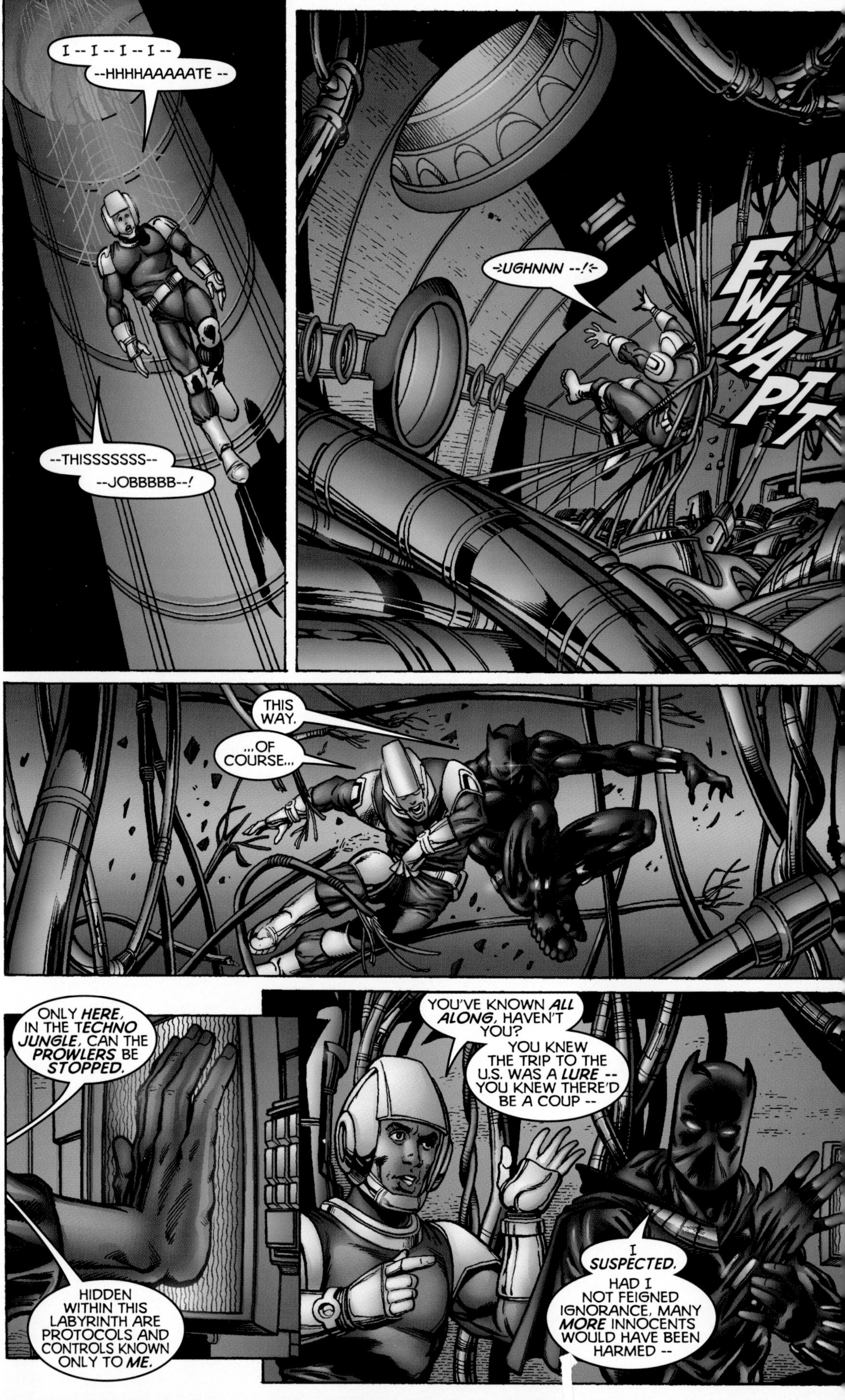

I -- I -- I -- I --
--HHHHAAAAATE --
--THISSSSSSS--
--JOBBBBB--!
UGHNNN --!
FWAAPTT
THIS WAY.
...OF COURSE...
ONLY HERE, IN THE TECHNO JUNGLE, CAN THE PROWLERS BE STOPPED.
HIDDEN WITHIN THIS LABYRINTH ARE PROTOCOLS AND CONTROLS KNOWN ONLY TO ME.
YOU'VE KNOWN ALL ALONG, HAVEN'T YOU?
YOU KNEW THE TRIP TO THE U.S. WAS A LURE -- YOU KNEW THERE'D BE A COUP --
I SUSPECTED.
HAD I NOT FEIGNED IGNORANCE, MANY MORE INNOCENTS WOULD HAVE BEEN HARMED --

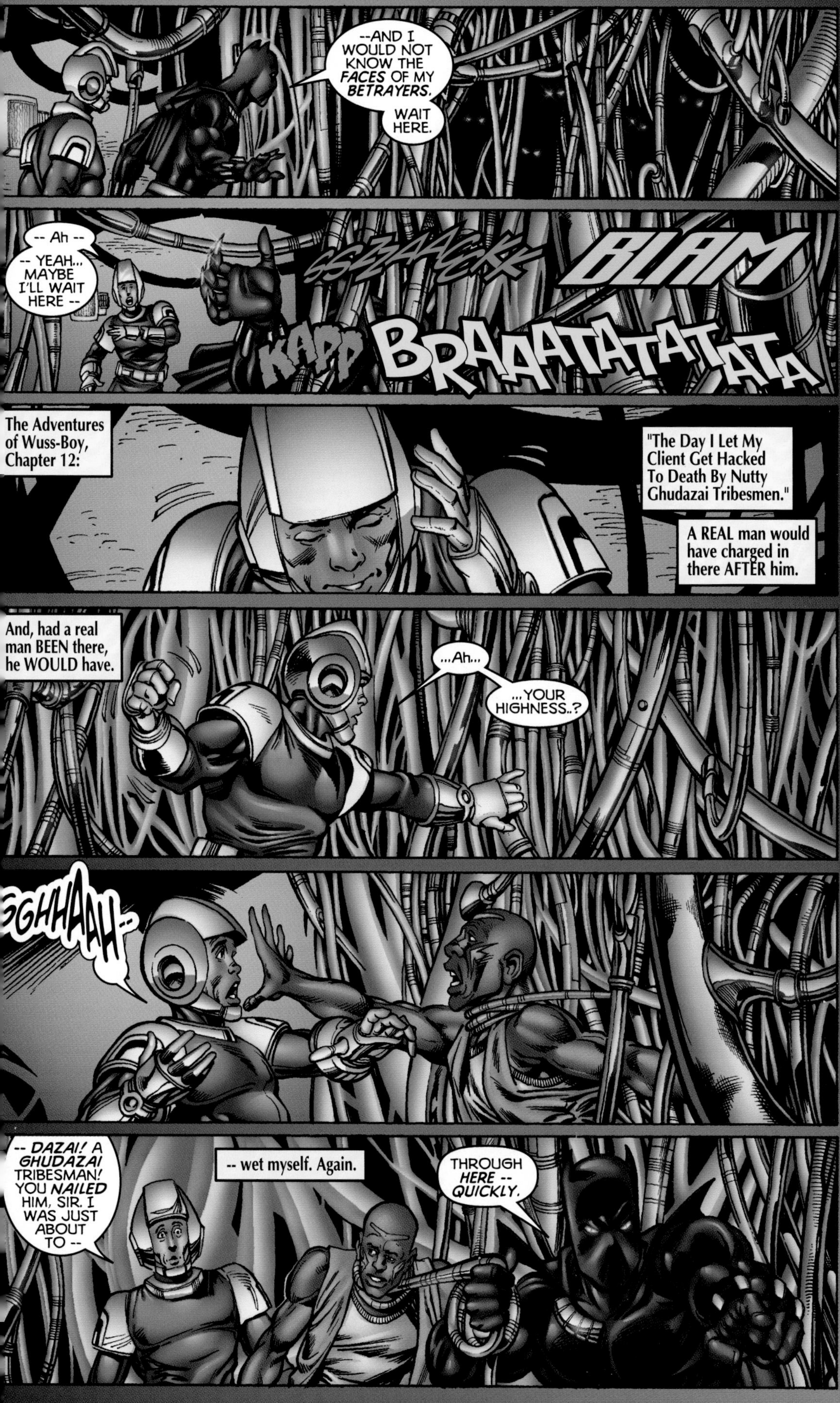
--AND I WOULD NOT KNOW THE *FACES* OF MY *BETRAYERS.*
WAIT HERE.
-- Ah --
-- YEAH... MAYBE I'LL WAIT HERE --
GSZZAACKK
BLAM
KAPP
BRAAATATATATA
The Adventures of Wuss-Boy, Chapter 12:
"The Day I Let My Client Get Hacked To Death By Nutty Ghudazai Tribesmen."
A REAL man would have charged in there AFTER him.
And, had a real man BEEN there, he WOULD have.
...Ah...
...YOUR HIGHNESS..?
GHHAAAH-
-- *DAZAI!* A *GHUDAZAI* TRIBESMAN! YOU *NAILED* HIM, SIR. I WAS JUST ABOUT TO --
-- wet myself. Again.
THROUGH *HERE* -- *QUICKLY.*

C'MON -- C'MON, YOU MUTTS --! *BRING* IT TO ME!

MNAAHAHAAHA!

SHOW ME WHAT'CHA *GOT!*

YOU KNOW -- FOR A *SCRAWNY WHITE MAN*, YOU ARE NOT *COMPLETELY* USELESS IN *BATTLE*, SERGEANT TORK!

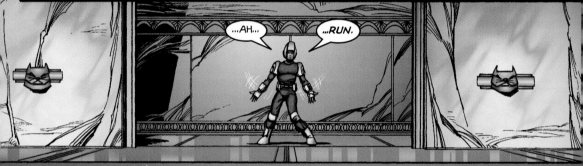

WELL, GEE, COMIN' FROM A BIG, OLD, GRITS-AND-CATFISH, FRED SANFORD- LOOKING SOUL BROTHER LIKE *YOU*, ZURI --

THOOOM

-- "THOOM?" UNIVERSAL ANNOUNCEMENT OF *MAJOR* BAD NEWS...

...AH...

...RUN.

RRAWWRRL

LEAVE THE *GHUDAZAI* TO MY WARRIORS, FRIEND ROSS.

IF... IF YOU INSIST...

ACHEBE SACRIFICES HIS *OWN* KINSMEN IN VAIN --

<NAKIA -- BELOVED -- REPORT.>

<I HAVE COME TO PROTECT MY KING, LORD.>

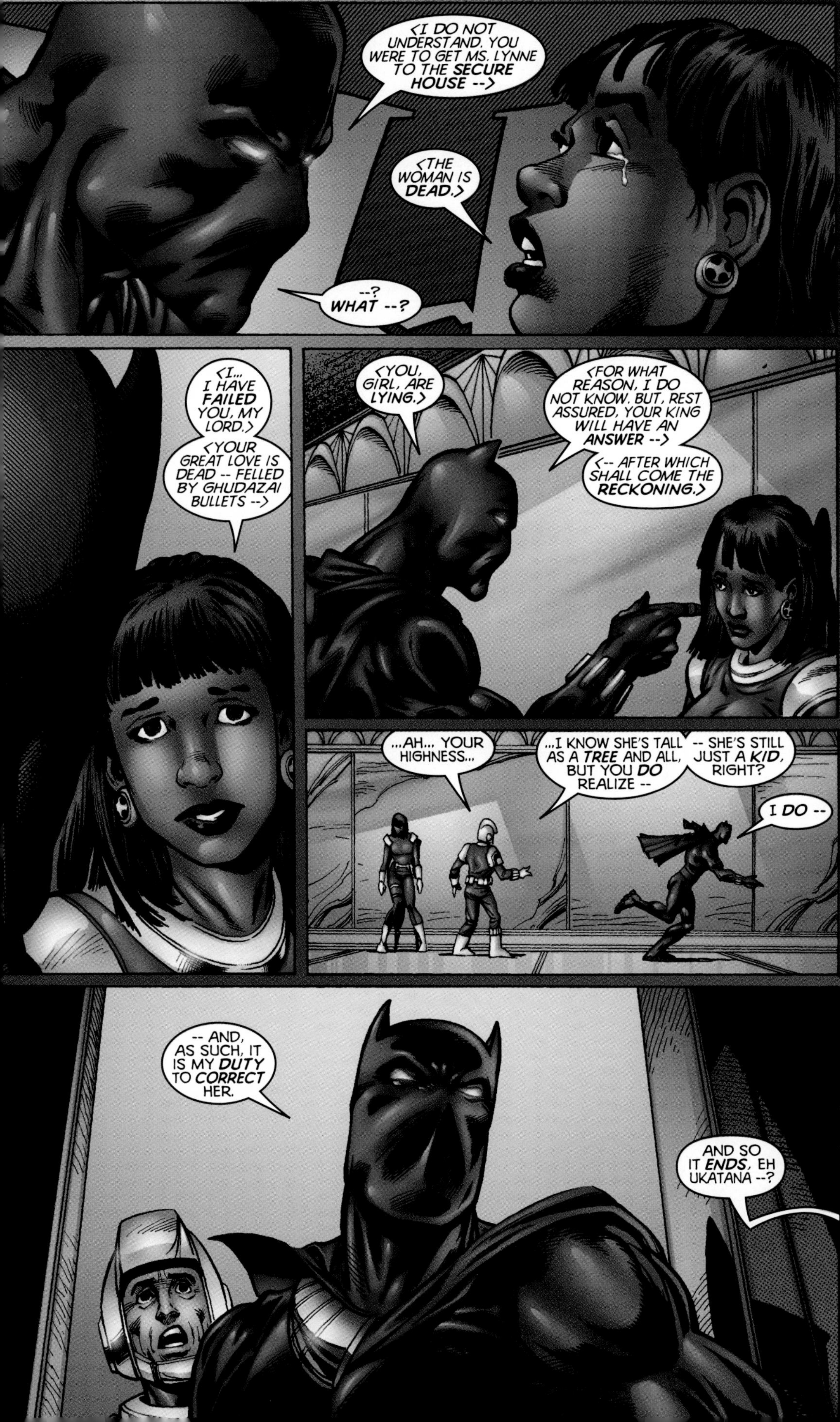
<I DO NOT UNDERSTAND. YOU WERE TO GET MS. LYNNE TO THE SECURE HOUSE -->
<THE WOMAN IS DEAD.>
--? WHAT --?
<I... I HAVE FAILED YOU, MY LORD.>
<YOUR GREAT LOVE IS DEAD -- FELLED BY GHUDAZAI BULLETS -->
<YOU, GIRL, ARE LYING.>
<FOR WHAT REASON, I DO NOT KNOW. BUT, REST ASSURED, YOUR KING WILL HAVE AN ANSWER -->
<-- AFTER WHICH SHALL COME THE RECKONING.>
...AH... YOUR HIGHNESS...
...I KNOW SHE'S TALL AS A TREE AND ALL, BUT YOU DO REALIZE --
-- SHE'S STILL JUST A KID, RIGHT?
I DO --
-- AND, AS SUCH, IT IS MY DUTY TO CORRECT HER.
AND SO IT ENDS, EH UKATANA --?

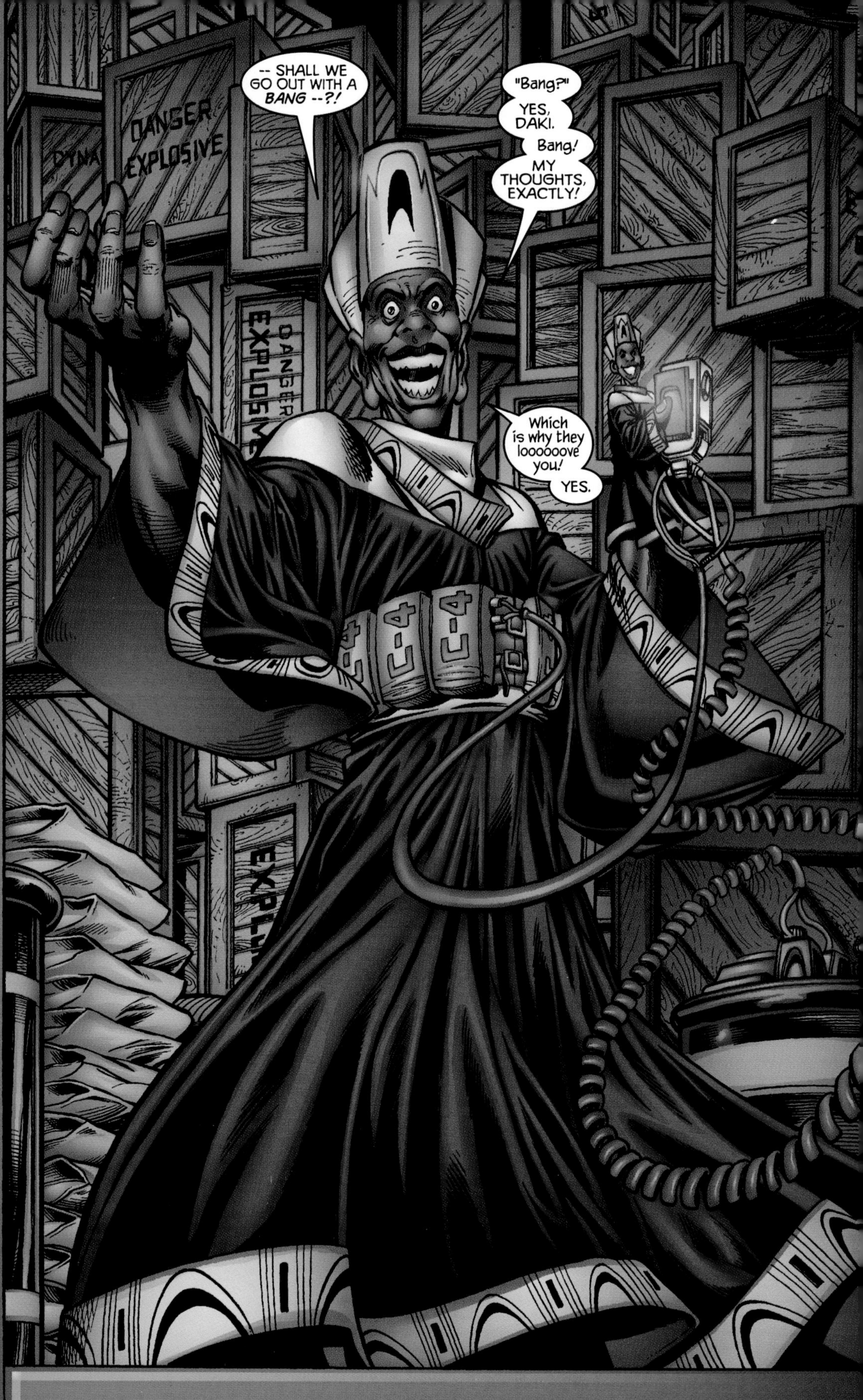
-- SHALL WE GO OUT WITH A *BANG* --?!
"Bang?"
YES, DAKI.
Bang!
MY THOUGHTS, EXACTLY!
Which is why they loooooove you!
YES.
DANGER EXPLOSIVE
DANGER EXPLOSIVE
C-4

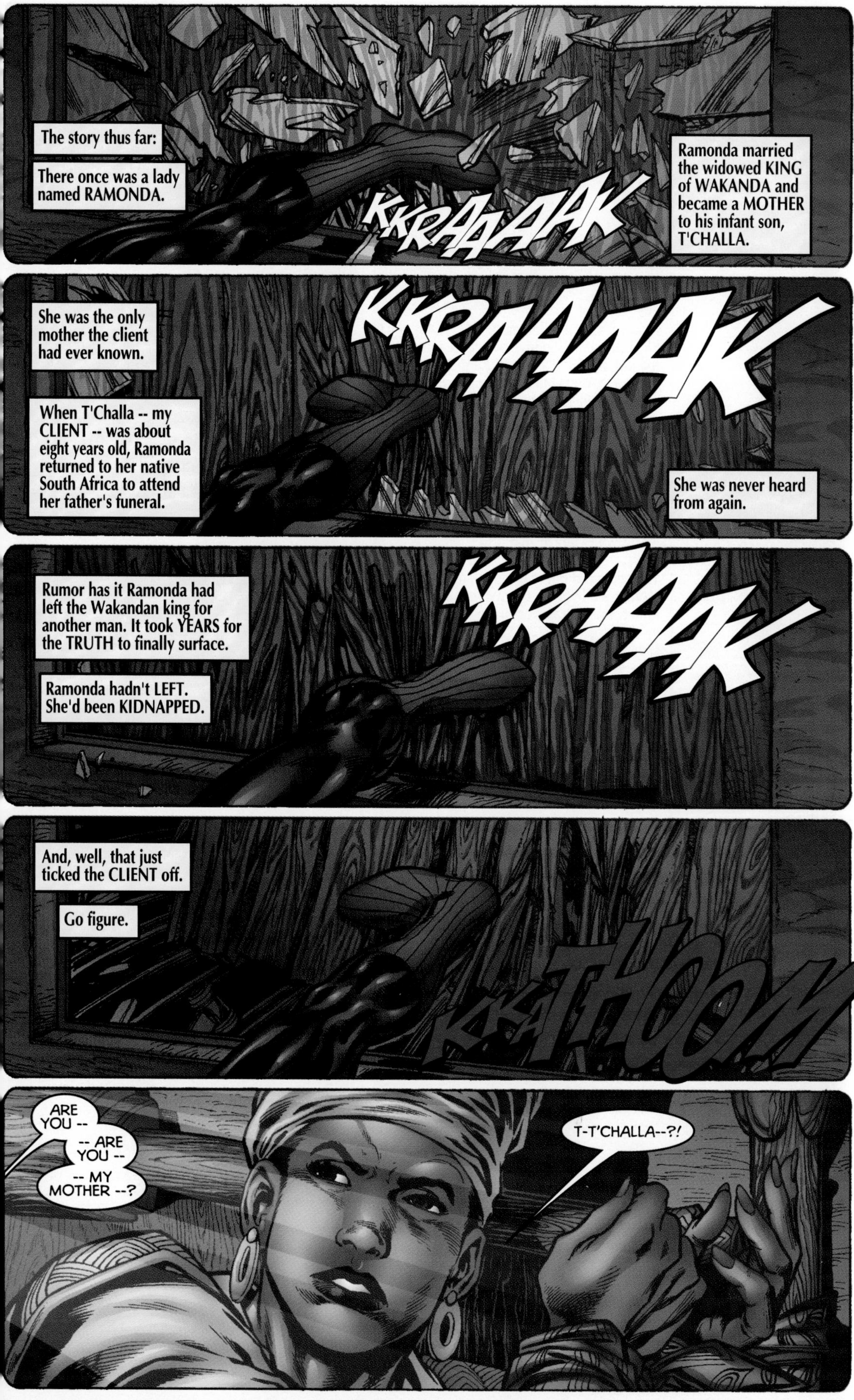
The story thus far:
There once was a lady named RAMONDA.
KKRAAAAK
Ramonda married the widowed KING of WAKANDA and became a MOTHER to his infant son, T'CHALLA.
She was the only mother the client had ever known.
KKRAAAAK
When T'Challa -- my CLIENT -- was about eight years old, Ramonda returned to her native South Africa to attend her father's funeral.
She was never heard from again.
Rumor has it Ramonda had left the Wakandan king for another man. It took YEARS for the TRUTH to finally surface.
KKRAAAAK
Ramonda hadn't LEFT. She'd been KIDNAPPED.
And, well, that just ticked the CLIENT off.
Go figure.
KKATHOOM
ARE YOU --
-- ARE YOU --
-- MY MOTHER --?
T-T'CHALLA--?!

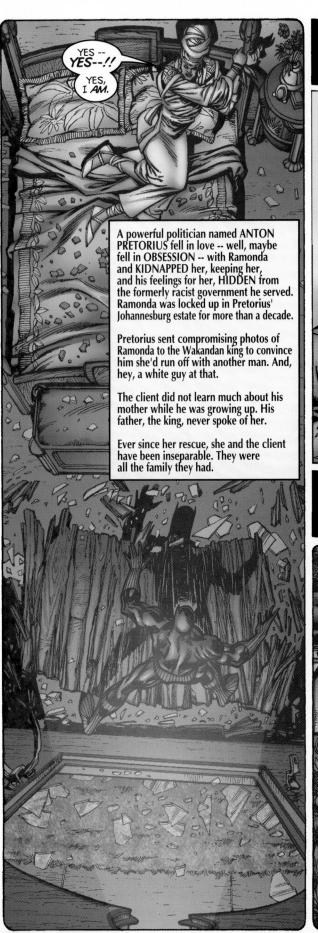

YES -- *YES--!!*

YES, I *AM.*

A powerful politician named ANTON PRETORIUS fell in love -- well, maybe fell in OBSESSION -- with Ramonda and KIDNAPPED her, keeping her, and his feelings for her, HIDDEN from the formerly racist government he served. Ramonda was locked up in Pretorius' Johannesburg estate for more than a decade.

Pretorius sent compromising photos of Ramonda to the Wakandan king to convince him she'd run off with another man. And, hey, a white guy at that.

The client did not learn much about his mother while he was growing up. His father, the king, never spoke of her.

Ever since her rescue, she and the client have been inseparable. They were all the family they had.

CAPTAIN REWIND

BUT, I'M GETTING AHEAD OF MYSELF AGAIN.

I KNOW... I KNOW, GUYS. IT'S A HARD HABIT TO BREAK.

I LEFT THIS PART OUT -- REMEMBER, EARLIER --

THE OTHER SON

Ramonda was mother to more than ONE son.

Remember I told you about HUNTER, the WHITE WOLF, orphaned when his parents' plane crashed in the jungle --

-- and ADOPTED by the Wakandan king?*

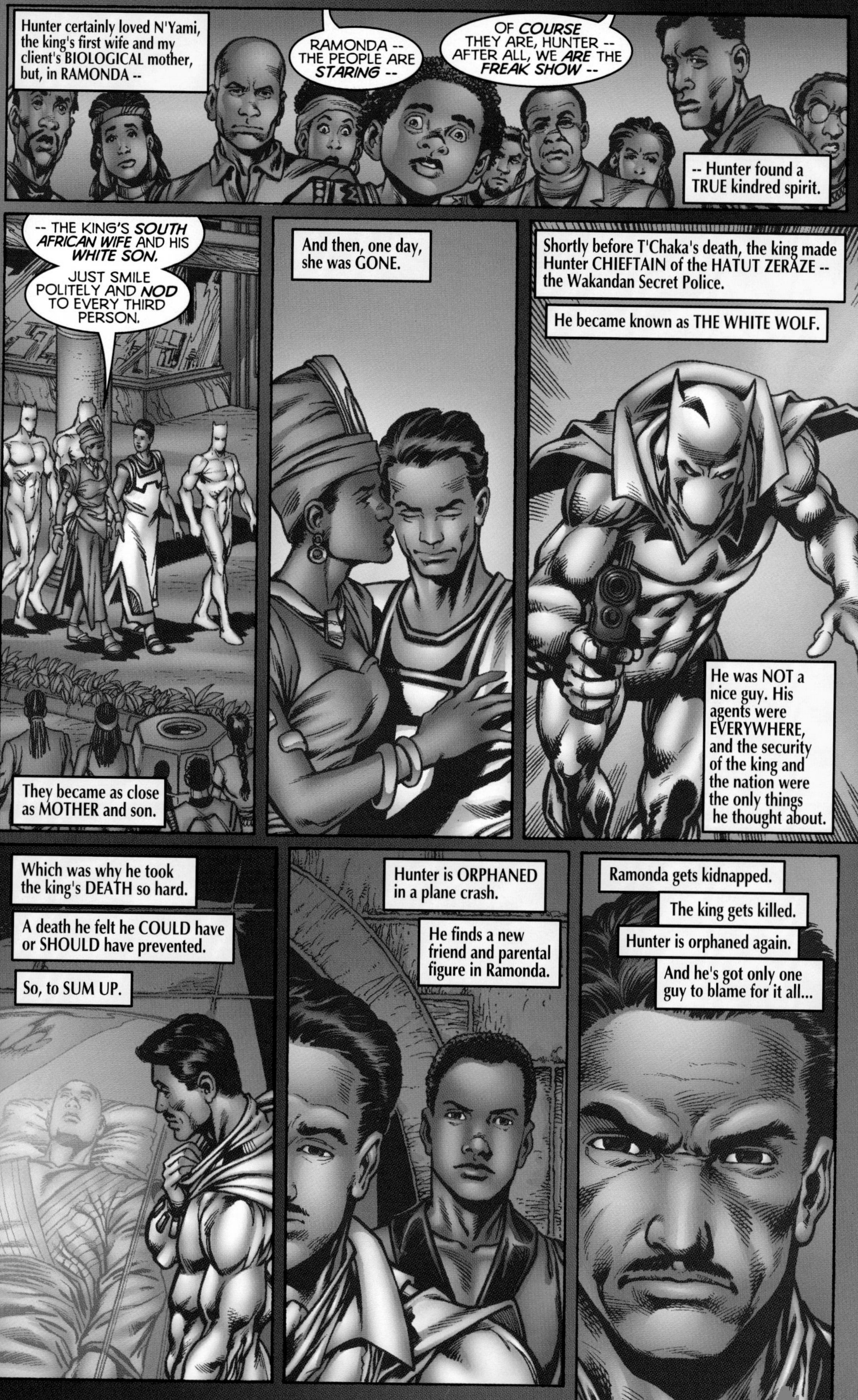
Hunter certainly loved N'Yami, the king's first wife and my client's BIOLOGICAL mother, but, in RAMONDA --
RAMONDA -- THE PEOPLE ARE STARING --
OF COURSE THEY ARE, HUNTER -- AFTER ALL, WE ARE THE FREAK SHOW --
-- Hunter found a TRUE kindred spirit.
-- THE KING'S SOUTH AFRICAN WIFE AND HIS WHITE SON.
JUST SMILE POLITELY AND NOD TO EVERY THIRD PERSON.
They became as close as MOTHER and son.
And then, one day, she was GONE.
Shortly before T'Chaka's death, the king made Hunter CHIEFTAIN of the HATUT ZERAZE -- the Wakandan Secret Police.
He became known as THE WHITE WOLF.
He was NOT a nice guy. His agents were EVERYWHERE, and the security of the king and the nation were the only things he thought about.
Which was why he took the king's DEATH so hard.
A death he felt he COULD have or SHOULD have prevented.
So, to SUM UP.
Hunter is ORPHANED in a plane crash.
He finds a new friend and parental figure in Ramonda.
Ramonda gets kidnapped.
The king gets killed.
Hunter is orphaned again.
And he's got only one guy to blame for it all...

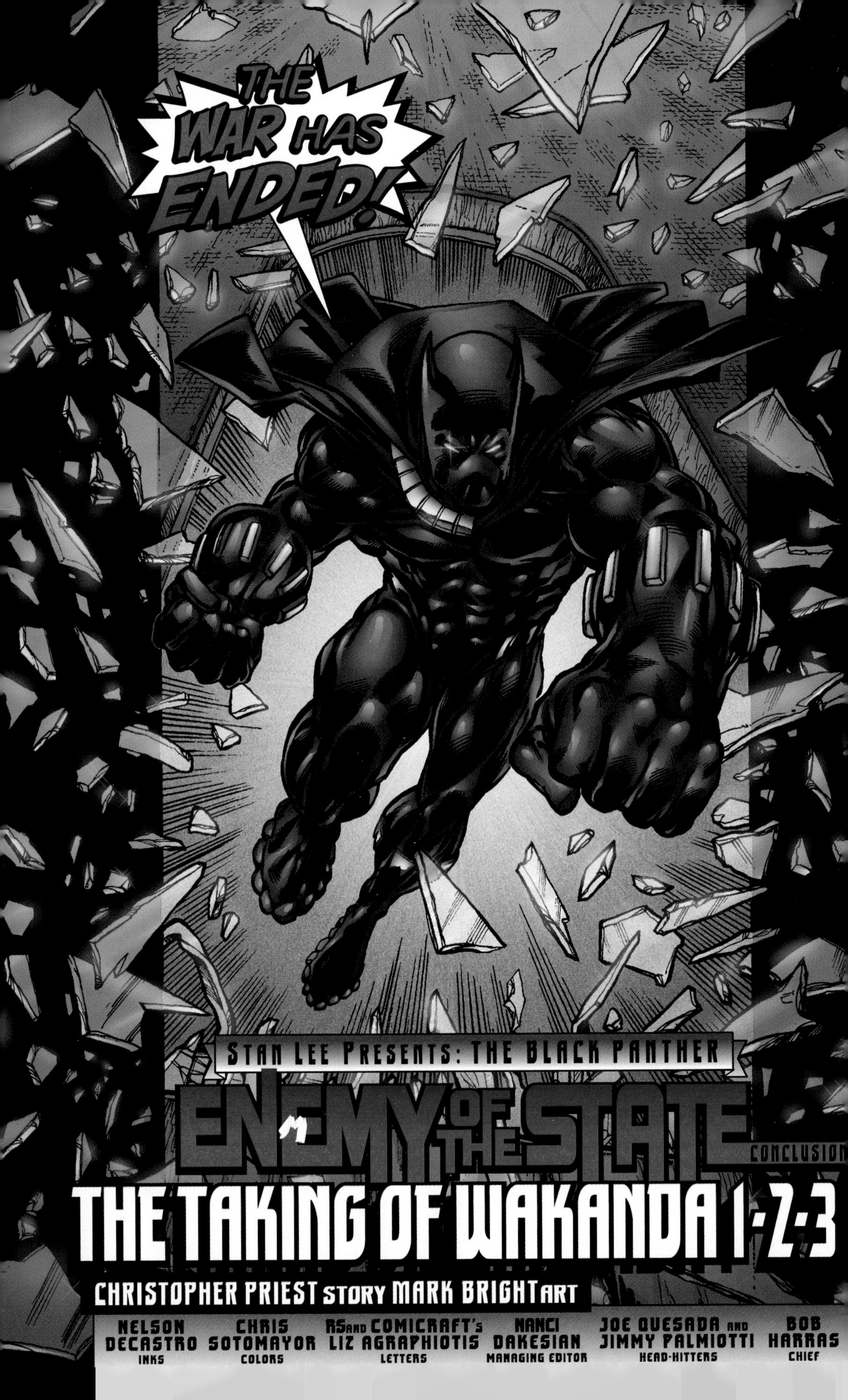
THE WAR HAS ENDED!
STAN LEE PRESENTS: THE BLACK PANTHER
ENEMY OF THE STATE
CONCLUSION
THE TAKING OF WAKANDA 1-2-3
CHRISTOPHER PRIEST STORY MARK BRIGHT ART
NELSON DECASTRO INKS
CHRIS SOTOMAYOR COLORS
RS AND COMICRAFT'S LIZ AGRAPHIOTIS LETTERS
NANCI DAKESIAN MANAGING EDITOR
JOE QUESADA AND JIMMY PALMIOTTI HEAD-HITTERS
BOB HARRAS CHIEF

LONG LIVE THE KING

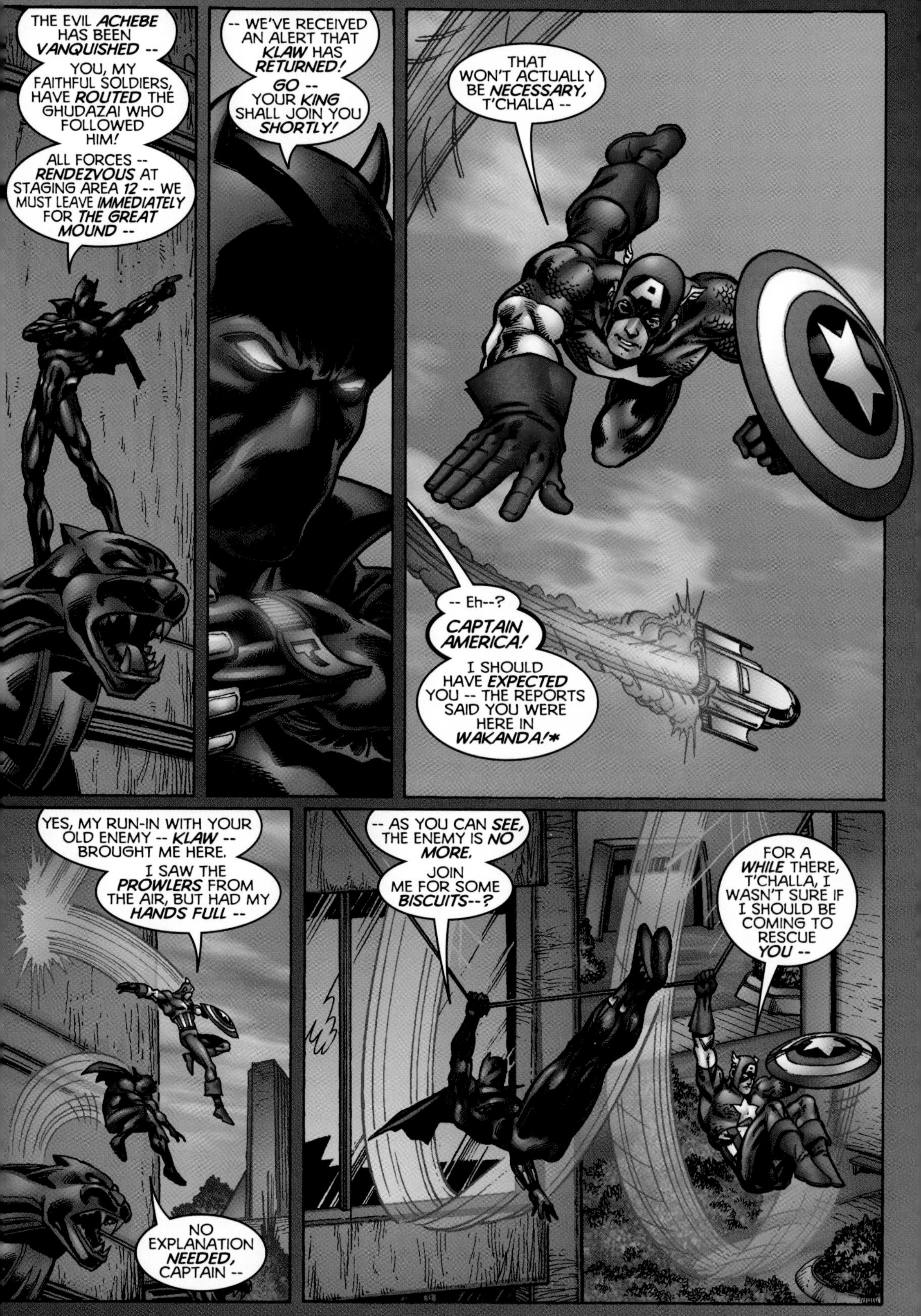

THE EVIL ACHEBE HAS BEEN VANQUISHED --
YOU, MY FAITHFUL SOLDIERS, HAVE ROUTED THE GHUDAZAI WHO FOLLOWED HIM!
ALL FORCES -- RENDEZVOUS AT STAGING AREA 12 -- WE MUST LEAVE IMMEDIATELY FOR THE GREAT MOUND --
-- WE'VE RECEIVED AN ALERT THAT KLAW HAS RETURNED!
GO -- YOUR KING SHALL JOIN YOU SHORTLY!
THAT WON'T ACTUALLY BE NECESSARY, T'CHALLA --
-- Eh--?
CAPTAIN AMERICA!
I SHOULD HAVE EXPECTED YOU -- THE REPORTS SAID YOU WERE HERE IN WAKANDA!*
YES, MY RUN-IN WITH YOUR OLD ENEMY -- KLAW -- BROUGHT ME HERE.
I SAW THE PROWLERS FROM THE AIR, BUT HAD MY HANDS FULL --
NO EXPLANATION NEEDED, CAPTAIN --
-- AS YOU CAN SEE, THE ENEMY IS NO MORE.
JOIN ME FOR SOME BISCUITS--?
FOR A WHILE THERE, T'CHALLA, I WASN'T SURE IF I SHOULD BE COMING TO RESCUE YOU --

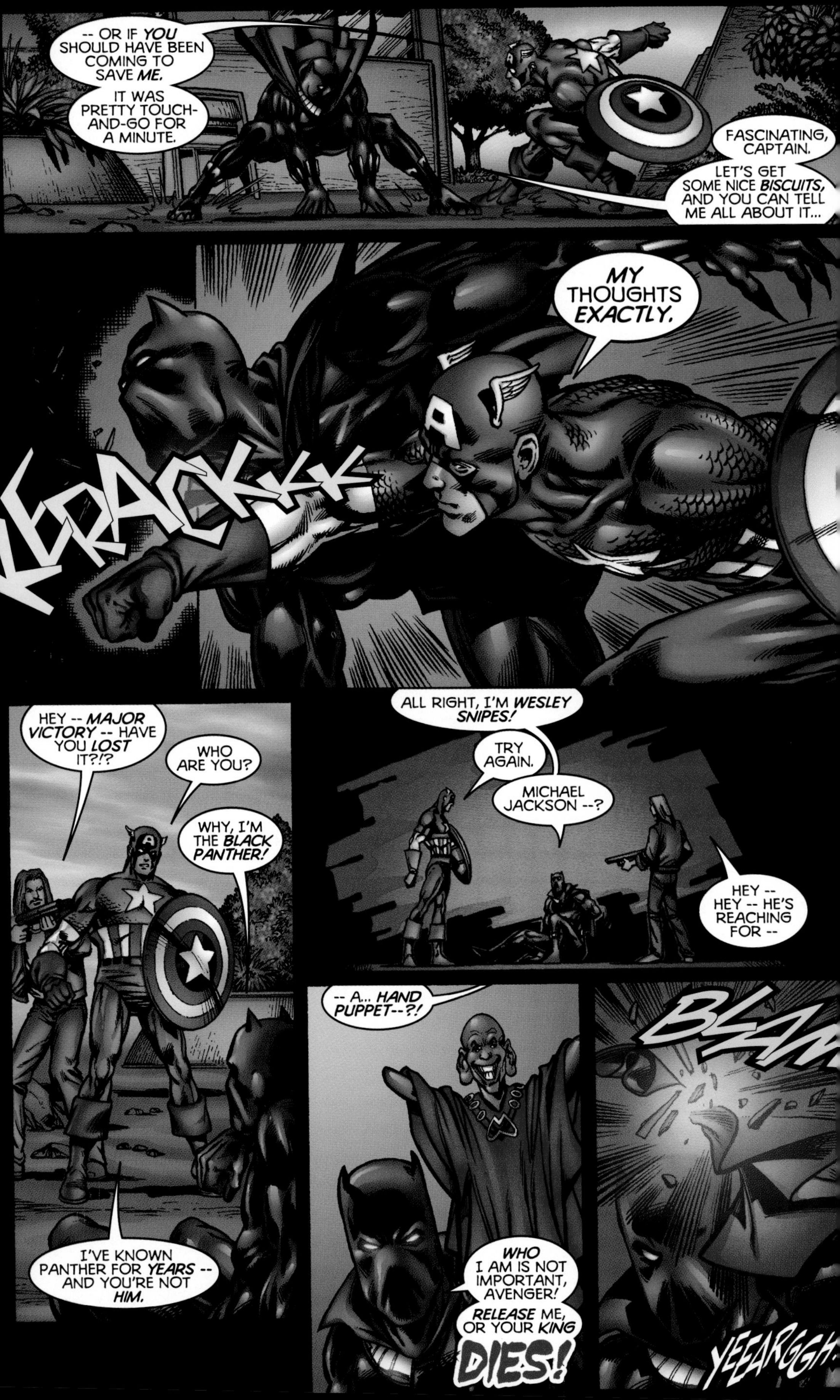

-- OR IF *YOU* SHOULD HAVE BEEN COMING TO SAVE *ME.*
IT WAS PRETTY TOUCH-AND-GO FOR A MINUTE.
FASCINATING, CAPTAIN.
LET'S GET SOME NICE *BISCUITS,* AND YOU CAN TELL ME ALL ABOUT IT...
MY THOUGHTS *EXACTLY.*
KRACKKK
HEY -- *MAJOR VICTORY* -- HAVE YOU *LOST* IT?!?
WHO ARE YOU?
WHY, I'M THE *BLACK PANTHER!*
I'VE KNOWN PANTHER FOR *YEARS* -- AND YOU'RE NOT *HIM.*
ALL RIGHT, I'M *WESLEY SNIPES!*
TRY AGAIN.
MICHAEL JACKSON --?
HEY -- HEY -- HE'S REACHING FOR --
-- A... *HAND PUPPET*--?!
WHO I AM IS NOT IMPORTANT, AVENGER!
RELEASE ME, OR YOUR *KING* DIES!
BLAM
YEEARGGH!

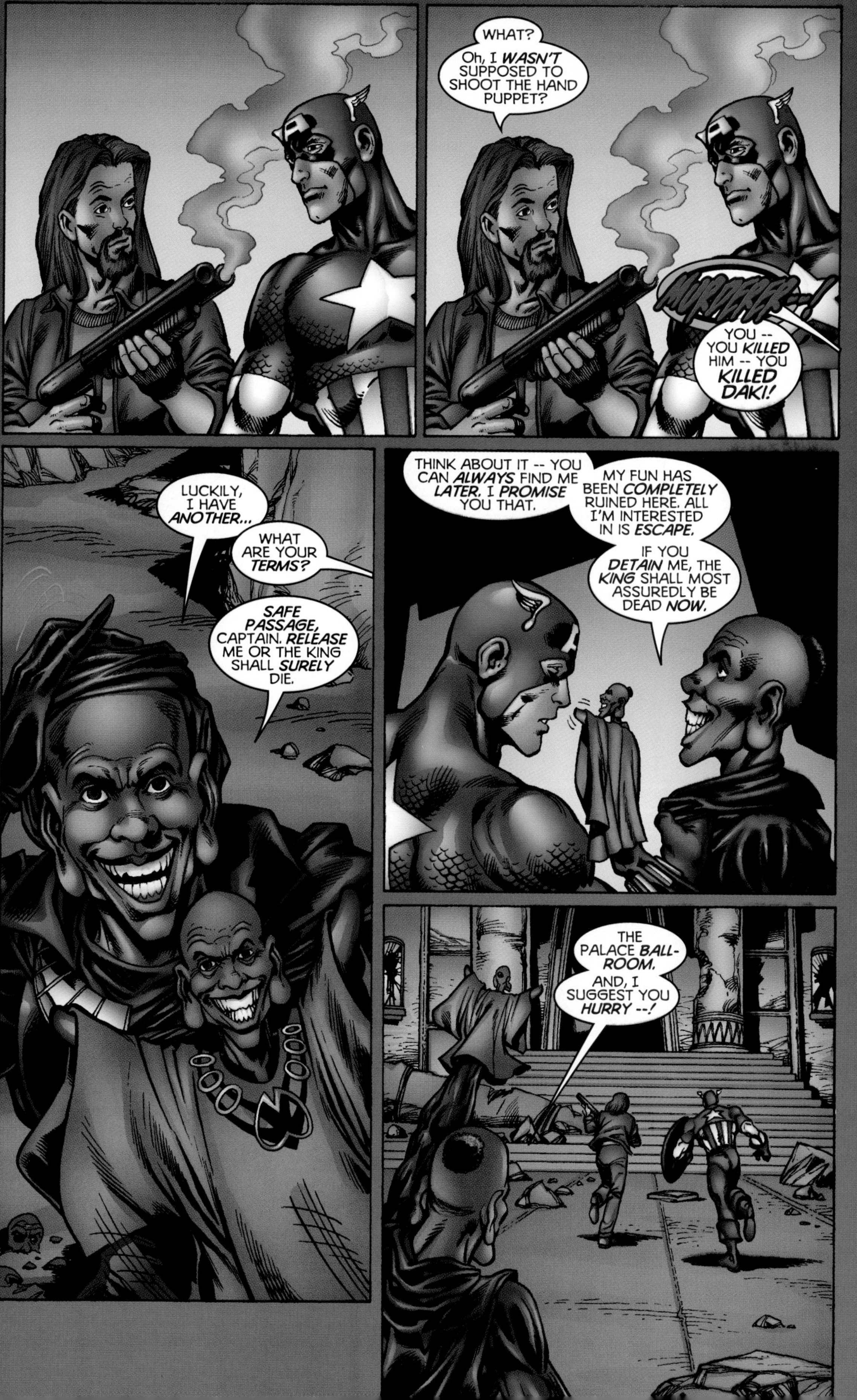
WHAT?
Oh, I WASN'T SUPPOSED TO SHOOT THE HAND PUPPET?
MURDERER--!
YOU -- YOU KILLED HIM -- YOU KILLED DAKI!
LUCKILY, I HAVE ANOTHER...
WHAT ARE YOUR TERMS?
SAFE PASSAGE, CAPTAIN. RELEASE ME OR THE KING SHALL SURELY DIE.
THINK ABOUT IT -- YOU CAN ALWAYS FIND ME LATER. I PROMISE YOU THAT.
MY FUN HAS BEEN COMPLETELY RUINED HERE. ALL I'M INTERESTED IN IS ESCAPE.
IF YOU DETAIN ME, THE KING SHALL MOST ASSUREDLY BE DEAD NOW.
THE PALACE BALL-ROOM.
AND, I SUGGEST YOU HURRY --!

And, so, there I was.

Stanford Law, Oxford masters, five years in Washington, Mr. Can-Do-Work-The-System-Fast-Track hotshot Beltway lawyer. Master of my Political Domain. On the short list for a cabinet post. The Pennsylvania Avenue Wunderkind.

... ah ...

Trapped inside a giant arcade game with a naked black man.

The BAD NEWS was, all of the beach-ball-sized TOY PRIZES were BOMBS. The WORSE news was EACH BOMB was powerful enough to LEVEL the palace. The EVEN WORSE news was there were HUNDREDS of bombs --

-- each with an INDEPENDENT TIMER set to a DIFFERENT TIME. The glass case was filling up with ACID and, in what I personally consider serious OVERKILL --

-- the grappling claw overhead was both ELECTRIFIED and RAZOR SHARP. Achebe REALLY could have chosen one or the other... but, I digress...

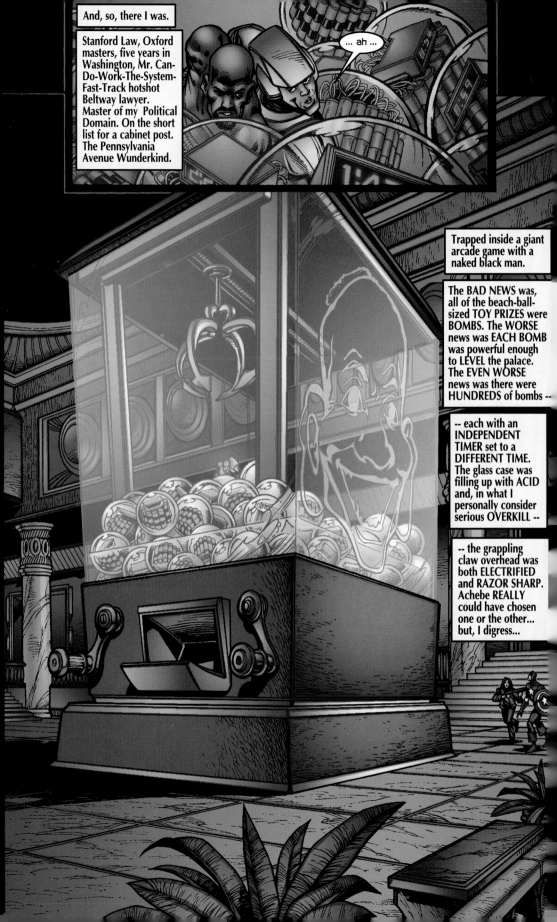

WHERE'S NELSON RIDDLE WHEN YOU REALLY NEED HIM?

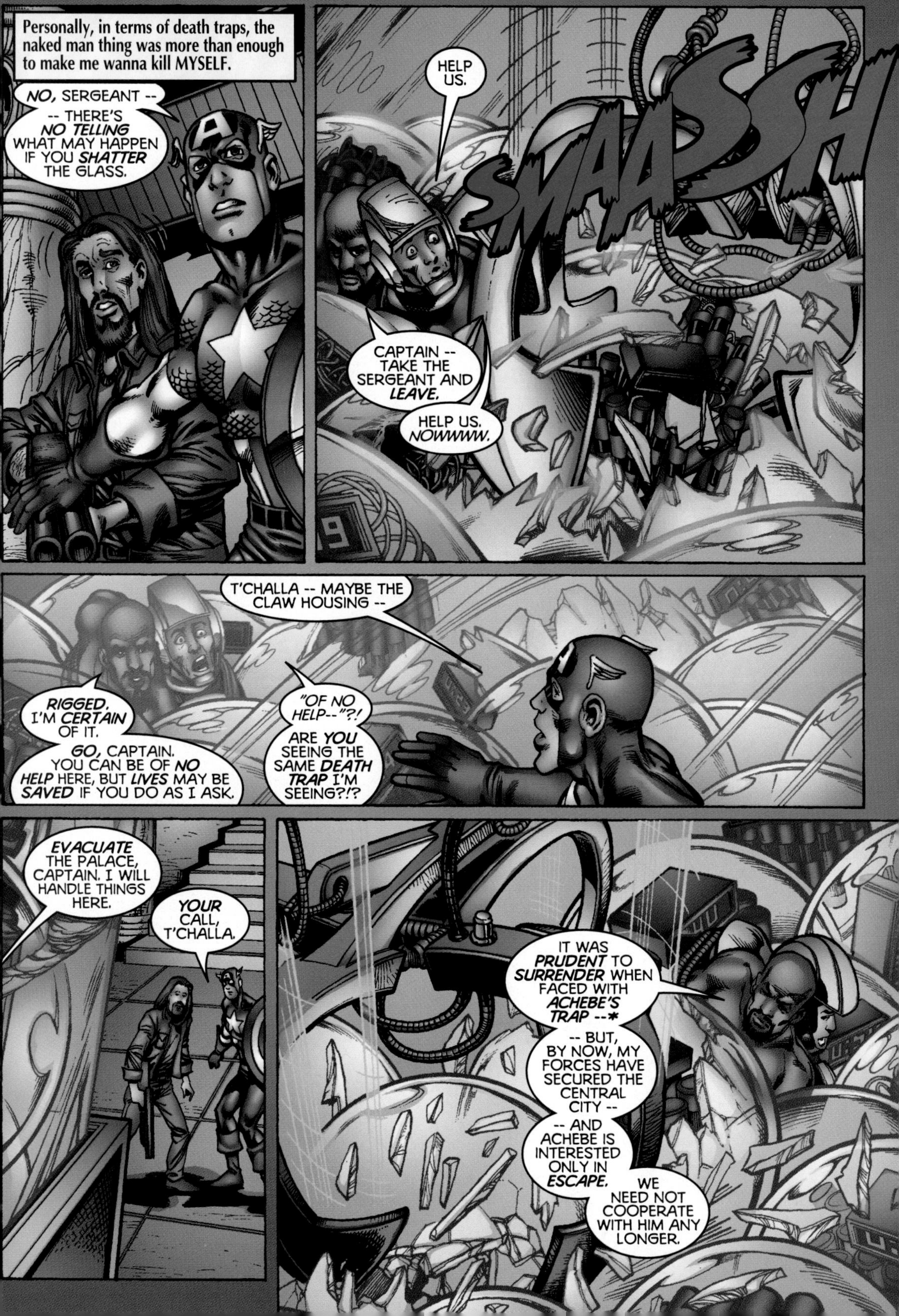

Personally, in terms of death traps, the naked man thing was more than enough to make me wanna kill MYSELF.
NO, SERGEANT --
-- THERE'S NO TELLING WHAT MAY HAPPEN IF YOU SHATTER THE GLASS.
HELP US.
SMAASH
CAPTAIN -- TAKE THE SERGEANT AND LEAVE.
HELP US. NOWWWW.
T'CHALLA -- MAYBE THE CLAW HOUSING --
RIGGED. I'M CERTAIN OF IT.
GO, CAPTAIN. YOU CAN BE OF NO HELP HERE, BUT LIVES MAY BE SAVED IF YOU DO AS I ASK.
"OF NO HELP--"?!
ARE YOU SEEING THE SAME DEATH TRAP I'M SEEING?!?
EVACUATE THE PALACE, CAPTAIN. I WILL HANDLE THINGS HERE.
YOUR CALL, T'CHALLA.
IT WAS PRUDENT TO SURRENDER WHEN FACED WITH ACHEBE'S TRAP --*
-- BUT, BY NOW, MY FORCES HAVE SECURED THE CENTRAL CITY --
-- AND ACHEBE IS INTERESTED ONLY IN ESCAPE.
WE NEED NOT COOPERATE WITH HIM ANY LONGER.

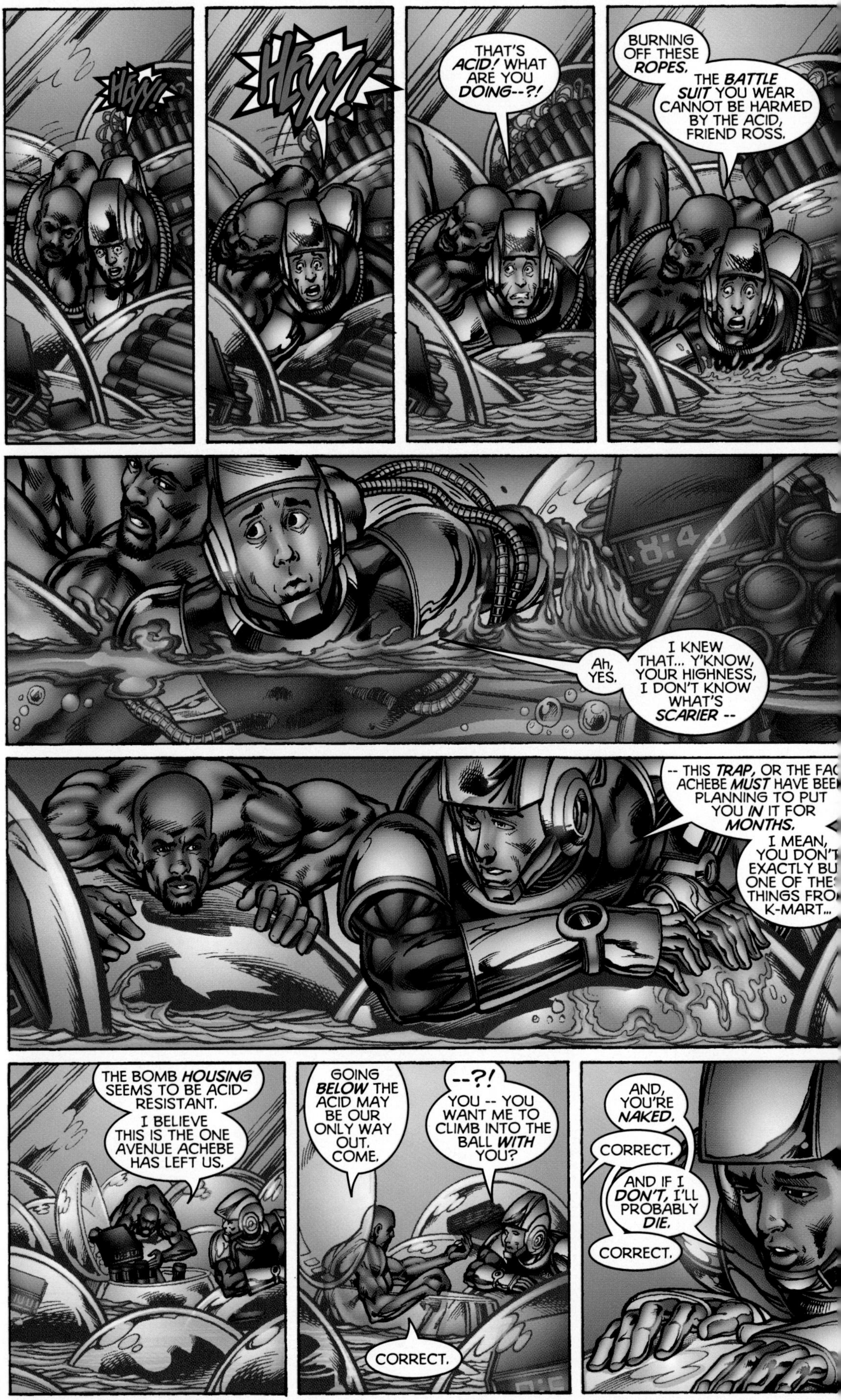
HEYY!
HEYY!
THAT'S ACID! WHAT ARE YOU DOING--?!
BURNING OFF THESE ROPES.
THE BATTLE SUIT YOU WEAR CANNOT BE HARMED BY THE ACID, FRIEND ROSS.
Ah, YES.
I KNEW THAT... Y'KNOW, YOUR HIGHNESS, I DON'T KNOW WHAT'S SCARIER --
-- THIS TRAP, OR THE FAC ACHEBE MUST HAVE BEE PLANNING TO PUT YOU IN IT FOR MONTHS.
I MEAN, YOU DON'T EXACTLY BU ONE OF THES THINGS FRO K-MART...
THE BOMB HOUSING SEEMS TO BE ACID-RESISTANT.
I BELIEVE THIS IS THE ONE AVENUE ACHEBE HAS LEFT US.
GOING BELOW THE ACID MAY BE OUR ONLY WAY OUT. COME.
--?!
YOU -- YOU WANT ME TO CLIMB INTO THE BALL WITH YOU?
CORRECT.
AND, YOU'RE NAKED.
CORRECT.
AND IF I DON'T, I'LL PROBABLY DIE.
CORRECT.

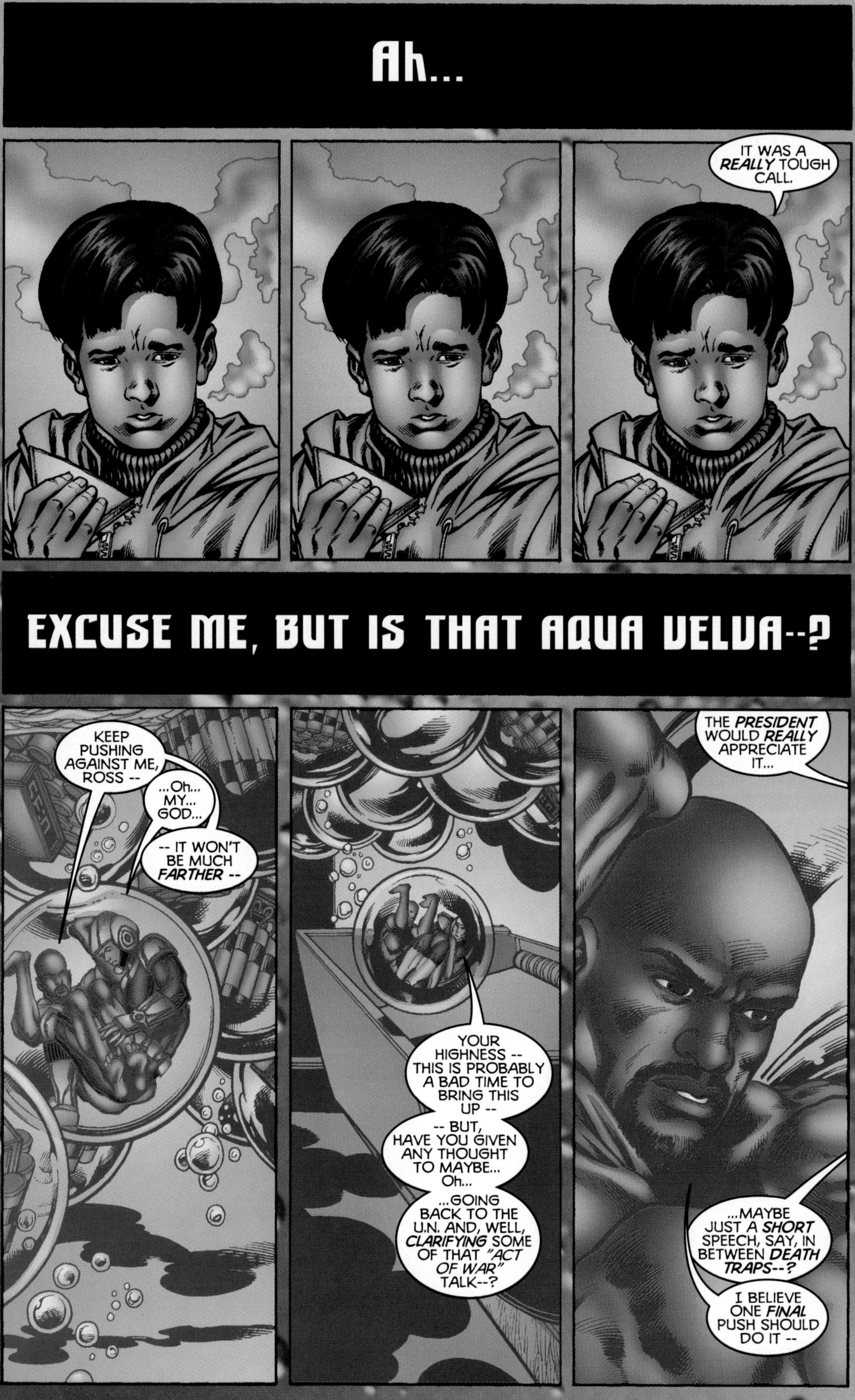
Ah...
IT WAS A REALLY TOUGH CALL.
EXCUSE ME, BUT IS THAT AQUA VELVA--?
KEEP PUSHING AGAINST ME, ROSS --
...Oh... MY... GOD...
-- IT WON'T BE MUCH FARTHER --
YOUR HIGHNESS -- THIS IS PROBABLY A BAD TIME TO BRING THIS UP --
-- BUT, HAVE YOU GIVEN ANY THOUGHT TO MAYBE... Oh...
...GOING BACK TO THE U.N. AND, WELL, CLARIFYING SOME OF THAT "ACT OF WAR" TALK--?
THE PRESIDENT WOULD REALLY APPRECIATE IT...
...MAYBE JUST A SHORT SPEECH, SAY, IN BETWEEN DEATH TRAPS--?
I BELIEVE ONE FINAL PUSH SHOULD DO IT --

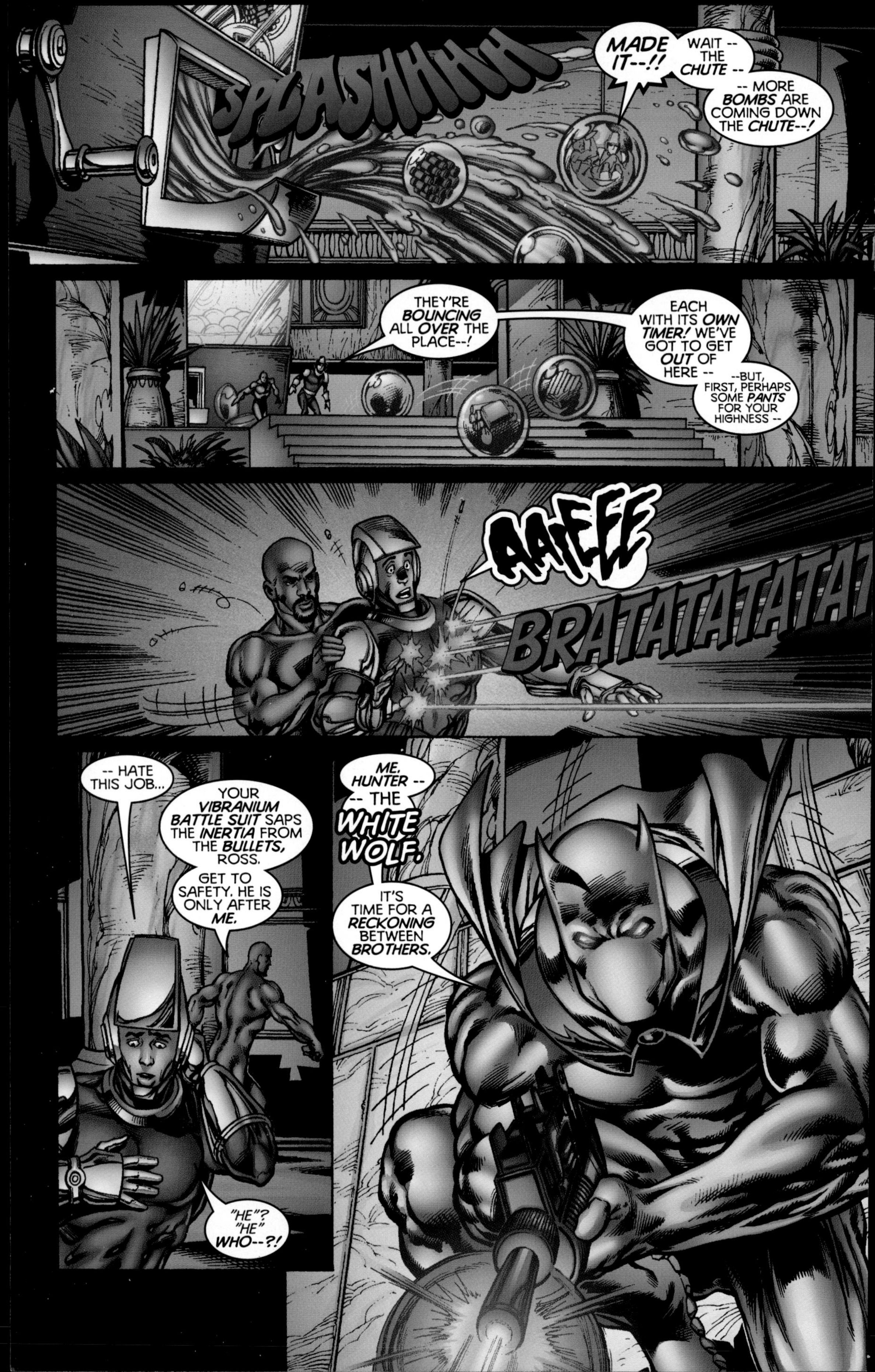
SPLASHHHH
MADE IT--!!
WAIT -- THE CHUTE --
-- MORE BOMBS ARE COMING DOWN THE CHUTE--!
THEY'RE BOUNCING ALL OVER THE PLACE--!
EACH WITH ITS OWN TIMER! WE'VE GOT TO GET OUT OF HERE --
--BUT, FIRST, PERHAPS SOME PANTS FOR YOUR HIGHNESS --
AAIEEE
BRATATATATAT
-- HATE THIS JOB...
YOUR VIBRANIUM BATTLE SUIT SAPS THE INERTIA FROM THE BULLETS, ROSS.
GET TO SAFETY. HE IS ONLY AFTER ME.
"HE"? "HE" WHO--?!
ME. HUNTER --
-- THE WHITE WOLF.
IT'S TIME FOR A RECKONING BETWEEN BROTHERS.

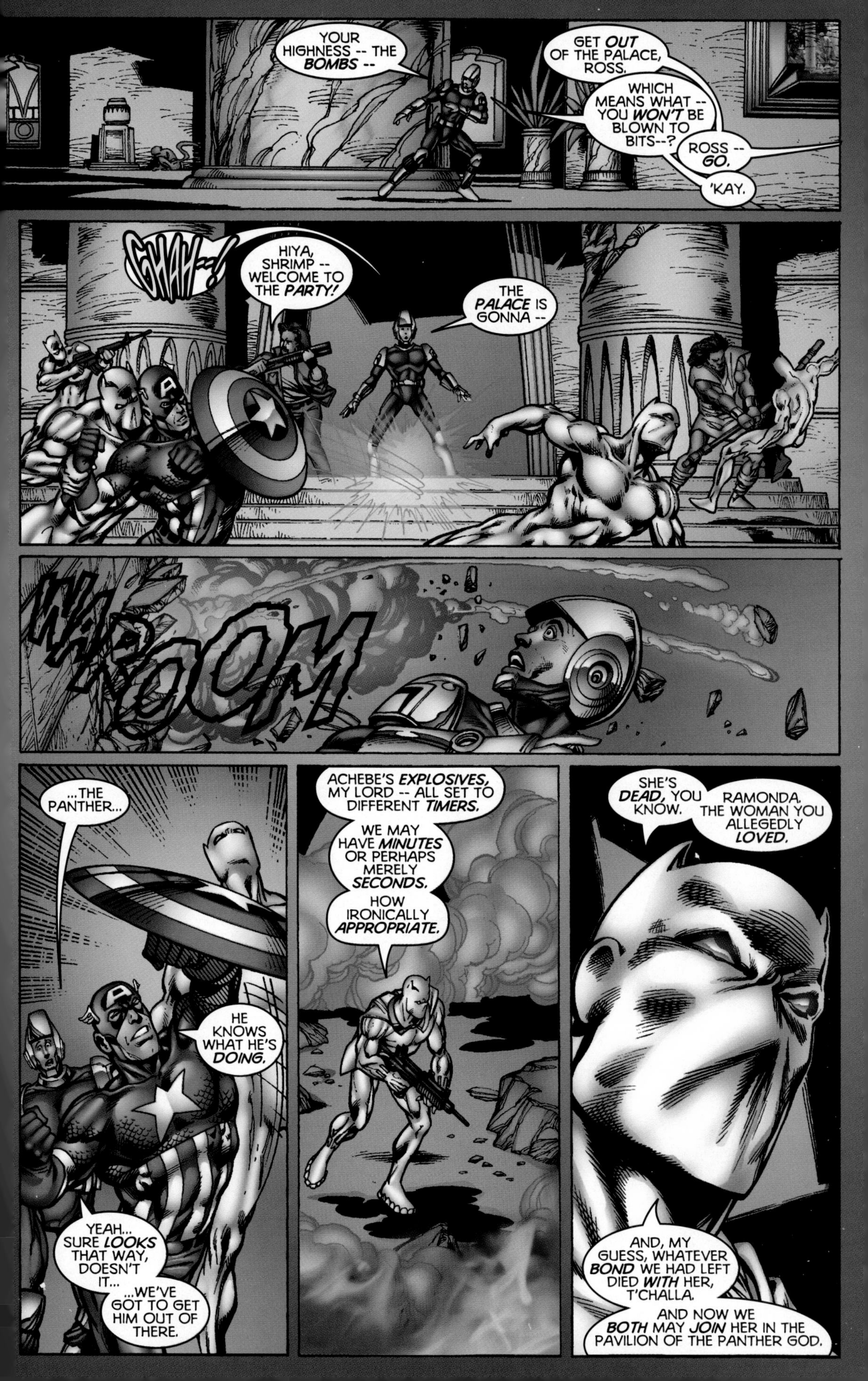
YOUR HIGHNESS -- THE BOMBS --
GET OUT OF THE PALACE, ROSS.
WHICH MEANS WHAT -- YOU WON'T BE BLOWN TO BITS--?
ROSS -- GO.
'KAY.
CHAK--!
HIYA, SHRIMP -- WELCOME TO THE PARTY!
THE PALACE IS GONNA --
...THE PANTHER...
HE KNOWS WHAT HE'S DOING.
YEAH... SURE LOOKS THAT WAY, DOESN'T IT...
...WE'VE GOT TO GET HIM OUT OF THERE.
ACHEBE'S EXPLOSIVES, MY LORD -- ALL SET TO DIFFERENT TIMERS.
WE MAY HAVE MINUTES OR PERHAPS MERELY SECONDS.
HOW IRONICALLY APPROPRIATE.
SHE'S DEAD, YOU KNOW.
RAMONDA. THE WOMAN YOU ALLEGEDLY LOVED.
AND, MY GUESS, WHATEVER BOND WE HAD LEFT DIED WITH HER, T'CHALLA.
AND NOW WE BOTH MAY JOIN HER IN THE PAVILION OF THE PANTHER GOD.

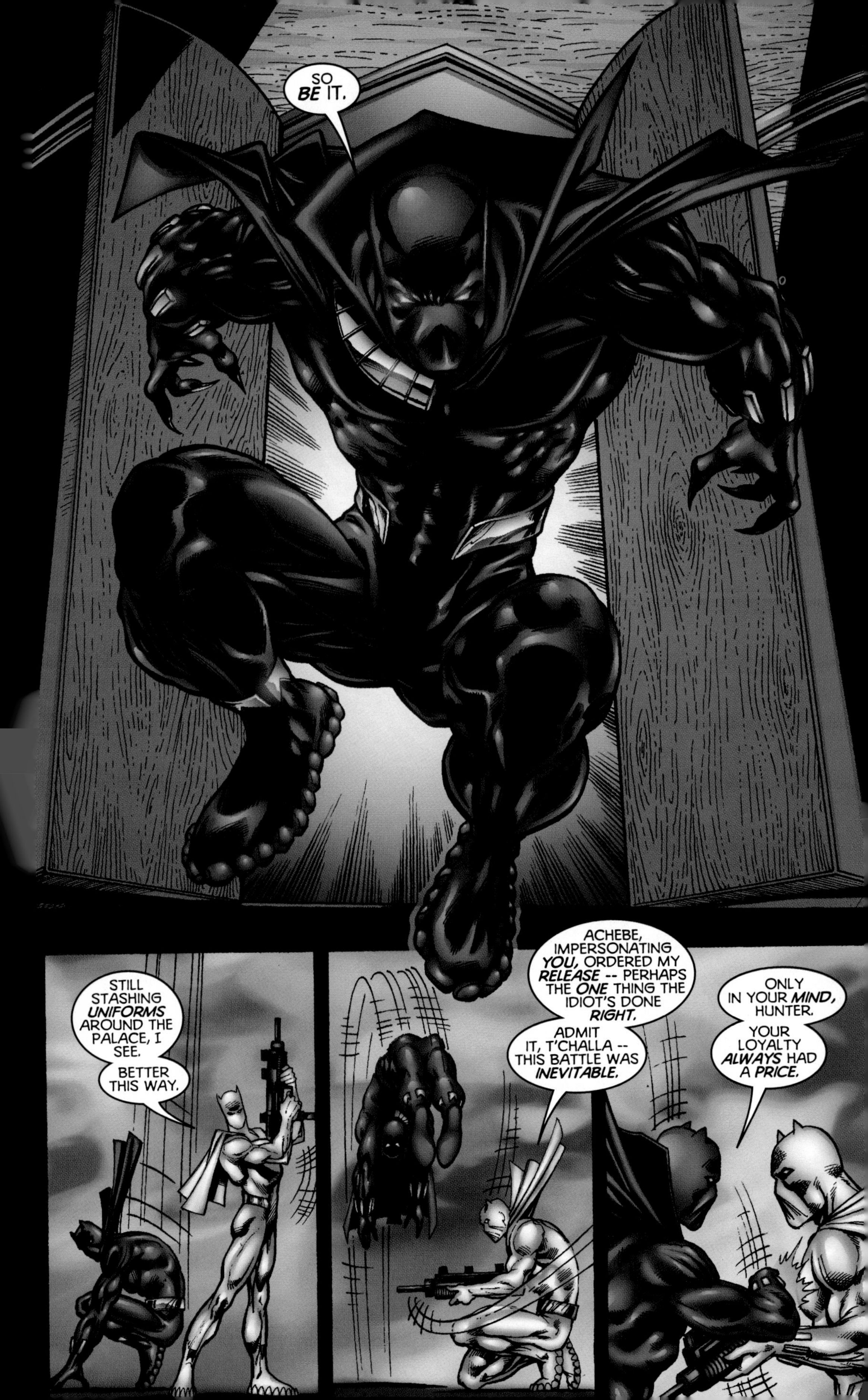
SO BE IT.
STILL STASHING UNIFORMS AROUND THE PALACE, I SEE.
BETTER THIS WAY.
ACHEBE, IMPERSONATING YOU, ORDERED MY RELEASE -- PERHAPS THE ONE THING THE IDIOT'S DONE RIGHT.
ADMIT IT, T'CHALLA -- THIS BATTLE WAS INEVITABLE.
ONLY IN YOUR MIND, HUNTER.
YOUR LOYALTY ALWAYS HAD A PRICE.

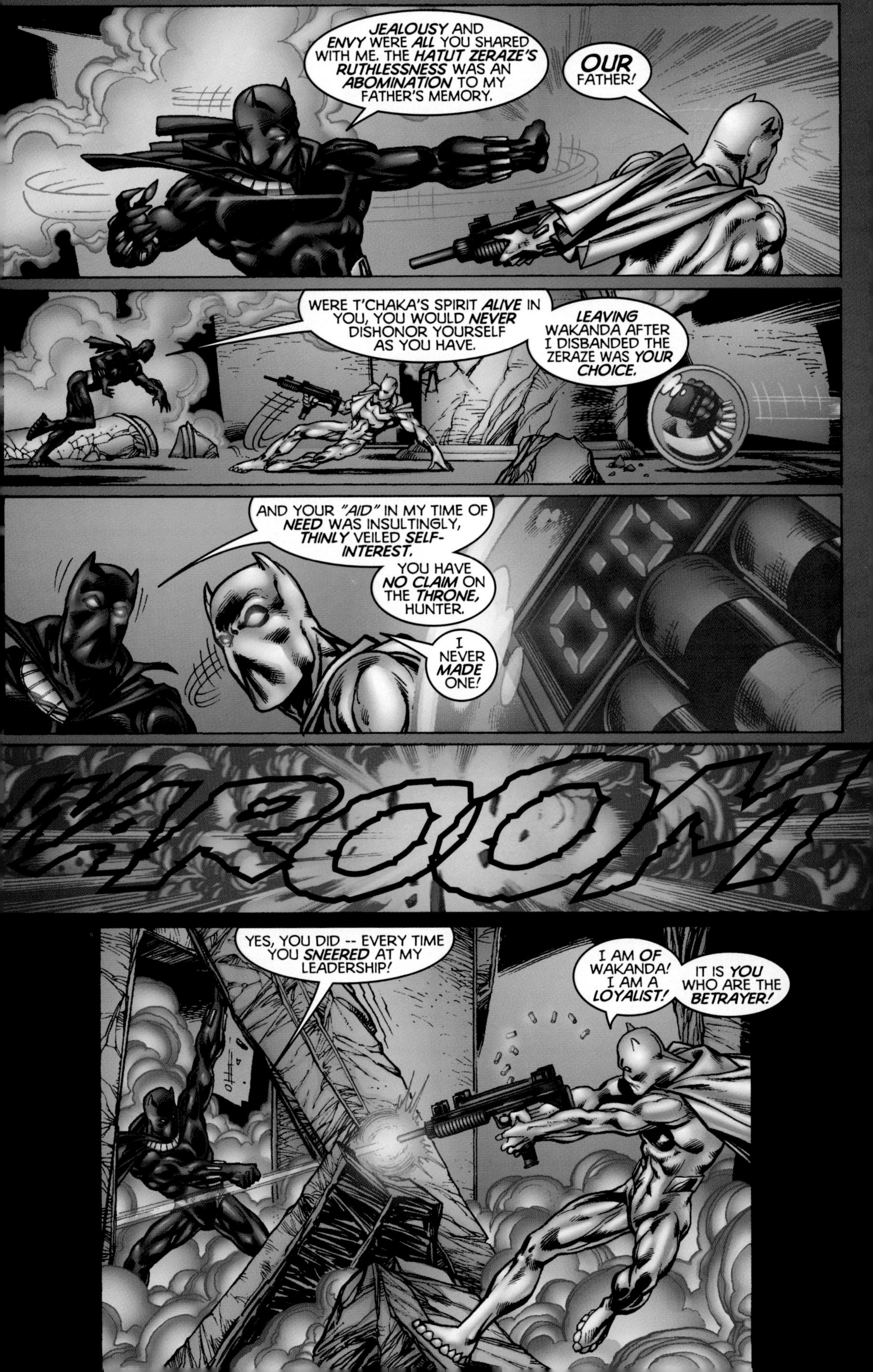
JEALOUSY AND ENVY WERE ALL YOU SHARED WITH ME. THE HATUT ZERAZE'S RUTHLESSNESS WAS AN ABOMINATION TO MY FATHER'S MEMORY.
OUR FATHER!
WERE T'CHAKA'S SPIRIT ALIVE IN YOU, YOU WOULD NEVER DISHONOR YOURSELF AS YOU HAVE.
LEAVING WAKANDA AFTER I DISBANDED THE ZERAZE WAS YOUR CHOICE.
AND YOUR "AID" IN MY TIME OF NEED WAS INSULTINGLY, THINLY VEILED SELF-INTEREST.
YOU HAVE NO CLAIM ON THE THRONE, HUNTER.
I NEVER MADE ONE!
KRROOM
YES, YOU DID -- EVERY TIME YOU SNEERED AT MY LEADERSHIP!
I AM OF WAKANDA! I AM A LOYALIST!
IT IS YOU WHO ARE THE BETRAYER!

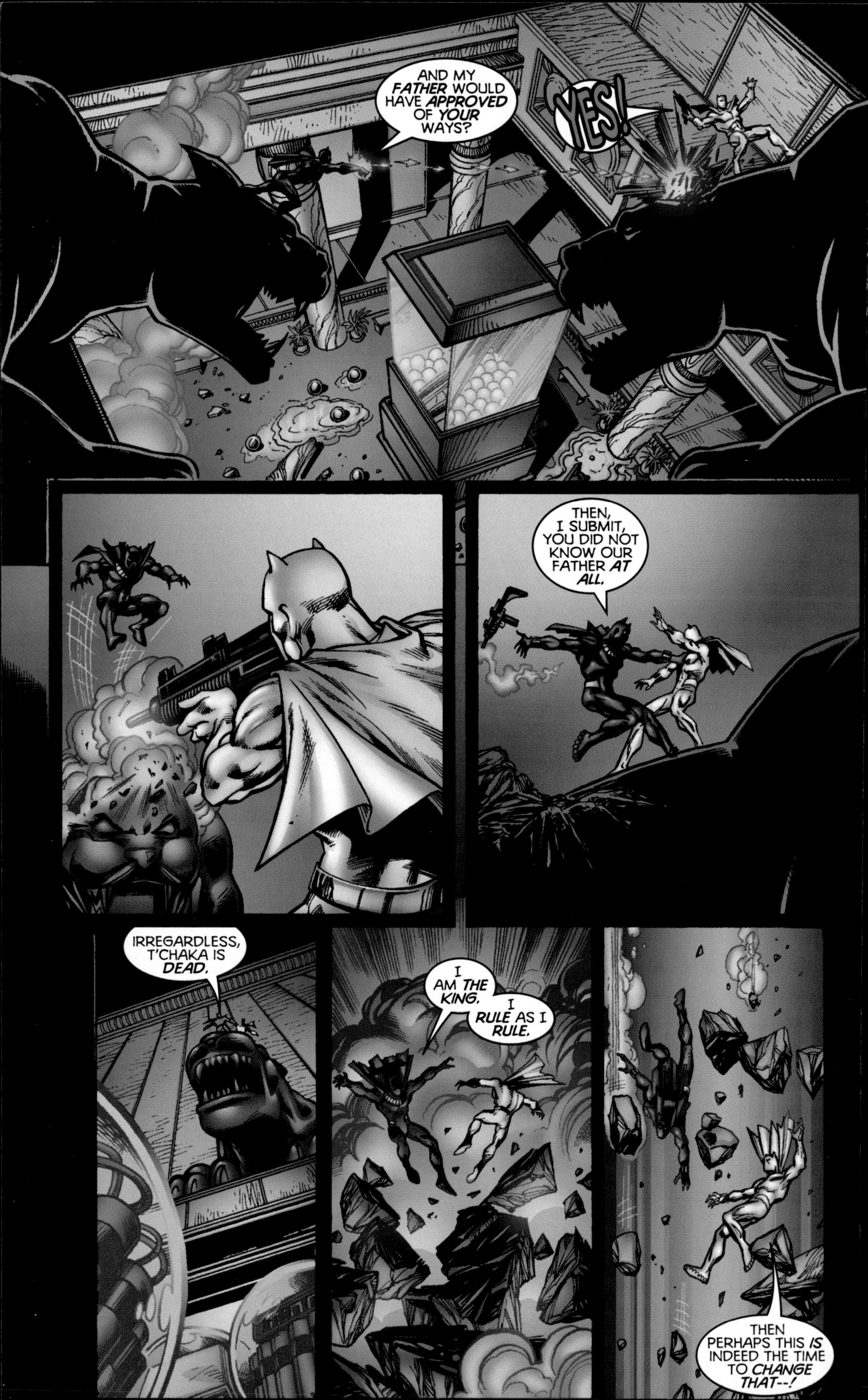
AND MY FATHER WOULD HAVE APPROVED OF YOUR WAYS?
YES!
THEN, I SUBMIT, YOU DID NOT KNOW OUR FATHER AT ALL.
IRREGARDLESS, T'CHAKA IS DEAD.
I AM THE KING.
I RULE AS I RULE.
THEN PERHAPS THIS IS INDEED THE TIME TO CHANGE THAT--!

Outside, the White Wolf's boys were making things fairly interesting.

...NOT THE HAIR... NOT THE HAIR...

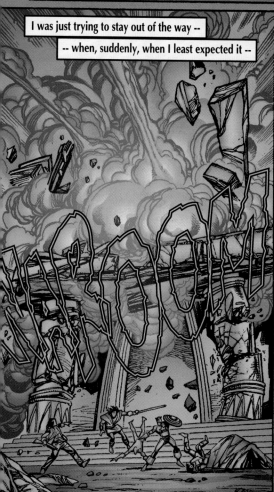

I was just trying to stay out of the way --

-- when, suddenly, when I least expected it --

-- I became a MAN.

ROSS -- NO -- IT'S TOO DANGEROUS--!

Don't ask me to EXPLAIN it, Nikki. It's just -- well -- I just couldn't LEAVE him in there.

WON'T... BE LONG NOW, MY LORD...

ACHEBE'S DEVILISH HANDIWORK HAS ALL BUT LEVELED YOUR GREAT HOME...

...TIME ... TO END THINGS BETWEEN US...

SO, HUNTER -- THIS -- THIS TREACHERY -- IS THE ACT OF A LOYALIST --?!

I AM LOYAL TO THE THRONE, T'CHALLA!

THIS IS A DISPUTE BETWEEN BROTHERS!!

COMMAND ME AS MY KING --

-- AND, OF COURSE, I WILL OBEY YOU.

THAT'S ALL IT WILL TAKE, T'CHALLA --

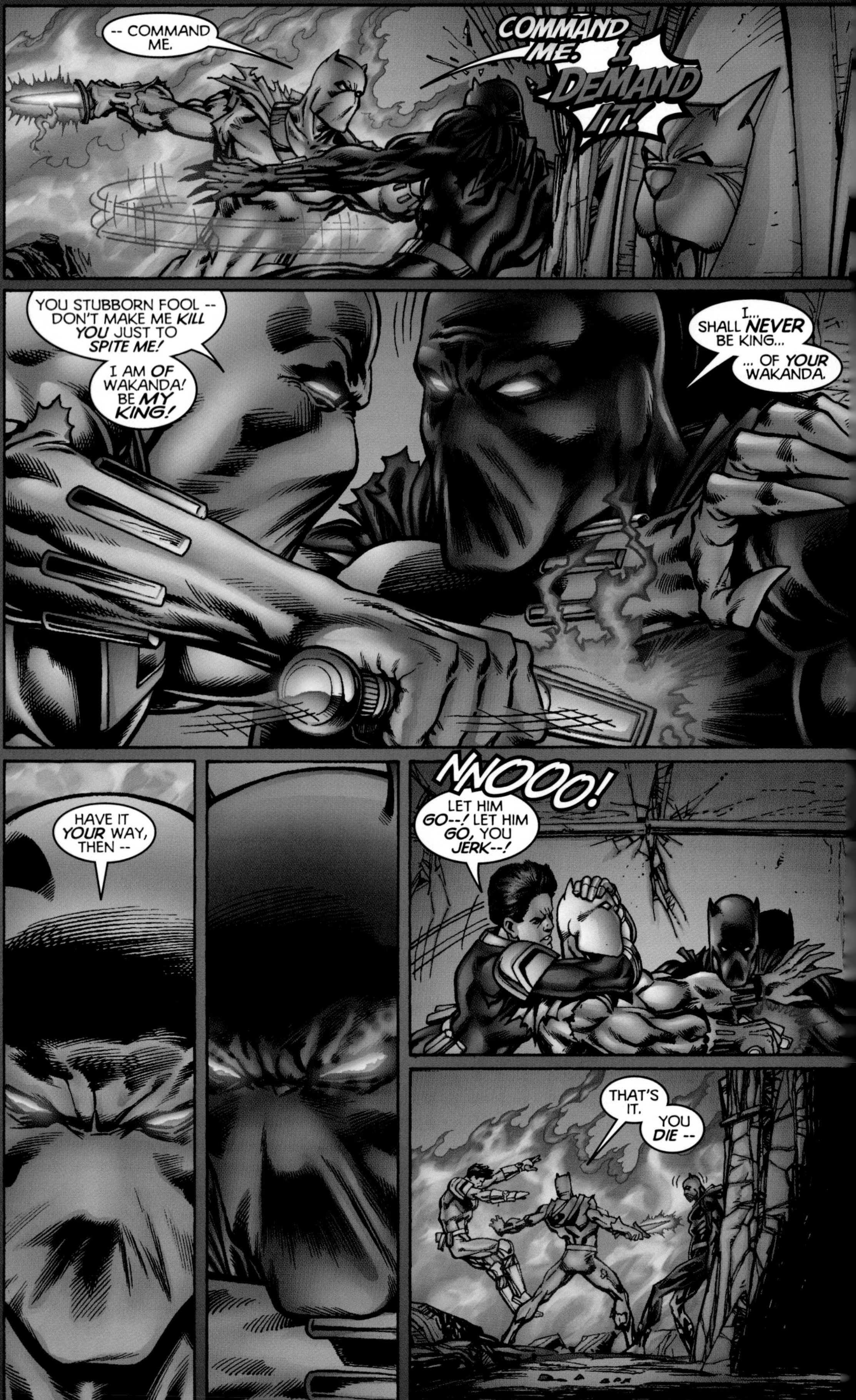

-- COMMAND ME.
COMMAND ME. I DEMAND IT!
YOU STUBBORN FOOL -- DON'T MAKE ME KILL YOU JUST TO SPITE ME!
I AM OF WAKANDA! BE MY KING!
I... SHALL NEVER BE KING...
... OF YOUR WAKANDA.
HAVE IT YOUR WAY, THEN --
NNOOO!
LET HIM GO--! LET HIM GO, YOU JERK--!
THAT'S IT.
YOU DIE --

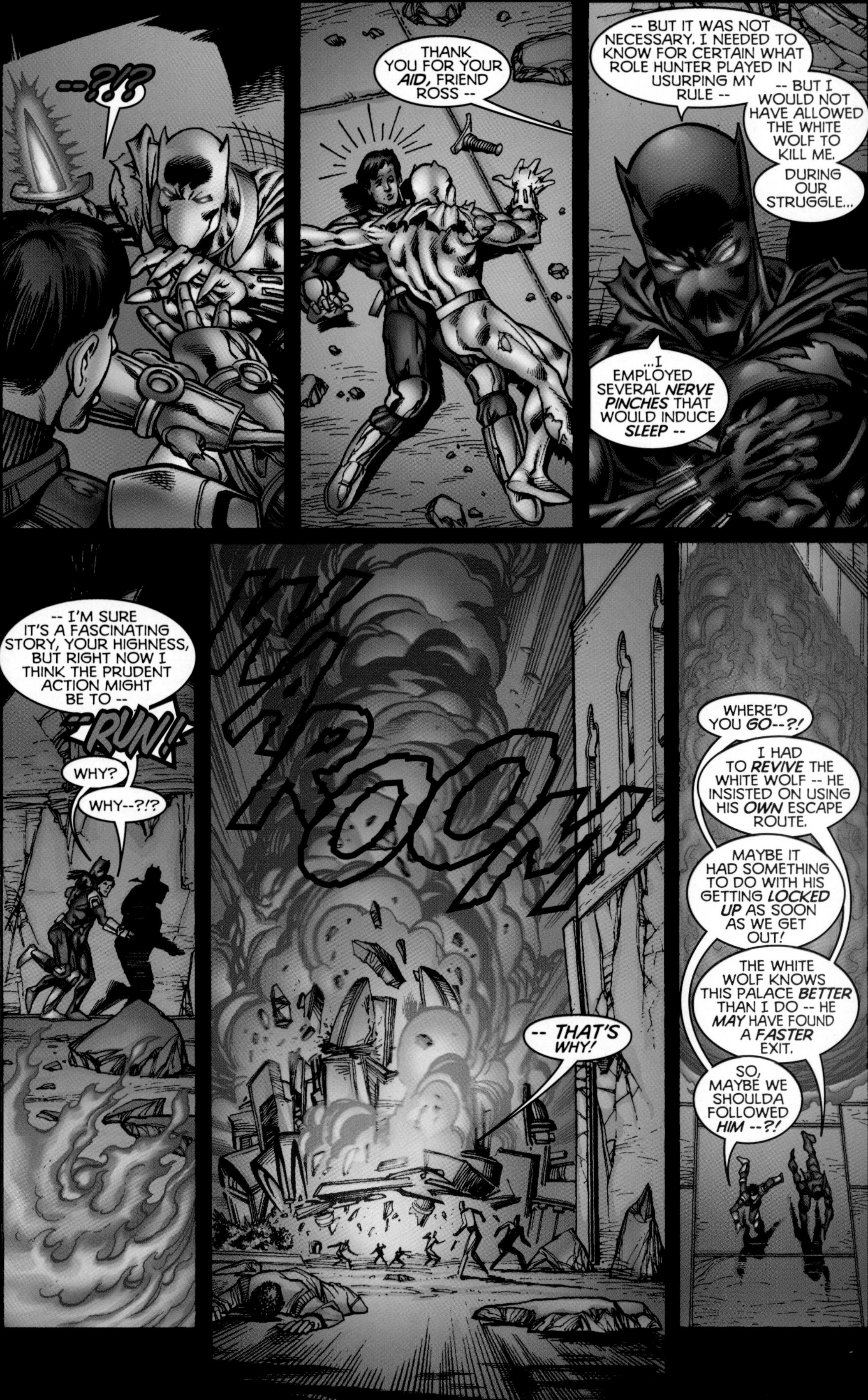

--?!?
THANK YOU FOR YOUR AID, FRIEND ROSS --
-- BUT IT WAS NOT NECESSARY. I NEEDED TO KNOW FOR CERTAIN WHAT ROLE HUNTER PLAYED IN USURPING MY RULE --
-- BUT I WOULD NOT HAVE ALLOWED THE WHITE WOLF TO KILL ME.
DURING OUR STRUGGLE...
...I EMPLOYED SEVERAL NERVE PINCHES THAT WOULD INDUCE SLEEP --
-- I'M SURE IT'S A FASCINATING STORY, YOUR HIGHNESS, BUT RIGHT NOW I THINK THE PRUDENT ACTION MIGHT BE TO --
--RUN!
WHY?
WHY--?!?
WHOOM
-- THAT'S WHY!
WHERE'D YOU GO--?!
I HAD TO REVIVE THE WHITE WOLF -- HE INSISTED ON USING HIS OWN ESCAPE ROUTE.
MAYBE IT HAD SOMETHING TO DO WITH HIS GETTING LOCKED UP AS SOON AS WE GET OUT!
THE WHITE WOLF KNOWS THIS PALACE BETTER THAN I DO -- HE MAY HAVE FOUND A FASTER EXIT.
SO, MAYBE WE SHOULDA FOLLOWED HIM --?!

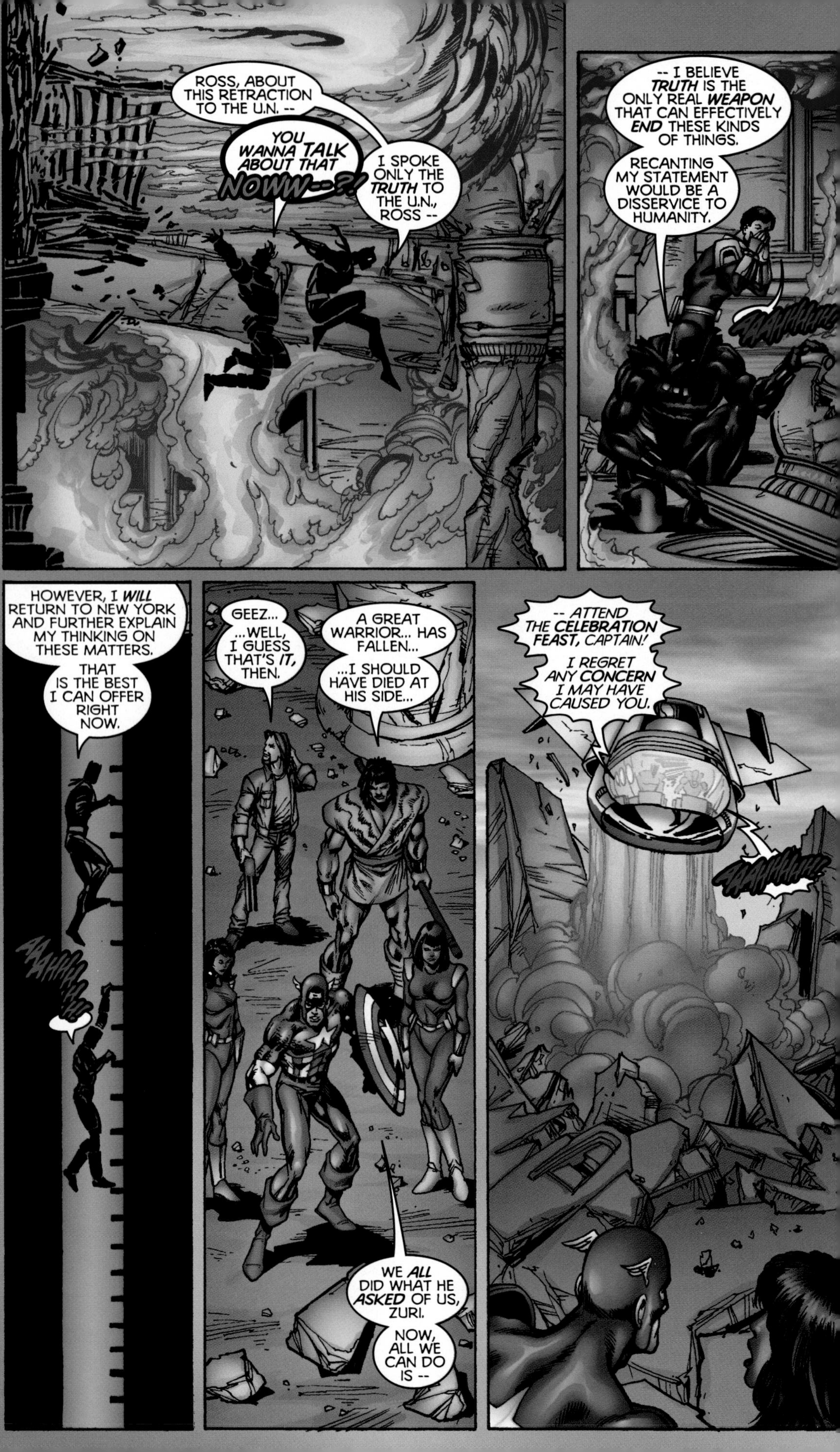
ROSS, ABOUT THIS RETRACTION TO THE U.N. --
YOU WANNA TALK ABOUT THAT NOWW--?!
I SPOKE ONLY THE TRUTH TO THE U.N., ROSS --
-- I BELIEVE TRUTH IS THE ONLY REAL WEAPON THAT CAN EFFECTIVELY END THESE KINDS OF THINGS.
RECANTING MY STATEMENT WOULD BE A DISSERVICE TO HUMANITY.
HOWEVER, I WILL RETURN TO NEW YORK AND FURTHER EXPLAIN MY THINKING ON THESE MATTERS.
THAT IS THE BEST I CAN OFFER RIGHT NOW.
GEEZ...
...WELL, I GUESS THAT'S IT, THEN.
A GREAT WARRIOR... HAS FALLEN...
...I SHOULD HAVE DIED AT HIS SIDE...
WE ALL DID WHAT HE ASKED OF US, ZURI.
NOW, ALL WE CAN DO IS --
-- ATTEND THE CELEBRATION FEAST, CAPTAIN!
I REGRET ANY CONCERN I MAY HAVE CAUSED YOU.

AWAKENINGS

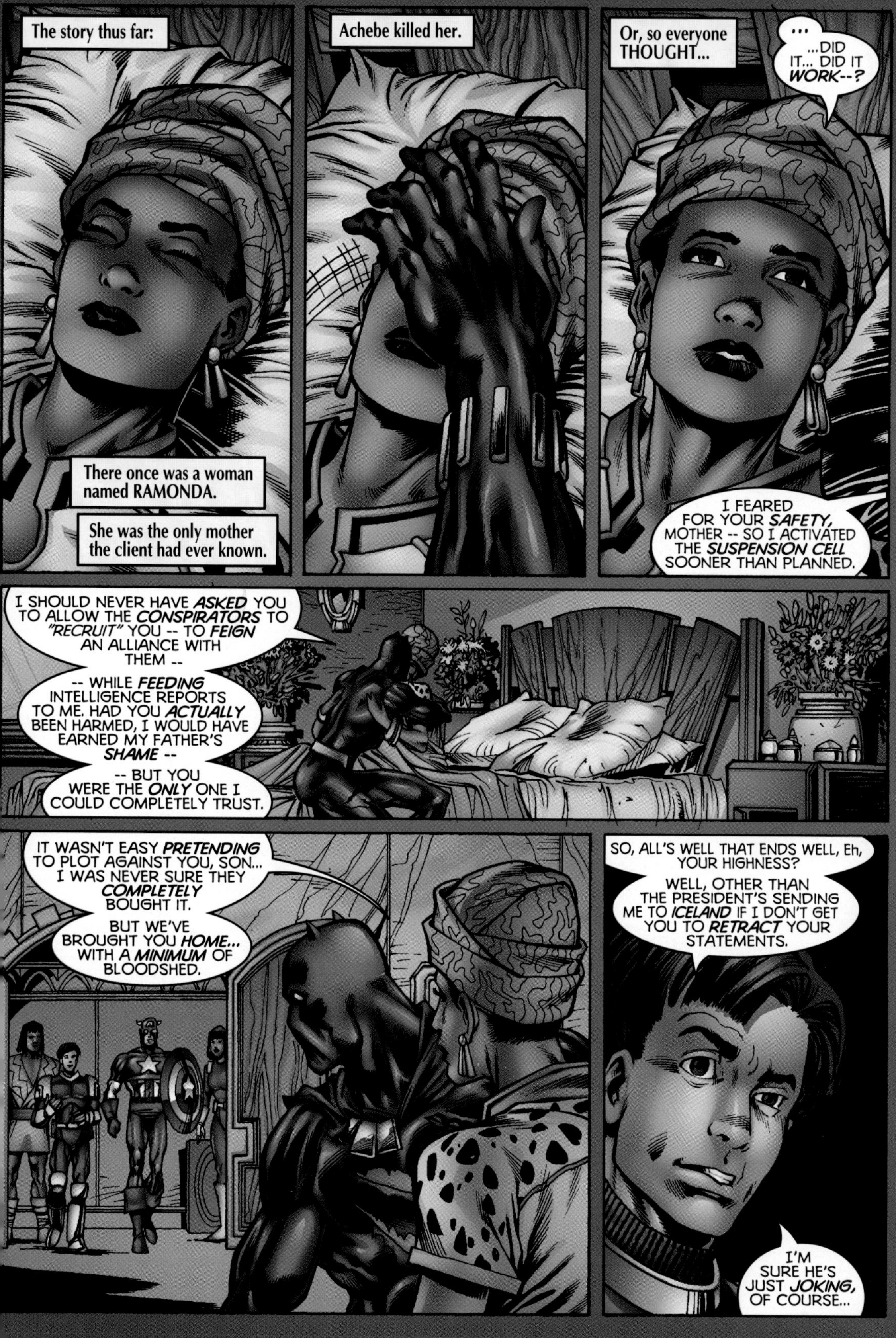

The story thus far:
There once was a woman named RAMONDA.
She was the only mother the client had ever known.
Achebe killed her.
Or, so everyone THOUGHT...
... ...DID IT... DID IT WORK--?
I FEARED FOR YOUR SAFETY, MOTHER -- SO I ACTIVATED THE SUSPENSION CELL SOONER THAN PLANNED.
I SHOULD NEVER HAVE ASKED YOU TO ALLOW THE CONSPIRATORS TO "RECRUIT" YOU -- TO FEIGN AN ALLIANCE WITH THEM --
-- WHILE FEEDING INTELLIGENCE REPORTS TO ME. HAD YOU ACTUALLY BEEN HARMED, I WOULD HAVE EARNED MY FATHER'S SHAME --
-- BUT YOU WERE THE ONLY ONE I COULD COMPLETELY TRUST.
IT WASN'T EASY PRETENDING TO PLOT AGAINST YOU, SON... I WAS NEVER SURE THEY COMPLETELY BOUGHT IT.
BUT WE'VE BROUGHT YOU HOME... WITH A MINIMUM OF BLOODSHED.
SO, ALL'S WELL THAT ENDS WELL, Eh, YOUR HIGHNESS?
WELL, OTHER THAN THE PRESIDENT'S SENDING ME TO ICELAND IF I DON'T GET YOU TO RETRACT YOUR STATEMENTS.
I'M SURE HE'S JUST JOKING, OF COURSE...

...WHICH PRETTY MUCH BRINGS US UP TO *DATE.*

NOW, I'M NOT ENTIRELY SURE GUARDING A DECREPIT *MONITORING STATION* FITS IN MY *JOB DESCRIPTION.*

I MAY HAVE SOME BASIS FOR AN *EEOC* TITLE 4 COMPLAINT.

YOU'RE RIGHT. WHY BOTHER.

WELL, IT WAS A FUN CAREER WHILE IT LASTED.

YOU KIDS *ENJOY* THAT, NOW.

FRIEND *ROSS--!*

MY *MASTER* HAS SPOKEN TO YOUR *STATE DEPARTMENT!*

THEY HAVE REQUESTED YOU REMAIN AT THE KING'S SIDE!

WHAT SAY YOU--?

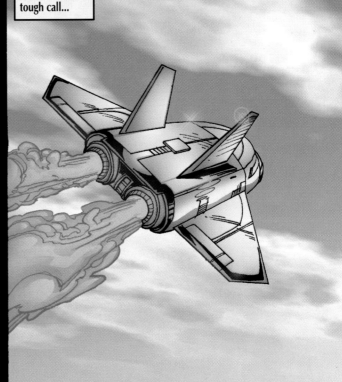

It was a REALLY tough call...

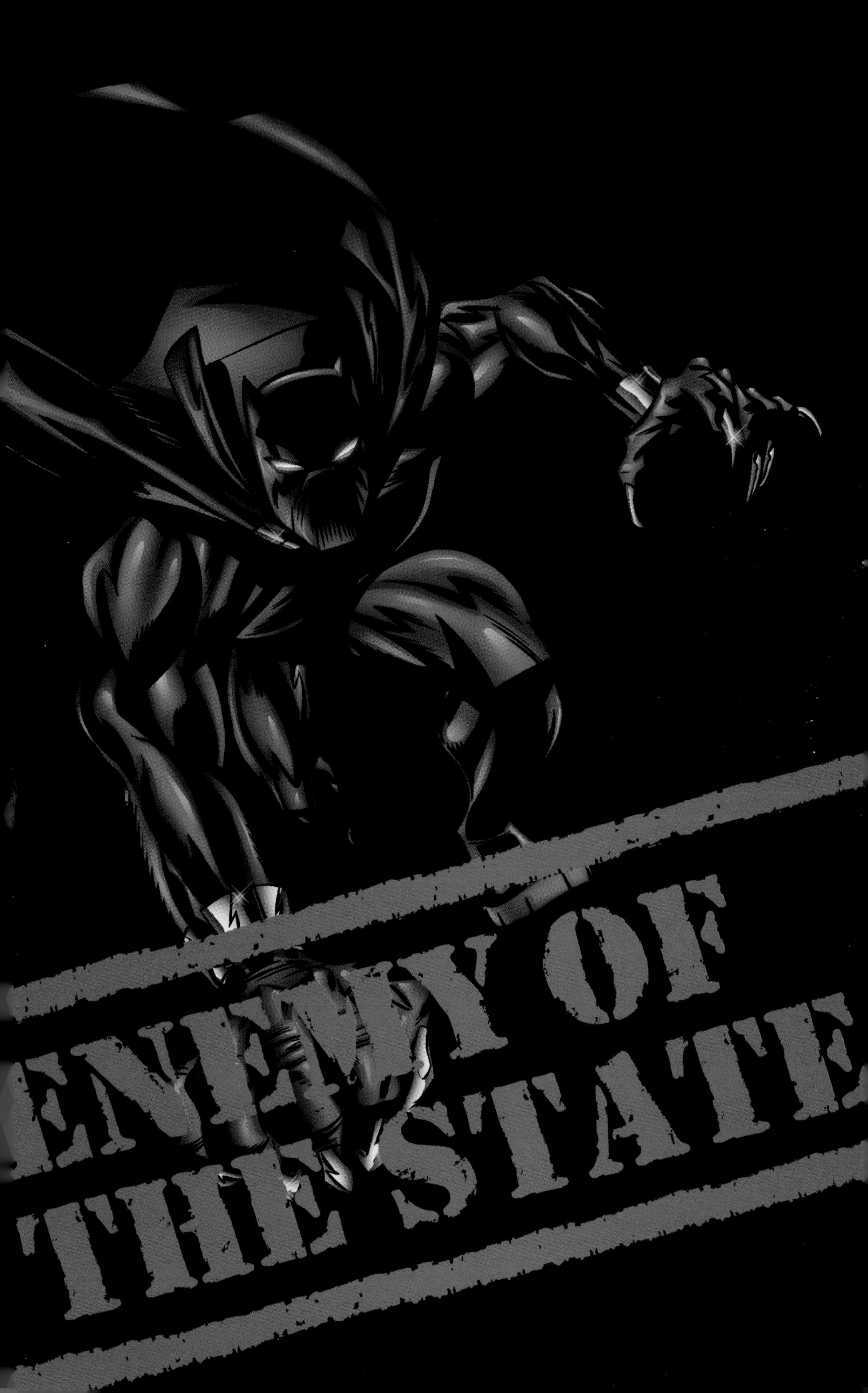
ENEMY OF
THE STATE

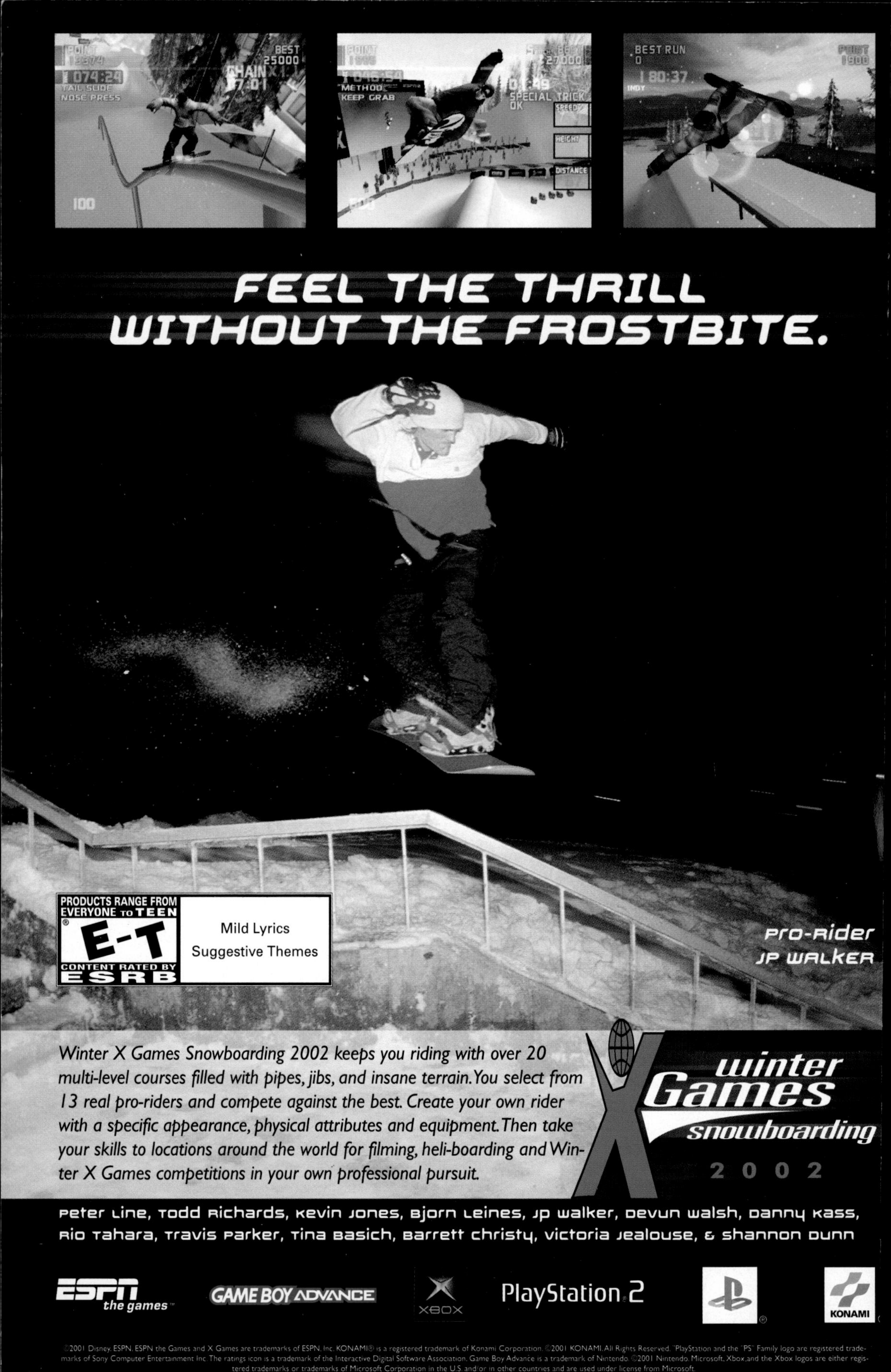
FEEL THE THRILL
WITHOUT THE FROSTBITE.
PRODUCTS RANGE FROM EVERYONE TO TEEN
E-T
CONTENT RATED BY ESRB
Mild Lyrics
Suggestive Themes
pro-rider
JP WALKER
Winter X Games Snowboarding 2002 keeps you riding with over 20 multi-level courses filled with pipes, jibs, and insane terrain. You select from 13 real pro-riders and compete against the best. Create your own rider with a specific appearance, physical attributes and equipment. Then take your skills to locations around the world for filming, heli-boarding and Winter X Games competitions in your own professional pursuit.
winter X Games snowboarding 2002
peter line, todd richards, kevin jones, bjorn leines, jp walker, devun walsh, danny kass, rio tahara, travis parker, tina basich, barrett christy, victoria jealouse, & shannon dunn
ESPN the games
GAME BOY ADVANCE
XBOX
PlayStation 2
KONAMI
©2001 Disney. ESPN, ESPN the Games and X Games are trademarks of ESPN, Inc. KONAMI® is a registered trademark of Konami Corporation. ©2001 KONAMI. All Rights Reserved. "PlayStation and the "PS" Family logo are registered trademarks of Sony Computer Entertainment Inc. The ratings icon is a trademark of the Interactive Digital Software Association. Game Boy Advance is a trademark of Nintendo. ©2001 Nintendo. Microsoft, Xbox, and the Xbox logos are either registered trademarks or trademarks of Microsoft Corporation in the U.S. and/or in other countries and are used under license from Microsoft.